STUDIES IN
PEERAGE AND
FAMILY HISTORY

"Genealogical enquiries and local topography, so far from being unworthy the attention of the philosophical enquirer, are amongst the best materials which he can use, and the fortunes and changes of one family, or the events of one upland township, may explain the darkest and most dubious portions of the annals of a realm."—PALGRAVE.

"The expansion and extension of genealogical study is a very remarkable feature of our own times. Men are apparently awaking to the fact that there are other families besides those described in the peerage, that those families have their records, played their part in history, furnished the bone and sinew of national action, and left traces behind them which it behoves their descendants to search out and keep in remembrance. There is nothing in this that need be stigmatised as vain and foolish; it is a very natural instinct, and it appears to me to be one of the ways in which a general interest in national history may be expected to grow."—STUBBS.

"Let no one deem that, because a false pedigree is a thing to be eschewed and scouted, therefore a true pedigree is a thing to be despised. A true pedigree, be it long or short, is a fact. . . . To those to whom it belongs it is a possession ; and, like any other possession, it is to be respected. It is only the false imitation of the true which is to be despised."—FREEMAN.

"Falsum committunt viri docti, qui hominibus de plebe nobilitatem, insignia et antiquitatem generis adfingunt . . . Et potest profecto debetque mercenariorum illorum pœna tunc, quum reipublicæ valde per eos nocitum, atque fides monumentorum et historiæ turbata est, ad ultimum supplicium proferri."—LEYSER.

STUDIES IN PEERAGE
AND FAMILY
HISTORY

By J. HORACE ROUND M.A

AUTHOR OF "THE COMMUNE OF LONDON"
"FEUDAL ENGLAND" ETC

BALTIMORE:
GENEALOGICAL PUBLISHING COMPANY
1970

Reproduced from the
Original Edition
London, 1901

International Standard Book Number 0-8063-0426-X
Library of Congress Catalog Card Number 72-124475

American Publishers
GENEALOGICAL PUBLISHING COMPANY
Baltimore, Maryland
Published in conjunction with
THE TABARD PRESS
Trowbridge, England

Printed in Great Britain
Bound in the United States of America

Contents

CONTENTS

Erratum et Addenda

Page 13. The Irish earldom of Llandaff (1797) is now similarly assumed, if not the barony of Cahir.

Pages 126-7. Too late for insertion in the text I discovered that Jordan Fitz Alan (Fitz Flaald) and his son Alan Fitz Jordan were lords of Tuxford, etc., in Notts, and that Alan was succeeded there, as in Norfolk, by his daughter and heiress Olive. Further, Olive is there found to be identical with that Olive who was wife (1) of Robert de St. John, of St. Jean-le-Thomas (see my paper on "The Families of St. John and of Port" in *Genealogist* [N.S.], XVI. 45), and (2) of Roger de Monbegon, who gave 500 marcs for her and her inheritance in 1 John. This completes the pedigree of the line.

Their Nottinghamshire estate consisted of Tuxford, with lands in Walesby and Kirton, together with West Markham and Warsop, all of which had formed part of the escheated fief of Roger de Busli (see Thoroton's *Notts*, III. 213, 214, 219, 220, 227, 354, 369), and must have been bestowed by Henry I. on this favoured family. It was as holding the 6 carucates at which these lands were assessed that Jordan had his 12 sh. of danegeld remitted in 1130. Alan Fitz Jordan enfeoffed Geoffrey de le Fremunt at Walesby and Kirton, and his daughter Olive (who occurs in the Rufford Cartulary) kept her court at Tuxford.

This discovery enables us to identify two of the churches given to the abbey of Tiron by Alan Fitz Jordan as "seneschal of Dol." In my *Calendar of Documents preserved in France* they occur as 'Tophor' and 'Garsop' (p. 358); but they were clearly Tuxford and Warsop. The scattered character of tenures in this obscure period is illustrated by this seneschal of Dol holding land independently in the counties of Lincoln, of Norfolk, and of Notts.

Page 152. The elder Eustace must, however, have been dead

ERRATUM ET ADDENDA

in 1088, for Florence speaks of the then count as Eustace "junior," and the Anglo-Saxon chronicle styles him "the younger."

Page 169. Among the Crown lands bestowed by Stephen on his son earl William were Woking, Godalming, Gomshall, Stoke, and Walton, in Surrey, valued in all at £95 a year in 1155 (*Liber Rubeus*, p. 654).

Page 171, line 14. *For* Maud *read* Mary (as on p. 172).

Pages 385-6. With reference to Glamorgan's 'commission patent' of 1 April 1644,—which Mr. Gardiner insists is genuine, and which I denounce as a forgery,—Mr. Gardiner holds that Endymion Porter was concerned with Glamorgan in the sealing of it, and observes that "Endymion Porter, it will be remembered, was believed to be associated with a similar performance in affixing the great seal to a document despatched to Ireland in 1641" (*Eng. Hist. Rev.*, II. 692). Unfortunately, this latter document is described by Mr. Gardiner himself as an undoubted forgery (*History* [1884], X. 92-3).

Pages 454-5. Another case of assumption and subsequent recognition by the Crown is that of Powys. After the barony of that name had fallen into abeyance (1427), the title, like those of Mowbray and Segrave, was assumed by both the co-heirs, and this assumption was inadvertently recognised by the Crown in the case of Lord Tiptoft (1449), if not also in that of the Greys, the other co-heirs. This case has a direct bearing on that of Mowbray.

Preface

THE studies contained in this volume are intended to illustrate that new genealogy which is of comparatively recent growth, and to stimulate the movement for honesty and truth in peerage and family history. It is evident that, both in England and America, there is an increasing interest in genealogical research, and, with the rapid growth of the published materials available, it is likely to increase further. If it is conducted on the right lines, that is, on the modern system, such research is wholly praiseworthy, and is in no way liable to the taunts levelled against that older genealogy which consisted either in inventing pedigrees or in repeating without question the unsupported statements of a herald. Works, indeed, of this character, as will be shown in these pages, are still produced even now ; but the efforts of the new school of genealogists are surely, if slowly, bearing fruit. The hold, however, on the public at large of the old fables and the old beliefs would seem, from the newspaper press, to be almost as strong as ever.

That this is so is doubtless due to the sanction they appeared to receive from their quasi-official and persistent repetition in the pages of *Burke's*

PREFACE

Peerage and of other 'Burke' publications.[1] But, for the source of these fables, or at least of the worst and the most venerable, we have to penetrate behind 'Burke' to the authors of these fabrications, the heralds and the antiquaries of the sixteenth and the seventeenth centuries. The joyous age of the old genealogy ranged from the days of Henry VIII. to those of Charles I.; and, of pedigrees published in modern books, many were concocted at that period and duly certified as true by officers of the Heralds' College.

A glimpse of the gulf that severs the 'old' from the 'new' genealogy is afforded by the ancient house of Lyte of Lytes Cary. Under queen Elizabeth and James I., the Lytes, father and son, were unrivalled exponents of the former. Henry Lyte, the father (d. 1607), compiled

A table wherby it is supposed that Lyte of Lytescarie sprange of the race and stocke of Leitus (one of the five capitaynes of Beotia that went to Troye) and that his ancestors came to England first with Brute.

The family's seat Lytes Cary was alleged to derive its name from "Caria in Asia," and its members bore upon their coat "Three sylver swannes, as

---

[1] Even as this preface goes to press the *World* (17 Oct. 1900), in an article on "Sir Humphrey de Trafford at home," asserts that "Randolf, Lord of Trafford, was the patriarch of the family, which for nearly nine centuries after him has produced an uninterrupted line of heirs male. The first recorded Trafford lived in the reigns of King Canute and Edward the Confessor, being succeeded by his son Ralph," etc. This grotesquely impossible tale is duly found in *Burke's Peerage*, although it is shattered by Domesday Book.

from the shield which Leit at Troy did beare,"[1]
Thomas Lyte, the son, drew up for James I. his
genealogy "from Brute, the most noble founder of
the Britains," which was not only graciously accepted by the king in 1610, but was hung up
at court "in an especiall place of eminence," and
extolled by the great Camden, Clarencieux king
of Arms. It was in gratitude for this pedigree
that James bestowed upon its author the famous
Lyte jewel, which, purchased by Baron Ferdinand
de Rothschild for nearly £3,000, is now preserved
among the Waddesdon gems in the British
Museum.

It is an interesting, indeed a unique circumstance that the present representative of the same
house, the Deputy Keeper of the Public Records,
has himself compiled a history of the Lytes which
is a masterpiece of modern genealogy.[2] The
'old' and the 'new' are thus brought into
strange and direct contrast. But, wide as is the
gulf that divides them, the former lingers on.
Pedigrees compiled in the age of the Lytes and by
heralds contemporary with Camden are still published year after year, are still valid at the College
of Arms. Indeed, within the last few years, one

---

[1] A learned Dominican, Father O'Daly, published even so late
as 1655 a history of the Geraldine earls of Desmond, which
began with the assertion : "It is a fact beyond questioning that the
Geraldines, Earls of Desmond—a race renowned for valour—
derived their origin from the ancient Trojans," their "founder"
having fled to Italy, after the siege, with Æneas.

[2] "The Lytes of Lytescary" (*Somerset Arch. Trans.* [1892],
XXXVIII. [2], 3–101).

family has " proved and recorded," in the archives of that institution, 323 quarters to its coat of arms, consisting largely of coats assigned to " British kings " (in Planché's words) " as visionary as those in Banquo's glass." We are indebted for this remarkable information to Mr. Fox-Davies' *Armorial Families*, in which this monstrous shield is depicted as well as described.[1] Among the arms there recognised as authentic by the Heralds' College are those of a potentate who died in 318, as well as those of Coel Godebog, that primitive and convivial soul. We further learn that—

The present representative is 67th in descent in an unbroken MALE line from Belinus the Great (Beli Mawr) King of Britain, as shown by the Records fully registered down to the present time in Her Majesty's College of Arms.—See Norfolk xvi. 45 Coll. Arms.[2]

The arms of Beli himself appear repeatedly in the shield, on the strength, of course, of this pedigree, proved by " Records " to what must be the early days of the Christian era. One is glad to learn what " Records " mean at " Her Majesty's College of Arms." [3]

---

[1] Ed. 1899, pp. 512–4. Compare p. xiv. :—" Some families are undoubtedly entitled to a very great number [of quarterings]. . . . Anyhow, at the Heralds' College, I believe, the record is held by the family of Lloyd of Stockton, who have proved and recorded 323." In the 1895 edition of the same work, "the record " is assigned to the family of Lane-Fox, with 136, the Lloyds of Stockton having then only 102. This enables us to date [1895–1899] the proving and recording of the rest.

[2] *Ibid.*

[3] Since the above passage was written Mr. Gwenogvryn Evans

PREFACE

It would seem desirable to point out that even so ardent a champion of the College as the author of *The Right to Bear Arms* maintains that "we are still without any definite evidence that such a thing as a coat of arms, in the sense we now understand the term, had any existence whatsoever at the time of the First Crusade" (p. 4). Mr. Fox-Davies, also, holds that such heraldry "had no existence at the time of the Norman Conquest,"[1] while he stoutly proclaims that "Planché is the truest writer who has yet set pen to paper on the subject of Heraldry."[2] Now Planché not only ridiculed the coats of "British kings," but placed the beginning of armorial bearings a century at least after the Conquest.

has expressed himself, on the subject of Welsh pedigrees, as follows :

"When a pedigree reaches back beyond the third generation of the time in which it was originally drawn up, unless supported by independent documentary evidence, the work of even the most honest men cannot be trusted. Take for instance the vellum roll (some seven yards long) of pedigrees at Mostyn Hall, in the hand of Guttyn Owen, a man thoroughly trustworthy as to the matters of his own time, and yet, in that roll, certain pedigrees are traced back to 'Adam son of God,' without any conscious sense of the incongruous. It does seem as if reason took its leave of every genealogist sooner or later" (Report to Commission on Historical MSS. on the Peniarth collection, p. vi.). Even in our own famous volume, *The Red Book of the Exchequer*, the official who compiled it, Alexander Swereford, solemnly records that he wrote in the year 1230, in the 15th year of king Henry III., whose pedigree he proceeds to trace, through Noah, to Adam "son of the living God."

[1] *Armorial Families*, p. v.

[2] *Ibid.* p. xxix. Mr. Woodward also, in what is perhaps the leading work on English heraldry, gives his "entire adherence" to Mr. Planché's conclusions (I. 32).

PREFACE

Yet, having thus proclaimed his faith, Mr. Fox-Davies accepts as genuine the "bogus" coats of British kings because "proved and recorded" at Her Majesty's College of Arms.[1]

Are not, indeed, the "bogus" arms assigned to Edward the Confessor, in right of his kingdom of England—the arms for using which the gifted earl of Surrey suffered death upon the scaffold—found in a 'record' at the Heralds' College ? We read of the alleged grant of these arms by Richard II. to Thomas Mowbray, then duke of Norfolk, that—

The authority for this statement is doubtless an entry in one of the records of the College of Arms (R. 22, 67), which is itself a copy of another record, and which runs as follows . . .

"Et dedit eidem Thome ad pertandum (*sic*) in sigillo et vexillo quo (*sic*) arma S[ti] Edwardi."[2]

We have only to turn to the *Monasticon* (VI. 321) to learn that this precious 'record' is not a record at all, but is a mere copy of a monastic narrative, which is grossly and demonstrably inaccurate. Moreover, when the writer, whose

---

[1] "There are many people who grandiloquently assert that 'they don't recognise the authority of the College of Arms.' Such a statement may sound very big, but it is pure nonsense" (Preface to *Armorial Families*).

[2] *Genealogical Magazine*, II. 401 (signed "F.-D.") ; and *The House of Stourton*, II. 811. As bearing on the authorship of the latter work, it will be found interesting to compare these two volumes, especially the illustrations on pp. 378, 398, 399 with those on pp. 812, 808, 810, and the text of the following pages, 397 with 746, 397–402 with 808–813, 402–3, 438–9 with 832–834, and 439–441 with 828–830. In the Latin extract cited above we find "pertandum" and "et utraque" (for "ex utraque") in both volumes (see further p. 61 below).

PREFACE

initials, I may repeat, are " F.-D.," assists us on "the arduous journey in pursuit of heraldic knowledge," by informing us that the alleged grant was a " grant of the arms of Plantagenet, which thus technically became thereafter the arms of Mowbray,"[1] he betrays extraordinary confusion.   He is even good enough to explain to us that—

the knowledge that the arms of Plantagenet had been re-granted to the Mowbrays is not very general, and we take it that there are very few who are aware that in the strictly technical sense, and also, by the way, in strict conformity with the laws of arms, the Duke of Norfolk and his predecessors of the House of Howard bear and have borne these Royal Plantagenet arms, not as the quartering for " Thomas of Brotherton," but as a quartering for Mowbray, to which family the arms of Plantagenet were granted, as we have seen, to be borne (with the arms of King Edward the Confessor) as their chief and principal arms.[2]

But "we have seen" nothing of the kind.   For it is not even alleged in the above monastic narrative that Richard II. granted more than the arms of Edward the Confessor, with which the arms of " Plantagenet " had nothing in the world to do.

The critical treatment, in this volume, of the heralds and their so-called " records " has been made necessary by recent efforts to exalt the authority of their documents and to terrorize the public, in the matter of arms, by crude and violent language.[3] Those who may have been impressed by this *ex parte* clamour will learn with some surprise, from

[1] *Genealogical Magazine*, II. 401 (cf. p. 439) ; and *The House of Stourton*, II. 813.
[2] *Genealogical Magazine*, II. 442 (see also II. 509).
[3] See *The Right to Bear Arms*, by ' X,' and Mr. Fox-Davies' *Armorial Families*.

the evidence here collected, that heralds themselves have been among the worst of purveyors of spurious pedigrees, and have taken advantage of their official position to give these productions a *cachet* they would never otherwise have obtained. It will further be found that, in arms also, they have been grievous sinners. The modern officer of arms will say that all this is now changed, and that pedigrees and proofs of right to arms are subjected to close scrutiny. But the point on which I have to insist is that the College is handicapped by its past ; the follies and the frauds of past heralds are binding on its present members, for are they not " on record " ? One of the greatest snares in genealogical study is the putting of " new wine " into " old bottles," the combination of the new genealogy, based on record evidence, with the old heraldic pedigrees teeming with fiction and with error. These two methods of genealogy cannot possibly be combined, and, however strict the officers of arms may now be in admitting proofs, they are bound to accept, at the same time, the pedigrees " recorded " by heralds in the past ; and thus the " records " of the College are a millstone about its neck.

Of this assertion we have recently been afforded the most conclusive proof. For one of the heralds has himself published, within the last two or three years, an elaborate account of his own family "from the Norman era to the present day."[1] The pedigree he gives for the modern period is, doubtless,

---

[1] *Genealogical Magazine* (not to be confused with *The Genealogist*), I. 459.

absolutely correct ; but, having claimed as his direct ancestor a John in the Lane ("en la Lone") —a surname common enough in the 14th century —he produces as his father "Adam de Lona of Hampton, co. Stafford, and of Halton, co. Chester, son and heir of Sir Richard de Lone." Moreover, like the ancestor of most of the Smiths—"Sir Michael Carington" to wit, this Adam was "among the Crusaders who went to the Holy Land," we read, "under the banner of Cœur de Lion" (1190).[1] It is true that beyond Adam's grandfather, that gallant knight "Sir Reginald de Lona, of Halton, co. Chester," the descent of "this ancient and loyal family" has not as yet been proved ; but of him at least they are the heirs-male,[2] while one of them, it is added, under William Rufus, married into one of those "leading families" whose daughters have always been kept in stock at Her Majesty's College of Arms. Now, in spite of the fact that "Sir Reginald de Lona" is, we learn, "upon record," the history of the family is this. They were townsfolk of Wolverhampton in the 14th century, townsfolk who derived their name from the 'lane' in which they dwelt. The pedigree can, it is probable, be proved up to John 'in the Lane,' whose father is said to have been Adam ; but Adam cannot, even as a farrier, have taken part in a crusade before he was even born. His alleged grandson is known to have been living in the reign of Edward

[1] *Genealogical Magazine*, I. 130.
[2] *Ibid*. I. 130, 459.

III.   In the same reign the "ancient and loyal"
house of "in le Lone" were displaying an energy
at Wolverhampton worthy of a Boxer clan.   One of
them was long 'wanted' for felony, and three others
were among the rioters who plundered and assaulted
an unfortunate man, "cut out his tongue," and
"plucked out his eye"; they were also charged
by John de Sutton with having "assaulted his men
and servants and cut off their tongues and noses."[1]
This is the house that, we now read, "has been
seated in the county of Stafford for seven hundred
years," and in that of Cheshire earlier still.   The
worst of it is that the true pedigree has long been
perfectly known,[2] and that there is nothing to suggest a descent from alleged Cheshire knights.   But
need one add that the latter origin is duly asserted
as a fact in Burke's *Landed Gentry*, where Wolverhampton is, with much judgment, idealized as
"West Hampton"?   Thus it is that a family
pedigree, which is by no means devoid of interest,
is made by the heralds merely absurd.

But indeed the whole system of "record" badly
needs the light of day.   I have never been able to
ascertain the actual meaning of "on record," or on
what principle some documents are so dignified
and others not.   It is pretty certain that if a
scholar, trained to deal with documents and to
gauge their authority and value, were let loose on
the College "records," we should have some

---

[1] *Calendar of Patent Rolls*, 1338–1340, pp. 364, 366.
[2] See Shaw's *Staffordshire* (1798), II. 97, and *Salt Archæological
Society* (1880), I. (2), p. 325.

strange revelations. This remark applies specially to the evidence of grants of arms. When the College has to send to Oxford for particulars of such grants, when it offers to " record " at the present day grants that were made, but were not recorded, two or three centuries ago, when it picks up stray manuscripts in auction-rooms in the hope of filling some of the gaps in its vaunted, but imperfect "records," we can afford to smile at the daring statement by the author of *The Right to Bear Arms* that " arms are good or bad as they are recorded or unrecorded" at the Heralds' College. And when, further, the same writer deems it his duty to "insult publicly"[1] those who use arms which are not there recorded, it becomes desirable to enlighten the public on a state of things which destroys his case, and which shows that the absence of such record is no proof that the arms are ' bad.'

It is a different matter when these writers denounce the flagrant abuse by which the arms of old families, belonging to them alone, are assumed, or rather pirated by those who happen to possess the same name, but are not descended from them. In this denunciation one is bound to join, although it is possible that one may exaggerate the heinousness, in practice, of this assumption, which often springs from ignorance, for it would probably be unnoticed by the vast majority of men. Moreover, in such extreme cases as those of Stuart and Mont-

[1] " One has to insult him publicly in black and white " (*The Right to Bear Arms*, p. xiv.).

morency it has received the official sanction of heralds themselves.[1] It does, however, amount to an assertion that one is a member of a family to which one does not belong, and this is why the above writers denounce it as the act of a snob. But of a wholly distinct character is the use of arms which are not those of any other family of one's name, but which do not happen to have been 'recorded' (or 'registered') at the Heralds' College. In this case there is no pretension to belong to another family, and, therefore, no possible ground for denouncing the act as snobbish. The above writers, however, have endeavoured to confuse the public on the subject and to class together all those whose right to the arms they use is not 'registered' at the College.[2] The object is to compel them alike to take out fresh grants, these being, as is well known, a lucrative matter for the heralds.[3]

As a matter of fact, the oldest and the purest right to arms was that conferred by user. In the heyday of chivalry, when heraldry was still a living science, in the age of Crecy and Poitiers and of the founders of the Garter, it was user that determined the right to arms. In the well-known case of Scrope and Grosvenor (1389), as in that of Warbleton and Gorges (1347), the decision was based on

[1] See pp. 20, 144 below.

[2] Mr. Fox-Davies classes them together as all "bogus pretenders." (See Introduction to *Armorial Families*, p. xxx.)

[3] See Mr. Hutton's article on "A Reformed College of Arms": "A considerable proportion of the fees exacted go into the pocket of the official who happens to have the particular job in hand" (*Contemp. Rev.*, July 1900, p. 97).

user alone.[1] The Crown was only appealed to to decide who could prove the prior user. When coats were used to distinguish their bearers, it was essential that no two should be the same, and some authority had to be invoked to decide, where this was so, who had the prior claim. And the authority invoked was the king. It was only thus, and for this purpose, that the Crown came to intervene. The evidence in the cases cited above proves that it was on the king's "viages" (*i.e.* military expeditions) that controversies arose from the same coat being borne by more than one person.[2] Consequently, when he was preparing for a great *viage* into France, Henry V. ordered the sheriffs (2 June 1417) to see that no one should appear with 'coat-armours' at the musters " unless he possesses or ought to possess them by ancestral right (*jure antecessorio*) or by the gift of some one having the power to give them (*ad hoc*)." Now this order, which had in view only the *viage* in question (*in presenti viagio nostro*), distinctly states on what depended the right to bear arms. A man had either to prove user, *i.e.* that his forefathers had used them ; or he had to show that they had been given him by someone who possessed

[1] As it was also in that of Fakenham and Sitsilt (1333), which, however, I do not cite, as the documents are only known to us through Bossewell (*Workes of Armorie* [1597], pp. 79–81).

[2] The great importance, in war, of armorial bearings for recognition is illustrated by the well-known story of Simon de Montfort's barber being sent up into a tower, before the battle of Evesham, to identify, as an expert, the advancing host by their arms.

that right.[1] Of grant by the Crown there is no word. And yet this is the one document on which those who assert that no arms can be borne except by a grant from the Crown are compelled to take their stand.[2]

As a matter of fact, the right conferred by established user continued, on the most reluctant showing of ' X ' himself, to be recognised. In his opinion, at the Heralds' visitations,—

The definite production of a specific grant for the arms in question was not necessarily insisted upon by the Heralds, who allowed and confirmed arms as borne by right when the right to these was established to their satisfaction. . . . What proofs the Heralds required the production of to establish this legal right I am utterly unable to say. . . . One can only surmise. . . . In the case of less important families using arms which in no way interfered with the rights of other people, one's experience leads one to suppose that the claimants were treated more easily and the arms admitted (that is, they were recorded and confirmed with little or no alteration) upon the strength of usage for a certain period.[3]

---

[1] This, as is well known, was sometimes done.

[2] "Certain is it that in the year 1418 (*sic*) he [Henry V.] issued a writ. . . . It is on this writ that I take my stand," etc., etc. (*The Right to Bear Arms*, pp. 17, 20). The writer ekes out his case (pp. 21–2) by a warrant of Charles II., reciting *inter alia* that the descendants of Lord Ogle, by the heiress of the Percys, could not quarter the arms of Percy " according to the law of Armes without the special dispensation and license of us." And yet, according even to Mr. Fox-Davies, they would be "entitled by the English law" to do so without permission. (See *Armorial Families*, p. xiii.) On p. 159 the above writer goes further and asserts, in general terms, that "Charles II. says of the assumption of name and arms," etc., etc., as proof that a man cannot assume arms for himself. But the king is merely speaking of the old arms of Percy, not of a man assuming fresh arms himself.   [3] *The Right to Bear Arms*, pp. 87, 99.

PREFACE

No attempt is made by the writer to give any reason why the Heralds should not now do what, he himself admits, they seem to have done then. And yet they avowedly decline to do it, apparently in order that they may be able to obtain the fees on a grant *de novo*.[1] And, meanwhile, the above writer classes arms which are not pirated, and for which user can be proved, with those which are stolen from another family, as no less "bogus" and "illegal" (p. 116). As there is, in spite of the writer's bluster, no law in existence against such arms being borne, it is probable that county families who have borne them, as such, for generations, will continue to do so until such time as the College of Arms consents to revive its ancient practice. They only profess, by so doing, that their position entitles them to use arms, a fact which the Heralds would themselves admit, if they should apply for a grant; and they will but find themselves in company with two and twenty peers, and over thirty baronets, who, according to the author of *Armorial Families*, "have no right whatsoever to the arms they bear." That those whom he describes as "prominent people, whose social position is undoubted," may even esteem more highly the arms their ancestors have borne than those which a retired tradesman has lately been induced to purchase, may indeed be inconceivable to a person of vulgar mind.[2] But the fact remains. Indeed,

[1] I take this suggestion from their own mutual recriminations about the time of James I.

[2] 'X,' for instance, exclaims that they "in their lunacy prefer a bogus coat" (*The Right to Bear Arms*, p. 165).

in a sudden burst of emotion the writer himself exalts "the aristocracy of birth," and admits that "the *cachet* of birth" is what "the plebeian" lacks.[1] But, as it is the object of his work to prove that plebeians are those, of whatever birth, who have not had a grant of arms (or been included in its limitation), it is obvious that the poor man is simply contradicting himself.

There is one more point on which I may enlighten the public. Loud assertion is not evidence, although it may impose upon the timid. Mr. Fox-Davies loudly asserts that "*nothing* can alter the fact that the officers . . . of the College of Arms . . . have the *sole* authority and control of armorial matters" . . . [are] "the sole *authority* upon matters of arms."[2] And the author of *The Right to Bear Arms* closes his work with the confident assertion " that matters armorial have been delegated in England in all due form to the control and supervision of the Earl Marshal and the College of Arms " (p. 83). Yet he himself cites Dallaway for the fact that " Appeals from the Earl Marshal's Court could be carried into the King's Bench " (p. 38), and Dallaway (whose work is dedicated to the Earl Marshal himself) tells us that—

Appeals from its jurisdiction . . . were referred to the

---

[1] *Armorial Families*, pp. xviii.–xix. So too : " Money will do much. . . . But money cannot purchase real ancestry " (an observation admirably true). Unhappily it can and does purchase a grant of arms.

[2] *Armorial Families*, pp. viii., xxx. (the italics are his own).

king's bench, by which the awards were sometimes superseded, and always liable to revision, which . . . invalidated the general opinion of the necessity of the existence of the court.[1]

To this I may add the interesting fact that in 1625 (or 1624) the law officers of the Crown (to whom the matter was referred) "uppon long serch of recordes and presidentes" certified that it was "just and lawfull" to appeal from the Court of Chivalry to the Court of Chancery in a suit concerning the bearing and quartering of certain arms.[2] So much for what Mr. Fox-Davies terms the "legal side."

The fact is that, in harping on "the legal apart from the scientific and antiquarian view of the study of Armory" (p. xxix.), Mr. Fox-Davies does but reproduce the attitude of modern heralds, one of whom was the first, he tells us, to impress on him that there is "a legal side to Armory as well as an antiquarian" (p. xxxi.). The "scientific" side, we are told, "might well have been left" for the present. To the real student and lover of heraldry nothing, on the contrary, can be more uninteresting than its modern commercial development in the hands of the Heralds' College. To certain members of that corporation, as also to 'X' and Mr. Fox-Davies, the most interesting thing in heraldry may be the modern grant; but the result is that the present movements in favour of the intelligent study of the science, of the revival ot

[1] *Inquiries into the Origin and Progress of the Science of Heraldry in England*, pp. 95, 289-90.
[2] Pixley's *History of the Baronetage*, p. 138.

PREFACE

pure and artistic design, and of the new honest genealogy, have all originated not within, but without the walls of the Heralds' College.[1]

"As a lover of Armory," Mr. Fox-Davies pleads for an Act of Parliament which "would in some measure restore the ancient respect for Arms." In stirring words the prophet cries:

> When the glory of knightly honour once more shall hold sway in these kingdoms three, and these marks of honour take their rightful place, let it not be said that whilst in our charge we have allowed their splendour to be tarnished or their lustre to be dimmed (p. xxxii.).

After which it is painful to return to the facts of everyday life, and to be reminded, as we recently were, how these "marks of honour" are obtained.

> It is a matter of common knowledge that payment of the fees claimed will always secure a grant, apart from the rule, now somewhat meaningless, . . . that grants are not made to retail shopkeepers.[2]

Mr. Hutton rightly ridicules the pretence, in these circumstances, that a grant is a special favour from the Crown. As strenuous efforts are made to bamboozle the public on the point, it is needful to insist upon the fact that the Crown knows nothing of the grant. Take for instance this passage from *The Right to Bear Arms* (pp. 165–7, 170):

> A grant of Arms is a patent of gentility in precisely the same

---

[1] See further, for the Heralds and their ways, pp. 144–146, 308–321 below.

[2] "A Reformed College of Arms" (by Mr. Hutton), in *Cont. Review*, July 1900, p. 98.

PREFACE

manner as the letters patent creating a peerage constitute a patent of what we here in England commonly and colloquially call nobility. . . . Each of them grants a definite honour. . . . But every Peerage patent that is issued carries with it the obligation of certain fees. . . . When a Patent of Arms is applied for, certain fees are payable. . . . But the cases of a Patent of Arms and a Patent of Peerage are identically the same, inasmuch as on the issue of either patent certain fees are required to be paid. . . . Consequently, if a coat of arms granted by patent is to be stigmatised as bought from the Crown, then of a surety every Peerage granted by Patent is equally ‘bought.’

The writer, of course, is well aware that no such parallel exists. In the first place, the grant of a peerage proceeds directly from the Crown, and involves its special sanction ; in the second,—and this is the essential point,—a peerage cannot be purchased by the mere payment of fees. Even a man who has no pretentions to be, by birth or breeding, what is termed a gentleman can obtain a grant of arms by merely paying the fees. Let him, if he accepts the above writer’s statements, attempt to obtain a peerage dignity by similarly offering to pay the fees. If he should actually be led to do so, his faith in the above writer is likely to be rudely shaken.

And this is the essence of the case. A peerage is the object of ambition, because but few can obtain it ; a grant of arms is of no account, because nobody values what “anyone” can obtain. And no amount of rhodomontade can alter or obscure the fact. ‘X,’ indeed, wildly exclaims :

Why do people object to have their arms described as ‘bogus’? . . . Because in the frantic struggle to get into Society nine

PREFACE

men out of ten will tell lie upon lie, to prove that their fathers were not labourers or 'dans cette galère,' and will therefore use bogus arms, to show that they and their people are not of the vulgar crowd. That is what I call snobbery, rank, utter and absolute.[1]

But even if the right to bear arms gave the *entrée* to any 'Society' but that which he himself adorns, the anonymous author must be aware that there is nothing to prevent a labourer's son from becoming "a gentleman of coat-armour," if, in the sarcastic language of the *World*, he has "a few pounds to spare to the accommodating fossils of Queen Victoria Street."[2]   The above writer, who angrily complains that the word 'gentleman' is "applied in an idiotic manner" to those not entitled to it, and "even to a man of polite and refined manners and ideas," insists that—

Nothing a man can do or say can make him a gentleman without formal letters patent of gentility—in other words without a grant of arms.[3]

May one not venture to suggest to composers of comic operas that they might introduce a chorus of heralds with some such refrain as this ?—

> Seventy-six pound ten !
> Seventy-six pound ten !
> The sum isn't large,
> Yet it's all that we charge
> For making you gen—tle—men.

Solvitur ridendo.   It is only by showing its ridiculous aspect that one can effectually expose "a

[1] *The Right to Bear Arms*, pp. x.–xi.
[2] Article entitled "Order Arms !" in *World* of 16 Aug. 1899.
[3] *The Right to Bear Arms*, p. 8.

PREFACE

standard of social and personal measurement which makes plebeians of men of county family and established position, and 'gentlemen' of all the 'bounders' in the kingdom" who care to pay the fees.[1] What I am exposing is not the practice of granting arms, but the effort to persuade the public that the grant is a special privilege, when it is notoriously obtained by the mere payment of cash.

It is hoped to show in these pages that genealogy and the study of the peerage may, when intelligently pursued, be useful handmaids to history. The paper, for instance, on the Counts of Boulogne will explain the devolution of some great territorial 'Honours,' and will throw what seems to be a fresh light on the acceptance by Stephen and his son of Henry II.'s succession. The study on the family of Ballon introduces the Norman Conquest of South Wales; and that on the Peers under Henry VIII. involves a new theory on his action in 'the Reformation Parliament.' In "Charles I. and Lord Glamorgan" a famous problem in English history is approached from the standpoint of a student, not only of the peerage, but of documents. Without professing to have demolished Mr. Gardiner's conclusions on the subject, one may claim that the evidence in the case, when scientifically stated, raises at least grave doubts, and proves that his arguments are not consistent, while his treatment of the documents concerned has been neither critical nor exact. "The succession to the

[1] *World*, 16 Aug. 1899.

PREFACE

Crown " raises the question whether that succession, in certain contingencies, is at present clearly provided for. It is argued that the wording of the Act of Settlement was based on a misconception, and that its legal interpretation might involve the vacancy of the throne.

In view of the points of law discussed in these pages, it is perhaps desirable to mention that I am not, directly or indirectly, connected with the legal profession. I may also explain that publication has been unavoidably delayed, and that these papers were in type before Lord Mowbray and Stourton had " claimed to be heir of line and senior [?] co-heir general to the ancient earldom of Norfolk created in 1312."[1] His lordship's petition to the Crown to determine the " abeyance " of the earldom is of great interest for peerage history, and the last paper in this volume will be found to bear on the question. For the same reason there is no mention, on p. 184, of Miss Bateson's valuable papers in the *English Historical Review* on the " Laws of Breteuil," while the last edition (1900) of Burke's *Landed Gentry* has also appeared too recently to be noticed in these pages.

I have to thank Mr. Murray for permission to incorporate in the paper on " the Peerage " the bulk of my article on that subject which appeared in the *Quarterly Review*. " Our English Hapsburgs " is reproduced, with some additions, from

[1] *Times*, 21 July 1900. It will be seen that on p. 436 I have questioned whether any proof of the alleged seniority of the Howard co-heiress has been adduced.

PREFACE

the *Genealogist,* and the argument on the Mowbray barony, which is here enlarged and developed, originally appeared in the pages of the *Law Quarterly Review.* With these exceptions the contents of the volume are now published for the first time. Mr. Lindsay, Q.C., Windsor Herald, was good enough to allow me to collate Dugdale's extracts from the College of Arms MS. H. 13 with the original manuscript, and thereby to detect the errors and alterations in the printed text.

J. H. R.

I

The Peerage

NEARLY a quarter of a century ago Professor Freeman, in a famous article, set himself to expose, in
language of almost unexampled scorn, the fables
and the fictions which passed current for genuine
family history in the well-known 'Peerage' of Sir
Bernard Burke, Ulster King-of-Arms.[1] The state
of things, as it then existed, was described by him
as follows :

When we turn over an English peerage, or a book of English
pedigrees of any kind, we are tempted to put Juvenal's question
. . . What are pedigrees worth ? when stage after stage,
not in mythical, but in recorded ages, not among gods and heroes,
but among men who ought to be real, is purely mythical—if
indeed mythical is not too respectable a name for what must be
in many cases the work of deliberate invention. I turn over a
peerage or other book of genealogy, and I find that, when a pedigree professes to be traced back to the times of which I know
most in detail, it is all but invariably false. As a rule, it is not
only false, but impossible . . .   The historical circumstances,
when any are introduced, are for the most part not merely fictions,
but exactly that kind of fiction which is, in its beginning, deliberate and interested falsehood.

Mr. Freeman then proceeded to make his posi-

---

[1] "Pedigrees and Pedigree-Makers" [*Contemporary Review*,
XXX. 11–41].

tion clear; he explained that there was "no reason to blame the present representatives of the families concerned" for accepting "tales which they have heard from their childhood, and which it is a kind of family honour to believe"; his quarrel was with the peerage editor, who gave not only currency but a quasi-official stamp to tales of "manifest falsehood," and who made himself responsible "for the monstrous fictions which appear as the early history of so many families." That this position was a fair and just one is shown by the very different attitude of two peerage editors whose works, we shall see, have been published since Mr. Freeman wrote, and who have rejected without hesitation whatever appeared to them false. But, apart from this justification for the criticism of published pedigrees, it seems to me that a wrong is done to those families who endeavour to give a truthful account of their origin and history—sometimes at the sacrifice of beliefs handed down for generations—when, by the side of their honest pedigrees, there are printed, year after year, the exploded fictions which the public and the press accept as no less genuine on the strength of their appearance in that well-known work which is subjected, as they are assured, to constant revision and amendment.

By the side of what has been termed this "gorgeous repertory of genealogical mythology," there have appeared, since Mr. Freeman wrote, two works devoted to the Peerage, of which honesty and even frank scepticism have, throughout, been distinctive notes. The first is the *Peerage and Baronetage* of Mr. Joseph Foster (1880–1883) ; the second is the great *Complete Peerage* of ' G. E. C.' (1884–1898). Mr. Foster, whose services to genealogy were recognised by an honorary degree conferred by Oxford University, on the completion of his great work, *Alumni Oxonienses*, confined his labours to the members of the existing Peerage and Baronetage ; the *Complete Peerage*, in its eight volumes, comprised, on the contrary, the whole Peerage, extinct, extant, dormant, or in abeyance, of all three realms. The first attempt, in modern times, to produce a work of this character was that of Sir Harris Nicolas, whose useful *Synopsis of the Peerage* (1825)—re-edited by Courthope as the *Historic Peerage*, in 1857—was restricted to English dignities. Although he gave no pedigrees, and had, therefore, not much temptation to deviate from history or from truth, Nicolas deserves all credit for his manful statement of his principles, made, as it was, when the study of genealogy was still at its lowest ebb, and when peerage writers had brought their craft into well-deserved contempt.

To the merit of sedulous care, of rigid impartiality, and to having acted upon the resolution of not stating a single word which he did not believe to be strictly true, with the view of flattering the pride or gratifying the ambition of others, he conscientiously feels that he is entitled. . . . He has felt that with respect to hereditary honours, more than with any other worldly possession,—

" Rien n'est beau que le vrai,"

3

and that to attribute a dignity to an individual who has no legal right to it, is a species of falsehood which, if not so injurious, is at least as morally culpable as any other deviation from truth.

Since that time there has arisen a school of critical genealogists, whose work, unfortunately much scattered, is now chiefly represented by that recognised organ of research in the field of family history, the *Genealogist*. To the labours of these devoted students in clearing away the false, and substituting for it the truth, the *Complete Peerage*, as its footnotes show, has been very largely indebted.

Before discussing *Burke's Peerage* by the side of this great work of reference, I am anxious to explain that the criticisms I may offer will be no mere *réchauffé* of Mr. Freeman's article. The Professor admitted that he wrote only as the historian of the Norman Conquest. "I shall keep myself," he wrote, "strictly to those pedigrees which touch the English history of those times of which I believe myself to have some minute knowledge," though, as he added, "the period in which I am most at home happens to be the period where it is most needful unsparingly to wield the critical hatchet against the thick growth of genealogical falsehood." It has, indeed, if I remember right, been somewhere wittily said by the present bishop of Oxford that "it would seem that everybody whose ancestry didn't go away in the *Mayflower* must have come over with the Conqueror's ships"; but many a spurious pedigree begins later than the Conquest, while even within the field to which Mr. Freeman confined himself there are still fictions to be exposed. Moreover, the Professor did not understand scientific genealogy ;[1] while, as for the Peerage, although he was entrusted with the article on that subject in the *Encyclopædia Britannica*, he knew hardly anything of peerage law and history. As evidence of this I may appeal to his almost incredible blunder on the doctrine of ennobling the blood. In a violent pamphlet against the House of Lords he told the people (to whom it was addressed) that

when a certain body of men go on, age after age, making inferences, laying down rules which are altogether in their own interest and not at all in the interests of the other powers in the State, we are tempted to call that process corruption or usurpation rather than healthy growth or development. Now this is what the House of Lords has been doing ever since it began to be a distinct House of Lords. *The Lords laid down the rule that the King's writ " ennobled the blood " and bestowed a hereditary seat in Parliament—a thing which nobody would have found out from the writ itself.* . . . The body which thus disloyally, almost rebelliously, flouted the Crown has no right to claim respect on any grounds of antiquity or traditional dignity when, in the like spirit, they turn round and flout the people. They have, to be sure, their "noble blood," strange effect of King Edward's writ

---

[1] He wrote, for instance, in this article : "There is, we will say, a deed . . . which is done, say, by John of Sutton, with the consent of his wife Agnes and his son Richard ; there is another deed done by Richard of Sutton with the consent of his mother Agnes and his son William ; here is real evidence for three stages of the pedigree." But, with names so common as these, it is quite possible that there might be two men named Richard of Sutton, each of them with a mother Agnes. It is the proof of identity in such cases as these, that is, as the expert knows, the usual *crux* in genealogy.

of summons. Let us wait and see what their "noble blood" can do for them when they have turned every other power of the State against them.[1]

The assertion italicized above is absolutely contrary to fact. "Whenever," Mr. Freeman wrote, "the Lords have decreed or resolved or acted in any way by themselves and for themselves, they have always acted with the very narrowest aim of narrowing the access to their own body, in the interest of the phantasy of 'ennobled blood.'" Now the doctrine or "phantasy" of "ennobled blood," for which the Lords were abused by Mr. Freeman, was not, as a matter of fact, laid down by them at all, but by the judges of England! We have only to refer to the original authority, the Journals of the House of Lords (XII. 629–630), to learn that the doctrine on which is based the right to many baronies by writ, the doctrine that when a man had received a "writ of summons . . . his blood was thereby ennobled," was "laid down" in a *unanimous* 'opinion' of the judges, to whom the Lords had referred the question as a point of law. We also find that the Lords' resolution in this (the Clifton) case did *not* contain anything about 'ennobled blood,' and was not even accompanied by any *rationes decidendi*. Lastly we learn from the *Third Report on the Dignity of a Peer* (Ed. 1829), pp. 31–2, that the above 'Opinion' was discussed by the Lords in no favour-

---

[1] *The Nature and Origin of the House of Lords.* By Edward A. Freeman, D.C.L., LL.D., Regius Professor of Modern History in the University of Oxford.

able spirit, the question being even raised how far it might be still binding on them. But perhaps the most astounding of the Professor's statements on the subject is his assertion that

it is the same doctrine which has led to the anomalous position of the judges with regard to the House of Lords. . . . It was possible to keep them from ever winning a full parliamentary position, and they have never won it. . . . It was the superstition, perhaps one should rather say the cunningly devised fable, about hereditary right, ennobling of blood, and the like, which kept them out for ages.

When we learn that the authors of this injustice to the judges, of this " cunningly devised fable," were no other than the judges themselves, we realize the recklessness of the misrepresentation into which the writer was betrayed by his almost frantic prejudice.[1]

It will be seen, therefore, that, in citing Professor Freeman's criticisms, I do so merely in order to show that the statements found in *Burke's Peerage*, as to the origin and early history of certain great families, would be even more preposterous than they are at the present time, if he had not, by his public and merciless exposure, compelled, here and there, a tardy and reluctant amendment. How hard it is to bring about any improvement in the pages of ' Burke ' is shown by its persistent repetition of errors, misstatements, and absurdities, exposed by me in the *Quarterly*

---

[1] See my communication to the *St. James' Gazette* of 24th June, 1885, on "Professor Freeman and the House of Lords." No reply was made to this exposure by himself or any one else.

Review seven years ago.[1] With very few exceptions, no advantage has been taken of the information I then placed at the disposal of the editors of ' Burke,' in spite of the announcement that, last year, a " more thorough revision than usual of its contents was possible." We shall find, indeed, that this ' revision ' has resulted in the actual revival of certain exploded fables.

The extreme difficulty of improving ' Burke ' is shown also by comparison, not only with the infinitely superior *Complete Peerage*, but even with 'Debrett,' of which the editor is far more ready than those responsible for *Burke's Peerage* to correct his work. It would not be necessary to insist at such length upon the point were it not that, owing to it having been edited by the late Ulster King of Arms, and connected after his death with a member of the Heralds' College, the book has acquired, in the eyes of the public, a semi-official status, for which, in spite of its cover, there is absolutely no warrant. Most of the absurd statements in the press on the subject of noble families can be traced to those fables which have obtained currency through its pages.

The *Complete Peerage*, of which the modest author prefers to be known by his initials only, is distinguished further from other works dealing with ennobled families by involving many points of peerage law and history, with which only a few students are familiar and on several of which

---

[1] Article on " the Peerage," October, 1893.

THE PEERAGE

there still exist uncertainty and doubt. On some
of these I advanced views in my *Quarterly Review*
article at variance with those expressed in that
work, and in the ' Corrigenda '[1] its author has
accepted, on most of these, my conclusions. Indeed, he has been content, for the baronage of the
feudal period, to rely chiefly upon others, his own
studies having been directed to more modern
periods. He tells us, in his preface, that " Mr.
Courthope's work is an almost infallible guide as
far as it extends," and he has clearly treated it as
such. The consequence is that, on some points,
he is, as indeed are others, hopelessly behind the
times. Thus, for instance, in a matter of such
importance as the earliest writs of summons, he
simply follows Courthope (1857), who had virtually copied from Nicolas (1825). Accordingly,
his work is based throughout on the belief of
Nicolas that there was no record of any valid writs
of summons between the Parliament of Simon de
Montfort in 1264 and that held by Edward I. in
1295 ; also that the writs of 1294 and 1297 were
for Parliaments of doubtful validity. All this has
now been changed. It is, however, right to mention that the late Deputy-Keeper of the Records
(Sir T. D. Hardy) held the same belief, as is evident from the Minutes of Evidence on the Hastings
case (1841) :—

---

[1] Vol. VIII. pp. 250–537. It has long been difficult, if not
impossible, to obtain complete copies of the book, its high value
as a work of reference having been quickly recognised.

Q. Have you made any search whether there are any writs of summons to Parliament from the forty-ninth of Henry the Third to the twenty-third of Edward the First ?
A. I have.
Q. Do you find any ?
A. I do not.

Moreover, in his *Constitutional History* (1875) Dr. Stubbs himself followed Courthope, writing as follows :—

The importance of 1264 and 1295 arises from the fact that there are no earlier or intermediate writs of summons to a proper Parliament extant ; if, as is by no means impossible, earlier writs addressed to the ancestors of existing families should be discovered, it might become a critical question how far the rule could be regarded as binding.

Yet Sir Francis Palgrave had long before (1830) published his *Parliamentary Writs*, containing those of summons to the Parliament of Shrewsbury in 1283. These, which every one, we have seen, had completely disregarded, were, in 1876, sprung by Counsel on the Committee for Privileges, and accepted by them without question, and apparently without the slightest conception that they were establishing a precedent of the most momentous consequence. When it is added that the contested writs of 1294 and 1297 were also allowed to be put in evidence without question, and that the writ of 1283 affects a hundred baronies, it will be seen that the Mowbray decision (1877) unconsciously wrought a revolution, and that the history of baronies by writ must now be undertaken *de novo*. This decision has also finally disposed of the 1264 writs, which had been accepted in the cases of Le

Despencer and De Ros, and thereby raised a question of precedence as yet insoluble. But G. E. C. has overlooked the fact that the Hastings decision (1841) had already ignored those writs, and set up a wholly new date by recognising sittings, in lieu of writs, in 1290. This barony is assigned by him, we find, to 1295, and by Courthope to 1264, though, as I have said, the authorized date is 1290 (18 Edward I.).[1] These changes are so important, and are clearly so imperfectly understood, that I have thought it well to explain them in detail.

We may now select some test cases of the verdicts on doubtful titles, now, happily, few in number. 'Burke' recognises the assumption by Lord Mar of the title 'Lord Garioch,' although significantly unable to assign to it any creation: G. E. C., however, denies "that any Parliamentary Barony ot that name was ever vested in" the Earls of Mar. In this conclusion he had the support of the late Lyon [Mr. Burnett], although they both sided with Lord Mar in the matter of his earldom. Again, at the death of the late Lord Eglinton (1892), it was asserted by those who claimed to be specially well informed that his father had succeeded in 1840 to the Scottish Earldom of Winton (1600).[2] 'Burke' admits this succession, although the only proof is that, after the title had been dormant

---

[1] My correction has been accepted by the author in his 'Corrigenda.'

[2] This was one of the points noted by me in the *Quarterly Review* article.

nearly a century, Lord Eglinton caused himself to be "served heir male general" to the earls of Winton : G. E. C. does not admit the validity of this proof, and pronounces the title of earl of Winton (United Kingdom), conferred on the family in 1859, to have been "a very improper one" under the circumstances. We observe that G. E. C. considers the attainder of 1716 (ignored by Ulster) a bar to the succession, though Mr. Riddell, I believe, held that. it was saved by a specialty. Into the thorny subject of Scottish retours and services, their trustworthiness and their validity as proofs of extinctions, or even as instructing the right to a peerage, under the present dispensation, I do not propose to enter ; but, as the sympathies of G. E. C. are clearly with the Scottish school, I do not think he is quite consistent in opposing himself to that unhappy system which was responsible (as even its advocates admit) for the fact that there was in Scotland no "salutary check to undue assumption or usurpation." Indeed, under 'Angus,' he boldly assigns that historic earldom to the dukes of Hamilton, although they have, as yet, only claimed it. Turning to the dukedom of Châtellerault, we find that, according to 'Burke,' it is vested in the duke of Abercorn, while the late duke of Hamilton was only said to "claim" that ghost-like relic of a distant past.[1] Neither of the dukes, though holding between them nearly thirty Peerage dignities, would waive his claim to

---

[1] This is omitted in ' Burke ' since the late duke's death.

this shadowy title ; and 'Burke,' while assigning
to the Irish Duke, "in the point of honour, over
all," the *escocheon* of the French Duchy, engraves it
also on the arms of his rival, observing with courtly
felicity that "his Grace places" it there. But in
the painfully candid *Complete Peerage* the duke
of Abercorn himself is only recognised as a claimant, an elaborate note reminding us that it is even
quite doubtful whether the contested title was ever
created at all. The Irish Viscountcy of Valentia
is another of those cases in which the *Complete
Peerage* appears to great advantage by the side of
the careless 'Burke.' On the death of the 9th
Viscount (1844), the title was assumed by "his
distant cousin," who, adds G. E. C., "took no steps
to establish his right thereto." According to the
same authority there were senior branches of the
family of which the extinction "has never been
proved."[1] Of all this we learn nothing, under
" Valentia," in 'Burke,' though reference to a roll
hidden away at the end of the volume will show that
the right to this title is as yet unproved, and that,
consequently, no vote can be given in respect of
it at elections of representative peers for Ireland.
However valid the claim may be, it is surely, in the
highest degree, unsatisfactory that its validity should
thus remain unproved indefinitely. The same remark applies to the Scottish Barony of Belhaven.
It is stated by G. E. C. that the 9th Lord, who
died in 1893, was succeeded by his "4th cousin

---

[1] Vol. VIII. p. 15, note *b*.

and heir male . . . who succeeded to the
peerage 6th September, 1893, his claim thereto
being established in July, 1894."[1]   But, the error
having been pointed out to him, he substituted for
" established " the words : " recognised so far as
having been served heir and as voting for Scotch
Representative Peers, but not by the Committee for
Privileges in the House of Lords.[2]   Here again
the claim may be valid, but 'Burke' gives us no hint
of the actual state of affairs.[3]   The far more remarkable case of the Barony of Ruthven of Freeland will be discussed separately below.   Here it
need only be said that its existence is energetically
denied by G. E. C., as it was by Mr. Foster in his
'Peerage'; Debrett also admits the title only as
" claimed and assumed by Walter James Hore
Ruthven as 8th 'Baron'" and pronounces it "more
probable" that the barony " really ceased with the
extinction of the direct male line."   The cause of
all this trouble, as I have repeatedly insisted, is the
absence of any valid check on the assumption of
Scottish and Irish titles.   The last case I select is
that of the exalted, but mysterious, foreign dignities claimed by the earls of Denbigh.   These
noblemen are descended, in the words of Professor
Gardiner, from " the plain country gentleman who
had the good luck to marry Buckingham's sister in
the days of her poverty."   Rising with Buckingham, he became a peer, and, in due course, the

---

[1] Vol. VIII. p. 307.   [2] Vol. VIII. p. 532.
[3] It is only right to add that this criticism applies to 'Debrett'
also in the case of these two titles.

family revealed a fact which they had hitherto kept to themselves, namely, that they were not of English origin, but were descended in the male line from the mighty house of Hapsburg. It was this illustrious descent that inspired the pen of Gibbon when, alluding to their pedigree of a thousand years, he wrote that "the successors of Charles V. may disdain their brethren of England; but the romance of Tom Jones, that exquisite picture of human manners, will outlive the palace of the Escurial, and the imperial eagle of the House of Austria." Lord Denbigh, according to 'Burke,' down to the present year, is "count of Hapsburg, Laufenburg, and Rheinfelden," and, as such (it was added), "a count of the Holy Roman Empire." An eagle of Austria bore his arms, and the antiquity of his countship is so great that its date of creation is unknown. Yet on all these honours G. E. C. is mute, though he hints in a footnote that no "mention of this illustrious origin is made in the Heralds' visitations." As will be seen below,[1] I have critically examined the story and pronounced it an absolute concoction, without, strange as it may seem, one shred of truth. This year, 'Burke' at last abandons under 'Denbigh' the countships and the arms (as indeed 'Debrett' had previously done); but under "Foreign Titles of Nobility" (p. 1894) we still find "Hapsburgh, etc., see Denbigh," while even under "Denbigh," the family pedigree is still traced to "Geffery, count of Hapsburgh."

[1] See the paper on "Our English Hapsburgs."

These cases are, of course, conspicuous, but the
little points which tempt the honesty and test the
accuracy of peerage writers are more easily overlooked.   It is by his treatment of such points that
G. E. C. inspires confidence, especially when his
statements are fortified by a dense array of dates.
If Sir Bernard Burke inclined to mercy, and flat-
tered the vanity of his patrons, the opposite tendency is visible in G. E. C.   He takes a positive
delight in explaining that the first Lord Kensington
was the son of "a purser," that Lord Kingsale
(1759–1776) was "bred a carpenter," or that the
founder of Lord Carrington's family was a "respectable draper at Nottingham."   For pretentious
affectations he is pitiless.   Thus he very sensibly
observes of the title 'Ffrench' :—

The ludicrous mode of spelling the name with a *double* "f"
has been stereotyped by its adoption in the patent of 1798.   It
probably arose from ignorance that the form of the capital "F"
was that of the small "f" *duplicated*,   .   .   .   and, considering
the spread of education, is not likely to occur again.

We note, however, that under "De Freyne" he
accepts the statement that "this title is merely an
archaic form of the family name, otherwise *de Freigne*
or *de Fraxinis*."   Now this is simply absurd.   "The
family name" was plain "French," and its derivation obvious.   When Playfair composed his Baronetage as a monument of sycophantic folly, he discovered that Smith was derived from *Smeeth*, "a
level plain," but confessed that he could find for
Baker no possible derivation.   In the same spirit
the French family, discarding its obvious origin,

assumed an imaginary descent from " De la freigne "
(*De Fraxineto*). Yet on the rage for ' De ' in the
last hundred years, G. E. C., we find, is unsparing
in his sarcasm. Such titles as ' De Tabley,' ' De
Mauley,' and ' De Ramsey ' arouse in him the
same scorn as a " modern Gothic castle." Even
' De Grey,' as he points out, is a modern innova-
tion on Grey. Supplementing the cases he quotes,
one may here attempt a list illustrating the manu-
facture of the imitation article in feudal nobility.
The immortal creator of ' Jeames,' who from
' Yellowplush ' became ' De la Pluche,' did but
satirize that process of conversion which has
changed the names of Smith, Bear, Hunt, Robin-
son, Aldworth, Smithson, Wilkins, Wigram,
Morres, Lill, Smith, Supple, Mullins, Green, and
Gossip, into Vernon, De Beauchamp, De Vere, De
Grey, Neville, Percy, De Winton, Fitzwygram,
De Montmorency, De Burgh, De Heriz, De
Capell Brooke, De Moleyns, De Freville, and De
Rodes. Bottom is indeed translated. The marvel
is that such tempting examples have not been more
widely followed.

> What can delay
> De Vaux and De Saye,
> *   *   *   *   *
> Fitzwalter, FitzOsbert, FitzHugh, and FitzJohn ?

It is alleged in *A treatise on the law concerning names and changes of names* that " an application to assume the particle ' De ' in front of a
name is usually granted where unquestionable evidence can be produced of descent from some

ancestor who so wrote his name." [1] Yet, so recently as 1863, the Irish family of Power, which holds a Papal countship, obtained a Royal license to change its name to 'De la Poer.' Count 'de Poher de la Poer' claims to be lord 'le Power (and Coroghmore)' as heir male of the body of ' Sir Richard Power, Kt.,' who was so created in 1535.[2] Here then we have four forms of the name, three of which—le Power, de Poher, and de la Poer—contradict one another. And the origin of this dreadful jumble is simply the desire of a family as old as the Conquest of Ireland to repudiate their purely personal surname and to claim for it a territorial origin. The name is very frequently met with, in the 12th century, in England, and in Ireland after the Conquest, and when it has a prefix at all, that prefix is *le*. Therefore, whatever its meaning, the name must be personal. A Mr. Redmond, who wrote an account of this family, calmly overcame the difficulty by changing 'le' into 'de' in the case of its early members, which enabled him to arrive at the conclusion that "it may fairly be presumed that the family sprang from the counts or princes of Le Poher." [3] This indeed is what it claims, and, accordingly, it has now adopted the names of Alan, Rivallon, and Yseult.

It is only fair, however, to observe that, so far

[1] *Genealogical Magazine*, II. 451.
[2] See *Burke's Peerage*, *Burke's Landed Gentry*, and *Genealogical Magazine*, I. 140, 207, 270.
[3] Le Poher was a *Comté* in Britanny which ceased to exist as a separate organization in 937.

back as 1767, the idiotic form of 'la Poer' crept in at the time of Lady Tyrone's claim, although that claim was made under a writ to 'Nicholas le Poer' (1375), and since that time the Beresford family have used it as a Christian name in the developed form of 'De la Poer.' The Trench family, one of whom had similarly married a Power heiress in the last century, have, with more regard for facts and grammar, used (as earls of Clancarty), 'Power' and 'Le Poer' as Christian names. I have elsewhere shown that this name has no more to do with a Breton *Comté* than has Smith to do with " *Smeeth*, a level plain," and that it is purely personal.[1] Count 'de Poher de la Poer' has twice replied,[2] but has not even attempted to prove that the name had 'De' before it, or to deny that its prefix, when it had one, was 'Le.' Indeed, he very frankly quoted the verdict of M. de Guyencourt (Secrétaire de la Société des Antiquaires de la Picardie) :—

Il est absolument certain que les Pohiers sont les habitants de Poix en Picardie. Aujourd'hui encore on leur donne ce nom ; ils se le donnent à euxmêmes. Le mot Pohier était Latinisé en *Poherus* : " Pontivi comitem sequuntur in arma Poheri."

This would be one origin of the name ; but there are others, though I do not go so far as Mr. Rye, who approves of my strictures on the tampering with the name and asserts that it meant 'the poor man.'[3]

---

[1] *Genealogist*, [N.S.] XII. 215, XIII. 15–16.
[2] *Ibid*. XII. 221–3, XIII. 131–2.
[3] *Ibid*. XII. 288.   See also Eyton's *Shropshire*, III. 197–8.

It is Ireland also that provides the most monstrous case of all, that of ' De Montmorency.' Mr. Freeman scoffed at

the singular fact that a family named Morres, dissatisfied with a very respectable name . . . thought proper in the last century to change it into *Montmorency*, and to give out that a branch of the house of the first Christian baron followed the banner of the Norman.

With grim humour he pointed out that this " is one of the very few cases where the faith, even, of Sir Bernard Burke gives way," and " when he comes to this monstrous fable," we find that "there is somewhere a last pound which breaks the back even of an Ulster King-at-arms." [1] The alleged descent, indeed, is ignored by *Burke's Peerage* and absolutely laughed to scorn by G. E. C. Yet it is not fair to treat the claim as a mere private assumption. As Colonel Morres boasted at the time, his proofs were " verifiés avec la plus scrupuleuse attention par l'autorité compétente et sanctionnés désormais par l'autorisation du prince qui gouverne aujourd'hui l'empire britannique." [2] But, unfortunately, " l'autorité compétente " was, as ' X ' and Mr. Fox-Davies are always so loudly insisting, the officer-of-arms concerned. Sir William Betham, Deputy-Ulster, certified, in his official capacity, that the alleged pedigree was

[1] *Cont. Rev.*, XXX. 38.
[2] "Les Montmorency de France et les Montmorency d'Irlande, ou Précis historique des démarches faites à l'occasion de la reprise du nom de ses ancêtres par la branche de Montmorency-mariscomorres" (Paris, 1828), p. 25.

"established on evidence of the most unquestionable authority, chiefly from the ancient public
records." May one not apply to this certificate
the words that 'X,' as the heralds' champion,
applies to the unfortunate public :—

> The Psalmist in his haste remarked that all men were liars,
> and spoke with no experience of armorial bearings or of the
> temptation they afford to depart from the truth.[1]

For the absolute falsehood of Betham's certificate
is demonstrated, beyond the possibility of question,
in my article on "The Montmorency Imposture,"[2]
where I have proved that, on its own showing, the
entire pedigree collapses. Yet the Crown, naturally,
could only accept the statement of its own officer of
arms, and it accordingly described the alleged descent
as duly proved and recorded.[3] The energetic protest
of the French house was wholly disregarded, and so
perfect was this "modern antique," which dates,
like others, from the Wyatville period, that the
family assumed not only the arms, with the name,
of that historic house, but also its motto, "Dieu
Ayde," as if conscious that the proof of their
claims was beyond the power of man. And now
there has crept in the name of 'Bouchard,' the
tenth-century patriarch of the French house. It
was bound to come. Have not the Douglases
stereotyped in 'Sholto' the legend of the 'dark-grey
man,' the Ashburnhams in 'Bertram' the victim of

---

[1] *The right to bear arms* (p. 176).
[2] *Feudal England*, pp. 519–527.
[3] *London Gazette*, Sept. 9, 1815 ; *Dublin Gazette*, Aug. 12, 1815.

the Conquest, the Stourtons in 'Botolph' its
English hero, and the Fieldings in 'Rudolph' their
glorious descent?   The mythical Otho is commemorated in the family nomenclature of Fitz-
geralds, and in that of the Grosvenors has appeared
a most traditionary 'Lupus,' while the Russells
perpetuate in 'Odo' their imaginary Norman
origin.   Although this fashion is modern, it was
strangely forestalled by the Percys, whose well-
known 'Algernon' referred to the supposed sobri-
quet of their founder, and began some four
centuries ago, though not, there is reason to believe,
as a true Christian name.   But in even earlier days
the Beauchamps had shown the way, Guy de
Beauchamp, earl of Warwick, who was born in
1278, being named after the famous Guy, the
mythical ancestor of the Earls *temp*. Athelstan,
whose adventures with dragons and with pagan folk
were long the joy of the romancer.   The name has
been revived in our own time, being borne by the
present earl of the Greville house.

Apart from the " modern antiques " at which
we have glanced above, the *Complete Peerage* is
severely critical of the efforts made by certain
families to connect themselves, by title or by surname, with houses of older standing to which they
are unrelated.   The most glaring of these cases is
that of the banking family of Smith, originating,
as observed above, in " a respectable draper at
Nottingham." [1]   When raised to the peerage by

[1] Martin's *Stories of Banks and Bankers*, quoted by G. E. C.
It is interesting to learn, of the barony conferred on this family,

Pitt about a hundred years ago, it selected as the title of its barony 'Carrington,' doubtless, as is pointed out by G. E. C., because an older family of Smith, " in no way connected with the family of the grantee," had borne that title from 1643 to 1706.[1] And this latter house had itself selected that title because of a 'cock-and-bull' story that its real ancestor was Sir Michael Carrington, standard bearer to Richard I. in Palestine, a descendant of whom, John Carrington, "fled out of England and named him selfe Smith."[2] As if this were

that " According to Wraxall, this was the only instance in which George III.'s objections to giving English peerages to those engaged in trade were overcome " (*Dictionary of National Biography*).

[1] It was, perhaps, unfortunate that in the person of Lord Boringdon, the Parkers of Devonshire should have taken 'Morley' as the title of their earldom (created 1815), in view of the fact that the ancient barony of Morley (1299), now in abeyance, had been held by a family of Parker, with which they had no connection, for two and a half centuries. But this can hardly be held to justify the violent note on the subject in the *Complete Peerage* (V. 374):—" It is impossible to speak too strongly of the contemptible and vulgar vanity and want of all right feeling which induced the grantee of 1815 to select his title . . . in the hope of [fraudulently] palming himself off as being of the ancient stock." Such violent language as this is not only excessive, but is a subject for regret in a work of reference.

[2] The authority of Elizabethan heralds was vouched for this story : " Of whose family I may not omit to observe what I have seen attested by Sir William Dethick, sometime garter principall King of Armes, and Robert Cooke Clarenceux ; viz., that the said John Smyth (the baron) was grandson to John Carington ; and the said John Carington lineally descended from Sir Michael Carington, knight, standard-bearer to the famous King Richard the First in the Holy Land " (Dugdale's *Warwickshire*, p. 601). Subsequently, however, in his *Baronage*, Dugdale only asserted

not enough, the above modern family of Smith, though not even claiming connection with the descendants of the alleged standard bearer, changed its name, in 1839, to 'Carrington' (and subsequently to 'Carington'), presumably because it sounded nicer, and without even a baseless tradition to support the change. Another branch of the same family now appears among the Baronets, as 'Bromley,' while a third has recently been ennobled under the title of 'Pauncefote.' This latter creation gave rise to a wondrous paragraph, which appeared on all sides in the press, tracing the new peer's descent from a Sir Grimbald Pauncefote living in the Middle Ages, whose name indeed used to appear at the head of the family pedigree in Burke's *Landed Gentry*.[1] The distinguished diplomatist in question, however, is in no way descended from the Pauncefotes, and in *Burke's Peerage* the pedigree begins, in the most straight-

that the family "do derive themselves" as above. Their actual founder, Sir John Smith, a baron of the Exchequer, who died 1547, is alleged to have been a great-grandson of Sir Thomas de Carington, who died 1383 ! But the family arms have mysteriously changed more than once (see *Complete Peerage*, II. 167).

As might be expected, many a Smith turned with longing eyes to "Sir Michael Carington" as an ancestor. The 1886 edition of Burke's *Landed Gentry* guardedly observed that "Several families [of Smith] claim descent from the earlier branches" of "the Caringtons, who are stated to have changed their surname to Smith," among them one whose "immediate ancestor" died in 1795. This modest claim had developed in the 1894 edition into the five-columned pedigree of "Smith-Carington," traced back to "Sir Mychell de Carinton," and thence to the Conquest.

[1] See the editions of 1886 and 1894.

forward manner, with his actual ancestors, the Smiths.

In sharp contrast with such instances as this of an honest and straightforward descent, Lord Lytton's pedigree in 'Burke' still commences with "Sir Robert de Lytton of Lytton, in the county of Derby, comptroller of the household to King Henry IV.," although it will be found, on close scrutiny, that the present owner of Knebworth descends from "William Robinson," *tout court*, a stranger in blood to the old Lyttons, who obtained the property by bequest, in 1710, to the exclusion, as is pointed out by G. E. C., "of the heirs at law and representatives of the race of Lytton."[1] Bearing in mind that the present family have not, in the words of the same authority, "*any* descent from the old family of Lytton of Knebworth," there is something exquisitely comic in this sonorous passage from the panegyric of Alison the historian on Sir E. Bulwer Lytton.

"Born of a noble family, the inheritor of ancestral halls of uncommon splendour and interest, he has received from his Norman forefathers the qualities which rendered them noble. No man was ever more thoroughly imbued with the elevated thoughts, the chivalrous feelings which are the true mark of patrician

[1] The present Lyttons, though descended in the female line from an old Norfolk family, the Dallings, are in the male line Wiggetts, a family on which Mr. Walter Rye, in his *Popular History of Norfolk*, has something to say. It is a singular coincidence that another branch of the same family (the Wiggetts) has now become 'Chute of the Vyne,' inheriting that most interesting old Hampshire seat, like their kinsmen at Knebworth, without any descent from the Chute family.

blood ; and which, however they may be admired by others, never perhaps exist in such purity as in those who, like the Arab steeds of high descent, can trace their pedigree back through a long series of ancestors."

"The dining-room at Knebworth, in Hertfordshire, Sir E. Bulwer Lytton's noble family mansion, originally built by a Norman follower of the Conqueror, is fifty-six feet long and thirty high, hung round with the armour which the family and their retainers wore at the battle of Bosworth, and ended by the gallery in which the minstrels poured forth their heart-stirring strains." [1]

The admiration here expressed by Disraeli's " Mr. Wordy " contrasts quaintly with Thackeray's bitter caricature of the aristocratic novelist.

" Look again at me friend Bullwig. He *is* a gentleman, to be sure, and bad luck to 'im, say I ; and what has been the result of his litherary labour ? I'll tell you what, and I'll tell this gintale society, by the shade of Saint Patrick, they're going to make him *a Barinet."*

" And pray what for ? "

" What faw ? " says Bullwig. " Ask the histowy of litwatuwe what faw ? Ask Colburn, ask Bentley, ask Saunders and Otley, ask the gweat Bwitish nation, what faw ? The blood in my veins comes puwified thwough ten thousand years of chivalwous ancestwy . . . and the Bwitish government, honowing genius in me, compliments the Bwitish nation by lifting into the bosom of the heweditawy nobility the most gifted member of the democwacy." [2]

Whether the solemn Scottish writer was hoaxed or not by his host, it adds to the humour of the whole story when we find that even the old Lyttons did not purchase Knebworth till after Bosworth fight. It was bought, according to ' Burke,' in 7 Hen. VII. (1491–2), by " Sir Robert de Lytton of Lytton,"

[1] Alison's *History of Europe* (1852), I. 480.
[2] *Yellowplush Papers.*

son of the above Sir Robert de Lytton, who lived, we learn, under Henry IV. (1399–1413). The editor's notions of regnal chronology seem to be as strange here as they are in the case of the St. Johns. Nor is our confidence increased when we find that this Lytton (a property in Tideswell, then valued at forty shillings a year) was held, in 1431, not by a Robert, not by a knight, not even by an esquire, but by Richard Lytton, ' gentilman.'[1]

An instance of the scrupulous exactitude of G. E. C. is afforded by the title of Warwick. He points out that this should rightly be Brooke and Warwick, the Earls taking precedence under Brooke (1746). Though adopting the style of Warwick (1759) alone, their petition for assigning to Warwick the precedence of Brooke was never, he observes, granted. He is further careful to explain that when these honours were conferred, the family, in spite of the flourishes of peerage writers, were not even co-heirs of a younger branch of the old earls of Warwick, whom therefore they in no way represent, although their coat-of-arms is decked with the swan and the bear of the Beauchamps, together, he adds, with the suggestive motto, " Vix ea nostra voco." We must also agree with him on the impropriety of granting the baronies of Lovel and Holland to Lord Egmont's ancestor (1762), when he was in no way a co-heir to the ancient baronies of these names. The Lovel quartering on Lord Egmont's coat is most mis-

---

[1] *Feudal Aids*, I. 287.

leading, implying, as it does, a non-existent representation in blood.

Nor is it only on names and styles that G. E. C. is outspoken. He reminds us of the origin of the earldom of Orkney, and is careful to explain that Lord Winchilsea's Viscountcy of Maidstone was obtained (1623) by bribery, and that so recently as 1747 the viscountcy of Folkestone was purchased for £12,000 through the notorious countess of Yarmouth, who "is stated to have derived considerable sums from the sale of peerages." Holles, we see, according to him, bought his barony (1616) through Buckingham for £10,000, and the coveted earldom of Clare (1624) for an additional £5,000. I had imagined that the latter cost him more, but, though the purchase system was as fully recognised in the peerage then as in the army afterwards, the facts are not easy to ascertain. The barony of Teynham (1616) was undoubtedly said to have been purchased for £10,000, but I have seen it stated that the earldoms of Devonshire (1618), Northampton (1618), and Warwick (1618) cost no larger a sum. The Scottish barony of Fairfax (1627) is also said to have been paid for.[1] G. E. C., by the way, would seem to be unaware of Dugdale's letter on the difficulty (surmounted by a bribe to courtiers) of inducing Charles II. to recognise at the Restoration the suspicious Dudley patent of 1644. Again, under 'Guilford,' G. E. C. revives the North

---

[1] Markham's *Life of the great Lord Fairfax*, p. 14.

ecclesiastical scandals ; though under ' Feversham '
he does not allude to the origin of the Duncombe
wealth. Macaulay and Professor Freeman, between them, were outspoken enough on the subject, the latter writing :—

> Lord Macaulay's readers know how "the once humble name
> of Duncombe" got transferred to the lands which had once been
> the reward of Fairfax ; and students of local genealogy may
> know how the name passed, not only to the lands—the lands
> which the House of Commons proposed to confiscate as a punish-
> ment of their owner's fraud—but also to their later possessors.
> Now, if Brown chooses to call himself Duncombe, or if Dun-
> combe insists that Brown shall call himself Duncombe, no great
> harm is done to anyone, and Brown most likely is pleased. But
> when the lands of Helmsley were made to take the name of
> Duncombe, a real wrong was done to geography. . . .
> The thing is a fraud on nomenclature as great as any of the
> frauds which the first Duncombe, "born to carry parcels and to
> sweep down a counting-house," contrived to commit on the
> treasury of the nation.[1]

An unsparing footnote is suggested to G. E. C.
by the restoration of the earldom of Devon (1831),
contrasting strangely with the famous panegyric of
Gibbon on the Courtenays, who " still retain the
plaintive motto, which asserts the innocence, and
deplores the fall, of their ancient house." Another
note carefully explains that, in 1837, a jury "only
took 15 minutes to determine upon their verdict"
implying that the Premier Baron of England had
cheated at cards.[2]

But the limit of what is permissible is reached
in such comments as these, and one cannot but
regard that this limit is passed in certain objection-

[1] *English towns and districts*, p. 310.   [2] Vol. VI. p. 407.

able notes. It is possible to compile an honest Peerage without making it a *chronique scandaleuse*, and a work of reference is only disfigured by remarks which offend, surely, against good taste.

A point upon which G. E. C. permits himself to speak strongly is the practice of calling out of abeyance certain ancient baronies in favour of modern co-heirs but distantly connected with them. His remarks on this subject (under ' Beaumont') deserve quoting :—

The early years of the Queen's accession were the halcyon times for the Peerage lawyers. Supporters of the Whig Government (Lord Melbourne's) who, under other Ministers, might have entered the peerage from *below*, had now good reason to expect to be placed *over* the heads of almost the entire Baronage (*e.g.*, over such families as Stourton, St. John, Dormer, Roper, Clifford, Byron, etc.), provided only that the Peerage lawyer could prove that there was in them . . . some small fraction of co-representation of some one of the prodigious number of early Baronies, which (according to modern interpretation) were created in fee by the numerous writs of summons issued by the Plantagenet kings. Before the time of George III. (passing over the anomalous case of Le Despencer) no abeyance had been terminated that had existed more than the space of some thirty years or so ; that king, however, in four (Botetourt, Zouche, Roos, and Howard de Walden) out of the eight Baronies [*sic*] he thus terminated, introduced the pernicious practice of reviving Baronies whose estates had been entirely alienated, and where the dignities themselves had lapsed for a century or more. It was reserved, however, for the short space of little more than three years (March 1838 to May 1841) to terminate the abeyance of *six* Baronies—of which five had long been disused, the 'caput Baroniæ' and all estates belonging to them having been alienated and their very names become unfamiliar. These five were : VAUX, which had been in abeyance about 175 years ; (2) BRAYE, about 300 years, the newly established Baroness representing one of the younger of the *six* sisters and co-heirs (all of whom left issue) of the second Lord ; (3) BEAUMONT, about 350 years ; (4) CAMOYS, above 400 years ; and, finally, (5) HASTINGS, which, though in abeyance *only* 300 years, had been *dormant* for about 450 years. . . . Had this pace of terminating abeyances been continued, the Peerage would, since the Queen's accession, have by this time been 'adorned' with about 100 such (strange) Baronies . . . but, happily, the good sense of the Crown itself preserved the Peerage from being thus swamped.

This most objectionable system . . . is admirably described by Disraeli in his novel called *Sybil* (1845), where Mr. Hatton, the famous Peerage lawyer of the Inner Temple, explains how *he* can make a Peer. . . . "If you wish to be Lord Bardolph, I will undertake to make you so . . . it will give you precedence over every other Peer on the roll, except three (*and I made those*)."

This complaint is repeated by the writer as he comes to each of the obnoxious baronies, and as a protest against the abuse of the prerogative it has much justification. There is also a good deal of truth in his comment on the modern barony of Fitz-Walter, granted in 1868 as a consolation to Sir Brook Bridges on his failing to establish his right to the ancient barony of that name :—

A very different treatment was shown to this (*Conservative*) claimant of a peerage to what had been, a few years previously, shown to the (*Liberal*) claimants of the Baronies of Vaux, Camoys, Braye, Hastings, etc. . . . while in *this* case the Barony had continued *uninterruptedly* from 1295 to 1755, and the claimant represented an undoubted moiety, if indeed not the entirety thereof.

Another case, one may add, of contrasting treatment in the matter is afforded by the barony of Ferrers. With the exception of short spells of abeyance, 1646–1677 and 1741–9, this barony existed continuously from 1299 to 1855. But it is not so much upon that ground that it might have been selected as an ideal case for the determination of the abeyance as from the singular and happy circumstance that its senior co-heirs, the family of Ferrers of Baddesley Clinton, were also the heirs *male* of the great house of Ferrers, as is shown by G. E. C. in an admirable chart pedigree (III. 334–5). It is hard enough for our ancient houses to trace an undoubted male descent from even the humblest Norman mentioned in Domesday Book, but the house of Ferrers was already mighty when the Conqueror filled the throne, and had attained the dignity of an earldom in the early days of Stephen. The heir male of such a house as this would be worthy indeed to take his seat among the ancient barons of the realm. And yet the existence of such a line, outside the House of Lords, serves to remind us that, in England, a simple country gentleman can still look down in calm disdain, from the heights of immemorial *noblesse*, on the scramble for the newest of peerage dignities or for those baronetcies which are fast becoming the peculiar perquisite of the *nouveau riche*.[1]

---

[1] I am tempted to allude to the little-known fact that the royal instructions to the special Commissioners, at the foundation of the order (1611), commanded them to " proceed with none, except it shall appear unto you, upon good proof, . . . that they are, at the least, descended of a grandfather (by the father's side) that bore arms." And those admitted were, accordingly, gentry of high position and ancient lineage. The *status* of these early baronetcies is, therefore, quite different from that of those conferred, according to the modern practice, on persons who—to

THE PEERAGE

The first two Stuart kings are often charged with the degradation of hereditary titles of honour, not only by creating them too profusely, but also by virtually selling them.[1] There is, unfortunately, in this charge a good deal of truth ; but it would be grievous hypocrisy to pretend that the practice was restricted to those monarchs, or that even in these decorous days peerage dignities are invariably conferred for public services alone.[2] The question involved is a very wide one ; indeed, for those who look ahead and who watch the signs of the times, it is one of national importance. That the highest honours which the Crown has it in its power to bestow should at all times be granted with jealous care, if their value and their dignity are to be maintained, is a self-evident proposition ; but the point that is apt to be overlooked, the now growing danger, is the risk that " the trail of finance " should sully the honour of the Peerage, should hasten the ever-increasing tendency to substitute a plutocratic for an aristocratic class. That this country has been saved from much that is, beyond dispute, deplorable in the public life of the United States is, it may be confidently and boldly asserted, due to the existence of a social standard other than that of mere wealth. This is a matter

quote the *Quadripartitus* [Ed. Liebermann], describing the *novi homines* of 1114—" vera morum generositate carentes et honesta prosapia, longo nummorum stemmate gloriantur."

[1] See p. 28 above, and compare Pike's *Constitutional History of the House of Lords*, p. 355.

[2] See, for instance, the significant note in *Complete Peerage* (VIII. 47) on the notorious " resignation honours " of 1895.

not of prejudice, but of observation and of fact. The social standard of this country may, like others, have its faults, but it has, at least, saved us, thus far, from making the accumulation of wealth, however acquired, the sole national ideal. Nor is it among the least of the services rendered to the nation by its army and its navy that the officers of those great professions have kept before us, in a corporate form, the conception of a life of which the aim was, not the making of money, but the discharge of duty.

It is, and always has been, easy to sneer at the claims of birth, but if English political and social life is not to be degraded to the level reached in the United States, if great abilities are still to be attracted to the service of the public and the State rather than to that of Mammon, there is absolutely no means by which this can be effected other than that of maintaining barriers which wealth alone cannot overleap, of rewarding service by distinctions which money cannot buy, of upholding a social standard based on something else than the dollars a man has acquired by fair means or foul.

We are not called upon to settle what should be the social standard in Utopia ; what we have to do is, here in England, to see that wealth does not usurp the position of that standard. And this, because its doing so would lower the whole tone of national life.

When Mr. Gladstone urged the argument, in the House of Commons, on the Royal Grants Bill, that " the habits of society have in the course of

THE PEERAGE

years become more and more expensive, and, as I
may say, luxurious,"[1] he was taken to task by one
of his followers, the member for Sunderland, as
follows :—

When the right hon. gentleman tells me that the cost of living
has increased, I admit that the cankerworm of extravagance, the
precursor of decay and ruin of nations, has eaten deeply into London Society.

Mr. Storey proceeded to urge that a member of
the Royal Family should rather " by an honourable
simplicity of life attempt to discourage luxury than
. . . undertake a race of competitive extravagance
with the plutocrats and aristocrats of the time."
One need not approve of Mr. Storey's taste, one
need not share his political opinions, to feel that a
great truth underlay his words. It would be hard
to vulgarize royalty, or to degrade aristocracy, more
effectually than by stooping to compete, on its own
level, with wealth alone. The whole matter is one
of standard, and we cannot wonder that the newly
rich should strive to make that standard what it is
in the United States.[3] Here, as yet, even a baronetcy, at least when Conservatives are in power, is
not always to be bought, as we learned the other
day, for £50,000. That no money, under any
circumstances, should be able to buy a peerage

[1] *Hansard*, 4th July, 1889, col. 1483.
[2] *Ibid.* 25th July, 1889, cols. 1307–8.
[3] To close observers it is a sign of the times that, of late, the
term 'middle class,' which formerly denoted those beneath the
rank of gentry, has been largely applied to those of moderate
fortune irrespective of their birth.

dignity is, if a dream, at least a dream which, in the national interest, men of both parties might well combine to realize. There at least a barrier might be found, if in social life no leaders can be found bold enough to stem the flood. If society is doomed, we may at least strive to avert the degradation of the Peerage, not in the interests of a class, but in those of the whole people.

The Stuart kings might plead, if arraigned at the bar of history, that whether they received money or not, they bestowed their peerage dignities on those qualified by birth to receive them, on men who already belonged to the ranks of the English gentry.[1] Nor, it may be added, was the danger from the tyranny of mere wealth one that had then to be reckoned with. And Charles, quick to make his point, would doubtless turn to such a charter as that which he granted to the borough of Colchester, excluding even from the franchise itself brewers and all those connected with the traffic in drink, and, with an air of well-bred surprise, would inquire if it were indeed the fact that a peerage was now the reward for the acquisition of a fortune by the sale of a recognised source of national poverty and crime.

There are few points connected with the Peerage on which so much misconception prevails, among the general public, as the doctrine of abeyance. It appears to be usually considered imma-

[1] See the cases above on p. 28.

terial whether a dignity is spoken of as 'dormant' or 'in abeyance.' Yet the two conditions are radically distinct. A dignity is said to be 'dormant' when it is in existence but is not assumed : it falls into 'abeyance' when, being descendible (as in the case of a barony by writ) to heirs-general, its heirs are two or more sisters, who, having an equal share in the dignity, can neither of them assume it. In Scotland, where the eldest daughter inherits such dignities, such a state of affairs cannot arise ; but in England, where—except for vague traces of an *esnecia* or *droit d'aînesse*—the sisters rank equally, it has led to curious developments. Lady Otway-Cave, in whose favour the barony of Braye was called out of abeyance in 1839, had four sons and five daughters, so that the succession seemed well secured. Yet, at her death (1862), the barony fell into abeyance, and only emerged in 1879, on four of the five daughters having died childless, so that the fifth became sole heir. This case aptly illustrates the two methods by which the abeyance of a dignity can be 'determined,' viz. (1) by the intervention of the Crown in favour of one of the co-heirs ; (2) by the natural extinction of all the co-heirs but one.

Instructive, and in many respects memorable, was the determination of the abeyance of the historic baronies of Mowbray and Segrave in favour of Lord Stourton (1877–8), which will be the subject of a separate study in this volume. I have already referred to its bearing on the dates of baronies by writ, but I cannot pass over the novel principle it enunciates, with equal unconsciousness, in the doctrine of abeyance. Yet, apart from the points of law involved, it was eminently fitting that these ancient dignities should be ' called out ' in favour of one whose ancestors had already been peers of the realm for more than four hundred years. Moreover, it served to accentuate the fact that the heirship in blood of that *colluvies gentium* which had made the fortunes of the Howards had long passed from the dukes of Norfolk, although they had succeeded in diverting in their favour the historic estate and some of the dignities so acquired. So too the anomalous barony of Percy, vested in the duke of Athole, similarly reminds us that the dukes of Northumberland have ceased to represent the Percys, whose estates, however, they retain. It is, perhaps, as little realized that the right heir of Nelson is not the holder of the Nelson earldom, who is descended from a sister of the admiral, but Lord Bridport, who represents his brother, and is accordingly duke of Bronté. So also the dukes of Marlborough are but the junior co-heirs of Churchill, the representation of his elder daughter (*suo jure* duchess of Marlborough) being vested in the late Lord Conyers. We are not told on what grounds the princedom of the Empire is alleged to have descended with the dukedom to a junior co-heir. G. E. C., indeed, appears to doubt the fact (V. 255).

The consideration of the Mowbray descent brings me to a question of heraldry never, so far as I know, raised till I wrote in the *Quarterly Review*

(Oct. 1893) as follows. Few coats are more familiar than that of the house of Howard, with its famous Flodden augmentation. For the benefit of non-heraldic readers one may explain that, like the scalp that adorns the Indian brave, an 'augmentation' granted for a victory commonly bore an armorial allusion to the vanquished leader. Accordingly, the Howards' victory at Flodden, and the death on the field of the King of Scots, were commemorated by the grant of an augmentation adapted from the King's arms, but so imperfectly described in the original as to make the accepted blazon somewhat open to question. My point, however, is that this honourable distinction was granted to the duke of Norfolk " et heredibus suis temporibus futuris imperpetuum." Dugdale renders this as a grant in tail male, and the late Dr. Brewer, in his official calendar of Henry VIII. papers (vol. I. p. 729), similarly terms it a " grant in tail male." Now this is a rather serious matter. Rightly or wrongly, Dr. Brewer enjoyed a great reputation, and it may appear incredible that he should so misread the grant. Yet there is no doubt about it ; I have examined the original roll (Pat. 5 Hen. VIII., pars 2, m. 13, *alias* 18) more than once. It is possible that,—as in the grant of the dukedom, which precedes it, and that of estates, which follows it, the *habendum* is to heirs male of the body,—Dr. Brewer hurriedly took the words of inheritance to be the same in all three cases. The augmentation, however, we have seen, was granted in fee simple, and would therefore descend to heirs general. In this case the Lords Mowbray and Petre are now alone entitled to it, and it is wrongly borne by the duke of Norfolk, whose shield so proudly figures in front of the College of Arms, of which, as Earl Marshal, he is the hereditary head. The vision of the Earl Marshal of England summoning himself before his own court for using a coat to which he is not entitled, is irresistibly suggestive of a Savoy libretto. But, seriously speaking, if mine is not, as it surely must be, the right interpretation, the alternative is that the coveted distinction ought to be forthwith removed from the coats of Lord Mowbray and Lord Petre. But in either case, be it observed, it is wrongfully assumed by all the other Howards, although invariably assigned to them by ' Burke' and every one else. The difference between a grant to a man and his heirs and a grant to all his race is well seen in the case of the Seymour augmentation (15th Aug. 1547), which was granted not only to the Duke and his heirs, but also " omnibus posteris suis totique familie." I may add that the lions in this augmentation were not (as proudly blazoned by 'Burke' and others) 'lions of England,' but lions regardant (not gardant) and " langued and armed with azur "—a correction which revives our doubts on the blazon of the Howard augmentation.

Since I wrote the above passage, the question has been independently approached by Mr. Fox-Davies, who has arrived, I find, at the same conclusion on the actual facts as myself. In two articles dealing with "the arms of Mowbray and Howard,"[1] he observes that the grant of the Flodden augmentation is

especially remarkable inasmuch as whilst it is contained in the same Letters Patent creating the dukedom of Norfolk with a limitation to the heirs male of his body, the augmentation is given to the Duke 'et heredibus suis.' . . . Now, the meaning of 'heredibus suis' is 'heirs general.' Of that there can be no question. The 'heirs general' of the said Duke at the present time (1899) are Lord Mowbray, Segrave, and Stourton, and Lord Petre, and it has frequently been stated that the augmentation has descended to them and to them only, such devolution being of course the strict and proper interpretation of the grant (p. 441).

I cite the passage because its writer is the ardent and avowed advocate of the jurisdiction of the heralds and of their head in all armorial matters. He adds, it is true, that "Probably, however, subsequent records and exemplifications have regularized its use by other members of the Howard family"; but as he does not even hint that the limitation has been changed, he can only mean that the Earls Marshal now bear by collusion with the heralds what he would term a "bogus" distinction.

One may further add, while on heraldry, that 'Burke' persists in repeating that story of the Percy arms which has long been conclusively disproved. The heiress of the Norman Percys married, in the 12th century, "Joscelin of Lovain," we read, "son of Godfrey Barbatus, duke of

[1] *Genealogical Magazine*, vol. II. [1899], pp. 396–403, 438–443.

Lower Brabant, and count of Brabant, who was descended from . . . the Emperor Charlemagne." Of this heiress we then read, with characteristic anachronism,—

Her ladyship (*sic*), it is stated, would only, however, consent to this great alliance on condition that Joscelin should adopt either the surname or arms of Percy ; the former of which, says the old family tradition, he accordingly assumed, and retained his own paternal coat in order to perpetuate his claim to the principality of his father should the elder line of the reigning duke at any period become extinct.

Alas for "the old family tradition" ! Joscelin, it is known, did not take, as alleged, the name of Percy, and indeed it is even doubtful whether his wife was an heiress in his lifetime or, at any rate, when he married her. As to his 'paternal coat,' which 'Burke' describes, in its blazon of the present duke's bearings, as "the ancient arms of the duke of Brabant and Lovaine,"[1] it was never the coat of that potentate (who, by the way, is wrongly described) and, so far from having been borne by Joscelin, the shield of his descendants the Percies, as Mr. Longstaffe has observed,[2] shows no trace of "the blue lion until the reign of Edward I." Joscelin, whose legitimacy has been questioned, was the son of Godfrey 'Barbatus' duke of Lower Lorraine, and previously count of Louvain,[3] who

---

[1] This statement has been also made by Mr. Fox-Davies in his *Armorial Families*.   [2] *The Old Heraldry of the Percys.*
[3] He is styled in 'Burke,' as above, "Duke of Lower Brabant and Count of Brabant" ! Louvain is the 'Lovaine' of the heralds, which is perpetuated in the barony of 'Lovaine' (1784) now vested in the duke of Northumberland.

was also father of Adeliza queen of Henry I. No arms of the house are known for fully half a century after Godfrey's death, and when they appear they are "sable, a lion rampant, or," while those borne by the dukes of Northumberland, in the first quarter, are " or, a lion rampant azure." The account in ' Burke,' therefore, is wrong on every point.[1] Its version of the origin of the Percys is no less wildly erroneous. "The family," we read, " of Percy of Normandy deduced its pedigree from Geoffrey (son of Mainfred, a Danish chieftain), who assisted Rollo in 912 in subjugating that principality." This gigantic fable can be traced, one need scarcely add, to an Elizabethan herald. Such also, no doubt, is the source of the statement as to William de Percy, founder of the house in England, that

his wife, Emma de Port, (was) a lady of Saxon descent, whose lands were among those bestowed upon him by the Conqueror; and according to an ancient writer, " he wedded hyr that was very heire to them in discharging of his conscience."

As a matter of fact, Emma was the daughter of a Norman from the Bessin, Hugh de Port, who obtained a large fief in Hampshire, on which he gave a solitary manor with her in marriage to William ! Even, therefore, for the origin of this famous English house ' Burke' can give us nothing better than exploded fables. I may take this opportunity of

---

[1] It is further complicated by the arms in question being also described as the "arms of Hainault," which were wholly different. See, on this point, Mr. Watson's note in *Complete Peerage*, VI. 228-9.

mentioning the interesting fact that the service due
to the Crown from the fief of the early Percys was
that of 30 knights. Some nine or ten other
great English fiefs owed the same quota, the whole
system being based, as I have shown, on a unit of
5 (or 10) knights.[1] On the death of William de
Percy, the last male of his line, each of his sisters
inherited half the fief; the quota of each, therefore,
became 15 knights. Joscelin of Louvain, who had
married one of them (by whom he was ancestor of
the later Percys) was himself by no means a bad
match, having secured from his sister's husband
(the earl of Arundel) the honour of Petworth, part
of the great Arundel fief, which he held, in the
days of Henry II., by the service of 22½ knights.
Thus these Sussex estates came to be united with
the Percy fief; and united they remained till about
the middle of the 18th century, when Petworth
passed away by will to the Wyndhams, earls of
Egremont, and from them to their illegitimate
descendants, the Lords Leconfield.[2]

The mention of Joscelin de Louvain above reminds me of a story that will probably be new to
most of my readers. The ambitious founder (*ne*
Smithson) of the present line of dukes, boldly
refusing a marquessate as a " modern rank," asked
for a dukedom of Brabant in right of his wife's
descent. The king promised to " give satisfaction
to a very respectable person," and eventually be-

---

[1] *Feudal England*, pp. 246–262.

[2] Their Sussex estates are given by G. E. C. as over 30,000
acres in 1883.

stowed on him, as a compromise, that of North-umberland (1766).

But it is time that I should more particularly address myself to that familiar volume which is yearly issued, bearing on its title-page the insignia of the late Ulster King-of-Arms.

Of *Burke's Peerage* I desire to speak with all fairness. It has long been the fashion to pour contempt on peerage writers' pedigrees, and it cannot be denied that it was fully justified by the absurd fables which the Burke family, like the Randle Holmes in the past, have recklessly repeated in their productions. But, in justice, it is right to add that these fables were, at the worst, repeated rather than invented, and that slowly but steadily, under the pressure of ridicule and competition, they are being weeded out. The Temples, for instance, are no longer derived from earl Leofric of Mercia, though here again 'Burke' succeeds in stultifying itself, for the arms, under Temple of Stowe, 'Baronet,' are given as "Quarterly, 1st and 4th, or, an eagle displayed sa., bearing the arms of the Heptarch [!] kingdom of Mercia, which have been borne by the family since their ancestors were earls of that county."[1] This statement is actually made at the foot of

---

[1] These arms, invented by some herald, must be recognised as valid at the College, for Mr. Fox-Davies assigned them to Sir Richard Temple of the Nash, and blazoned them, under the Duchess of Buckingham, as borne "for Leofric" (*Armorial Families*, 1st Ed., pp. 961, 962), though his own Introduction denies the use of armorial bearings in Leofric's times.

a pedigree beginning somewhat humbly in the days of Henry III. The absurd legend of the origin of the Berties has been so ruthlessly demolished that the pedigree now modestly begins about the time of Henry VII. This last instance calls to remembrance the article on " Pedigrees and Pedigree Makers," in which the alleged origin of the family was ridiculed so ruthlessly. We may note, in several other cases, the wholesome effects of that bitter attack, but some families, obdurate still, cling sturdily to the legends it exposed. The Ashburnhams, proud of their " stupendous antiquity," persisted that " there is scarcely a pedigree deduced from so remote a period so capable of proof as " theirs. We were still assured, so recently as 1895, that Bertram de Esburnham was " Sheriff of the counties of Surrey, Sussex, and Kent, and Constable of Dover Castle in the reign of King Harold," and was beheaded, with his sons, by the Conqueror for his defence of that fortress. I observed in my *Quarterly Review* article that Sir Bernard would find it difficult to name those " ancient records and trustworthy writers " where any such facts are recorded or even hinted at. From later editions of his ' Peerage ' we learn at last that his authority for the story that so enraged Mr. Freeman was simply " Francis Thynne writing in the reign of Elizabeth." And Thynne, I need hardly add, was a herald.

One of the stories in *Burke's Peerage* which specially stirred Mr. Freeman's wrath was that with which the pedigree of Fitz-William then began in its pages. " Sir William Fitz-Godric, cousin to king Edward the Confessor," was made father of " Sir William Fitz-William," ambassador to Normandy, who, joining duke William " in his victorious expedition against England," fought with great valour at the battle of Hastings. This drew from the Professor one of his fierce outbursts :

It is perhaps needless to say that all this is a pure fable ; but one really stands aghast at the utterly shameless nature of the fable. . . . When one is inventing falsehoods about a family, it is as easy to invent falsehoods to its credit as falsehoods to its dishonour. Whoever invented the pedigree of Earl Fitzwilliam was of another way of thinking. He had the strange fancy of wishing to be descended from a traitor.[1]

The explanation clearly was that the fashion of the time required that the founder of a family should have fought on the duke's side at the Conquest. Now the founder in this case was William Fitz-Godric living under Henry II. As his name implied an English, not a Norman, origin, the pedigree-maker threw him back more than a hundred years, and invented the story of the embassy to Normandy, to account for his coming over with William and to do so by an explanation which assigned him eminence at the time.

Something of course had to be done after the Professor's outburst ; so the pedigree was overhauled. There was not the slightest difficulty in ascertaining the facts. One of our ablest historical antiquaries in the early part of this century was the

Rev. Joseph Hunter, whose 'South Yorkshire'
stands high among our county histories. The
first volume of this work (1828) was dedicated to
Lord Fitz-William, and the origin of the family
was there discussed and established on record
evidence (pp. 332-3). It was founded by the
marriage of William Fitz-Godric (as her second
husband) with Albreda de Lisoures, a Yorkshire
heiress, whose father's lands, including Sprotborough, passed to her son by him, William Fitz
William.[1] This marriage took place about
1170.[2] In spite, therefore, of its Norman name,
this family can claim the very rare distinction of
descent from an English thegn, Godric by name.[3]

These being the known facts, how was the
pedigree reconstructed by the editors of *Burke's
Peerage*? The above William Fitz-Godric, the
husband of Albreda de Lisoures, was transformed
into William Fitz-William, and then, in mathe-
matical language, 'produced' to the days of the
Conqueror. This is done by providing him with

[1] The great Laci inheritance, to which she succeeded through
her mother, passed to the descendants of another husband.

[2] Mr. Hunter found William Fitz-Godric paying £6 13s. 4d.
for it in 1178 (Pipe Roll 24 Hen. II.), but held that it must
have been earlier. I connect it, therefore, with the appearance
of this William Fitz-Godric on the Roll of 1170 (16 Hen. II.).
I cannot agree with Mr. Hunter's suggestion that this William
may have been identical with another husband of Albreda,
William de Clerfait, founder of Hampole Priory. Godric was so
essentially an English name that, when Henry I. married a queen
of native birth, his courtiers bestowed it on him as a nickname.

[3] The persistence of English thegns and drengs, after the
Conquest, in the North of England is a very interesting fact.

a father, a grandfather, and a great-grandfather, each of them named Sir William Fitz-William and all of them alike fictitious. Each of these fictitious knights is made lord of Sprotborough, and the second is provided with the one piece of definite evidence vouchsafed us. We read that he was

living 1117, as appears from a grant made by him of a piece or wood in Elmley to the monks of Piland (*sic*). To this grant is a round seal, representing a man on horseback, completely armed and circumscribed, *S. Willmi Filii Willmi Dni de Emmalaia* ; and on the reverse the arms of Fitzwilliam ; viz., Lozengy.

Really this addition to " the genealogical and heraldic value " of the work [1] compels one to ask whether Somerset Herald possesses any trustworthy book on heraldry, and, if so, whether he actually believes that armorial seals, such as this, were in use in 1117. As a matter of fact, the seal belongs, as was fully explained by Mr. Hunter, not to 1117, but to 1217. And thus the only scrap of evidence for these imaginary Fitz-Williams is at once demolished. As for ' Piland,' it would seem to denote the well-known Abbey of Byland.

But not content with this performance, the pedigree in *Burke's Peerage* makes the third of our imaginary knights marry " Ella dau. and co-heir of William de Warren, Earl of Surrey, and d. 1148." Here again Mr. Hunter had explained most carefully that this match was impossible, as "there is abundant evidence " that the earl left but

---

[1] See preface to the 1900 edition.

one daughter and heiress. The fact is that there has been a muddle between two earls William living at different epochs. Hence this imaginary marriage. And yet "the heralds of Elizabeth's reign not only admitted the fact, but allowed the quartering of Warren to the later Fitz-Williams."[1] Precisely what one would expect of them ![2]

Mr. Freeman, again, in his famous article, was no-where more severe than in dealing with the origin of the Stourtons. He dealt with it at some length as a type of those pedigrees "which bring in large pieces of professed history which are nothing in the world but sheer invention." The story which excited his wrathful indignation was this :—

This noble family, which derives its surname from the town of Stourton, co. Wilts, was of considerable rank antecedently to the Conquest ; for we find at that period one of its members, Botolph Stourton, the most active in gallantly disputing every inch of ground with the foreigner, and finally obtaining from the duke his own terms. . . . From this patriotic and gallant soldier lineally descended——[3]

On this story (of which I omit the strategic details), Mr. Freeman thus commented (pp. 25–6) :—

Now if we did not know that a pedigree-maker will do any-thing, it would really be past belief that anybody could have ventured on such monstrous fiction as this. It would have been more respectable to trace the house of Stourton to Jack the Giant Killer, or Jack and the Beanstalk, for they have at least a received

---

[1] Hunter's *South Yorkshire*, I. 335.
[2] Compare Dugdale's erroneous allowance of the earl of Richmond's coat, as a quartering, to the Stapletons.
[3] *Cont. Rev.* XXX. 25.

THE PEERAGE

legendary being, while Botolph Stourton and his exploits are invented of set purpose to swell the supposed credit of a family whose real beginnings seem to be in the fourteenth century, . . . the whole thing is fiction. There is nothing of the kind anywhere in history or in legend. We have a *Gesta Herewardi*, mythical enough to be sure in part ; but we have no *Gesta Botolphi*. Yet the exploits of Botolph greatly surpass the exploits of Hereward. . . . If William granted to Botolph whatever he demanded, it was clearly not land that he demanded, least of all the lands of Stourton. At page 72 of Domesday, we find Stourton in Wiltshire plainly enough ; but its lord is not any Botolph ; its actual holder is not any Botolph ; its former owner is not any Botolph. . . . So Botolph Stourton vanishes from Stourton, and he equally vanishes from every other spot ; for not a man of the name appears in Domesday as holding, or having held, a rood of land anywhere. The tale is sheer invention ; it is mere falsehood, which might at any time be confuted by the simple process of turning to Domesday. . . . When the pedigree was invented, Domesday was doubtless still in manuscript ; but is it possible that there is no copy of those precious volumes in the library of Ulster King-at-Arms ?

Mr. Freeman's fierce outburst could not be disregarded, and so, down to the present year, *Burke's Peerage* was content to begin the Stourton pedigree with "Sir William Stourton," living 1325 and 1341, and even pointed out that Dugdale began it with "John de Stourton," who lived in 1377, though it added that "*Brydges's Collins* carries back the pedigree, however, to Botolph Stourton *temp. Conquestoris*." But now, in 1900, Mr. Freeman being dead, the "laborious researches" of Somerset Herald,[1] a son of Sir Bernard Burke, are seen in the resuscitation of the rudely evicted 'Botolph,' and in the discovery that his namesake, the present

[1] See Preface to 1900 Edition.

Lord Stourton, is his direct descendant. The story now runs thus :—

> The aforesaid BOTOLPH, 'primus Dominus de Stourton post Conquestum' (from whom the present Lord Mowbray Segrave and Stourton is 29th in the direct line of male succession) *m.*, according to the ancient pedigrees, Anne, dau. of Earl Godwin, sister of King Harold II., of which marriage there was issue, ROBERT and Galfridus (*sic*). The elder son,
>
> SIR ROBERT DE STOURTON is believed to have built the mansion or castle of Stourton, etc., etc.

It is frightful to think of what the effect of this crowning outrage would have been on Mr. Freeman's mind, and, above all, on his language. If Botolph and his exploits led him to write of " monstrous fiction " and " mere falsehood," what would he have said of the " pedigree-maker " who had dared to assign to Botolph for a wife a daughter of his beloved Godwine, a sister of his adored Harold ? " When in doubt, try ' Anne.' " This maxim, I sometimes think, was dear to the pedigree-maker's heart ; but in Harold's ' sister Anne ' he overshot the mark. More than twenty years ago it was Mr. Freeman's complaint that

> The readers of the book accept the stories on the faith of the author or editor . . . . Indeed Sir Bernard Burke himself tells us, in his ' Prefatory Notice ' prefixed to the thirty-second edition of his Peerage and Baronetage, that he has " again subjected its pages to searching revision and extensive amendment." Here, then, Sir Bernard Burke distinctly takes on himself what reason would have laid upon him even if he had not taken it upon himself, namely responsibility for his own book. It is the Ulster King of Arms, not the unknown persons who send him the accounts of this or that family, whom we must blame for the monstrous fictions which appear as the early history of so many families.[1]

---

[1] *Cont. Rev.* XXX. 12–13.

But what shall we say when the Botolph fiction appears in *Burke's Peerage*, not as a relic of a careless age, but as the result, in 1900, of "a more thorough revision than usual" of its pages?

Is it possible that we owe this increase of its "genealogical value" to the access enjoyed by Somerset Herald to the priceless records of the college? What, one wonders, is their verdict in the matter? Luckily, Sir Richard Colt Hoare, when he was writing his history of Wiltshire, "procured from the College of arms" its authorized Stourton pedigree.[1] And, even more luckily, he gave it not only in narrative form, but in chart form also,[2] heading the latter:—

This pedigree, down to the year 1721, was ratified and confirmed under the Seal of the College of Arms, on the 26th day of September, A° 1722.

This delightful composition duly begins with "Botolph or Bartholomew de Stourton, temp. Will. Conq.," who married "Ann, dau. of Godwin, earl of Kent." The story, therefore, must be true; for is it not ratified and confirmed by the seal of the College of Arms? And yet, Mr. Fox Davies cries,—

There are very many people who grandiloquently assert that 'they don't recognise the authority of the College of Arms.' Such a statement sounds very big, but it is pure nonsense.[3]

---

[1] Vol. I. p. 43. [2] *Ibid.* pp. 43, 47–8.
[3] Preface to *Armorial Families.* The same protest recurs, of course, in *The right to bear arms* by 'X': "and yet there are some silly fools who don't recognise the authority of the College" (p. 163). The pure and classic style of these twin writers should be noted.

PEERAGE STUDIES

Surely it is not without a cause that, in the great history of the Stourtons, which has just made its appearance, the head of the house is shown in its frontispiece with his hand resting on the book from which these words are taken.

Of the two gorgeous volumes in which that history is contained I speak here with some hesitation. For they are only a private production, and they have for their wholly meritorious object the setting on record a trustworthy account of an ancient English house. It is, indeed, to be wished that more of our historic houses would, as in Scotland, produce such histories, and would, like Lord Mowbray and Stourton, resolve to give us facts only, in the place of so-called "tradition." His lordship's preface is emphatic on the point :—

There can be no question of unsubstantiated statements having been intentionally or carelessly inserted as facts upon the mere strength of family tradition ; and throughout the progress of the book I have always insisted upon absolute accuracy, etc., etc.

It is with some surprise, in view of these words, that one reads in the same preface the unqualified assertion (as in *Burke's Peerage*) that

The Stourton pedigree commences at the Conquest, since which time there has been an unbroken male descent (I am the 29th in the direct male line of succession).

But it is with more than surprise—it is with bewildered amazement—that one finds even the legendary Botolph, with whom the pedigree commences at the Conquest, insufficient as an ancestor. 'Tradition' is invoked for the existence of a far

earlier Botolph, himself descended from a long line
of fighting and Heptarchic Stourtons.

The Stourtons of Stourton, co. Wilts were traditionally a
powerful and warrior family in the Saxon period, and are stated
to have fought under the banner of the Saxon line of the Kings of
Wessex, and, after the Saxon divisions of the Heptarchy became
united, under the Kings of England. According to tradition,
King Alfred the Great made the head of the Stourton family a
Saxon Thane—and this probably testified to the ownership of the
lands of Stourton—for his great valour and bravery while fighting
in the service of the King, probably at Bonham, in the county of
Somerset.

*   *   *   *   *

The Lord of Stourton who fought under King Alfred is traditionally said to have been a Botolph de Stourton, ancestor of that
Botolphus de Stourton who flourished during the reigns of Edward
the Confessor, Harold, and William the Conqueror, and who is
said to have obtained a settlement from the last named King on
his own terms, by which he presumably retained possession of
part of the parish of Stourton (p. 5).

Should we entertain the slightest doubt, the writer
is prepared to smite the Philistines (such as was
Professor Freeman), not indeed with the jawbone
of an ass, but with the thighbone of an ancestor.
At Warwick Castle they show the rib of the cow
slain by the ancestor ; at Stourton they preserved
the thigh of the ancestor himself. The only
question that can possibly arise is what ancestor it
was. Let us continue the quotation.

One of these Botolphs of Stourton was a man of gigantic
stature. The positive reiteration of this fact is one of the few
surviving traditions of the Stourton family, and it is proved (*sic*)
by two circumstances, namely, this tradition and the actual existence of a large thigh-bone, the *os femur* of a human being,
. . . which was positively and confidently asserted to have

belonged to him. The general belief is that this bone may have belonged more correctly to the Botolph *temp. Conquestoris.*

That a human thighbone, though now lost, was actually in existence is proved by the evidence of two witnesses who had seen it with their own eyes. Aubrey, who saw it in the buttery at Stourton, declared that it " exceeds the proportion of human thigh-bones, and, besides, . . . not of the figure or shape of a human bone." A Benedictine father, consulted by Lord Mowbray and Stourton, wrote, in reply, that he remembered—

the existence of the (so-called) thigh-bone of your ancestor, . . . a very large bone, almost as much as one could lift ; it was sometimes called Lord Stourton's thigh-bone, or the thigh-bone of a giant, but little credence was put in the designation, which was used to ' gull ' the innocents. By people of mature age it was regarded as the bone of some enormous animal.

Such is the evidence on which avowedly rests the existence of Botolph's thigh-bone, and that bone seems to be the best proof forthcoming of Botolph's own existence.

The net conclusion at which we arrive is that

the settling of the Stourton family at Stourton must, according to tradition, date at least from the time of king Alfred the Great.

When the country, after the defeat of the Danes at Stourton and elsewhere, in 1016, was eventually under the government or the Saxon Kings, the Lords of Stourton again came into prominence, and another Botolph of Stourton was deemed of sufficient status and estate to marry a daughter of Godwin, Earl of Kent, etc. . . .

The position of Botolph, Lord of Stourton, who lived during the reigns of his two royal brothers-in-law, Edward the Confessor and Harold II., and took an active part against the Norman invaders, and who himself made such a strong resistance against the Conqueror personally, led that monarch to arrange with Botolph on his own terms when the Conqueror invaded the Western parts of England. . . . All this is history, and it has been chronicled that it was actually at the residence of Botolph at Stourton that the Conqueror came to meet his opponents to arrange there the terms which these Saxon warriors had demanded and actually obtained from him (p. 12).

One shudders to think what treatment these statements would certainly have received at Professor Freeman's hands ; for we have already seen what language he applied to such history. The 'Botolph' story, in these volumes, is actually more elaborate and positive than that which the Professor chastised.

Botolph de Stourton, being a brother-in-law of Harold, no doubt took part in the battle of Hastings. . . . In fact, the tradition which has survived is that he was present at both the battles of Stamford Bridge and Hastings (p. 13).

That Botolph Stourton was a great personage and Saxon warrior cannot be denied . . . seeing he was brother-in-law respectively to Edward the Confessor and Harold II.

To Botolph Stourton tradition has attributed the thigh-bone, but whether it really belonged to him, or to his ancestor of the same name, who fought under Alfred the Great, cannot for certain be determined.

That is where the caution of the true historian comes in. Confidence, however, at once returns :—

It is clear, however, that the Stourton family must have been settled at Stourton early in the Saxon period, and also were there at the Norman Conquest. . . .

Unfortunately the grants of William the Conqueror, or any of his sons, are not in existence, and, therefore, one has only to fall back on Doomsday and the most able authorities to ascertain facts (pp. 18–19).

Just so ; and what Domesday tells us we have heard in Mr. Freeman's words. With the ex-

PEERAGE STUDIES

ception of a weird 'Paul Plod,' who is much
cited for the early history, the "able authorities" seem to resolve themselves into a 'painter-
stainer,' Munday by name, living in the time of
Charles I.,—who suggested that perhaps Ralph,
the Domesday holder of Stourton, was not Ralph,
but Bartholomew,—and a certain Mr. William
Turner, who wrote a book on 'remarkable pro-
vidences' in 1697, and who is gravely cited as
evidence for facts of Norman history. There
was also, no doubt, the Heralds' pedigree with
its Botolph lord of Stourton, unknown to history or to Domesday. But that was all.

Stay! There was, we find, another authority,
and one whose date carries back the first appearance of the story. It is very difficult to say why
Lord Mowbray and Stourton should not have
appealed to this authority, for it is not only of
respectable antiquity, but carries back the origin
of the Stourtons to even earlier times. All the
writers who have dealt with this old Roman
Catholic house are fairly surpassed by the famous
Jesuit, Robert Parsons (1546–1610). According
to him, at the coming of Augustine (597),

there flourished among the first converts and benefactors [of
the Church] two satraps *Sturtonus* and *Sturleius*, who so favoured
the divine work, that they were the first to establish the Catholic
Church at Canterbury. . . . Wherefore they received and
still bear a representation of their benefactions in their arms (*scutis
gentilitiis*) . . . the other (Stourton) a monk girt with a
girdle, and armed with a scourge. . . . This antiquity induced Botolph Sturton, in the time of William the Conqueror,
to combine with the abbot of Glastonbury and Stigand archbishop

58

of Canterbury, and, meeting with success, he obtained from the Conqueror, for himself and for the whole tract in which he lived, conditions of peace.[1]

Canon Jackson, the well-known Wiltshire antiquary, who quotes the original passage in Latin, observes thereupon :—

It is stated in some of the 'Peerages' that the Stourtons were 'of considerable rank before the Conquest, and dictated their own terms to the Conqueror'; but of this there is no evidence in Wiltshire County History. If there was any such family in this County at the Conquest, it was not by their position, or extent of property here, that they were qualified to be formidable to the Conqueror. The name is found, apparently for the first time, among Wiltshire landholders in the reign of Edward I., when a Nicholas Stourton was holding one knight's fee here, under the Lovells of Castle Cary.[2]

In the *Complete Peerage* its learned editor goes even further, observing that

The manor of Stourton, which in the 14th century was held by the family of Fitzpayne, was, however, acquired before 1427 by that of Stourton (vii. 252).

It is, indeed, a singular fact that the family of Fitz Payne is found, for several generations, holding Stourton of the lords of Castle Cary precisely as the Stourton family held it before and afterwards.[3] This tenure has yet to be explained ; but in the meanwhile one may point out that Canon Jackson (followed by G. E. C.) was unjust (accidentally) to the Stourtons in beginning their history only "in the reign of Edward I." The

---

[1] 'A treatise of the three Conversions of Paganism to the Christian religion.'

[2] Aubrey's Wiltshire *Collections*, Ed. Jackson (1862), pp. 390–1.

[3] See Hoare's *History of Wiltshire*.

record in question[1] can be shown, from internal
evidence, to belong to the winter of 1242–3,
some thirty years before Edward's reign began.

Nor is this all. On the one hand, we have
'unsubstantiated statements' based on 'family
tradition' or the guesses of painter-stainers ; on
the other, we have mere negation. But it is not
enough to destroy 'fiction' ; the modern scientific
genealogist must give us facts instead. And facts
can be given. Stourton appears in Domesday
book as a portion of the great fief held by
Walter de Douai, which included, in Somerset,
Castle Cary, where he can be shown to have
had a castle, and in Devon the great manor of
Bampton, which had belonged to Edward the
Confessor. Walter's tenant Ralph, who had succeeded 'Alwacre' at Stourton, had also succeeded
him (as 'Elwacre') in three Somerset manors.[2]
This throws some light on the dispossessed thegn,
by whom Stourton had been held before the Conquest. Moreover, Walter's great fief is found, in
the next century, divided into the 'Honour of
Bampton,' which passed to the Paynel family, and
the 'Honour of Castle Cary,' held by the Lovels.
Stourton formed part of the latter, and it is strange
that those who have sought to carry back the
Stourton family have not observed that Robert
'de Sturtone' was the chief tenant of Henry
Lovel in 1166, holding from him three fees.[3]

---

[1] *Testa de Nevill*, p. 153.   [2] *Domesday*, I. 95*b*.
[3] *Red Book of the Exchequer*, p. 234.

Thus, if Lord Mowbray and Stourton, instead ot consulting Richmond Herald or possibly (as his frontispiece suggests) the author of *Armorial Families*, had employed a competent record agent or asked an historian to assist him, he might have produced genuine evidence that his house was of greater antiquity than Mr. Freeman and the writers quoted above believed to be the case. But the *ignis fatuus* of 'Botolph' and the wife found for him by the heralds has led him to make an ancient house a prey to just ridicule. Whether, in the future, *Burke's Peerage* will continue to publish the baseless pedigree it has now taken from his lordship's work time alone can show. But its repetition will be most unjust to the genuine pedigrees in the same work. And that is one of the reasons why a protest is required.

Let me now turn to certain fables that I have myself noted as needing revision and correction. Of these the majority, as might be expected, are traceable to the old eagerness for descent from a companion of the Conqueror, and are the fruit of invention tempered only by the worthless Battle Roll. How familiar they are, these old friends! Here is that 'very strong man'—not Mr. Thomas Atkins—who, "according to the venerable and almost uniform tradition, . . . landed in England with his master in the year 1066," and "protecting him with his shield from the blows of an assailant" at the Battle of Hastings, became known as Fortescu, and was progenitor to the family of that name. Here, too, is the patriarch of the St. Legers, though he no longer gives his arm to the Conqueror as he steps ashore. Lord Bolingbroke's pedigree still begins with the Conqueror's " grand master of the artillery and supervisor of the wagons and carriages " ; a tale to which I shall recur below. Lord Alington, however, since the appearance of my article, no longer seeks his progenitor in " Sir Hildebrand de Alington "—a name that would have gladdened Sir Walter Scott— ' under-marshal to William the Norman at the Battle of Hastings ' ; but Lord Verulam still traces to " Sylvester de Grymestone, . . . standard-bearer in the army of William the Conqueror." In this last case the descent was actually recognised in the preamble to the patent of creation (1719), in which the grantee (who had taken the name of Grimston) is asserted to be descended *non interruptâ lineâ* from this hypothetical *vexillifer !* Some of these strange stories contain their own refutation ; and the growing tendency to appeal to Domesday, in deference to modern historical research, is powerless to save them. Thus " Sir Mauger le Vavasor," we read, occurs in Domesday Book " as holding in chief of the Percys, earls of Northumberland." But the Percys were not then earls of Northumberland ; and if Sir Mauger was their tenant, he could not hold ' in chief,' and if he did he would not be a *vavassor (i.e.* an under-tenant). " Sir Elias de Workesley," who " it is stated in an old family record," was the founder *(longo intervallo)* of the Worsleys, is unknown to chroniclers or to Domesday Book. As for Lord Derby's progenitor, who came over with his sons at the Conquest, their coming "from Aldithley in Normandy" is one of the curiosities of geography; and the 'portgrave of Hastings' under the Conqueror, who is claimed as Lord Huntingdon's progenitor, is an official unknown to history.

The pedigree-maker, I observe, in these latter days, has found a way of adapting Domesday Book for his purpose. Any family — they are countless in number—of which the name is derived from a locality mentioned in Domesday Book is now assumed to descend from the tenant who was then holding there. Under 'Valentia,' for instance, we read of the Annesleys that "This family derives its surname from the Lordship of Anneslei, co. Nottingham, where its patriarch RICHARD DE ANNESLEI was seated at the time of the general survey." Now 'Anneslei' was certainly held by a 'Richard,' but there is nothing to show who he was, nor could a descent from him be proved. As this point is of some importance, I may illustrate it further by the case of "Sandford of Sandford." Mr. Eyton, who devoted much study to the early history of this ancient house, came to the conclusion that "Richard de Sandford, the first known representative of his line, occurs in 1167."[1] No one could know so much as Mr. Eyton on the subject, and yet Burke's *Landed Gentry* makes a genuine pedigree absurd by carrying back the family for three generations to the Conquest, and asserting that—

[1] *Shropshire*, IX. 222.

THOMAS " DE SAUNDFORD," a Norman, held the manor under Gerard de Tournay, a powerful Baron, whose name is in the *Domesday Book*.

This statement is sheer fiction; Sandford is entered in Domesday as held by " Gerard," of the Earl ; Domesday knows nothing of Thomas, and still less of " Thomas de Saundford." An even worse case is that of the pretentious pedigree of Smith-Carington,[1] which is carried up, in its latest development (1898), to " Hamo, Lord of Carinton, co. Chester, *temp*. William I." As a matter of fact, Carington (Cheshire) is not mentioned in Domesday Book, but it was appurtenant to Dunham, which, with six other estates, is entered in Domesday as held of the earl of Chester by ' Hamo.' Now this Hamo was the well-known founder of the Massys, barons of Dunham ' Massy,' and had nothing to do with a Carington or a Smith. As if to attain a climax of confusion, the name of the family having been accounted for by its connection with Carington in Cheshire, the ' Lineage ' in ' Burke ' commences with the statement that " The family derives its name from the castle, town, and port of Carenton (*sic*) in Normandy " !

Wilder, however, than the claims to descent from Norman invaders are those of the families who would ' go one better' by asserting an earlier origin. What is to be said to such a passage as this ?—

There still remain in England a few families, and Wolseley of Wolseley is one, that can prove by authentic evidence an unbroken

---

[1] See p. 24 above.

descent from Saxon times, and show the inheritance of the same lands in the male line from a period long anterior to the Norman Conquest. A legend in the family narrates that their ancestor was given the lands of Wlselei (now Wolseley) for destroying wolves in co. Stafford, in the reign of King Edgar, when wolves were finally destroyed in England.

And so the "authentic evidence" consists of "a legend in the family," itself dependent on another legend, namely, that wolves were "finally destroyed in England" under Edgar, whereas I have seen them alluded to as in existence in twelfth-century charters, while they were not extirpated, of course, till an even later date. Wolseley (in Colwich), as a matter of fact, was held at the time of Domesday (1086) by the bishop of Chester, whose under-tenant was a certain Nigel, unknown to the Wolseley pedigree. Equally absurd is the statement that the Derings are "one of the very few houses still existing in England of undoubted Saxon origin; an origin confirmed not only by tradition, but by authentic family documents." What possible family documents can establish the history of the house before the Conquest? As for "Randolphus de Trafford," who lived *ante Conquestum*, "as the family pedigree sets forth," we may leave him to the company of an impossible 'Eduni,' the "earliest known ancestor" of the Trelawnys, who is alleged, on the authority of Domesday Book, to have held "Trelawny or Treloen in the time of Edward the Confessor." Eadwig, who seems to be intended, was no more connected with 'Treloen' than he was with several other manors, and in no instance were their

Norman possessors descended from him. An equally impossible "Hugh Fitz Baldric, a Saxon thane," was a well-known Norman tenant-in-chief. As for the Pilkington who survived the Conquest as the Duc de Lévis weathered the Deluge, he is a 'worthy peer' of that early Fitz William who was already using an armorial seal when no one else possessed one, and who set up, "engraven in brass," some lines of sorry doggrel, thoughtfully composed in the English of a far later age.

Let us now examine the statements at the head of Lord Bolingbroke's pedigree.

WILLIAM DE ST. JOHN (the name was taken from the territory of St. John near Rouen), who came into England with the CONQUEROR, as grand master of the artillery and supervisor of the wagons and carriages; whence the horses' hames or collar was borne for his cognizance (*Brydges' Collins*, vol. VI. p. 42). He m. Oliva, da. of Ralph de Filgiers, of Normandy.

It can be positively shown, as to these statements: (1) that the St. John family did not come in with the Conqueror, but, in the next century, under Henry I; (2) that their name was taken from St. Jean-le-Thomas, near Mont St. Michel, which was far away from Rouen; (3) that the William de St. John who married the above 'Oliva' was living a century after the date of the Conqueror's death, and was in fact the imaginary patriarch's alleged great-grandson; (4) that Oliva herself was the mother, not the daughter, of Ralph de Fougères (not Filgiers) of Britanny (not Normandy).[1]

---

[1] See, for all this, my article on "The families of St. John and of Port" in *Genealogist* for July, 1899.

As for William the Conqueror's artillery and army service corps, the tale is obviously one of those venal herald's fables which even Dugdale, in his *Baronage*, was ashamed to repeat.

A few lines further down we read that :—

JOHN ST. JOHN was killed at the battle of Evesham 43 (*sic*) Henry III. He had been in the Holy Wars with Richard I., who at the siege of Acon, in Palestine, adopted the device of tying a leathern thong, or garter, round the left leg of a certain number of knights (one of whom was this John de St. John) that they might be impelled to higher deeds of valour.

One can only ask in blank amazement whether the brothers Burke possess a primer of English history. From it they would learn that the battle of Evesham was fought not in 43, but in 49 Hen. III., and that they have made a man who fought "in Palestine" in 1190 fight and fall at Evesham in 1265! That 'Acon' was Acre is more, perhaps, than any herald could understand ; but what is the authority for John de St. John receiving a distinction which cruelly suggests that Richard urged him to greater valour by curling a whipthong about his legs ?

But even when we pass to Ireland, where Ulster, one would have thought, should have been specially at home, we meet under the earldom of Fingall with a statement so grotesque as that "so early as the eleventh century we find John Plunkett was seated at Beaulieu, or Bewley, co. Meath, the constant residence of the elder branch of his descendants." What business either John or

'Beaulieu' could have had to be in Ireland at the
time passes the wit of man to discover. But as his
successor, a John Plunkett "living *temp.* Henry III."
(1216-1272), was father, we learn, of a man who
sat in the Parliament of 1374, the family history
was clearly unique. Now, why should this ancient
and distinguished house be made ridiculous by such
statements, when its name occurs both in England
and Normandy in authentic records of the twelfth
century, which are here completely ignored ? Or,
again, why should the ancestor of the Dillons,
one of the Irish *conquistadores*, be assigned the
absurd and impossible title of 'Premier Dillon,
Lord Baron Drumrany' ? And what authority can
there be for 'Sir Geoffrey de Estmonte, Knt. of
Huntington, in co. Lincoln,' being one of " the
thirty knights who landed at Bannow " in 1172 ?
Again, 'Burke' has yet to learn that the Burkes
themselves are not descended, as stated under
'Clanricarde,' from 'William Fitz-Adelm' [*i.e.*
Audelin][1]—governor of Ireland under Henry II., a
legend, as is now known, devoid of foundation. Perhaps, however, one ought to be thankful that they
are not still derived, as they used to be, in direct male
descent from Charlemagne himself. Betham, Sir
Bernard Burke's predecessor in the office of Ulster,
actually issued a formal certificate under his " seal
of office," as " Ulster King of Arms and Principal
Herald of all Ireland," certifying that this monstrous
concoction rested on " original documents of un-

---

[1] See my *Feudal England*, pp. 517–8.

quéstionable authority " and " is registered in the Archives of Ulster's Office of Arms " ! [1]

Again, under Leinster, " Premier Duke, Marquess, and Earl of Ireland," the pedigree of Fitz Gerald still begins with a story which is not only absolutely, but also demonstrably false :—

> The Fitz Geralds are descended from " Dominus OTHO," who is supposed to have been of the family of the Gherardini of Florence. . . . This noble passed over into Normandy, and thence, in 1057, into England, where he became so great a favourite with Edward the Confessor, that he excited the jealousy of the Saxon thanes. However derived, his English possessions were enormous, which, at his death, devolved on his son, WALTER FITZOTHO, who, it is somewhat remarkable, was treated after the Conquest as a fellow-countryman of the Normans. In 1078 (sic) he is mentioned in Domesday Book as being in possession of his father's estates.

Such circumstances are certainly " somewhat remarkable," their explanation being that they are at complete variance with the facts. " Walterius filius Otheri " (sic), the undoubted founder of the house, first occurs in Domesday Book (not 1078, but 1086), where he is found in several counties as a tenant-in-chief. It nowhere styles him a son of Otho (of which ' Otto ' was the Domesday form), and it does not state that his possessions had belonged to his father, but, on the contrary, proves them to have belonged to forfeited Englishmen. Thus the ' Otho ' story is shown to be absolute fiction. Will Sir Bernard, I asked in my review of the 1892 edition of his Peerage,[2] continue to

---

[1] See my paper on " The Barons of the Naas " in *Genealogist* [N.S.], XV. 5. [2] *Quarterly Review*, as above.

PEERAGE STUDIES

repeat it while assuring the public that he has "endeavoured to render minutely correct the ancestral details of the lineages"? We turn to the edition for 1900, subjected, as we are informed, to a "more thorough revision than usual," and we read with awe of "the laborious researches" by which Somerset Herald has so greatly increased "the genealogical value of this work." And then we find the whole fiction repeated word for word, including the gross blunder on the date of Domesday Book.

Let us take—also from the Irish Peerage—an instance of another kind. In the pedigree of the ancient house of Howth we still find this statement :—

Nicholas St. Lawrence 23rd Lord of Howth. His lordship *d.* in 1643, and was succeeded by his surviving son—William 24th Lord.

In editing the Register of Colchester Grammar School, for the Essex Archæological Society, I made the startling discovery, with the help of a parish register on the Essex and Suffolk border, that there had flourished there a Lord of Howth, between the above two peers, who had, in 1643, succeeded his brother Nicholas, and who was the real father of the above William. A discovery so unlikely as this is not only "part of the romance of gene-alogy,"[1] but is of much potential importance for the heirship to this barony, of which the heir-presumptive is, apparently, so remote as to be un-known. The *Complete Peerage*, in its 'corrigenda'

[1] Preface to my edition of the above Register.

70

(viii. 425–6), accepted the discovery and observed that it had been made by me. 'Burke' wholly ignores it. Is it pride that prevents the editor from availing himself of the results of genealogical research ? Or is it, in spite of all professions, just mere indolence ? The case below of the barony of Kingsale, so closely associated, by tradition, with that of Howth in its origin, points to the latter conclusion.

To see how a genuine pedigree can and should be constructed, we need only turn to that of Lord Wrottesley, the work, no doubt, of that excellent antiquary, General Wrottesley, in which the family's possession of Wrottesley is carried up to within a century from the Conquest, while the pedigree itself is traced to the days of the Conqueror. Injustice is done to those who can prove such a pedigree as this, when the wild traditions we have glanced at are published as sober history ; nor have families of undoubted antiquity, such as those of Lord Hereford or Lord Iddesleigh, anything to gain by appealing, in support of their earliest history, the former to pipe rolls which do not exist,[1] and the latter to 'an ancient record' which appears to have been nothing of the kind.[2]

---

[1] "The great roll of the Pipe 35 Hen. I. and 5 Stephen." The pedigree opens with an odd reference to "the theory of the Heralds' College, London."

[2] The Northcote pedigree is asserted (ed. 1900) to be "clearly proved by an ancient and copious pedigree preserved in the College of Arms . . . which pedigree is continued down to the Visitation of 1620." The character of this precious document may be gathered from such of its contents as are rashly

On the other hand, in one or two instances, the pedigree, instead of being carried too far, is not carried far enough. The founder of the present house of Berkeley is bluntly introduced as 'Robert Fitzhardinge,' who, like Melchizedek, had no father, although competent genealogists have held, and Professor Freeman thought it "in the highest degree probable," that he was the son of Harding, son of Eadnoth, the latter being, the Professor held, no other than Eadnoth the Staller, a magnate under Edward the Confessor. The probability of so unique a descent might at least have been referred to.

Again, the ancient and well-known house of Tichborne is traced only to Roger Tichborne "who flourished in the reign of Henry II." But I could take it back to his father Walter living under Henry I. and Stephen. Moreover, as descents in the female line are in some cases given, —as those, for instance, of the duke of Northumberland and Lord Beauchamp (perhaps because the houses of Smithson and of Pindar are comparatively modern)—it is strange that under 'Rutland' we have only a pedigree of the Manners family. For the boast, too often falsely made, that lands have descended from the days of the Conquest in an un-

given to the public. The first ancestor " on record," is 'Galfridus Miles,' who 'had his seat at Northcote' in 1103, and whose *second* successor was seated there in 1118 (*sic*), a record being actually vouched for the fact. As a grandson of this latter gentleman was married in 1288–9 (17 Ed. I.), the whole pedigree is doubtless worthy of the heralds and the College of Arms.

broken line, is absolutely true in the case of the historic estate of Belvoir. I was lately enabled to ascertain its true descent in the Norman period, which, as I had long suspected, has always been wrongly given.

And now for the house of Howard. Fiercely fighting the hydra of falsehood which he found resplendent in *Burke's Peerage*, Mr. Freeman, in the name of historical truth, smote the pedigree of Wake.[1] The singular feature in this pedigree is that it betrayed the usual desire to begin with a companion of the Conqueror, and yet hankered after claiming a forbear so famous in story as Hereward "the Wake." Hence much confusion and 'hedging,' which the Professor mercilessly printed in full. One need only quote this passage :—

> Hence the family is supposed to have been of importance prior to the Conquest. The celebrated Archbishop Wake wrote a history of the Wake family, in which he ascribes to Hereward le Wake the feat of having successfully opposed and finally made terms with William the Conqueror. As Augustine (*sic*) also mentions Wakes in Normandy, it is probable that there were two parties in the family at that time.

As Mr. Freeman forcibly observed, "it does very directly touch the historian when pedigree-makers . . . lay their hands on one of our national heroes in the form of Hereward." Vigorously denouncing this "trumpery piece of genealogical fiction," the Professor exclaimed with indignation :—

> Nor can the historian calmly look on while Hereward becomes

---

[1] *Cont. Rev.*, XXX. 31–3.

the sport of pedigree-makers. His authentic history is short, but he has an authentic history. . . . But as for connecting him with the family of Wake or any other existing family, there is not a scrap of evidence for it.[1]

The Wakes, however, appear to have 'declared to win' with Hereward, reviving his name, as that of their ancestor, together with that of his legendary wife "Torfrida," just as "Sir Brian Newcome ot Newcome" set the seal to his family legend by giving his children "names out of the Saxon calendar." Kingsley, moreover, had made their alleged descent famous by inserting this passage in his well-known novel on Hereward :

> Hereward the Wake, Lord of Bourne, and ancestor or that family of Wake the arms of whom appear on the cover of this book. These, of course, are much later than the time of Hereward. Not so, probably, the badge of the 'Wake Knot.' . . . It and the motto 'Vigila et ora' may well have been used by Hereward himself. . . .
>
> Hereward's pedigree is a matter of no importance save to a few antiquaries, and possibly to his descendants, the ancient and honourable house of Wake.[2]

---

[1] Reference may also be made to articles on Hereward in the *Saturday Review* of 1st Nov. 1862, and 19th May, 1866, which seem to be from Mr. Freeman's pen.

[2] It is a striking instance of the firm hold that these legends obtain on the imagination of the public that, even as I write, this statement appears in the columns of a newspaper :—"Sir Hereward Wake bears one of the oldest names in England, being a descendant of the famous 'Hereward the Wake.' Perhaps one of the most interesting things in connection with this family, especially in these days when lands change hands so frequently, is the fact (*sic*) that the Wakes have had the same property from generation to generation ever since the days of the Saxons, and echoes of those times are still to be heard in the Christian names of all the Wakes" (11th March, 1900).

But we see the fruits of Mr. Freeman's scorn in the guarded phrase which now appears at the head of the Wake pedigree :—" The Wakes claim Saxon origin " ; while the actual pedigree modestly begins in the latter part of the 14th century.[1] This is scarcely worthy treatment of one of our oldest families, one of the very few that belonged to the feudal baronage, and that can be traced back with certainty to within a century of the Conquest.[2]

I spoke above of ' the hydra of falsehood ' in this unfortunate compilation. No sooner had the Wake pedigree been thus mercilessly lopped than the gallant Hereward reappeared as the founder of quite another family, indeed of no less famous a house than the Howards, dukes of Norfolk.

As might have been expected, the Howards— or, at least, the heralds on their behalf—have tried hard to extend their pedigree beyond the known founder of their house, William Howard, who rose by the law, becoming a judge towards the close of the 13th century. *Collins' Peerage* (1779)

---

[1] *Burke's Peerage*, 1900.

[2] Its founder was Hugh Wac, who married the daughter and heiress of Baldwin Fitz Gilbert, and thus acquired Baldwin's fief. This Baldwin was son, not of Gilbert de Gant as alleged by Dugdale and other antiquaries, but, as I have shown (*Feudal England*, p. 474) of Gilbert de *Clare*, the head of that famous house. Hugh Wac was in possession of the fief in 1166, but I have urged that he is the "h'Wac" who attests a charter of king Stephen that I assign to 1142 (*Geoffrey de Mandeville*, p. 159).

As I have shown elsewhere (*Feudal England*, p. 161), Hereward, who was never known as "the Wake," had that name bestowed on him by some early pedigree-maker, who wished to annex him as the ancestor of the Wake family.

gives us "the descent as settled by Mr. Harvey, who was Clarencieux King of Arms in the reign of Queen Elizabeth, and with whom Glover (Somerset Herald), Philipot, etc., agree" (I. 52–3). This was the wild descent from "Auber, Earl of Passy" spoken of by Mr. Rye in a passage quoted below. In 1638, Lilly, then "Rouge Dragon," produced quite a different story, compiling "The genealogie of the princelie familie of the Howards, exactly deduced in a right line from the xvth yeere of the raigne of King Edgar, sole monarch of England in the yeere of our redemption DCCCCLXX. before the Norman Conquest 96 years, etc."[1] Dugdale, however, as in other cases, ignored the work of the officers of arms, the value and character of which he was, doubtless, competent to judge, and, in his *Baronage*, wrote this :—

There are those perhaps who will expect that I should ascend much higher in manifesting the greatness of this honourable and large-spreading family of Howard in regard I do not make any mention thereof above the time of King Edward I., some supposing that their common ancestor in the Saxon time took his original appellation from an eminent office or command ; others afterwards from the name of a place. And some have not stuck to derive him from the famous *Hereward*. . . . I shall, therefore, after much fruitless search to satisfy myself as well as others on this point, begin with William Howard, a learned and reverend judge of the court of common pleas.

In 1879, Sir Bernard Burke was still quoting

[1] "A finer heraldic volume than this need not be wished for ; the drawings and their colourings are of the first class." This MS. is said to be in the possession of Lord Northampton.

these words of Dugdale at the head of his Howard pedigree, though he added that :—

Despite, however, of Dugdale's inability to discover the parentage of the judge, it appears clearly proved from various charters that that learned personage was son of John Howard and grandson of Robert Howard or Herward, 'filius Hawardi,' and that the name was originally Herward.

But in 1880 there was substituted this version :—

The Ducal and illustrious Howards . . . represent a family undoubtedly of Saxon origin. Recent enquiries enable us to trace the ancestors of the Howards to a period much more remote than Sir William Dugdale thought possible and to establish the pedigree by undoubted evidence. Ingulph and Matthew Paris concur in stating that Howard or Hereward was living in the reign of King Edgar, 957 to 973, and that he was a kinsman of Duke Oslac, and that his son, Leofric, was the father of Hereward, who was banished by the Conqueror. The very ancient book of the church of Ely entirely confirms the statement. It appears that Hereward was subsequently allowed to return, and it is certain that his family retained Wigenhall and other portions of their inheritance in Norfolk. Hereward's grandson, Hereward or Howard, and his wife Wilburga, in the reign of Henry the Second, granted a carucate of land in Terrington in Norfolk to the church of Len (Lynn), and directed that prayers should be said for the souls of Hereward his father, and of Hereward the Banished, or the Exile, his grandfather. Robert Howard, the son of Hereward, was seized of Wigenhall, Terrington, and other estates in Norfolk, and was the father of John Hereward or Howard of Wigenhall, who, by Lucy Germund his wife, was the father of SIR WILLIAM HOWARD.

Of this audacious story one can only say that no statements of the kind are made by Mathew Paris, while what 'Ingulf' really says (under 1062) is that Leofric lord of Brunne married

Ediva, 'trinepta' of "that magnificent duke Oslac,
the contemporary of king Edgar."[1] To Leofric
himself, who is made to die in the days of William
I., no father is assigned, and, even if it contained
(which it does not) the alleged statement, the
whole chronicle called Ingulf's is now known to
be a forgery! Yet this mixture of ignorance and
falsehood is set forth, in 1900, as the fruit of
" recent enquiries " and as proved by " undoubted
evidence." Strong language, it may be said; yet
not a whit too strong. For so far back as 30th
January, 1886, Mr. Walter Rye wrote to the
Athenæum on the subject of the wild story in
' Burke,' and urged that "surely the pedigree of
the Head of the College of Arms should be above
suspicion," while in the same widely-read journal
(13th March, 1886), I denounced it " as a scandal
to our historical and antiquarian scholarship that
the ridiculous farrago of this ' mythical descent '
should be thus annually repeated to the public in
a quasi-official form." Again, in my *Quarterly
Review* article (October, 1893), I pilloried " that
wildly impossible story " to which " Ulster steadily
adheres," and complained that he " persists in
publishing this nonsense, and justifies, so long as
he does so, the sternest criticism of his work."[2]
Yet the story is still repeated when its falsehood
has been publicly denounced. It is not, we shall

[1] Ed. Gale, p. 67.

[2] The *Almanac de Gotha*, naturally misled, proclaims the Howards a " maison féodale Anglo-Saxonne que l'on fait remonter à
Leofric . . . vers 950."

find, in pedigree alone that revision is required in the history of the ducal house of Norfolk.

We have seen above the strange shifts to which the makers of Howard pedigrees have been put, in their efforts to get beyond the judge who founded the family toward the end of the 13th century. But we have not seen them all. In his well-known popular *History of Norfolk* (1887), Mr. Walter Rye selected " a few of the worst cases " of spurious pedigrees in Norfolk, and placed at their head that of " Howard, Duke of Norfolk, Premier Peer and Earl Marshal of England."

This family descends from Sir William Howard, who was a grown man and on the bench in 1293, whose real pedigree is very obscure and doubtful, and who invariably spelt his name Haward.

. . . Two *Coram rege* rolls, referred to by the heralds as mentioning William 'de' Howard and William 'Hauward,' have each been tampered with to make them so read—the 'le,' which was undoubtedly in the first, having been cut out,[1] and the tail of the 'y' in the second having been also removed with a knife, to make 'Hayward' read 'Hauward.'

Mr. Rye then continues:—

The pedigree itself was concocted very carelessly, and can deceive no one. It traces the Howards to 'Auber, Earl of Passy, in Normandy,' whose grandson, Roger Fitz Valerine, is said to have owned the castle of Howarden, or 'Howard's den' (!). Alliances with the Bigods, the St. Meres, the Bardolphs, the Brus, and the Trusbuts are liberally provided, to bring in nice-looking quarterings, while an alternative descent from Hereward the Wake is also put forward.

---

[1] Compare the remarks in this paper on the efforts to change 'le' Poher into 'de' Poher.

Well might the writer urge that such concoctions as this form " an instructive commentary on the value of the work of the older heralds and of the ' visitations.'" [1]

But now we come to the strangest part of the whole Hereward story, one of the quaintest episodes, I think, in modern genealogy. In 1896 there appeared a fresh claimant for the honour of descent from Hereward. In his *Hereward the Saxon Patriot*, Lieut.-General Harward not only claimed the patriot as his own " illustrious ancestor," but fiercely denounced the other families which had made a like claim and all who had aided and abetted them. " No weaker claim, or one supported by more unreliable evidence," could be imagined than that of the " grasping family " of Howard ; " the claim of the Temples . . . is too weak and frivolous to be seriously entertained " ; and " the last, and weakest, not to say most ludicrous claim . . . is that of Wake of Courteen Hall, Northampton." Poor Charles Kingsley, as the chief abettor of this claim, was charged with " utter incapacity," with writing " unintelligible nonsense," and with a " mad escapade as Professor of English History in twisting the hero of these pages, the renowned Hereward, into a peg on which to hang a Northampton family named Wake or Jones." Worse than ," a silly archbishop of their name," this " still more foolish

---

[1] For some criticisms on the value of these belauded ' visitations ' see the papers in this volume on the families of Stewart and of Spencer.

prebendary turns a somersault over the professorial chair," and " was most liberally remunerated " for doing so !

From Kingsley the gallant and fiery author turned to "the shortcomings of the Heralds' Office," and insisted "that a public office should cease to disseminate barefaced fabrications."[1] This demand was perfectly justified ; but when we turn from the heralds' "fabrications" to the author's own descent, what, to our amazement, do we find? On the authority of a heralds' visitation of Warwickshire (1619), it is traced up to "John Hereward de Pebwith" *circa* 1235, but no higher.[2] "Pebwith" can only be Pebworth in Gloucestershire, and the great Hereward, who lived at the time of the Norman Conquest, was connected, so far as records go, with Lincolnshire and with Lincolnshire alone.[3] A century and a half has to be covered before we come to the Gloucestershire man alleged to have lived *circa* 1235, and of evidence to connect him with the great Hereward there is not one scrap.[4] Yet on the assumption of such descent the author constructs his pedigree and denounces, as above, those families who claim a baseless connection with "Hereward the Saxon patriot." Of the genealogical curiosities contained in this extraordinary book it would be difficult to

---

[1] " The so-called ' visitations' and the records in the Heralds' College derived from them are in numerous cases untrustworthy and always suspicious " (p. 64).

[2] *Hereward the Saxon Patriot*, p. 91.

[3] *Feudal England*, pp. 160–162.

[4] The name, of course, was in no way distinctive.

give an idea.   One can only draw attention to the really significant fact that it is possible to publish, even now, a work of this character and to have it seriously, and even favourably, reviewed by uninstructed scribes.

A pleasing contrast to the Howard pedigree is afforded by that of the duke of Fife.   Its rise and fall is so curious a story that one may be pardoned for giving it in detail.   When William Duff was raised to an earldom in 1759, he selected the titles of Viscount MacDuff and Earl Fife ; 'evidently,' as G. E. C. observes, "to indicate a descent from the ancient earls of Fife of the house of Macduff." The same descent was implied in the marquessate of Macduff and dukedom of Fife granted so recently as 1889.   Accordingly, till some years ago, ' Burke ' gave as the origin of the family :—

This noble family derives from Fyfe Macduff, a chief of great wealth and power, who lived about the year 834, and afforded to Kenneth II., King of Scotland, strong aid against his enemies the Picts.

This descent was traced through the Duffs of Muldavit, of whom the first, living in 1404, was said to be a cadet of the old earls of Fife.   Baird, who wrote a genealogical history of the family about 1773, set forth the pedigree without question, as did others ; in 1783 Lord Fife procured a charter giving the name of MacDuff to the port he had created at Doune ; and, finally, the family, who had adorned their mausoleum with inscriptions proclaiming it and with the crest of the old earls of Fife, ventured on a crowning step.   Incredible though it may seem, 'a fine stone effigy, with a singularly well-preserved inscription,' erected, it is supposed, to an Innes of Innes about 1539, was removed from Cullen Church to the Duff mausoleum, where, by altering the inscribed date to 1404 (in Arabic numerals !) it was made to figure as that of the first Duff of Muldavit. No less an authority than the late Mr. Stodart, Lyon Clerk Depute, informed 'G. E. C.' that this was probably done in 1792 "to add to the glory of [the then] Lord Fife" ! Moreover, an imitation antique inscription was cut at the same time recording in detail the spurious descent. The credit of unmasking these remarkable proceedings belongs to Mr. William Cramond, who, with indefatigable zeal, established the real facts. The descent from the old earls of Fife was soon seen to be untenable, but the family was still traced to Duff of Muldavit in 1404, and the *Almanac de Gotha* preserves this version ;[1] Mr. Cramond, however, eventually disproved this also and showed that the family could not be traced beyond the middle of the 17th century. 'Burke' has at last surrendered at discretion, and now begins the pedigree with Adam Duff, who died between 1674 and 1677, and "laid the foundation of the prosperity of the family." *Sic transit gloria mundi*. If, as we presume, the present pedigree appears with the sanction of the duke of Fife,

---

[1] It is only just to Mr. Foster to mention that he from the first, in his 'Peerage,' had independently refused to admit even the Muldavit descent.

he has set an example to others, by this frank recognition of facts, which we hope may be widely followed.

The story of the translated effigy and the manufactured genealogical inscription is not, though startling, unique. Tampering has not been confined to the will or to the parish register. Only students of genealogy, perhaps, remember the famous Coulthart imposture, in which the evidences for the pedigree were one and all forged, "monuments to the imaginary line of the Coultharts" being erected in two Scottish churchyards in the shape of altar-tombs commemorating successive lairds of Coulthart! Even this performance was eclipsed by the Deardens at Rochdale, who, according to a writer in the *Gentleman's Magazine* (1852), had constructed in Rochdale Church an apocryphal 'family chapel,' with sham effigies, slabs, and brasses to the memory of imaginary ancestors. This statement, I may add, was actually true, the work having been executed about 1847; and although most of these monstrosities have now been buried, "five imitation antiques" were allowed to remain. A similar performance, so far back as the days of Henry VIII., was exposed not long ago, in a learned paper on "the Hughenden effigies," by Mr. E. J. Payne.[1] He showed that monuments in Hughenden church, which had successfully imposed on Stothard and other antiquaries, even in the present

[1] *Records of Buckinghamshire*, vol. VII. (1896), pp. 362–412.

century, were spurious, having been erected by
a family of Wellesbourne to connect themselves
with the Montforts. One existing effigy was
'adapted' and the others fabricated for the purpose. His conclusions were :—

that they caused a monumental effigy of this imaginary ancestor
to be carved in the style of the thirteenth century . . .
that they adapted the plate-armour effigy to their purpose by
cutting similar arms on the skirts, and that they had the three
rude effigies fabricated by way of filling up the gap between the
fourteenth and sixteenth centuries.

Oddly enough, the same county contains a church
in which, within the present century, monumental
inscriptions have been erected for the purpose of
asserting a descent which is now known to be
spurious. I can supplement these cases by yet
another. An American family of Sears, in search
of English ancestors, laid violent hands on a family
of Sayer, formerly of Colchester, and having constructed for themselves a spurious descent from
that house, obtained permission to erect in St.
Peter's, Colchester, a brass (appropriate metal !)
recording that descent—and testifying to a human
weakness *ære perennius*.

Indeed, even since my article appeared, the now
notorious 'Shipway frauds' have revealed the fact
that such proceedings are still quite possible. The
extraordinary story is thus told by one of the clergy
of the parish :—

In the fall (*sic*) of 1896, by an elaborate system of impudent
frauds, an unscrupulous attempt was made to claim these
monuments for one who was an entire stranger to the parish.

An agent from London[1] was employed in a *search for a pedigree*. He, by fraudulent means, concocted a very plausible story. Genealogies were manufactured, tombs were desecrated, registers were falsified, wills were forged : in a word various outrages were committed with many sacred things in this parish and elsewhere. These two figures, as part of the pedigree, were deposited in a niche in the chantry ; . . . on either side were huge brass tablets on which were engraven various untruthful and unfounded statements.

In this case, we learn,—

the Bishop of Bristol directed [1898] that a faculty should be applied for to remove the glass case and inscriptions, and to restore the tombstones in the churchyard to their proper places. He further directed that the forged inscriptions, etc., in various parts of the church should be removed.[2]

We shall find, in dealing with 'the origin of the Stewarts,' that among the adornments of Ely cathedral is a prominent inscription similarly intended to support " untruthful and unfounded statements." Nothing, however, can be done in the case of these statements, for is not their truth vouched for by the records of the Heralds' College?

One of the victims to this weakness was Lord Brougham himself. It was said of another ardent Radical, who had compiled a voluminous genealogy, that he sat under the largest family tree to be found in Christendom. But Lord Brougham's tree, in its rapid growth, rivalled the Indian mango. Perhaps the *Dictionary of National Biography*, to which G. E. C. triumphantly appeals,

[1] Dr. Davies, who was the author of the frauds of which he was subsequently convicted.

[2] *Our Parish : Mangotsfield* (1899).

errs on the side of incredulity ; but those who are curious in such matters may turn with advantage to the *Gentleman's Magazine* for 1848, where they will find that the same romantic genealogist was a friend of Mr. Dearden and of Lord Brougham, and will read the wondrous story of the so-called ' Crusader's tomb.'

What Mr. Cramond accomplished for the pedigree of the duke of Fife, Mr. Foster did for that of Lord Tweedmouth. Certainly there has been, in our time, no genealogical question of purely academic interest so bitterly and so stubbornly contested as that of the Marjoribanks pedigree ' recorded ' in the Lyon Office. On the creation of the Tweedmouth peerage in 1881, the pedigree of the new peer was duly communicated to the two rival Peerage editors, Sir Bernard Burke and Mr. Foster. The former, after his wont, published it without question ; the latter, as a critical genealogist, deemed it unsatisfactory, and warned his readers that it was wanting in proof and there-rore doubtful. Thereupon the Lyon Clerk Depute ridiculed him for daring to question a " proved and registered pedigree." Despising him as a merely ' English ' genealogist, the Scottish authorities were wholly unprepared for the result of this rash challenge. One after another they entered the field to be overwhelmed in turn. Mr. Foster was found, to their great surprise, to have at his fingers' ends their public and burghal records. He could tell them more than they ever knew ; and he tore their pedigree (or rather pedigrees) to shreds. His straightforward on-slaught contrasted strongly with the pitiful subter-fuges of his opponents. As an example of these he was accused by the then Lyon king of arms of fabricating a date (1688) which " occurs in no printed account of the family except Mr. Foster's," for the purpose of demolishing it. As a matter of fact, the date, so far from being his fabrication, was given by Ulster in his ' Peerage,' and remains there, it will be found, to this day ! Mr. Foster's determined honesty had, of course, made many enemies, who joined eagerly in the attack ; but, finding it at length useless to uphold the discredited descent, they coolly abandoned it as a matter " of little interest to genealogists " ! My readers may be left to draw their own conclusion, and to estimate from this the value of pedigrees ' proved and registered' in the Lyon Office.

We shall have, however, to wait till Mr. Foster resumes the publication of his ' Peerage ' for a trustworthy account of Lord Tweedmouth's de-scent, ' Burke ' having altered it, it is true, but only in matters of detail. The founder of the family, Joseph Marjoribanks of Edinburgh, mer-chant burgess, is still made the grandson of a Lord Clerk Register " of that ilk and of Ratho," although, as Mr. Foster has proved, his parentage has not been traced.[1]

The Marjoribanks pedigree reminds us, by the

---

[1] Mr. Foster's article (*Collectanea Genealogica*, I. 94-107) may be recommended to those interested in the subject as a brilliantly destructive criticism of official genealogy.

way, that there are several problems of Scottish genealogy for light on which we turn in vain, as ever, to the pages of 'Burke.' We still read of Lord Polwarth that "by failure of the *male* heirs of Sir Robert Scott of Murthockstone (from whom derives the noble house of Buccleugh), his lordship claims the chieftainship of all the Scotts in Scotland"; and yet, under 'Napier and Ettrick,' our accommodating editor traces the male heirs of Sir Robert, through the Scotts of Howpaisley and Thirlestaine, and duly assigns them the Scott coat with the Murdochstone bend. Turning to another coveted heirship, the male representative of the Stewards (Stuarts) of Scotland, we find Lord Galloway's undoubted ancestor, Sir William Stewart of Jedworth (executed in 1402), asserted to be the son of Sir John 'of Jedworth,' whose father was slain at Falkirk in 1298. But there is well known to be no proof that Sir William was the son of this Sir John ; the missing link has still to be found, and even a generation, it may be, is omitted. It is unfortunate also that the 'Peerage' opens with a characteristic passage (under 'Abercorn') where, instead of frankly deriving the Hamiltons from Walter Fitz Gilbert, who first appears on the 'Ragman Roll' of homage (1296), 'Burke' temporizes after its wont. It discreetly drops the time-honoured legend, originating in, or commemorated by, the crest of the family ; but, while declining "to trace the exact descent of the illustrious Scottish house of Hamilton from the great and powerful stock of the ancient de Bellomonts (*sic*), Earls of Leicester," the editor, as did his father, still leaves it to be supposed that somehow or other the Hamiltons did descend from that " magnificent Norman race." And he persists in beginning their definite pedigree a generation too soon.

From Scottish pedigrees I pass to two Scottish titles. I hope my readers will not be alarmed by the name of the earldom of Mar, suggesting, as it does, Lord Palmerston's *dictum* on the Schleswig-Holstein question, that only one man really understood it, and that he went mad. I shall not enter, of course, into the merits of the original decision by the House of Lords (1875), which, as Lord Selborne and the Lord Chancellor observed in the 1877 debate, " must be considered as final, right or wrong, and not to be questioned." Nor shall I discuss the wild pretension that an existing earldom was created " before 1014," for it is admitted that the first undisputed earl of the house died about 1244.[1] My remarks will here be confined to the ' Restitution Act ' of 1885, based as it is on what one of its ardent advocates has described as " a hypothesis which can with difficulty be apprehended—even as a legal fiction

---

[1] *Genealogist* [N.S.], IV. 181. It is uncertain whether he inherited the earldom through his father or his mother, nor can the connection of either with the previous holders be established (*Ibid.* II. 68–9 ; IV. 178–180). The idiotic anachronism, " creation, before 1014," still appears in *Burke's Peerage*, but G. E. C., in his *Complete Peerage*, sensibly treats a ' Ruadri ' who appears in 1115 as the first bearer of the title.

—by a Scottish historical antiquary." [1]   At the commencement of this great controversy, it had been admitted, on all hands, that there was but one earldom of Mar, the dignity which figured on the Union Roll and which was undoubtedly vested in the earl of Mar and Kellie who died in 1866.   At his death that dignity was " assumed by Mr. Goodeve-Erskine [*né* Goodeve], sister's son and next of kin, or heir-at-law, to the deceased earl "—to quote the words of his champion, Lord Crawford — as a dignity of medieval origin, descending to heirs of line.   But it was subsequently claimed by Lord Kellie, as the late earl's heir-male, on the ground (to quote the same writer) that it was " a new creation by Mary, Queen of Scots, in 1565 . . . descendible . . . to the heirs-male of the body of the patentee." The question at issue was thus clear ; and the House decided in favour of Lord Kellie, on the avowed grounds (as Lord Crawford admitted) that " the earldom of Mar which now exists on the Roll of Scottish Peers, and which was held by the earl of Mar and Kellie who died in 1866, was a new creation by queen Mary, and not the restitution by her of an ancient dignity ; and [that] the new dignity created by queen Mary was limited to heirs-male of the body, and not descendible to heirs-general."

In any other case this would have settled the question.   But Mr. Goodeve-Erskine, having assumed the title, declined to drop it, though

[1] *Genealogist* [N.S.], III. 22.

the House of Lords, holding rightly " that his assumption was without warrant " (as Lord Crawford wrote), had ordered him to drop the title when appearing before them. This raises the whole question of the assumption of Scottish titles, and, as strenuous efforts have been made to represent the Restitution Act as the sanction of this assumption, it is important to observe that, on the contrary, it styled Mr. Goodeve-Erskine by that name throughout, thereby denying the validity of his assumption (1866–1885), and involving the corollary that but for this Act he would not be earl of Mar.

And now for the Act. As it was impossible to undo, at least in form, what the Lords had done, it was resolved by Lord Mar's supporters to resort to what his own champion termed " an equivocation on the facts of the case." The letter of the Lords' resolution was accepted, while repudiating the *rationes* on which alone it was based. All that was needed was to assume that the earldom of Mar could not possibly have been created in 1565 (which was precisely what the Committee decided, *teste* Lord Crawford, it had been), and that, consequently, Lord Kellie had been awarded a dignity which, as G. E. C. (one is sorry to see) puts it, was " apparently a creation by the Committee for Privileges in 1875." Although this language betrays the absurdity of the position (the Committee of course awarding an existing, not creating a new, dignity), it was treated as a brilliant discovery that the 'ancient' earldom of Mar was vested in Mr. Goodeve-Erskine, and on this daring *petitio principii* the Act of 'Restitution' was based.[1] As might be expected, a measure which avowedly represented an 'equivocation' failed to satisfy either party, because, while virtually revoking the decision of 1875, it pretended to do nothing of the kind. Hence protests at Holyrood, hence debates at Westminster, and all because clamour and agitation had been allowed to render ridiculous a decision which they could not reverse.

The Mar case, apart from the points of law involved, evoked a good deal of false sentiment, owing to the apparent injustice of a title which had come to the Erskines "through a lass," being retained by them as heirs-male instead of passing to the heir-general. But the peculiarities of the Scottish system have wrought in other cases the same or greater injustice, without protest being made. Another Erskine title, the earldom of Buchan, although nominally the old earldom of 1469, has been held, since 1695, by a branch of the family which, as G. E. C. observes, is "in no way connected with any of the previous

---

[1] I would particularly invite attention to the fearful confusion and contradiction into which counsel, 'Lyon,' and even law lords plunged, when the pedigree was 'proved,' before the Committee for Privileges in 1885. This was demonstrated by me, in an article on "Janet Barclay wife of Sir Thomas Erskine" (*Genealogist* [N.S.], IX. 131–137), to which no reply has been, or can be, attempted, for it is based throughout on the official "Minutes of Evidence, Mar Restitution Bill" themselves.

earls," to the detriment of their descendants and
heirs-general. This case, therefore, is even
stronger than that of Mar, to which Moray,
however, is a good parallel. The earldom of that
name came through an heiress to the family
who now possess it, but they diverted its descent
in favour of their heirs-male. It is alleged that
this was done by a re-grant of the 'comitatus,'
upon resignation, in 1611 ; but when the right to
the title came incidentally (not on a remit) before
the House of Lords (1790-1793), the decision
in favour of Lord Moray was based, it is virtually
known, not upon this charter (1611)—which
according to the Sutherland decision (1771)
could not have carried the honours—but upon the
same principles as the Mar decision (1875)
itself. And indeed, apart from those principles,
the construction of these charters, at the very
period of transition, is notoriously a moot point.
The parallel is carried further by the fact, that
however the charter might operate on the
honours, it undoubtedly vested the estates in the
heir-male. In England, owing to the absence
of the system of resignation and re-grant, such
cases do not arise, the only successful attempt in
that direction being the special Arundel entail
of 1627. Yet, through the whole of the 17th
century, the main issue in peerage cases was the
famous doctrine that an earldom 'attracted' a
barony in fee ; that is, diverted its descent in
favour of the heirs-male. 'The British Solomon,'
I may add, curiously justified that name by divid-

ing the contested dignity in such cases as Abergavenny (1604), Roos (1616 and 1618), and
Offaley (1620), awarding a barony to the heir-
male and another to the heir-general. Thus,
he divided the barony of Roos into those of
' Roos' and ' Roos of Hamlake.' Yet in this he
only followed the precedent which gave us such
twin dignities as Dacre of the North and Dacre of
the South ; and it is practically the same illogical
and bewildering compromise which has given us
in our own day two earls of Mar. And yet it was
James himself who gave us the sound maxim that
" it cannot stand with the ordour and consuetude
of the countrie to honnour two earlis with ane title."

My next Scottish dignity is the barony of
Ruthven of Freeland. Now this is a subject of
some delicacy, on which it is, unhappily, necessary to speak plainly. This dignity is on a
different footing from any other in the Peerage,
and is the greatest of all its curiosities. For,
wrongfully assumed in the first instance, it has
been wrongfully borne ever since. This fact, I
hasten to add, is no new discovery : Riddell, to
whom Sir Bernard appealed as " the most eminent
of Scottish Peerage lawyers," went into this matter
in his *Remarks on Scotch Peerage Law* (1833);
and though denouncing the ' apologies ' for the
assumption of the title as " too trivial and flimsy
for criticism," he condescended to expose them
in all their absurdity. They have also, we have
seen, been rejected by Mr. Foster and by G.E.C.
and called in question by ' Debrett.'

PEERAGE STUDIES

The facts, apart from these 'apologies,' are few and simple enough. The barony is said to have been created " in 1651," but even the date of the patent is unknown. The original document has long been lost—it is not proved how or when— and, as it was never registered, nor a copy made of it, and as moreover there is no " docquet or sign-manual thereof," its contents are wholly unknown.[1] Under these circumstances there is unconscious satire in the motto of the family : " Deeds show." For there is no adminicle of evidence to show what the limitation of the dignity really was.

When this is the case, as is well known, the law presumes a limitation to heirs-male of the body, this being, as Lord Cranworth observed in the Herries case (1858), " a settled rule of law." This would agree with the only clue we possess to the terms of the patent ; namely, a contemporary MS. in the Advocates' Library, which states that the limitation was to 'heirs-*male*.' On the extinction, however, of the direct male line in 1701 or 1704 (for even this date is uncertain) the title, though described as 'extinct' in Crawfurd's *Peerage of Scotland* (1716), seems to have been tentatively and fitfully assumed by the last lord's youngest sister, who had succeeded to his estates. At her death the estates passed to

[1] It is very singular that if, as alleged, it was preserved for a hundred years, no attempt was ever made to set its terms on record, as was done in the similar case of Rollo, a barony created the same year (1651).

96

their nephew, Sir William Cunningham, who, already heir of line, became thereby heir of tailzie as well to the last lord. Yet he did not assume the title. But his cousin and heir, Mrs. Johnston, tentatively revived the assumption, and —receiving a summons to the coronation of George II.—"in a jesting way," according to Lord Hailes, "she said that this was her patent, and that she would preserve it as such, in her charter-chest." It was not, however, till 1764 that Douglas—"a most indifferent peerage-writer," says Riddell, " and little, indeed, to be ever trusted "— gave a half-hearted recognition to this curious assumption. And now comes the striking point. In order to homologate the assumption and present a consistent story, the pedigree had to be falsified by cutting out both ' Baroness' Jean and Sir William Cunningham, and passing straight to 'Baroness' Isabel ! The existence of the two former being a fatal flaw in the case, they were carefully kept. out of sight by Douglas, Wood, and ' Burke' in turn down to 1883. But by that time the terrible Mr. Foster had unearthed these individuals, and had openly impugned the assumption. Accordingly, Sir Bernard had to shift his ground ; and, in his ' Peerage' for 1884, the account of the assumption was entirely re-written, and the old ' apologies' for it revived, thereby revealing the fact that apology was needed. I need only print side by side the two versions of the critical period in order to prove my point :—

PEERAGE STUDIES

Burke's Peerage, 1883.

David, 2nd baron, a lord of the Treasury, died without issue in 1701, when the barony devolved upon his niece, The Hon. Isabella Ruthven, as 1st baroness.

Burke's Peerage, 1884.

David, 2nd lord. . . . He entailed his estates, etc. etc. . . . Dying unmarried 1701, he was succeeded by his youngest sister Jean, who as Baroness Ruthven made up her titles to the estates,[1] and whose right to the peerage was unchallenged in her lifetime. She *d.* unm. 1722, and the next holder of the title was her niece Isabel, Baroness Ruthven.[2]

But even now the intervention of Sir William Cunningham between the two 'Baronesses' is carefully ignored.

I cannot, of course, enter here into all the details, but must refer the editor of 'Burke,' or anyone else desirous of really learning the truth, to the elaborate article I wrote on the subject in Part XIII. (pp. 167–186) of Mr. Foster's *Collectanea Genealogica* (1884), where all the 'apologies' are discussed *seriatim*, and clearly shown to be inept.[3] The *Complete Peerage* refers throughout (VI. 457–462) to this article as dealing "exhaustively" with the case and as "amplifying Riddell's crushing demolition of the 'apologies' for such assumption." Its editor asserts that "On the death of the second

---

[1] Yet it was only as "Mrs. Jean Ruthven" that she petitioned the Court of Session to record the entail, 1721.

[2] This version still appears (1900).

[3] Reference may also be made to papers by G. E. C. and myself in *Notes and Queries*, 6th S. VII. 153, 168 et seq., 290, 389, etc.

THE PEERAGE

Lord the title was arbitrarily assumed," and he refuses to accept any of those who have assumed it since 1701 as entitled to do so.

This title, in fact, is a solitary survival of those assumptions of Scottish dignities which formed in the last century so grave a scandal that repeated but unsuccessful efforts were made to check it. Owing to the peculiar Scottish system these assumptions passed 'unchallenged' unless a counter-claim brought the question to an issue, or votes tendered in respect of them turned the scale at an election. This was frankly admitted by the Lord Clerk Register in his evidence before the Select Committee of 1882 :—" As the law now stands, the title may be held for generations by persons who have never taken any steps whatever to establish their claim";[1] while even Lyon, though devoted to the system, conceded that " in Scotland there are individuals as to whom it may be matter of dispute as to whether they are Peers."[2]   Even in England, though the intervention of the writ of summons offers a safeguard against such assumptions, there is no such check in the case of a Baroness ; and it is a most remarkable fact that there were at least three wrongful assumptions of that dignity during the last century. 'Baroness Cromwell,' by whom that title was erroneously assumed from 1687 to 1709, actually walked as a Peeress at the funeral of queen Mary and the coronation of queen Anne ; 'Baroness Dudley' assumed that title from 1757 to 1762 ; and 'Baroness le Despencer,' as Lady

[1] 'Minutes,' 71.   [2] *Ibid.* 185.

Austen styled herself from 1781 to 1788, was also
a title erroneously assumed. All three cases will
be found in the admirable work of G.E.C., where
the origin of the error in each case is explained.
The whole subject of dignities assumed, recognised,
and even created in error, is one of curious interest.
Thus the Scottish Barony of Lindores was successfully assumed, like that of Ruthven, from 1736—
and those who assumed it allowed to vote—till the
accident of the vote being challenged at a close
election led to the assumption being stopped in
1793.[1] So the Barony of Willoughby of Parham
was actually held from 1679 to 1765 by a younger
son, summoned in error, and his descendants. But
this being an English barony, it is held that the
writ of summons, though issued in error, created a
dignity ; and the same famous doctrine of the ' ennobling of the blood,' by (rightly or wrongly)
sitting in the House, is responsible for the existence
of three baronies—Clifford (1628), Strange (1628),
and Percy (1722)—created by writs of summons
issued under a misapprehension. With these we
may perhaps compare the Irish Barony of ' La
Poer,' allowed to Lady Waterford and her heirs in
1767, although it was limited to heirs-male by the
creation of 1535. It would thus be virtually

---

[1] On this important case I follow Riddell (*The Law and Practice in Scottish Peerages*, pp. 777–9) : " In this case, the assumption
of the honour, from 1736 to 1790 . . . a period of fifty-
four years, with voting at Elections of the Sixteen Peers, were
held to go for nothing, which bears upon the law as to prescription
in honours."

parallel to the cases of Cromwell (1687) and Percy (1722).[1]

Passing from Scotland to Ireland, we observe with satisfaction that G. E. C. dwells, in his preface, on our imperfect knowledge of its peerage, of which " no comprehensive account exists." The subject has, indeed, been strangely neglected, and, when investigated by a competent scholar, will yield extremely interesting and somewhat surprising results. But although so well informed on the peerage of modern times, G. E. C., as I have said before, is not at home in the feudal period. He has therefore found himself dependent partly on a worthless and misleading list of the early peerage in the *Liber Hibernie*, and partly on the works of Mr. Lynch, the ablest writer, no doubt, upon the subject, but, we must remember, a partisan. Lynch wrote with the object of establishing, as a rule of law, a presumption in favour of heirs-male in the descent of Irish dignities. Betham, in spite of his official position, was so poor an advocate of the opposite view, that we cannot wonder at G. E. C. following Lynch throughout. But this is a matter that cannot be narrowed to a question of decisions and precedents. A broader view will take us deep down among the roots of Anglo-Irish difficulties. The native tribal principle, invincibly in favour of agnates, strove, here as elsewhere, against the principles of English law. I imagine that at first the latter prevailed, especially within

[1] See further, upon this subject, the paper below on "The Barony of Mowbray."

the pale, but with the ebb of the English rule the native principle revived ; and even the Anglo-Normans, ' Hibernis Hiberniores,' adopted, in the wilder parts, the old tribal system—Bourke (Mac-William), Bermingham (MacPhioris), FitzMaurice (MacMorrish), for instance—or at least elaborately entailed their estates upon heirs-male. Thus there arose, in practice, a system of male succession, although, in my opinion, it had not prevailed at first. It is largely due to this development that the houses of the *conquistadores* present so long and illustrious a descent in the male line, instead of merging in heiresses, as in England would have been their fate.

G. E. C. adopts for his sheet-anchor the ranking of the Irish peers at Windsor, when summoned there by Henry VII. (1489), combining it with the ranking by the ' Lords Commissioners ' in 1615. From these rankings he endeavours to determine the probable antiquity of their dignities. But here we have the old mistake of trusting to secondary and late evidence instead of investigating the facts for oneself. The enemy of peerage history is peerage law. We are confronted under ' Athenry ' with the difficulties to which it leads. The right order of precedence was Athenry, Kingsale, Kerry, upon which G. E. C. remarks :—

As the Lords Commissioners (in 1613 [*rectè* 1615]) admitted that " the FitzMaurices, Lords of Kerry and Lixnaw, proved their possession of that dignity to be as ancient as the Conquest " (*i.e.* 1172), and as " the same Lords Commissioners adjudged the antiquity of the Lords Courcy of Kingsale to be still greater than

that of the Lords Fitzmaurice of Kerry," it follows that the antiquity of the Barony of Athenry, which immediately precedes that
of Kingsale, cannot be *later* than 1172; in which same year
(according to their Lordships' authority) we must suppose the
Barony of Kingsale, as well as that of Kerry, to have been also
created, for certainly no such Baronies could have been created
before the Conquest above named.

The writer fails to perceive that what really
'follows' is the *reductio ad absurdum* of the Lords
Commissioners' ruling. Under 'Kerry' he repeats
his dilemma, again observing that " 29 May, 1223,
which date is, in all probability, that of the origin
of the peerage of Kingsale," is incompatible with
the above conclusion. The origin of the difficulty
is, I would suggest, that while, in England, the
' creation ' of a barony is reckoned to date from the
first proved writ of summons, in Ireland the writ
of summons has been comparatively ignored, and
dignities traced to the earliest period at which
their possessors were barons by tenure. This
principle, though pressed upon them, has always
been rejected by our own House of Lords, so that
the apparent superior antiquity of Irish over English baronies has no foundation in fact.[1]

The most famous, probably, of early Irish dignities is the celebrated barony of Kingsale. Who
has not heard of its thirty lords descended in direct
male succession from that John de Courci, ' Earl of

---

[1] It is only right to mention that the editor of the *Complete
Peerage*, always anxious to improve his work and bring it up to
date, has cited the above criticisms on his views (which appeared
in my *Quarterly Review* article) in his Corrigenda (vol. VIII. p.
251).

Ulster,' whose wondrous deeds procured for them the right of remaining covered in the presence of the king ?   But it is not only 'butter and patriots' that are produced in county Cork : it has also given us in the Courci myth the wildest of peerage fictions.   It is certain, from the testimony of Giraldus, that John de Courci left no heir ; it is, further, certain that his wondrous *geste*, so elaborately related in *Burke's Peerage* is sheer and impossible fiction ; and it is, lastly, certain that the alleged privilege of remaining covered in the royal presence is an even later addition to this late legend.[1]   And yet ' Burke '—though it now admits that John de Courci probably died childless—continues to inform us that "Lord Kingsale enjoys the hereditary privilege (granted by king John to De Courcy, Earl of Ulster) of wearing his hat in the royal presence."   No instance, I believe, is known of this ' right ' being exercised before the days of William III., although it had become familiar by the middle of the last century, when Montagu wrote to Horace Walpole, of the new Lord Kingsale (1762), that "our peers need not fear him assuming his privilege of being covered, for till the King gives him a pension he cannot buy the offensive hat."   G. E. C. waxes merry over what he terms the ' hat trick,' but it was not he who detected the flaws in the Courci legend,

---

[1] See my articles on "John de Courci, Conqueror of Ulster," in *Antiquarian Magazine and Bibliographer*, February 1883, and subsequent numbers ; also my life of John de Courci in *Dictionary of National Biography*.

nor, we shall find, when left to himself, has he escaped disaster.

In spite of what Planché described as their " worthless and unmannerly " privilege, and of the falsehood of its alleged origin, the Lords Kingsale were undoubtedly seated in their baronial territory of ' Courcy's ' from the days of Henry III., and possess a peerage dignity of great antiquity. But what their title really was no one seems to know. It has bewildered G. E. C., who sets forth its various forms, but himself adopts, all through, that of ' Baron Kingsale and Ringrone.' ' Burke,' on the other hand, adopts the incongruous style, ' Lord Kingsale, Baron Courcy of Courcy, and Baron of Ringrone.' The true title, however, was not ' Kingsale ' but ' Courcy,' and so late as 1613 the then peer sat in Parliament as ' Lord Courcy of Ringroane.' In the list drawn up preliminary to that Parliament he is styled ' the Lord Baron Cursie ' ; and ' Lord Courcy,' simply, was the style by which these peers had always been known. The creation, however, of a Viscount Kingsale, in 1625, was resented by Lord Courcy as an encroach- ment on his own territory, and, in 1627, he obtained from Royal Commissioners a misleading report " that the Lord Courcy was not only Lord Courcy, but Baron of Kingsale and also of Ring- rone." In 1634 the Lords' Journals still style him ' Lord Courcy ' in their list, but eventually ' King- sale ' in lieu of ' Courcy ' was adopted as the title of their peerage dignity, which, however, continues to be but one.

What is the date of its creation? My readers might imagine that if anyone knew the date of the Premier Barony of Ireland, it would have been Ulster King-of-Arms. Not so. It used to be alleged (and is still, I believe, in some popular 'Peerages') that the barony of 'Kingsale' dates from 1181. This date Sir Bernard abandoned, although his Peerage still asserts that John de Courci "was created in 1181 (being the first Englishman dignified with an Irish title of honour) Earl of Ulster." The objection to this date, as an Irishman might say, is that John was never created earl of Ulster at all. But, as to the barony, we are now told, both in the narrative and at its foot, that its 'creation' was in '1223.' Now, in this case, G. E. C. is in complete accord with 'Burke.' He repeatedly traces 'the peerage of Kingsale' to a grant by Henry III., 29th May, 1223, which he treats as a fixed point bearing upon other dates. In my experience an exact date is hardly ever an invention: it has an origin somewhere. But this date long baffled me. Its actual origin is a marvel. Lodge had writen in his Irish 'Peerage,' that

King Henry [III.] conferred on him [Miles, son of John de Courci] the Barony of Kingsale, to hold *per integram Baroniam*, and confirmed all the lands of Ulster to Lacie by patent, dated 29 May, 1223, 7 of his reign.

This date, obviously, refers to the grant of Ulster to 'Lacie,' but has been carelessly read as applying to 'the Barony of Kingsale.' There is, however, no such grant of Ulster on that date. What is the solution of the mystery ? Simply that a genuine grant of 7 *John* (1205) has been stupidly given as of 7 Henry III. (1223). Therefore the date should be 1205, not 1223, and has, moreover, nothing to do with the Courcys or with Kingsale !

And with this imaginary date everything goes by the board. There is no evidence that Henry III. granted a ' Barony of Kingsale,' no evidence that it ever belonged to Miles de Courcy ' the first lord,' no evidence that he was the father of that Patrick de Courci who is the first of the family on record. The whole story has been patched together to connect this fatherless Patrick with John, the conqueror of Ulster.

It is not alleged that any Courcy actually sat as a peer in Parliament till 1339–1340, a date (if genuine) inferior, of course, to that of several English baronies ; and, whatever the family's status was, it required, we learn from ' Burke,' to be " confirmed by patent 1397." G. E. C. assigns this confirmation to " 1396–97, 20 Ric. II.," and both writers clearly copy from Lodge's statement that the then lord, " by the letters patent of the king, received a confirmation of the honours and titles of Baron of Kingsale and Ringrone." But here again they get their date by misreading Lodge, who does not supply one. As the earliest patent for an Irish barony is assigned to 1462, the terms of this Courcy patent would be of extreme interest, and it is much to be regretted that Lodge did not quote them. Possibly they implied a creation *de novo*, and would thus have been distasteful to his patrons. In any case, so long as it is kept *in retentis*, a doubt must surround this document, and I expressed, in 1893, the hope that Ulster King-of-Arms would give us the terms and the exact date either from the patent itself or from its enrolment.

The above criticisms on this barony, which appeared in my *Quarterly Review* article, have been frankly accepted by G. E. C. in the 'Corrigenda' to his *Complete Peerage* (vol. VIII. pp. 435–6). He also, on his own account, caused search to be made for the mysterious alleged patent of 20 Ric. II.; but no trace of it could be found either in Ireland or in England (*Ibid*. pp. 436–7). In striking contrast with his zeal for the truth is the fact that 'Burke' (1900) continues to repeat all the absurdities I have here exposed, thus illustrating its editor's conception of "a more thorough revision than usual."

But really, as to dates of creation, what can be said of the extraordinary carelessness in a matter most keenly discussed, with which 'Burke,' year after year, treats the barony of Hastings? In Garter's Roll, which is given in the work, Lord Mowbray is ranked above Lord Hastings; while in his own "relative precedence," Sir Bernard, when I wrote (1892), took upon himself to reverse this ranking, apparently on the ground that Hastings dates from '1264,' which was indeed the date assigned to its creation at the foot of his account of that barony. Now, however, the confusion is worse than ever. For, although, in its table of

relative precedence (p. 1657) 'Burke' now ranks
Mowbray above Hastings, it there still assigns to the
latter the date ' 1264,' though, under ' Hastings,'
it gives the creation, at the foot of its account,
as ' 19 Dec. 1311,' while actually, in narrating the
determination of its abeyance, speaking of it (in
that same account) as "created by Edward I. in
1290" ! The latter date, I may add, is the right
one, as there is proof of the first lord's sitting in
that year, and, though the writ is not extant, Lord
Cottenham presumed, and the House accepted, its
existence from the sitting. So *Burke's Peerage*,
in this instance, flatly contradicts itself.

The mention of Mowbray naturally leads me to
glance at those Howard titles from which that
barony has been severed. The guidance of
Burke's Peerage is here most untrustworthy.
The duke of Norfolk is Earl Marshal under a
'creation,' not of 1483, but 1672 ; he is earl of
Arundel, not 'by possession of Arundel Castle
only,' but under the special entail of the dignity,
created by Act of Parliament in 1627 ; finally, he is
duke of Norfolk, whatever any one may say,
under the 'creation' of 1514, not under that of
1483. Even 'Burke' speaks of his ancestor as
"created duke of Norfolk" in 1514, and that
creation by Henry VIII. naturally ignored the
Yorkist creation of 1483, which perished with
Richard III. Nor, even apart from creation,
is 1483 the date of the precedence implied.
Moreover, the final act of restoration (which
has modified, we shall find, the limitation of

the dignity) was passed, not (as 'Burke' states) in '1664,' but in 1660, being confirmed in 1661. The restored duke, by the way, was a lunatic living at Padua. As an instance of the extraordinary carelessness prevailing in these matters, I may add that Mr. Fleming, that most eminent Peerage counsel, in opening the case for Lord Stourton, asserted that this " restoration extended by express words to all who could claim under the first duke of Norfolk " (Proceedings on the Mowbray Peerage Claim, 30th May, 1876, p. 6), and that the Committee allowed this assertion to pass unquestioned. But the Act, as I read it, excludes the Effingham line (as they are also excluded from the dignity of Earl Marshal) ; so that only those who can claim under the ' fourth ' duke are now in remainder to either dignity.[1]

My original criticism of *Burke's Peerage*, written shortly before the death of the late Ulster King of Arms, closed with these words :—

We trust that what we have said may be of service to Sir Bernard Burke, by enabling him to correct still further what may be fairly described as our standard work upon the Peerage. Nor is it only correction that is needed. The sense of proportion is at present wanting, some families being assigned undue space and importance relatively to others. . . . But what we would specially press upon him is that he should follow the example set him by G. E. C. in honesty and fidelity to fact. Let him not wait till critics or rivals have compelled him to reluctantly abandon his legends one by one. Let him remember that his official

---

[1] The views I have expressed on the Howard titles are all, I believe, virtually accepted by G. E. C. (*Complete Peerage*, VI. 45–48, 59).

THE PEERAGE

position invests his book, in the eyes of the public, with a quasi-official character, which lays on him a grave responsibility for the statements it contains. We hope that, as an earnest of his desire for accuracy, he will investigate the Ruthven assumption and state the facts more fairly ; and if he should hesitate, from kindness of heart, between the desire to avoid offence and the wish to let the truth be known, we commend to him the words of Aristotle :—Ἀμφοῖν φιλοῖν ὄντοιν, ὅσιον προτιμᾶν τὴν ἀλήθειαν.[1]

Those who have perused the present article will agree, I think, with me that the result of this appeal has been singularly disappointing. It would seem that only Mr. Freeman's lash, wielded with a fierceness of which I have not ventured to illustrate the full measure, could extort from the editors of 'Burke' any real or substantial reform. The means of amendment placed at their disposal are persistently rejected or ignored, while the "thorough revision" to which the work, as the public is assured, has been subjected is found to involve the introduction or revival of fictions of the worst type.

And yet the 'Peerage' is by no means the most misleading of the books which appear beneath the name and the official insignia of the late Ulster King of Arms. Five and thirty years ago there appeared a pungent work on *Popular Genealogists : the art of Pedigree-making*, which is known to have proceeded from the pen of a well-known officer of arms. It was pointed out in that volume that—

while the 'Peerage' may be to a slight extent improving from

[1] *Quarterly Review*, as above.

year to year, the 'Landed Gentry' is deteriorating. The successive editions are marked by a gradual disappearance of families of *status* and historical repute, while their places are to a large extent filled by persons whose sole connexion with land arises from their having been purchasers of a few acres in a county where their very names are unknown.

The immense majority of the pedigrees in the 'Landed Gentry,' including more especially the Scottish pedigrees, cannot, I fear, be characterized as otherwise than utterly worthless. The errors of the 'Peerage' are as nothing to the fables which we encounter everywhere. . . .

The reader who has followed me thus far will probably be of opinion that the works which we have been examining are in no respect worthy of the present condition of genealogical science. It is a remarkable circumstance that side by side with the laborious and critical genealogists, there should have sprung up a set of venal pedigree-mongers, whose occupation consists in garbling truth and inventing falsehood,—a calling which they pursue with the most untiring assiduity. But it is unfortunate, indeed, that the easy credulity of Sir Bernard Burke should allow him to be led blindfold by these obscure persons, whose most palpable fictions he seldom shows the least hesitation in adopting. Statements which would never otherwise have obtained a moment's credit have been allowed to go forth with the imprimatur of the chief herald of Ireland, on the strength of which they are relied on by a large section of the public . . . both his 'Peerage' and 'Landed Gentry' are profusely quoted in books circulating on the Continent as well as in Britain. Year by year new fictions, belonging not to respectable legend, but to regular imposture, are obtaining general acceptance on their authority ; it is, therefore, high time that the public should be disabused of their faith in these works.

One would hesitate to repeat these words if matters had improved since they were written, but their caution to the public is, unhappily, even more imperatively needed now. As a mere record of the Landed Gentry, the work which bears their name has gone from bad to worse ; the acreage and the real social standing of the ' landed ' families now admitted would amaze the public if it were known ;[1] and, as observed in the above extract, the longest pedigrees are sometimes those of families with the least claim to figure in the work at all. Happily a project is now on foot to issue an absolutely truthful and in every way trustworthy record of the real landed families of standing, with their history and the acreage they hold. It will be curious, indeed, to see how many of Burke's ' Landed Gentry ' will be able to make good their claim to admission within the select covers of the first really exclusive and absolutely straightforward work that it has been attempted to produce.[2]

It is still, unfortunately, true that, as observed by the above writer, " the errors of the Peerage are as nothing to the fables which we encounter " in other works bearing the name of ' Burke.' For proof of this assertion we may turn to an absolutely crushing review of one of the latest of these productions, *Burke's Colonial Gentry*.[3] Its writer ventures to express his regret that—

---

[1] As an amusing instance in point, one gentleman in business, who is not a landowner at all, is actually credited with two ' seats ' (not mere ' residences '), one of which he used to rent, and the other of which (within the walls of a town) he rents at the present time. And his family is described as ' of ' the former.

[2] I refer to the great series of volumes on our county families in connection with the Victoria History of the Counties of England (Archibald Constable & Co.).

[3] *Genealogist* [N.S.], XII. (1896), 66–71.

PEERAGE STUDIES

Sir Bernard Burke's sons deem it consistent with their reputation to issue to the public works of this character, in which the same loose statements, the same unbridged chasms, the same apocryphal legends, sometimes, it is true, tempered with the qualifying "It is said" or "It is probable," appear in edition after edition.

Instance after instance is then given of statements such as even *Burke's Peerage* would hardly now venture to admit. Whether we approve or not of Mr. Freeman's strong language, it would really seem that nothing less can move the editors of 'Burke,' or open the eyes of the public at large to the worthless nature of the statements which it has been led to accept and repeat on the strength of their appearance in edition on edition of works appearing beneath the *ægis* of a herald and bearing the name of a King of Arms.

II

The Origin of the Stewarts

OF the problems upon which new light is
thrown by my Calendar of documents in France
relating to English history, none, probably, for
the genealogist, will rival in interest the origin
of the Stewarts. It has long been known that the
Scottish Stewarts and the great English house of
Fitz Alan possessed a common ancestor in Alan,
the son of Flaald, living under Henry the First.
This was established at some length by Chalmers
in his *Caledonia* (1807) on what he declared to be
" the most satisfactory evidence." [1] According to
him, " Alan the son of Flaald, a Norman, acquired
the manor of Oswestrie, in Shropshire, soon after
the Conquest," and " married the daughter of
Warine, the famous sheriff of Shropshire." Mr.
Riddell, the well-known Scottish antiquary, followed up the arguments of Chalmers, in 1843,
with a paper on the " Origin of the House of
Stewart," [2] in which he accepted and enforced
the views of Chalmers, including his theory that
Walter Fitz Alan brought with him to Scotland
followers from Shropshire and gave them lands

[1] Vol. I. pp. 572–575.   [2] *Stewartiana*, pp. 55–70.

there.   But research has hitherto been unable to determine the origin of Flaald father of Alan, or even to find, in England, any mention of his name.

No less an authority on feudal genealogy than the late Mr. Eyton devoted himself to a special investigation on the subject of Alan " Fitz Flaald," [1] and arrived at the conclusion that, after all, he was a grandson of " Banquo, thane of Lochaber," whose son " Fleance " fled to England.   " My belief is," Mr. Eyton wrote, " that the son of Fleance was named Alan . . . and that he whom the English called Alan Fitz Flaald was the person in question." [2]   He admitted, however, of the priories of Andover, Sele, and Sporle, cells of the Abbey of St. Florent de Saumur, that he could " show a connection between Alan Fitz Flaald or his descendants and each of these cells,[3] which suggested an Angevin origin, and for which he could not account.   But where he really advanced our knowledge was in showing that Alan Fitz Flaald married, not (as alleged) a daughter of Warine the sheriff, but Aveline daughter of Ernulf de Hesdin, a great Domesday tenant.   I have now been able to trace Ernulf to Hesdin (in Picardy) itself, in connection with which his daughter ' Ava ' also is mentioned.[4]   In 1874, an anony-

---

[1] *History of Shropshire* (1858), VII. 211–232.

[2] *Ibid*. p. 227.   It is essential to bear in mind that the old Scottish writers made Walter, the first Steward, a son of 'Fleance,' wholly *ignoring* Alan his real father (see p. 119 below).   This invalidates their whole story.

[3] *Ibid*. 219.   [4] See Preface to my Calendar, p. xlvii.

mous work, *The Norman People*, approached the problem from the foreign side, and adduced evidence to prove that Flaald was a brother of Alan, seneschal of Dol.   But there was still not forthcoming any mention of Flaald in England, while the rashness and inaccuracy which marred that book resulted in his being wrongly pronounced a "son of Guienoc."   The great pedigree specially prepared a few years ago for the Stuart exhibition by Mr. W. A. Lindsay (now Windsor Herald) still began only with Alan son of Flaald, to whom a daughter of Warine the sheriff was assigned as wife. Moreover, in the handsome work on *The Royal House of Stuart* (1890), which had its origin in that exhibition, Dr. Skelton could only tell us that "there was (if the conclusions of Chalmers are to be accepted) an Alan son of Flathauld, a Norman knight, who soon after the Conquest obtained a gift of broad lands in Shropshire" (p. 5).   Alan, we shall find, was not a Norman; the lands he was given were widely scattered; and he did not obtain them "soon after the Conquest."

The latest authoritative statement on the subject is that, it would seem, of Sheriff Mackay in the *Dictionary of National Biography* (1896).[1]   He tells us, of the House of Stewart, that

[1] This passage is found in the biography of the first Stewart king, so that I only lighted upon it after this paper was written. It gave me the clue to Mr. Hewison's book, of which I had not previously heard, but which I have now read just in time to add his results to this paper (24th Jan., 1900).

PEERAGE STUDIES

Its earlier genealogy is uncertain, but an ingenious and learned, though admittedly in part hypothetical, attempt to trace it to the Banquho of Boece and Shakespeare, Thane of Lochaber, has been recently made by the Rev. J. K. Hewison (*Bute in the Olden Time* [vol. II.] pp. 1–38, Edinburgh, 1895).[1]

Mr. Hewison's volume opens with the words :—

The origin of the royal house of Stewart has long remained a mystery, perplexing historical students, who feel tantalized at knowing so little concerning the hapless victim of the jealousy of King Macbeth—Banquo, round whom Shakespeare cast the glamour of undying romance, and to whom the old chroniclers of Scotland traced back the family of Stewart.

The author's ' glamour ' augurs ill, and in spite of the unique advantage he enjoyed in having access to the late Lord Crawford's MS. collections on the subject, we soon find ourselves wandering, alas, with Alice in Wonderland.

It may be concluded that Walter, the son of Fleadan, son of Banchu, is identical with Walter, son of [A]llan (or Flan), son of Murechach of the Lennox family, if not also with Walter, son of Amloib, son of Duncan of the other genealogy. Chronology easily permits of the equation of Murdoch, the Maormor of Leven . . . with Banchu . . . who might have survived even his son Fleance—we, meantime, only assuming that Fleance was slain in Wales. *Ban-chu*, the pale warrior, would be his complimentary title ; the old surname of his family . . . also descended to his son, *Flan-chu*, the red or ruddy warrior, known to his Irish kinsmen as Fleadan.

We are surely coming to the *Man-chu* dynasty. But no.

This Irish form of the name *Fleadan tan* (*i.e.* either Fleadan the Tanist or Fleadan the younger) imports a significant idea—

---

[1] Vol. XLVIII. p. 344.

namely, *flead* . . . a feast, which corresponds in signification
with *Flaald*. . . .

Then there bursts upon us yet another discovery :—

> *Fleanchus* . . . is the Latinised form of *Flann-chu*, the Red
> or Ruddy Dog . . . and is also a sobriquet—the Bloodhound.
> . . . This nomenclature is evidently a reminiscence of the dog-
> totem or dog-divinity, etc., etc.

There remains, however, the standing puzzle[1]
why Walter the first Stewart was made by the
old romancers a son of Fleance son of Banquo,
though his father was indisputably Alan son of
Flaald.   One solution offered by our author is
that " Ailin or Allan may have become the family
name " ; but his own view is that

> The native name of Banquo's son would be the common
> Goidelic one *Flann*, which signifies rosy or fair, and has an
> equivalent in *Aluinn*, beautiful, fair, to which the word Alan,
> both in Britanny and Ireland, may be traced.

Thus it was that ' Flann ' would become ' Alan ' in
Britanny, "more especially when, in the vulgar
tongue of Dol, the former, denoting a pancake,
would sound like a nickname."   And if we should
still have our doubts, is there not, at Dol, to this
day—

> an imposing edifice, built of granite, in the purest Norman
> style of architecture of the twelfth century, which tradition names
> ' La maison des Plaids,' and avers was the revenue office and
> court-house of the archbishops.   This name, " the House of the

---

[1] See p. 116, note 2, above.   It will be seen that to assert,
as here, that Alan and ' Fleance ' were the same will not overcome this difficulty.

Plaids," is touchingly significant of Fleance with the royal wearers of the tartan. . . .

But I really cannot pursue further these "ingenious and learned" new lichts. A dreadful vision of dog-totems, arrayed in the Stewart tartan, and feasting, with fiery visage, on pancakes in the streets of Dol, warns me to leave this realm of wonders and turn to the world in which we live. From "the House of the Plaids" I flee.[1]

Fortunately Flaald is a name, for practical purposes, unique ; and we need not, therefore, hesitate to recognise in "Float filius Alani dapiferi" who was present (No. 1136) at the dedication of Monmouth Priory (1101 or 1102) the long-sought missing link. We thus connect him with the fourth, the remaining cell of St. Florent de Saumur in England. But we have yet to account for his appearance as a 'baron' of the lord of Monmouth, William son of Baderon. The best authority on Domesday tenants, Mr. A. S. Ellis, confessed that he had failed to trace the lords of Monmouth in Britanny.[2] The key, however, to the whole connection is found in the abbey of St. Florent de Saumur and in its charters calendared in my work. In the latter half of the eleventh century many Bretons of noble birth were led to

[1] It is positively the fact that the author so renders the name of the 'Maison des Plaids,' where the (Arch)bishops are supposed to have held their pleas (" plaids ").

[2] *Domesday Tenants of Gloucestershire*, p. 46.

take the cowl. Among them was William, eldest
son of that Rhiwallon, lord of Dol, whom, on the
eve of the Norman Conquest, Duke William and
Harold of England had relieved when he was
besieged by his lord. Rhiwallon's son William,
who was followed by his brother John (No.
1116), entered the abbey of St. Florent de
Saumur, and became its abbot himself in 1070.
Zealous in the cause of the house he ruled, he
clearly urged its claims at Dol, receiving not only
local gifts, but also, as its chronicle mentions, the
endowments it obtained in England. Of the two
families with which we are concerned the lords
of Monmouth can, by these charters, be traced
to the neighbourhood of Dol, for William son of
Baderon confirms his father's gifts at Epiniac and
La Boussac (No. 1134), which places lay together
close to Dol. The presence among the witnesses
to these charters of a Main of La Boussac and a
Geoffrey of Epiniac affords confirmation of the
fact. Guihenoc, the founder of the house in
England (probably identical with " Wihenocus
filius Caradoc de Labocac),"[1] undoubtedly became
a monk of St. Florent,[2] and resigned his English
fief to his nephew William (son of his brother
Baderon), who is found holding it in Domesday.

Some charters were specially selected by me
from the *Liber Albus* of St. Florent (Nos. 1152–4)
to illustrate, about the end of the Conqueror's reign,

[1] Lobineau, *Histoire de Bretagne*, II. 219.
[2] *Calendar*, Nos. 1117, 1133.

the little group of Dol families who were about to settle in England.[1] Among the witnesses to one of them are Baderon and his son the Domesday tenant. But the one family we have specially to trace is that which held the office of " Dapifer " at Dol. " Alan Dapifer " is found as a witness, in 1086, to a charter relating to Mezuoit[2] (a cell of St. Florent, near Dol). He also, as " Alanus Siniscallus," witnessed the foundation charters of that house (*ante* 1080) and himself gave it rights at Mezuoit with the consent of "Fledaldus frater ejus," the monks, in return, admitting his brother Rhiwallon to their fraternity.[3] He appears as a witness with the above " Badero " in No. 1152, and in 1086 as a surety with Ralf de Fougères (No. 1154). Mentioned in other St. Florent documents,[4] he is styled in one, " Dapifer de Dolo.[5] And it is as " Alanus dapifer Dolensis " that he took part in the first crusade, 1097.[6] This style is explained in a charter of 1095, recording a gift to Marmoutier by Hamo son of Main, with consent of his lord " Rivallonius dominus Doli castri, filius Johannis archiepiscopi," in which we read :—

---

[1] It would, no doubt, be a rash conjecture that the "Herveus botellarius" of these charters (Nos. 1153, 1154) was the ancestor of those Herveys, from whom the Butlers of Ireland are descended. But if it should eventually prove to be no mere coincidence, the Butlership of Ireland would have had an origin curiously parallel to the Stewardship of Scotland.   [2] *Lobineau*, p. 250.

[3] *Ibid*. 137, 138, collated by me with the *Liber Albus* at Angers.

[4] *Ibid*. 232, 234.   [5] *Ibid*. 310.

[6] *Ordericus Vitalis* (Société de l'histoire de France), vol. III. 507.

THE ORIGIN OF THE STEWARTS

Hoc donum factum est per manum Guarini monachi nostri de Lauda Rigaldi tunc temporis prioris Combornii, testibus his : Alano siniscalco Rivallonii predicti, etc.[1]

His brother's son, Alan fitz Flaald (ancestor, as has been seen, of the Stuarts) also occurs, in these Breton documents, as releasing his rights in the church of " Guguen "[2] to Bartholomew abbot of Marmoutier ;[3] while two charters of Henry I. confirming the foundation of Holy Trinity Priory, York, as a cell of Marmoutier, and prior to 1108, contain his name as a witness (No. 1225). Again, a charter of donation to Andover Priory reveals him as present in the New Forest with William son of Baderon and " Wihenocus monachus " (William's uncle) early in the reign of Henry I.[4] It was Alan also who founded Sporle Priory, Norfolk (No. 1149), on land he held there, as another cell of St. Florent, the Bretons who witness his charter further attesting his origin. Among them is seen Rhiwallon " Extraneus," the founder of the Norfolk family of Le Strange, which, more than five centuries later, was so ardent in its loyalty to Alan's descendants, the Stuart kings of England.[5]

It will have been observed that " Float filius Alani dapiferi " is assumed above to have been the

[1] Transcripts from (Bretagne) cartulary of Marmoutier in MS. Baluze 77, fo. 134, and in MS. lat. 5441 (3) fo. 323. Alan is also brought into conjunction with this Hamo son of Main in No. 1152.   [2] Cuguen, near Dol.

[3] *Lobineau*, II. 310 ; MS. lat. 5441 (3) fo. 235.

[4] *Mon. Ang.* VI. 993.

[5] His name has hitherto remained doubtful, and is given as Roland in the *Dictionary of National Biography*.

123

brother, not a son, of the crusader. This assumption is based upon the facts that the crusader's gift at Mezuoit was ' conceded ' by his brother ' Fledald,' who was, therefore, his heir at the time, and that his office of " dapifer " at Dol was afterwards held—a fact hitherto unsuspected—by descendants of Alan fitz Flaald. The crusader, it must therefore be inferred, left no heir.

The sudden rise of Alan fitz Flaald and his evident enjoyment of Henry's favour from the early years of the reign, were thought by Mr. Eyton to be due to his (fabulous) Scottish origin. But it might, with some probability, be suggested that his Breton origin accounts for the facts. When Henry was besieged in Mont St. Michel, he is known to have had Breton followers ("aggregatis Britonibus ") and, after his surrender, " per Britanniam transiit, Britonibus qui sibi solummodo adminiculum contulerant, gratias reddidit " (Ordericus).[1] Dol was his nearest town in Britanny, and Alan may thus, like Richard de Réviers, have served him across the sea, when he was but a younger son.

It would seem, indeed, although the fact has been hitherto overlooked, that a group of families whom Henry had known when lord of the Côtentin were endowed by him when king with fiefs in England. In addition to Alan Fitz Flaald, founder of the house of Stewart, and to Richard de

---

[1] Elsewhere, Orderic observes that Henry, "dum esset junior . . . ut externus, exterorum, id est Francorum et *Britonum* auxilia quærere coactus est."

Réviers, ancestor of the earls of Devon,[1] the Hayes of Haye-du-Puits were given the Honour of Halnaker (Sussex), the Aubignys, afterwards earls of Arundel, obtained from him a fief in Norfolk ; the two St. John brothers, from St. Jean-le-Thomas, were granted lands in Oxfordshire and Sussex, and founded another famous house ;[2] while the family of Paynel also, sprung from the Côtentin, owed to Henry lands in England.

Among the documents calendered in my volume are Papal bulls to the abbey of St. Florent, ranging from 1146 to 1187 (Nos. 1124–9), which suggest that Alan's son William, who acquired by marriage Clun castle, must have bestowed its church of St. George, with all its dependent churches, on Monmouth Priory, a fact hitherto unsuspected. Mr. Eyton thought that the gift of this church to Wenlock Priory by his widow (*temp*. Ric. I.) represents the first occasion on which it is mentioned.

Alan fitz Flaald has hitherto been credited with two well-known sons, William and Walter, ancestors respectively of the Fitzalans and the Stewarts.[3]

---

[1] He is found, seemingly, in Domesday, holding a single lordship.

[2] See my paper on "The Families of St. John and of Port" in *Genealogist*, July, 1899, p. 1. And compare p. 66 above.

[3] A third son, "Simon," is claimed as the ancestor of the Boyds, and is assigned to him, with William and Walter, in Mr. Lindsay's great Stewart pedigree, the standard authority on the subject. But although a Simon 'brother' of Walter occurs as a witness in the Paisley cartulary, his name is very low on the list, and he may have been only a uterine or even a bastard

He had, however, another son, who needs to be
specially dealt with. This was Jordan, his heir in
Britanny, and, apparently, at Burton in England.
Mr. Eyton knew of his existence, but could state
little about him. In No. 1220 we find him, as a
" valiant and illustrious man," making restitution
to Marmoutier in 1130, with his wife Mary and
his sons Jordan and Alan. In the same year we
detect him entered on the English Pipe Roll in
several places, though one of the entries suggests his
Breton connection.[1] He may safely be identified
with that " Jordanus dapifer " who witnessed a
charter to Mont St. Michel in 1128–9 (No. 722);
and consequently he held the family office. We
find him also in a St. Florent charter,[2] and in one
of Marmoutier.[3] Of his sons, Jordan restored to
the priory of St. Florent at Sele the mill at Burton
given it by Alan fitz Flaald,[4] but was, probably,
soon succeeded by his brother Alan, who confirmed
to a priory of Marmoutier (No. 1221) another
gift of his grandfather, Alan fitz Flaald, at Burton,
mentioning his wife Joan and his son Jordan.[5] This

brother. The Empress Maud's bastard brothers are styled her
' brothers ' in her charters, nor was this unusual.

[1] Rot. Pip. 31 Hen. I., p. 11.
[2] *Lobineau*, II. 232.   [3] *Ibid*. 146.
[4] " Jordanus filius Jordani filius Alani hominibus suis de
Burt[ona]. Sciatis me reddidisse monachis S. Florentii de Sal-
mur molendinum de Burt[ona] sicut habuerunt tempore Alani
filii Flealdi et tempore Jordani patris mei " (original charter at
Magdalen College).
[5] It was either this Jordan or his grandfather who, as " Jordanus filius Alani siniscalli," confirmed a gift to Combourg
(MS. lat. 5441 [3] 437).

THE ORIGIN OF THE STEWARTS

Alan, who meets us also, as his father's son, in a Savigny charter (No. 824), is identical with that "Alanum filium quondam Jordani Dolensem senescallum," who confirmed the grant of his grandfather Alan (fitz Flaald) at Cuguen, and himself added the church of Tronquet[1] about 1160.[2] We have further in No. 1013 the confirmation by Alexander III. of his gifts to the abbey of Tiron, including the church of Sharrington and three others in England. He attested a charter of the lord of Dol in 1145,[3] and, in or about 1165, a royal charter at Winchester concerning a release by his fellow-countryman Geoffrey son of Oliver de Dinan.[4] He also leads the list of witnesses in a dispute about the abbey of Vieuville (in the parish of Epiniac) in 1167, as "Alanus filius Jordani dapifer."[5] His wife Joan and daughter Olive were benefactors to the abbey of Vieuville for his soul.[6]

With this clue we return to England, and detect the heiress of the Stewards of Dol in that Olive, daughter of Alan "filius Jordani," who in 1227 was impleaded by one of her Breton tenants,—his father Iwan had been enfeoffed by her own father Alan,—at Sharrington, Norfolk. The record of

[1] MS. lat. 12,878, fo. 248d., and *Lobineau*, II. 310.
[2] The gift is wrongly assigned in *Gallia Christiana* (XIV. 1074) to 1133–1147, as being made before Hugh archbishop of Tours. The prelate was Hugh "archbishop" of Dol, whose date was 1155–1161 (*Ibid.* 1050).
[3] *Lobineau*, II. 147.   [4] *Mon. Ang.*, VI. 486.
[5] *Lobineau*, II. 308 ; MS. lat. 5476, fo. 98d.
[6] " Johanna uxor Alani dapiferi de Dolo et filia ipsius Oliva." *Lobineau*, II. 310 ; MS. lat. 5476, fo. 91.

the suit gives us the name of Alan's mother, Mary, mentioned, as we have seen, in No. 1220.[1]

In the middle, therefore, of the 12th century, this family flourished simultaneously in Scotland, England, and Britanny.

A short pedigree (see page 129) will make the descent clear.

A chronological difficulty is created by Mr. Eyton's statement that Alan Fitz Flaald was "dead ante 1114," for his son (it will be seen) the Steward of Scotland lived till 1177. It is desirable, therefore, to examine his authority for this date. Dugdale was acquainted with a confirmation by Sybil, lady of Wolston (Warwickshire), of a gift by her mother Adeliza to Burton Abbey of land in Wolston. In his *History of Warwickshire* (p. 33) he held that she was probably a daughter of Alan Fitz Flaald, because Alan was "enfeoft of this Lordship" before her. Mr. Eyton accepted Dugdale's conclusion, and therefore identified her mother 'Adeliza' as that 'Avelina' de Hesdin, whom he had so skilfully shown to be the wife of Alan. Further, as the land *ex hypothesi* belonged to Alan himself, and yet was given by her, she must, he held, have been a widow at the time of the gift; and as the abbey was already in possession at least as early as 1114, Alan, he concluded, must have been dead before that date.[2] These conclusions

[1] *Bracton's Note-book*, III. 620. Compare 'Feet of Fines' (Pipe Roll Society), II. 160.
[2] *History of Shropshire*, VII. 221–223, 228.

THE ORIGIN OF THE STEWARTS

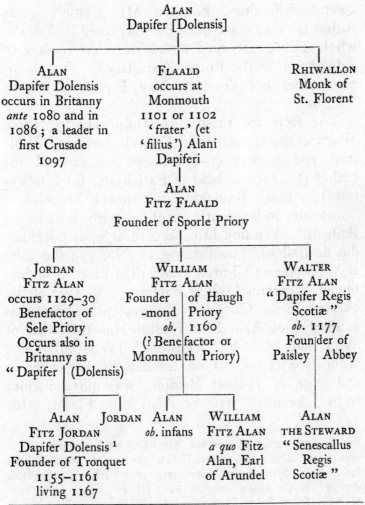

ALAN
Dapifer [Dolensis]

ALAN
Dapifer Dolensis
occurs in Britanny
ante 1080 and in
1086 ; a leader in
first Crusade
1097

FLAALD
occurs at
Monmouth
1101 or 1102
' frater ' (et
' filius ') Alani
Dapiferi

RHIWALLON
Monk of
St. Florent

ALAN
FITZ FLAALD
Founder of Sporle Priory

JORDAN
FITZ ALAN
occurs 1129–30
Benefactor of
Sele Priory
Occurs also in
Britanny as
" Dapifer (Dolensis)

WILLIAM
FITZ ALAN of Haugh
Founder Priory
-mond *ob.* 1160
(? Benefactor or
Monmouth Priory)

WALTER
FITZ ALAN
" Dapifer Regis
Scotiæ "
ob. 1177
Founder of
Paisley Abbey

ALAN
FITZ JORDAN
Dapifer Dolensis [1]
Founder of Tronquet
1155–1161
living 1167

JORDAN ALAN
ob. infans

WILLIAM
FITZ ALAN
a quo Fitz
Alan, Earl
of Arundel

ALAN
THE STEWARD
" Senescallus
Regis
Scotiæ "

---

[1] Among the obits at Dol we find that of another daughter of
Alan fitz Jordan : "Kal. Sept. obiit Ælicia uxor G[uillelmi]
Espine filia Alani Jordanis quæ dedit episcopo et capitulo Dol
. . . pratum senescalli," etc. (Gaignères' Transcript of Car-
tulary, MS. lat. 5211 C). A charter of her husband William
Spina, son of Hamo, confirms the donations made to Vieuville

PEERAGE STUDIES

created difficulties, but, on Mr. Eyton's great
authority, they have been duly accepted.[1] Yet the
whole edifice rests on Dugdale's careless reading of
a document in the Burton Cartulary.[2] That document does not connect Alan Fitz Flaald with
Wolston.

The facts are these. In Domesday the three
Warwickshire manors of Church Lawford, Wolston, and Stretton-on-Dunsmore are entered together (fo. 239) as held of Earl Roger (of Shrewsbury) by that 'Rainaldus,' whom the historian of
Shropshire so brilliantly identifies with Renaud de
Bailleul.[3] We find him, accordingly, as "Rainaldus de Bailoul,"[4] confirming in No. 578 the gifts
at Wolston and Church Lawford of his own undertenant, a certain Hubert Baldran. Another of the
charters in my Calendar (No. 579) proves that this
Hubert (not Alan Fitz Flaald), was the father of
Sybil, lady of 'Wlfrichestone' (Wolston), from
whom we started. Thus Adeliza, mother of Sybil,
and wife of Hubert Baldran, was quite distinct
from "Avelina" wife of Alan Fitz Flaald, with

"de feodo Aeliz uxoris mee filie Alani Dolensis senescalli . . .
concedente Alano filio nostro" (MS. lat. 5476, fo. 85). His
father Hamo Spina occurs immediately after "Alan filius Jordanis
dapifer" in the above letter of 1167 (*Ib.* fo. 98*d*). As we read
of "Gaufridus Spina Doli senescallus" (*Ib.* fo. 91*d*) it would
seem that the Dol office was inherited by the Spina family, and
the English estates by the other daughter.

[1] *Burton Cartulary*, Ed. Wrottesley (Salt Arch. Collections,
1884), pp. 32, 33.   [2] *Ibid.* p. 33 *bis*.
[3] *History of Shropshire*, VII. 206 et seq.
[4] See my Calendar, p. 202.

130

whom Mr. Eyton rashly identified her.[1] Alan may have lived, and probably did, beyond 1114; and his gift at Stretton to Burton Abbey was made after he was placed in the shoes (as Mr. Eyton has shown) of Renaud de Bailleul.

We have thus seen how a single charter may prove of great importance, not only in establishing the true facts, but in demolishing erroneous conclusions with the corollaries based thereon.

Within the last few weeks there has unexpectedly been revived that view of the origin of the Stewarts which had long, one thought, been abandoned. As the whole story is most curious, and has, moreover, an important moral, I propose to discuss it in some detail. The pedigree of the Stuarts "of Hartley Mauduit," who hold a baronetcy dating from 1660, began in *Burke's Peerage*, so recently as last year, with Sir Nicholas Stuart the first baronet, "son of Simeon Stuart, Esq." But now, in this year of grace 1900,—

A more thorough revision than usual has been possible. . . . To the laborious researches and experienced counsel of my brother, Mr. H. Farnham Burke, Somerset Herald, the genealogical and heraldic value of this work is much indebted and is gratefully acknowledged (*sic*).

The "laborious researches" of Somerset Herald have indeed developed the Stuart pedigree, thanks

---

[1] She has been even further promoted in the British Museum Catalogue of Stowe MSS., where, in the abstract of the original deed (Stowe charter 103), she is strangely identified with queen Adeliza, widow of Henry I.

to those " invaluable documents the Heralds' Visitations, documents of high authority and value." [1]

> The illustrious ancestry of this family is given fully in the Visitations of Cambridge (*sic*), 1575 and 1619, in which is traced their descent from the Royal Stuarts.
>
> ANDREW STUART, younger son of Alexander Stuart, 2nd son of Walter Stuart, seneschal of Scotland, great-grandson of Walter, 1st high steward of Scotland, grandson of Banquo Lord of Lochaber. He m. the daughter of James Bethe, and had an only son.
>
> ALEXANDER STUART, to whom Charles VI. of France granted an honourable augmentation of his arms.

And so the pedigree proceeds through another eight generations down to the first baronet.

Dear old ' Banquo,' " whom we miss " ! [2] What a pleasure it is to welcome him back among us once more, and to know that he, and not Flaald, was the founder of the house of Stuart on the unimpeachable authority of the Heralds and their ' Visitations ' ! It is true that, according to the " Royal Lineage " [3] contained in the same volume, it was not descended from Banquo at all, and that the " above Alexander Stuart, 2nd son of Walter Stuart," had no existence ; but these are details which the editor, doubtless, will see to in his next edition. It is also true that the new pedigree would at once make Sir Simeon Stuart heir-male of " the Royal Stuarts," an honour foolishly claimed by sundry Scottish families. [4] Let us hope that Somerset Herald will inform Lyon King of

---

[1] Preface to Burke's *Landed Gentry*, Ed. 1898.   [2] *Macbeth.*
[3] *Burke's Peerage*, 1900, pp. cliii.-cliv.   [4] See p. 89 above.

Arms that his "laborious researches" have decided this long-contested question.

But, seriously speaking, what is the origin of the new descent, which, this year, makes its appearance in *Burke's Peerage* ? Well, the story is, or ought to be, familiar to all genealogists. For, owing to Oliver Cromwell's mother having been a member of this family, his Stuart descent was alluded to by Carlyle, which has given genealogists the opportunity of making merry at his expense. The alleged descent was, for several years, discussed in the recognised organ of genealogical research ;[1] but of this discussion Somerset Herald is, no doubt, ignorant. So far back, indeed, as 1878 the very interesting heraldic glass of which I am enabled to give an illustration was exhibited to the Archæological Institute, and that well-known Scottish authority, Mr. Joseph Bain,[2] discussed the whole story thereon before it. He then observed of the alleged grant by " Charles VI. of France," to which Somerset Herald appeals :—

In M. Michel's *Les Ecossais en France*, published in 1862, he gives a drawing of this very design, and the text of the asserted grant by Charles VI. of France in the fifth year of his reign, conferring the strange coat of arms on Sir Alexander Stuart on account of the merits of his father Andrew. . . . M. Michel says that ' it is enough to cast the eye on these pretended

---

[1] *The Genealogist* [N.S.], vols. I. (1884), II., III., VIII., X. (1893).

[2] Editor of the ' Calendar of documents relating to Scotland,' the ' Hamilton Papers,' the ' Calendar of letters and papers referring to the Borders,' etc. etc.

letters of concession, to recognise the patois or an Englishman little familiar with the language spoken at Paris at the end of the fourteenth century, and to doubt the fact asserted by the writer '—an opinion which will be shared by anyone moderately versed in Old French.[1]

The alleged grant only exists in the form of a transcript in a private MS. of the 16th century;[2] but we shall see below that not only deeds, but even sealed deeds, were among the fabrications of those who concocted false pedigrees.[3]

That well-known critical genealogist, Mr. Walter Rye, set himself, a few years later, to destroy the alleged descent and all its wondrous tales in the Herald's "Visitation" and elsewhere. The conclusion at which he arrived was that the "Stywards," as these alleged descendants of the Scottish Stuarts wrote their name, were simply "a Norfolk family, probably of illegitimate descent, and certainly of no credit or renown, which had been settled at Swaffham long before the alleged Scottish ancestor is supposed to have landed in England with his royal master and kinsman."[4] He further held that three other deeds, in Norman-French, found in the above cartulary, were forgeries, and that Augustine Steward, a lawyer, to whom we owe the cartulary, was "the vagabond who, I suspect, concocted the whole pedigree in 1567." No one attempted to challenge Mr. Rye's conclusion; but Mr. Bain wrote that "Augustine

[1] *Archæological Journal*, XXXV. 302-3, 399.
[2] Add. MS. 15,644.
[3] See the paper on "Our English Hapsburgs."
[4] *Genealogist* [N.S.], II. 34-42.

Steward's pedigree of the Stewards prior to John is an absurd fiction ; that [portion] subsequent to him has been treated according to its deserts by Mr. Rye."[1]

I have satisfied myself, however, that, in details, Mr. Rye's conclusion is somewhat crude and is based on an insufficient knowledge of the above cartulary and other documents. The concoction was of earlier date than he supposed, and more than one member of the family was concerned in the matter. In the *Genealogist*[2] I was able to show that Robert Welles *alias* Steward, last Prior and first Dean of Ely, had far more to do with the matter than the above critics had known. It is recorded in Wharton's *Anglia Sacra* that

Decanatum adeptus, nomen gentilitium *Stewarde* homo ventosus deinceps adhibuit ; et nobilitatis suæ opinione inflatus, familiæ suæ genealogiam scriptis commendavit (I. 685).

The whole descent, set forth by himself, is, luckily, there preserved, and is alleged to be " breviter extracta e rotulis Heraldorum anno MDXXII." The heraldic tastes of Robert are confirmed by the armorial drawings found in his MSS.,[3] and the dean of Ely has been so kind as to verify for me Wharton's statement and to examine personally the MS. return of the Prior's possessions made by this Robert to Henry VIII., now in the muniment room at Ely.[4] On the vellum title-page is found

[1] *Ibid.* III. 111.   [2] [N.S.], vol. X. 18.   [3] *Anglia Sacra*, I. xlvii.
[4] It is headed " Annuus valor omnium terrarum et possessionum Prioratus de Elye anno Henrici Regis Octavi tricessimo secundo " [*i.e.* 1540-1541].

the coat as now borne by the family, that is, the arms of "the Royal Stuarts" with "le lion ruge batty de baston node d'or," as an augmentation of honour, in an inescutcheon of pretence. And this coat, I observe, hangs from a ragged staff (as in Add. MS. 15,644), this being the staff with which the feat depicted in the window was performed. The Dean informs me that the same coat is found elsewhere in the volume and that it is also depicted on the cover with "1549" and "Steward" below it.[1] It is clear, therefore, that the whole story can be carried back some twenty years further than Mr. Rye supposed, and that it began with this Robert, last Prior of Ely.

A short chart pedigree will show the connection of the members of the family concerned.[2]

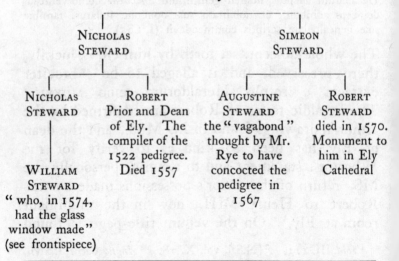

NICHOLAS STEWARD		SIMEON STEWARD	

| NICHOLAS STEWARD | ROBERT Prior and Dean of Ely. The compiler of the 1522 pedigree. Died 1557 | AUGUSTINE STEWARD the "vagabond" thought by Mr. Rye to have concocted the pedigree in 1567 | ROBERT STEWARD died in 1570. Monument to him in Ely Cathedral |
| WILLIAM STEWARD "who, in 1574, had the glass window made" (see frontispiece) | | | |

---

[1] The Dean has further been good enough to send me sketches of the arms. [2] See also my paper in *Genealogist* [N.S.], X. 18–19.

THE ORIGIN OF THE STEWARTS

In 1817 Mr. William Stevenson produced a supplement, with notes, to Bentham's *History of Ely*, in which he complained of Wharton charging the dean of Ely with " vanity," and offered this " apology in excuse of his vanity " :—

If the pride of ancestry be allowable and commendable in any-one, and if the genealogy of Dean Steward is to be depended upon, we believe very few can vie with him, or justly blame him on that score ; for an office copy of his pedigree, giving an history of the family, the patents, and grants of their arms, with their marriages into the first families of Norfolk, Suffolk, Cambridge-shire, etc., shows that he was descended in a direct line from Banquo, King of Scotland, in 1048. . . . The account is continued to the year 1576 (p. 121).

The " office copy " in Mr. Stevenson's possession must have been supplied by the Heralds' College, and the date he names (1576) is of importance ; for it points to the Visitation of Cambridgeshire in 1575. This Visitation was made by the notorious Cooke ' Clarencieux,'[1] and it was to Cooke that Augustine Steward had shown the alleged grant by Charles VI. of France.[2] We have now seen that (as indeed Somerset Herald implies)[3] the official recognition of this family's descent from " the Royal Stuarts " dates at least from the Visitation of 1575. Bearing this date in mind, we may turn to the two stately monuments erected in Ely Cathedral to Robert Steward (d. 1570) and his brother Sir Marcus Steward (d. 1603), who were cousins of the dean

[1] Gutch's *Collectanea Curiosa*.
[2] See p. 143 below.   [3] See p. 132 above.

of Ely. The latter bears a long inscription, setting
forth the whole story, together with a coat of arms
of twenty-three quarterings ; [1] but the other, I
observe, has but nine quarterings on the tabard
borne by the effigy and on the two shields below
it, and the famous coat of the Stewarts is not
among them.[2] The fact that the shield *above* the
effigy displays eleven quarterings, including the
Stewart coat, suggests to me a subsequent addition
as in the case of the monument erected to Sir
Robert Spencer (d. 1522).[3]

It is needless to repeat the absurd stories which
embellish the concocted pedigree ; but something
must be said of the glass window represented in
the frontispiece. It has been well observed that
as this window was set up by Oliver Cromwell's
grandfather, it was probably a familiar object to
the future Protector in his youth. He there saw
his maternal ancestor, bearing on his shield the
pure arms of the head of the house of Stewart,
smiting with a ragged staff,—for his sword had
broken,—" le faux et fatise usurpeur et coart Lion
de Balliol," while the hand of the French king,
extended from above, bestows on him, in memory
of his exploit, the " honourable augmentation " of
" le lion ruge batty de baston node d'ore." This
' striking ' scene, within the royal double tressure,

---

[1] A coat with the same number is found on the monument of
another brother (d. 1603) in Norfolk. Compare p. 86 above.

[2] See the illustrations of these monuments in Bentham's
History of Ely.

[3] See paper below on " The Rise of the Spencers."

was surrounded by a genealogical tree, not of Jesse, but of " Banquho." [1]

This, then, is how it comes to pass that Sir Simeon Stuart, at the present day, bears for arms " Or, a fess chequy arg. and az., on an escutcheon of pretence arg. a lion rampant gu. debruised by a bend raguly or,"—that is to say, the very coat which is conferred in the apocryphal grant by Charles VI. of France, and which is depicted, as so conferred, in the frontispiece to this volume. This coat, it should be observed, is that of " the Royal Stuarts," pure and undefiled, with the addition of an augmentation of honour, such as is granted, in modern times, to a victorious general.

We need not discuss the ingenious speculation of Mr. Walter Rye that the whole story originated in the Norfolk Stywards bearing a " bend sinister " over a rampant lion, as a mark of illegitimacy.[2] It will be found that a similar, though less artistic story, was invented to connect the Feilding arms with those of the House of Austria,[3]

Viewing the evidence as a whole, I arrive at the following conclusion. The family, as they rose in the world, were eager, as in certain other cases ancient and modern, to claim connection

[1] The centre piece is carefully depicted twice in the margin of Augustine Steward's cartulary (Add. MSS. 15,644).

[2] *Genealogist* [N.S.], II. 40–41. It is significant that on the monument of Robert Steward (1570), the lion debruised by a ragged staff is still found as his own coat ; and the concocted grant by Charles VI. seems to me to be so worded as to account for the awkward fact that these arms were used.

[3] See the paper, below, on " Our English Hapsburgs."

with some great house of the same or of similar name. With singular audacity they seized on the reigning house of Scotland. Their own name, it is true, was 'Styward'; they were of obscure Norfolk origin; and the arms they bore were as different as they could be from those of the house of Stewart. The first difficulty they overcame by representing the Scottish Stewarts as being rightly 'Stywards';[1] to meet the second they concocted evidences to connect certain members of the Scottish house with Norfolk;[2] the heraldic obstacle only evoked still greater daring. They had to account for the awkward fact that they did not bear the Stewart coat, but one wholly different. They invented, therefore, the story of the French king's grant; but as an ordinary "augmentation of honour" would not be sufficient for their purpose, they introduced a special clause which gave them the option of bearing "d'argent ov le lion ruge batty de baston node d'ore, *solement*, comme son escu de guerre." Having thus accounted for their discontinuing to bear the Stewart coat, and for their bearing in its place the lion coat alone, they further forged (in my opinion) a confirmation by Garter Wriothesley, purporting to be granted 14th Sept., 1520, to Robert 'Steward' of Ely, clerk, in which he officially certified from his 'Registers' that "thancestors of the said Robert for their first cote did bere in

---

[1] They are actually so entered in the Cambridgeshire Visitation (Ed. Harl. Soc.).

[2] Mr. Rye has dealt with this part of the story.

gould a fesse chekey of silver and azure,[1] being in truth proper to their bloud and name, quartered with a red lyoun offended of a ragged staff bendwise," but that sometimes this latter coat had been borne as the first quarter, and sometimes as an escutcheon of pretence. To make a good job of the concoction while they were about it, they further made Garter certify that their ancestors had borne a crest based on the story told in the picture :—

And there I also find the aunciest cognizance used with the armes to be a ragged staffe standing upon a broken sword crossed saltirewise.[2]

It was here, we shall find, that they overreached themselves ; but the question of the crest seems to have escaped previous critics. I do not say that Garter Wriothesley was not capable of anything. He himself claimed descent from a family with which he was in no way connected on the strength of a pedigree which the late Mr. Eyton, the learned historian of Shropshire, has styled " a tissue of falsification and forgery," containing at least one deliberately falsified document and one " detestable forgery." Still his alleged confirmation is so demonstrably untruthful, and supplies so exactly what the family required, that I place it in the same boat with the French king's grant.

Armed with these evidences and with their alleged deeds, the family approached the heralds

---

[1] This was what they coveted—the pure Stewart coat.
[2] Add. MS. 15,644, fo. 1. Compare p. 136 above.

seeking their acceptance of the story, and evidently hoping to "resume" (as it is termed in these cases) the coat of their alleged ancestors. The result, at first, was not encouraging. Augustine Steward transcribed in his cartulary a confirmation by William Harvie, Clarencieux King of Arms, 1 May 1558 (4 and 5 Philip and Mary), granted at the request of "Symeon Stewarde of Laking-heathe, in the Countye of Suffolke, Esquyer." Clarencieux certified that

I coulde not without theire greate Iniurye assigne unto him any other armes then those which from the begynninge did apperteyne and belonge to that howse and famylye, whereof he is descended.

And as he found no crest assigned to the family, he granted, "by waye of encrease," for crest, "a Roo bucke in his proper collers," etc. etc.[1] It is evident from the sequel that Clarencieux refused to recognise the crest alleged to have been confirmed by Wriothesley, and that he did not allow the Stewart coat. The next document transcribed (fos. 63 et seq.), is a detailed certificate, in Latin, by the same Clarencieux, 27 June 1558, for Robert 'Stywarde' of Ely, son of the above Symeon, setting out the whole descent from Banquho and reciting the grant by the French king. But he refuses to recognise the crest claimed, and mentions that, on this account, he had granted a new one. Then follows (fo. 70) a document of 9 May 1564 (6 Eliz.), in which

[1] Add. MS. 15,644, fo. 62.

the same Harvie Clarencieux certifies that Augustine 'Stewarde' of the inner Temple, gentleman, " port dargent un lion rampant gueles debruse dun baston noue dore et sur son healme un capriole proper," etc.[1]   Poor Augustine, therefore, was " no forwarder."   Lastly (fo. 71) comes the confirmation by Cooke Clarencieux in English, 14 February 1573 (15 Eliz.), reciting textually and exemplifying the alleged grant " by Charles the Frenche kinge," and setting forth, at the request of " Augustine Stywarde gent.," the whole descent from " Walter of Dundevayle,"[2] " because of itself the manifestation of trewthe is a vertuous and lawdable thinge, to the settinge forthe and avauncement whereof all men are of dutie bounde." I do not think that this heraldic Chadband thereby confirms to the family the Stewart coat, though Mr. Bain appears to have formed that impression. It is not till we come to the Cambridgeshire Visitations that we obtain at last heraldic authority for the coat now borne by the family—" or, a fess chequy az. and ar.[3] on an escutcheon of the third a lion rampant gu. debruised by a baston raguly, or."   This is the first of nine quarters, and it heads a pedigree of great magnificence deduced from Banquo, on one side, to James I.

[1] This document is in Latin.

[2] This odd form, which recurs throughout, is surely a misreading of ' Dundonal '[d], which seems to be the relative form in Boece.

[3] So printed. And *Burke's Peerage* (backed by Somerset Herald) so blazons it.   But Mr. Fox-Davies' *Armorial Families* (backed by Richmond Herald) blazons it ar. and az.

of England, and on the other to the Cambridge-shire Stywards, now Stuarts.[1]   In this instance the evasive plea that these are not the true Visitations cannot, as it happens, be urged, for it is precisely to those Visitations that *Burke's Peerage*, assisted, we have seen, by Somerset Herald, appeals for the above pedigree.   They must, therefore, contain it.

The point on which one has to insist is that here is " a Norfolk family, probably of illegitimate descent, and certainly of no credit or renown," [2] duly authorized by the heralds themselves to bear, with " an honourable augmentation," the arms of " the Royal Stuarts," with whom they were in no way connected.   It will not avail to plead that the arms were merely an imitation granted, as such, to a family bearing a similar name; for they were allowed, as indeed is seen in *Burke's Peerage* for 1900, in right of a spurious descent from the house to which they belonged.   The case, we shall find, is on all fours with that of the Spencers of Althorpe, who were similarly allowed an old coat on the strength of their alleged, but spurious, descent from the feudal house of Despencer.

We are now in a position to gauge aright the denunciation, in certain quarters, of those who break "the Laws of Arms" and disregard the heralds.   We read, for instance, in the Preface to Burke's *Landed Gentry* (1898) :—

---

[1] Visitations of Cambridgeshire, 1575 and 1619. (Ed. Harl. Soc.), pp. 7–11.   [2] See p. 134 above.

THE ORIGIN OF THE STEWARTS

Unfortunately, the laws of arms have been, in these later days, very frequently set at naught, and the well-known ensigns of our historic families have been assumed by strangers in blood if not in name, though by their own act they have but erected a permanent memorial to the obscurity of their origin.

Again, in *The right to bear arms*, ' X ' exclaims as the champion of the College,—

Better modern gentility, better even raw new gentility, if it be genuine, than a *bogus* claim to ancient ancestry. . . . Is it not contemptibly snobbish to proclaim yourself to be *related* to some noble family of your name, when even the name of your grandfather is perhaps unknown to you ? Yet this is done every day (pp. xii.–xiii.).

Mr. Fox-Davies goes further. Greatly daring, he tells us that the heralds did their best to check these frauds, which were the work of the "painter-fellows."

Centuries ago the heralds deplored and tried to keep in check the vagaries and usurpations of these " painter-fellows," as they then described them. . . . Had these handicraftsmen stopped their hands at these legitimate limits, little abuse, comparatively speaking, could have crept in, but they did not ; they hankered after the fees—in their eyes veritable flesh-pots of Egypt—of the official heralds. Then, as now, the true position and authority of the Officers of Arms was not properly known or understood. Then, as now, these " painter-fellows " encroached, and then, as now, they profited by the lack of heraldic knowledge current among the general public, and they purposed to grant, confirm, and assign Arms . . . which were perfectly legitimate, and which belonged to ancient families, which legitimate coats-of-arms these " painter-fellows " assigned to other families bearing the same or similar names, without the ghost of a pretence, and without the shadow of a possibility of establishing a descent from the *bona fide* holders. That was how the abuse began centuries ago. At the present time, at the close of the nineteenth century, this same abuse runs riot, and now, as then, it is in the forefront, and the most prominent of all heraldic follies.[1]

Surely, it is only " the lack of heraldic knowledge current among the general public" that could enable such statements to be made with any chance of acceptance. It was the heralds themselves who, " centuries ago," provided the Russells and the Spencers, we shall find, with spurious pedigrees " without the shadow of a possibility of establishing" the descent ; it was they who authorized the Norfolk Stywards, on the strength of a ' bogus ' grant, to bear the coat of " the Royal Stuarts" with an augmentation of honour ; and it is they who, at the present time, grant to ' new ' families such close imitations of the arms belonging " to other families bearing the same or similar names, without the ghost of a pretence" of a connection, that the public is deceived into the belief that such a connection exists. Let the pirating of arms, by all means, be denounced as strongly as it deserves ; but let it, at least, be denounced by those who have not shown the way.

[1] Preface to *Armorial Families* (1899).

III

The Counts of Boulogne as English Lords

WHEN, towards the middle of the eleventh century, Eustace "aux Grenons" count of Boulogne married 'Goda' daughter of Æthelred and sister of Edward the Confessor, "this prince, whom," Mr. Freeman writes, "English history sets before us only in the darkest colours," laid the foundation of a close connection, which lasted more than a century and a half, between his heirs and the English realm. That he, like other Frenchmen, enjoyed king Edward's favour is manifest from the warmth with which the king supported him in his quarrel with the men of Dover. But whether he was given lands in England is, to say the least, doubtful. His wife, indeed, as "Goda comitissa," is entered in Domesday, Mr. Freeman observed, as having held land in Sussex, Surrey, Dorset, Middlesex, Bucks, Gloucestershire, and Notts;[1] and it is his conjecture that "Eustace succeeded to the lands of his wife"

---

[1] I have grave doubts whether it was she who held in all these counties, as I think there has been confusion, especially in Sussex, with the mother of Harold.

at her death, in 1056 or earlier, and held them till he was forfeited by William for " his treason in 1067."[1]

The reader is invited to observe the difficulties which surround, at the very outset, such inquiries as that upon which I am now about to enter. Though the daughter and the sister of an English king, and the mother of a possible successor, in Mr. Freeman's view, to their throne, Goda's matrimonial career is involved, he will find, in doubt. Whose widow was she when Count Eustace married her ? Who was the father of her son ?

We have to make our choice between three versions. On the one hand, the *Art de vérifier les dates* makes her marry (1) Drogo count of the French Vexin, by whom she had several children, (2) Walter count of Mantes, (3) Eustace count of Boulogne. Our ablest writer on the Domesday tenants, Mr. A. S. Ellis, adopts the same version, in dealing with " Harold son of Earl Ralf," Goda's grandson, and a Gloucestershire tenant-in-chief. " Earl Ralf," he writes, " was the elder son of the Countess Goda sister of king Edward, by her first husband, Drogo count of the French Vexin, who died . . . in June, 1035 . . . She married, secondly, Walter II., count of Mantes, dead 1051, and thirdly Eustace ";[2] and no less eminent an authority on these subjects than Mr.

---

[1] See, for all this, the Appendix on " the possessions of Count Eustace " in *The History of the Norman Conquest*, vol. IV.

[2] *Bristol and Gloucestershire Archæological Transactions*, vol. IV. Mr. Ellis appends a chart pedigree based on this version.

Eyton himself adopted, in full detail, the same version.[1]

Second, there is William of Malmesbury's version :—

> Eustachius erat comes Bononiæ, pater Godefridi, etc. . . . habebatque sororem regis Godam legitimis nuptiis desponsatam, quæ ex altero viro *Waltero Medantino*, filium tulerat Radulfum qui eo tempore erat comes Herefordensis (*Gesta Regum*).

This misled Mr. Freeman into inadvertently terming earl Ralf of Hereford, " Ralf the Timid, the son of *Walter* and Godgifu." [2]

The third version is that of Mr. Freeman himself, who elsewhere ignores Walter of Mantes as a husband of Goda (' Godgifu ') and makes Drogo her only husband, before Eustace, and the father of her children. This is the right version, as we learn from Orderic, who writes (1063) :—

> Walterius Pontesiensium comes, filius Drogonis comitis, qui cum Rodberto seniore Normannorum duce in Jerusalem ierat et in illo itinere peregrinus obierat. Drogo, ut dicitur, erat de prosapia Caroli Magni regis Francorum, eique sepedictus dux Rodbertus in conjugium dederat consobrinam suam, Godivam, sororem Edwardi regis Anglorum, ex qua orti sunt Radulfus et Gauterius Comites et venerandus Fulco præsul Ambianensium.

The interest of determining the true origin of earl Ralf of Hereford consists in the fact that his descendants in the direct male line continued to our own time in the ranks of the peerage, and, indeed, still exist. The splendour of such a pedigree as this, covering a thousand years, attracted Mr.

---

[1] *Key to Domesday : Dorset*, p. 79.
[2] *Norman Conquest*, vol. II. (2nd Ed.), p. 562.

PEERAGE STUDIES

Freeman's special interest,[1] as indeed it may enlist our own.

We have now seen that Eustace aux Grenons married Goda or Godgifu, sister of Edward the Confessor, and widow of Drogo count of the French Vexin, who died 1035. The whole confusion, I expect, has arisen from William of Malmesbury speaking of Drogo as *Walter*, which was the name of his son and successor. As the French Vexin contained Mantes and Pontoise, its count might be styled from those towns, as, in England, the earl of Sussex was also styled, under Stephen, earl of Chichester or of Arundel.[2] Thus was evolved Goda's imaginary husband, " Walter count of Mantes."

The next point that we have to determine is the devolution of Goda's estates, as her husband Count Eustace long survived her. Mr. Freeman, holding that she probably died before 1056, argued that Eustace seems to have " succeeded to the lands of his wife, that they were confiscated by William after his treason in 1067, and that the estates which Eustace afterwards held were later grants after his reconciliation." [3] But Goda, who had no children by Eustace, had left, we have seen, a son and grandson as her rightful heirs ; and there is nothing to show, or even to suggest, that Count Eustace obtained her lands. Mr. Freeman, how-

[1] See his article on " Pedigrees and Pedigree-makers," in *Contemporary Review*, XXX. 24.

[2] See my *Geoffrey de Mandeville*, p. 320.

[3] *Norman Conquest*, IV. 746.

ever, urged that the above view was strengthened
by the fact that

three lordships in Dorset (85) were held at the time of the
Survey by Ida the second wife of Eustace, which she is also said
to have held T.R.E. This looks as if Eadward had made
grants to the second wife of his friend, which were not confiscated
by William along with the lands of her husband.[1]

Domesday, unfortunately, records most explicitly
(85) of these three lordships, that " Hæc tria maneria tenuit *Ulveva* T.R.E.," so that the statement,
with the argument based on it, falls at once to the
ground. Oddly enough, on the opposite page, Mr.
Freeman wrote of " Wulfgifu, who was also Ida's
predecessor in some *(sic)* of her Dorset lands " (p.
747). He had simply read his Domesday, as in
some other cases, hurriedly and without care.

The last point that we have to deal with is the
identity of the Count Eustace with whom we meet
in Domesday. Here Mr. Freeman was misled,
not unnaturally, by the usually accurate Ellis. We
find him writing (pp. 745–6):—

Sir Henry Ellis (I. 385, 416) quotes a charter in which his
second wife Ida is described as 'venerabilis Ida tunc vidua' as
early as 1082.

Ellis refers us to *Gallia Christiana* (X. 1594),
where, however, we only read that, according to
the editors—

Quippe, *post* annum 1082, adveniens illuc venerabilis Ida tunc
vidua, piissimi Gerardi Taruannensis episcopi assensu consilioque
roborata, etc. etc.

It seems clear to me that the editors got their

[1] *Ibid.*

date " after 1082 " from the name of the bishop,
for they say (X. 1541) that he was appointed " anno
1083 aut saltem 1084." His assent, therefore,
must have been given " after" 1082. The bishop's
name gives us the limit 1083–4—1096 for Ida's
appearance as a widow, which is quite compatible
with her husband living, as stated in the *Art de
vérifier les dates*, till 1093, and, at any rate, with
his being the Domesday count of 1086. Mr.
Freeman, however, held, on the above mistaken
ground, that

The count Eustace of Domesday is not Eustace the Second or
Boulogne, who plays so important a part in our history, but his
son Eustace the Third (IV. 745).

" Sainte Ide," as the French call her, brought to
her husband Bouillon, from which her famous son
Godfrey, the crusader king, was named. Through
her the counts of Boulogne traced their descent
from " the Knight of the Swan," and the town of
Boulogne, from the same source, bears to-day
the swan for its cognisance. At Feversham
Abbey, founded by Stephen and his wife, the
heiress of Boulogne, the legendary tale was on
record.[1]

The more prosaic record of Domesday shows us
Ida as holding five manors in England. All five
found their way into the hands of religious houses.

---

[1] See the *Red Book of the Exchequer*, pp. 753–4, where the
Feversham book is quoted. The swan-drawn knight appears beneath the walls of Bouillon, rescues its beleaguered heiress, marries
her, and becomes the father of Ida. Ida in turn marries " magnus
comes Boloniæ Eustacius [as Gernuns]."

Nutfield (" Notfelle "), Surrey, was bestowed on the canons of St. Wulmer de Boulogne ; Kingsweston (" Chinwardestone "), Somerset, on Bermondsey Priory ; and the three Dorset manors on another Cluniac priory, that of Le Wast in the Boulonnais. These three last manors, Winterbourne Monkton, Bockhampton in Stinsford, and Eightholes in Swanage, became one as Winterbourne-Wast, the Priory from which they took the name retaining them far on into the fourteenth century. The record of a case in Trinity term 1227 shows us the prior of Le Wast producing in court the charter of " Count Eustace " by which he " gave " the Priory this manor, together with the Kentish churches of Westerham and Boughton Alulf.[1] So the actual gift seems to have been made, not by " Saint Ide," but by her son. The monks of Le Wast were excused Danegeld on 11 hides, in Wiltshire, in 1130 ;[2] but the $11\frac{1}{2}$ hides of the Dorset manor seem to be assigned to Stephen, whose wife was Ida's heir.[3] The interesting incident in the history of the manor was its seizure by John, in grim irony, as a reward for Eustache le Moine, who fought for him against Boulogne.[4]

Turning now to Ida's husband, Eustace (" aux Grenons ") count of Boulogne, I have elsewhere shown that he first appears, after William's victory, in a very unexpected quarter. As " Eustace eorl "

---

[1] *Bracton's Note Book* (Ed. Maitland), II. 216.
[2] " Monachis de Sancto Michaele de Wasto " (Pipe Roll of 1130, p. 22). [3] *Ibid*. p. 16. [4] *Testa de Nevill*, p. 164.

he is addressed, with bishops Herman and Wulfstan, in an English writ of William, which I assign to the beginning of 1067.[1] The document implies that he already held an official, or at least a high, position in the counties of Wiltshire and Gloucestershire. But it was not in this region that he received his great possessions. Mr. Freeman held that "the Domesday holdings of Eustace were grants later than his reconciliation with William" after his condemnation and forfeiture "by the Gemot" at the close of 1067.[2] . It must be remembered, however, that, on his own hypothesis, the Domesday holder was not this Count Eustace, but his son. In one of those fine passages in which we see him at his best, he wrote of Eustace :—

He himself was dead at the time of the Survey, but his widow and son appear there as holders of lordships, both in various other shires in those western lands which on the day of his sentence were still unconquered. The names of Ida and Eustace, the widow and the son of the coward of Boulogne, the mother and the brother of the hero of Jerusalem, are found as owners of English soil on spots which would have a strange propriety if we could deem that they were ever honoured with the sojourn of the mightiest of the foes of Paynimrie. One of the western possessions of the house of Boulogne lies nestling at the foot of the north-western crest of Mendip, where the power of evil of the old Teutonic creed has left his name in Count Eustace's lordship of Loxton. Another, Kenwardston, the dowry of the widowed Countess, crowns the wooded height which looks full on that inland mount of the Archangel which shelters the earliest home of Christianity in Britain.[3]

---

[1] *Feudal England*, pp. 422–425.

[2] For his raid, in William's absence, on Dover, from Boulogne, earlier in that year.

[3] *Norman Conquest*, vol. IV. I must not be understood as com-

It is in these descriptive passages that Mr. Freeman's pen excelled.

The six or seven Somerset manors held by the counts of Boulogne were an outlying portion of their fief. With the exception of a manor apiece in Oxfordshire and Hants, the rest of their estates were in the east of England, and the bulk of them lay in Essex. These estates were partly those of a number of English 'predecessors,' and partly represented the lands acquired by Ingelric the priest. This man, it would seem, was one of those useful officials who enjoyed the favour of William as well as the favour of Edward.[1] He was dean of St. Martin's-le-Grand, a house of secular canons, and this connection led to trouble between Count Eustace, as his successor, and its canons. His lands were not confined to Essex, but extended into Hertfordshire and Suffolk. Count Eustace secured them all, including those which Ingelric, in the Domesday Survey, is charged with seizing wrongfully under William; and he also obtained lands in Kent, Surrey, Bedfordshire, Cambridgeshire, Huntingdonshire and Norfolk. Thus was formed the great fief which, for some centuries

---

mitting myself to the view that the 'Lochestone' (Loxton) of Domesday derives its name from Lok, "the power of evil"; or that the countess was widowed at the time and held Kenwardston in dower; or that Glastonbury was "the earliest home of Christianity in Britain."

[1] See my paper on "Ingelric the priest" in the *Commune of London and other studies* (pp. 28–36); also *English Historical Review*, XI. 740, and *History of the Norman Conquest*, vol. IV.

after, was known as 'the Honour of Boulogne.'[1]

On this fief Domesday shows us three interesting tenants. Four of its Somerset manors were held by Alvred de 'Merleberg' (Marlborough), lord of the castled mound at Ewias on the Welsh border. It would seem to have escaped notice that Alvred, an important tenant-in-chief in 1086, was already established in England under Edward the Confessor,[2] as was his uncle Osbern[3]—probably Osbern 'Pentecost.'[4] His successor was that Harold from whom Ewias takes its name, Harold the son of Earl Ralf, and the grandson of Goda, countess of Boulogne.[5] And this is why 'Harold of Ewias' is found among the knights of count Eustace under Henry I., and why his heir, Robert de Tregoz was a tenant of the 'Honour' under John. In Bedfordshire and Cambridgeshire, Ernulf de Ardres, a follower from the count's own country, was enfeoffed by him in six estates.[6] In Essex, no fewer than eleven estates were obtained by another of his followers, "Adelolf de Merc." Deeper than the counts themselves or than any other of their

---

[1] The memory of its double origin was preserved in its possession of two feudal courts, one of which, it is interesting to note, was that of St. Martin's-le-Grand. (See Morant's *Essex*, I. 309, where an Inq. p.m. of 1333 is quoted.) The monthly court of the Honour was held at Witham.

[2] See Domesday, fo. 175, where he is entered as having then held an important Worcestershire manor under St. Mary's, Worcester. [3] *Ibid.* fo. 186.

[4] See my *Feudal England*, pp. 322-4. [5] See above, p. 148.

[6] See my paper on "The Lords of Ardres" in *Feudal England*, (pp. 462-464).

vassals, have Adelolf and his heirs stamped their name on the East-Saxon land. This younger branch of the *vicomtes* of Marck, near Calais, which was at that time in the Boulonnais, is commemorated in the parish of Marks Tey, as in the manor of Merks or Marks in Dunmow, which was held by Adelolf himself in 1086, by his heir Enguerrand de Merc in 1258, and by the same family in 1340. Mark Hall, in Latton, is another of the manors which takes its name from this family, and was held by Adelolf, its founder, in 1086. His descendants increased and multiplied in the land : Fulc de Merc and M. de Merc attended the count's feudal court, in Essex, before 1120 ;[1] Geoffrey and Enguerrand de Merc of Essex are found on the Pipe Roll of 1130 (p. 57) ; Henry and Simon de Merc are recorded as holding lands on the Boulogne fief in the days of John.[2] As we have mention of a Eustace de " Oeys," son of Henry de " Merc," in connection with the manor of East Donyland, on the Boulogne fief, and as Oye adjoined Marck in the Calaisis, and was connected with it, we have here further evidence of the true origin of the names. Among the witnesses to this last document (which must belong, from the names of the leading ones, to 1190–1193) are John and William de Merc.[3]

Although the enfeoffment of Boughton, Kent,

---

[1] See below.

[2] *Testa de Nevill.* This family is also found in Northants in the 12th century.

[3] *Colchester Cartulary* (Roxburghe Club), p. 36.

was effected by the counts later than Domesday, we may note that its name of Boughton 'Alulf,' derived from one of its holders, preserves a Christian name then common in the Boulonnais.[1] Keeping, however, for the moment to Domesday, we find Count Eustace holding the great manor of Tring in Hertfordshire, which paid him £22 a year of assayed money, " ad pensum ejusdem comitis."[2] From this we learn that the count had introduced a standard of his own into England for weighing the money due to him.

Among the tenures created on the fief later than 1086, it is interesting to find two 'serjeanties,' one of them, at Boughton Alulf, being that of acting as ' veauttor,' ' veltrarius,' or ' falconarius ' to the count, and the other that of serving as his cook.[3] It might hardly be supposed that, in the 12th and 13th centuries, the connection with the Boulonnais was so close that its *seigneurs* could still be holding lands in the east of England. Yet this was actually the case. The hamlet of Austruy, in the Boulonnais, gave name to one of its *pairies*, the hereditary constableship of the *comté*. In England, the lord of Austruy was enfeoffed in five knight's fees, partly at Shopland and Chich (St. Osyth) in Essex, and partly at Cowley near Oxford.[4] When, in the

---

[1] Willelmus de Bouton cum Elya herede *Alulfi* de Bouton . . et est de honore Bolonie (*Testa*, p. 216).

[2] Domesday, fo. 137.

[3] *Testa de Nevill*, pp. 216, 217.

[4] " Baldewinus de Osterwic [*i.e.* Austruy] v. milites, scilicet, in Schopiland ii. mil. et dim. et in Chicche, quam abbas tenet, et

reign of Henry I., the great Augustinian Priory of St. Osyth had been founded at Chich, we read that, under Stephen, there was bestowed " ex dono Baldewini constabularii et ex confirmatione comitis Stephani et Matildis uxoris suæ et Willelmi comitis [Boloniæ] et heredis eorum tenementum de Chiche quod est de feodo Boloniæ." It was thus the constable of Boulogne himself, and not a cadet of his house, who held these lands in England. A later constable of the same name was among the prisoners captured by John, during the struggle with the barons, in Rochester Castle (30 Nov. 1215) and had to pay £120 for his ransom ;[1] but after the war we find Shopland recovered by him as Baldwin d'Austruy, he being styled its rightful heir.[2]

Another baronial family of the Boulonnais, that of Doudeauville, held estates in Huntingdonshire by the service of five knights to the Count, while a family which took its name from Wissant (" Whitsand ") held lands of the count at Parndon, Essex, by knight-service.[3]

But the greatest of the barons of the Boulonnais,

---

in Covel, quam Templarii tenent secus Oxoniam ii. milites et dim." (*Testa de Nevill*, p. 274). The entry is omitted in the parallel list on p. 273, and confused with a wholly different one in the *Liber Rubeus* (p. 576).

[1] Calendar of Patent Rolls, 2 and 19 May 1216.

[2] " Schopelaund . . . post guerram recuperavit Baldewynus de Ostrewic . . . sicut rectus heres . . . et tenet per servicium duorum militum " (*Testa de Nevill*, p. 268).

[3] *Testa de Nevill*, as above. Wissant was the predecessor of Calais as the landing place from England in the Middle Ages.

in the twelfth century, in England was Féramus or Pharamus *seigneur* of Tingry, whom I have made the subject of a monograph.[1] Known in England as Faramus " of Boulogne," he was the son of a William " of Boulogne," who held land in Surrey and Northamptonshire under Henry I., and a grandson of Geoffrey son — presumably natural son—of Count Eustace II. Maternally, Faramus was a grandson of a Domesday tenant-in-chief, Geoffrey de Mandeville, ancestor of the earls of Essex. A charter of his in the British Museum,[2] recording an agreement between him and a great citizen of London, has among its witnesses several Boulonnais, three of whom took their names from Hesdigneul, one from Questreques, and another from Liembronne. Their names show that Faramus was already in possession of the Tingry fief at a date not much later than 1130. He was prominent under Stephen in England as a supporter of the king and queen, but Henry II., after his accession, gave him lands, in Buckinghamshire, at Wendover and Eton. It is just possible that these were given as compensation for the constableship of Dover Castle, which may have been entrusted to him by Stephen. He was also a witness, about this time, to three charters of Count William of Boulogne, Stephen's surviving son, and the count bestowed on him the manor of Martock, in the county of Somerset, which then belonged to the honour of Boulogne.

---

[1] *Genealogist* [N.S.], XII. 145–151.
[2] Add. Cart., 28, 345.

He was thus a holder of land in three English counties. But, in addition to this, he held lands of the Honour of Boulogne in three other counties, Essex, Hertfordshire, and Cambridgeshire, for which he owed the count the service of six knights.

All these lands descended, with Sibyl, his daughter and heiress, to his son-in-law Enguerrand de Fiennes, another baron of the Boulonnais, who was killed at (St. Jean d') Acre in 1189. Thus the *châtelains* of Fiennes inherited valuable estates in England together with his fief at Tingry.

I have, however, denied in my last book[1] that they were, as has been always supposed, constables of Dover Castle from the time of the Norman Conquest. The Constable's Tower preserves their name, but the legend seems to be of late growth. It is the sort of tale that one would naturally assign to some Elizabethan herald. The family, I may add, were not forgetful of their 12th century ancestor, as we are reminded by the wondrous name of the Rev. Pharamus Fiennes, who lived in the days of Charles the Second.

From the families of the Boulonnais I turn to those of its religious houses which were then connected with England. Of these there were more than has been known. As we have seen, St. Wulmer de Boulogne obtained from 'Sainte Ide' Nutfield in Surrey, while the priory of Le Wast secured her three Dorset manors as one estate,

---

[1] *The Commune of London and other studies* (Constable & Co.), pp. 279–282.

which became known thence as Winterbourne
" Wast." It was not till 300 years after the
Conquest (1370) that the prior of Le Wast
finally parted with this estate, to which a Count
Eustace had added the churches of Westerham
and Boughton Alulf in Kent.[1] To the priory of
Rumilly-le-Comte Eustace III.[1] had given, in his
last illness, £10 a year from his English manor of
Fobbing (Essex), while it held at least one church
on the count's English fief, that of Coggeshall,
before Stephen there founded an abbey for monks
of Savigny. From Fobbing also £20 a year was
paid " to the monks of St. Wulmer," [2] that is St.
Wulmer de Samer, to which abbey also Stephen,
when count of Boulogne, gave the church at Fobbing as well. The same house possessed tithes at
Rivenhall, Essex, a Boulogne manor. The abbey
of St. Josse was given by Count Matthew (Stephen's
son-in-law) £10 a year from Norton ; the abbey
of La Capelle is said to have held English churches
named in a bull of Pope Pascal (28 Oct. 1110),
and the abbey of Licques received a small endowment at Caenby, Lincolnshire. Of other houses,
the ' Maladrerie ' de Boulogne received from Count
Eustace £20 a year payable from his manor of
Boughton Alulf in Kent, and this gift was confirmed by Stephen as count of Boulogne before he
became king of England. The hospital of Wissant received before 1156 £5 a year payable from

---

[1] See p. 153 above.
[2] 'Monachis de Sancto Wlmero' (*Liber Rubeus de Scaccario*),
p. 501.

crown lands in Buckinghamshire and Bedfordshire, and, shortly afterwards, Henry II., when visiting St. Omer, bestowed an endowment on the hospital of Santingefeld.[1]

Apart from endowments, there was a close connection through two religious houses, the abbey of Licques, which through its daughter-house at Newhouse, Lincolnshire, became the mother-house of the Order of Premontré in England, and the abbey of Arrouaise. Both in England and in the Boulonnais, there were several houses of Augustinian canons owing allegiance to Arrouaise and bound to attend its chapter.[2]

Let me now speak of the fief held by the Counts in England. This was augmented under Henry I., for he and Count Eustace the younger had both married daughters of king Malcolm of Scotland, and they were on friendly terms. The Queen's sister, the countess of Boulogne, who died 18 April 1118, was buried at Bermondsey Priory, a house belonging to that Order of Cluni, which was always in high favour with the house of Boulogne.[3]

It has, so far as I know, been hitherto unsuspected that, on the death of Eudo Dapifer (the son of Hubert of Rye), early in 1120, some of his estates were given by the Crown to Count Eustace

---

[1] On these somewhat confused grants, see much information in Cobbe's *Luton Church* (1899), a work of great erudition.

[2] For much local information on the families and religious houses of the Boulonnais, I have to thank my friend, M. V.-J. Vaillant of Boulogne, Officier d'Académie.

[3] See *Monasticon*, V. 94, for her epitaph.

of Boulogne. This is proved by the Colchester Cartulary.[1] The count's statement is confirmed by the return of the tenants of the Honour of Boulogne in the time of king John, in which all these manors are named as held of the Honour.

The list of witnesses to his charter deserves, from its interest, to be quoted :—

Test[ibus] ejusdem Comitis Eustachii filiis Rad[ulfo] scilicet et Eustachio, Baldwino constabulario,[2] Heroldo de Ewias, Roberto filio ejus, Rogero de Sumeri,[3] Baldwino filio Widonis,[4] Eustachio de Merc,[5] Willelmo de Curtone,[6] Eustachio de Pauc'be, Baldwino de Wizant,[7] Ernulfo de Q$^{\bar{u}}$uecultr$^{\bar{u}}$,[8] Willelmo camerario, Huberto.[9]

Ralf and Eustace, 'sons' of the Count, are, I

---

[1] In the possession of Earl Cowper (now privately printed for the Roxburghe Club), which contains (p. 47) a charter of "Eustachius Dei gratia Bolonie comes," confirming to St. John's Abbey, Colchester, the gift of Eudo "de decimis maneriorum suorum que mihi rex donavit" (fo. 19). The six manors named are :—'Lillechurch' (Kent), 'Gamelegeia' (Cambs.), 'Neuselle' (Herts), 'Roinges' (Essex), 'Widham' (Essex), 'Ereswelle' (Suffolk).

[2] This would be Baldwin d'Austruy (the fief of the constables of the counts) represented under John by Baldwin "de Osterwic" (Austruy).

[3] "Rogerus de Sumeri" was the Domesday tenant of Elmdon.

[4] Wido held of the count at Finchingfield and Little Chishall in Domesday.

[5] Adelolfus de Merc was one of the count's largest Domesday tenants (see above, p. 157, and *Feudal England*, pp. 463–4).

[6] 'Ogerus de Curtun' is found holding of the Honour in Tendring, Fifield, and Donyland *temp.* John.

[7] Represented under John by William de Witsand, who held a fee at Parndon of the Honour (see p. 159).

[8] This name is read, in the printed text, "Grauecultura."

[9] Probably the Huberto 'armigero' or 'scutario' of other charters.

believe, unknown. One can only suppose that, like that Geoffrey "filius comitis Eustachii" who figures in Domesday Book,[1] they were not of legitimate birth. The second may well have been, it seems to me, the father of that "Eustacius filius Eustacii filii comitis" who is charged 10 marcs for his relief, under Essex and Herts, on the Pipe Roll of 11 Henry II. (1165). By far the most interesting of the other witnesses are Harold of Ewias and Robert his son, whose appearance among the count's tenants is accounted for above (p. 156). The return *temp.* John shows us Robert de Tregoz, who married the heiress of their house, holding of the Honour by knight service.[2]

Of the six manors named in the charter, Lillechurch is specially to be noted, because its true descent is proved by this evidence, and the positive statement of Hasted shown to be without foundation. As "Hecham" (Higham in

---

[1] See my "Faramus of Boulogne" in the *Genealogist* (as on p. 160 above).

[2] For our knowledge of the "Honour of Boulogne," and of the manors of which it was composed, we are largely indebted to this return, which is found in two versions, both of them corrupt, in *Testa de Nevill*, pp. 273–275 (compare p. 265 for the record of its scutage). The first of these is also found in the *Red Book of the Exchequer*, pp. 575–583, and the other in the *Black Book of the Exchequer* (Ed. Hearne). It seems probable that both versions are derived from a common original return, and in any case (as I have shown in my *Studies on the Red Book of the Exchequer*) the editor of the Red Book is mistaken in asserting (p. 575) that the Black Book version represents a return of "earlier date," and is also mistaken in speaking of it as "hitherto unknown," for it was duly printed by Hearne in his well-known edition of the Black Book.

Kent) this manor had been held in Domesday by "Adam" of the bishop of Bayeux. On the bishop's forfeiture his tenants had become tenants-in-chief, and "Adam" (the son of Hubert) thus obtaining the manor, was succeeded, clearly, by his brother Eudo "Dapifer." Eudo gave some tithes there (as at "Lillecherch") to his abbey at Colchester, which must also have obtained the church,[1] for we find the convent granting it to the nuns of Lillechurch, at the request of Stephen and Matilda, and receiving, in compensation, from the queen, land at East Donyland belonging to her Honour of Boulogne. Meanwhile, they had need, for the abbey they founded at Faversham, of the manor of Faversham, which had been granted by them to William of Ypres. He, therefore, gave it back to them, receiving in exchange the manor of Lille-church (Higham).[2] This is destructive of Hasted's assertion that the manor had reverted to the Crown on the death of Bishop Odo, and had thus come to Stephen as royal demesne.

The Colchester Cartulary also contains the confirmation of the Count's charter by Stephen, his son-in-law and successor.

Stephanus comes de Moret' . . . Sciatis quod ego et mea

---

[1] Morant, in his account of the Abbey, took it by mistake for the church of Higham, Suffolk.

[2] "Dedimus ego et Mathildis regina mea Willelmo de Ipra in excambium pro manerio de Favresham Lillechirch cum pertinentiis suis de hæreditate reginæ" (*Mon. Ang.*, IV. 573). It was of her inheritance because Count Eustace, her father, had acquired it as above.

conjux Matildis concessimus monachis [1] . . . sicut illi monachi umquam tenuerint plenius et liberius de Eudone dapifero et de comite Eustachio, ita ego et uxor mea Matildis concedimus, etc. . . .

Testes isti concessionis fuerunt Robertus de Salkavilla, Galfridus camararius, Willelmus camararius, Warnerius frater ejus, Willelmus filius Hervei, Hubertus scutarius, Walterus Mascherel,[2] Wlfgarus de Cokeshale,[3] Eurardus de Colcestra, Galfridus nepos abbatis, Gilebertus et Osbertus frater ejus, Osbernus palmarius.

When the whole fief was complete, the counts received from that portion of it which they had granted out to tenants the service of more than 120 knights.[4] It became known afterwards as "the Honour of Boulogne," which was specially named in Magna Carta, and still existed in name at the beginning of the 16th century.

The existence of this great fief, as an appendage of the *comté* of Boulogne, leads us to consider a point which seems to have been overlooked hitherto by all historians. At the death of Henry I. his nephew Stephen was not only count of Boulogne, in right of his wife, and in Normandy count of Mortain (a very important *comté*), by grant from his uncle, but was also, perhaps, the greatest landowner in England itself. For he there possessed at least :—

(1) The whole Boulogne fief.

(2) The forfeited fief of Robert Malet ("the

---

[1] The church of 'Lillecherch' is included in this grant.

[2] Founder of the Benedictine nunnery at Wix, Essex.

[3] Coggeshall, Essex.

[4] *Testa de Nevill*, p. 275. But perhaps the right total should be rather smaller.

Honour of Eye "), containing over 250 manors, and supplying over 90 knights.

(3) The forfeited fief of Roger " de Poitou " (son of Earl Roger de Montgomeri), containing about 400 manors, and comprising " the Honour of Lancaster."

(4) Certain crown lands, which had been granted him (as had the two above fiefs) by his uncle Henry I.[1]

We find, accordingly, in the Pipe Roll for 1130 entries of remission of Danegeld on his lands in seventeen counties, although the returns for several counties are wanting.

Now the wealth and influence conferred by the possession of these vast fiefs must have greatly assisted Stephen in obtaining the throne, as they also did, after he was king, in providing for his greedy followers.[2] I hope to show that they were also to some extent the cause of his agreeing to the succession of Henry II. in the place of his own son. For his younger son William, who became his heir on the death of his brother Eustace (10 Aug. 1153), had himself married the greatest heiress in England, the daughter of the earl de Warenne. She brought him the castles of

---

[1] See my *Feudal England*, pp. 202–3, 211.

[2] Some instances of this are given in my *Geoffrey de Mandeville*. The possession of the Boulogne fief had also enabled him to found the abbey of Coggeshall, while that of 'the Honour of Lancaster' had placed at his disposal endowments for the abbey of Furness. Both these houses, of which the latter was founded before his accession, were affiliated to the order of Savigny, with which, as count of Mortain, he had doubtless been brought in contact.

Lewes (Sussex), Castle-Acre (Norfolk), and Conis-borough (Yorkshire), together with a whole "Rape" of Sussex and more than 200 manors in other counties. This vast increment would render his private possessions even greater than his father's. But, even in addition to this, his father had given him large estates in England, so that it might well seem better for the young count of Boulogne, as he was already styled, to have these estates secured to him by Henry of Anjou than to claim a contested crown. Moreover, Henry, as duke of Normandy, was in actual possession of the Warenne inheritance in Normandy, and of the *comté* of Mortain. As part of the bargain, therefore, he offered to give all this to William, and, in addition, further lands in England itself if he was allowed to succeed peaceably to the crown.

Thus it was that the terms secured by the young count of Boulogne occupied a very large place in the treaty arranged between Stephen and Henry in the autumn of 1153. Count William obtained a confirmation of all that his father had given him,[1] together with fresh grants as part of the bargain,[2] including the castle of Pevensey and

---

[1] "Incrementum etiam quod ego Willelmo filio meo dedi ipse Dux ei concessit, castra scilicet et villas de Norwico cum septingentis libratis terre . . . et totum comitatum de Nordfolk præter illa quæ pertinent ad ecclesias," etc. This addition to the Warenne fief in East Anglia and the great Honour of Eye placed the whole region in his power.

[2] "Item ad roborandam graciam meam et dilectionem, dedit ei dux et concessit quicquid Richerus de Aquila habebat de honore Peneveselli, et preter hec castra et villas Peneveselli, et

the ' Rape ' of Sussex adjoining his own. But under the terms of this treaty the count of Boulogne would be too powerful for Henry's safety as king. He had castles in the south, in the east, and in the north of England, in the east[1] and in the west of Normandy ; his estates were absolutely gigantic. Henry, even after mounting the throne, had, for a time, to temporize. But the policy he kept steadily in view was (1) to reclaim estates alienated from the Crown, (2) to obtain possession of the castles. Accordingly, in spite of the solemn treaty of 1153, the count of Boulogne had to surrender to him, in 1157, all his castles, together with all the additions to his inheritance guaranteed to him by Henry in 1153.[2] But the count of Boulogne, Mortain, and Warenne (as he always styled himself[3]) was allowed to retain the vast estates which his father Stephen held, we saw, before his acces-

---

servitium Faramusi preter castra et villas de Doure, et quod ad honorem Doure pertinet." (Compare p. 160 above.)

[1] At Bellencombre and Mortemer near Neufchâtel.

[2] " Guillelmus filius Stephani regis qui erat comes civitatis Constantiarum, id est Moritonii, et in Anglia comes Surreiæ, id est de Warenna, propter filiam tertii Guillelmi de Warenna, quam duxerat, reddidit ei Penevesel et Norwith et quicquid tenebat de corona sua et omnes munitiones proprias tam in Normannia quam in Anglia ; et rex fecit eum habere quicquid Stephanus pater ejus habuit in anno et die quo rex Henricus avus ejus fuit vivus et mortuus " (Robert of Torigny [abbot of Mont St. Michel], pp. 92–3 [Rolls Series edition]).

[3] The omission of one of these three titles (Mortain) in his very fine charter exhibited at the British Museum can, I think, be explained.

sion, together with those of his wife in England and Normandy. There is evidence that he was in actual possession of the ' Honours' of Lancaster,[1] of Eye,[2] and of Boulogne,[3] as well as of the *comté* of Mortain.[4]

At this point a brief chart pedigree may enable the reader more easily to grasp the descent of the Honour and of the accretions it received (see next page).

When in 1159 the count died in the Toulouse campaign, where he fought in Henry's host, his death presented a great temptation to the English king. The sole surviving child of Stephen was Maud abbess of Romsey, and the great domains of Count William were doomed, as it seemed, to be broken up. But, as her namesake and great

---

[1] *Cal. Rot. Chart.*, I. (1) 28, for instance.

[2] Stephen's possession of this great ' Honour' is proved by his charter, as king, to Eye Priory, confirming its possessions as held in the time of Robert Malet, " et tempore meo antequam rex essem " (*Monasticon*, III. 406). His son's tenure is similarly proved by his charter of confirmation to that same house as " comes Boloniæ, Warennæ, et Moritonii " (*Ibid.*).

The fact of the possession of this Honour by Stephen explains the remission to him, under Suffolk, in 1130, of nearly £46 for Danegeld (Rot. Pip. 31 Hen. I. p. 99), implying that his lands in that county were assessed at the vast sum of some 460 hides (or their equivalent) ; and it accounts for Fulcher ' de Pleiforda' paying to have his case tried " in Anglia in curia comitis Moriton'," (*Ibid.* p. 99). For Playford (Suffolk) belonged to the Honour of Eye, and Stephen, before his accession, had confirmed the gift of its church to Eye Priory (Harl. MS. 639 [D'Ewes' Transcript], fo. 59*b*). See also p. 176 below.

[3] See the important charter printed by me in " The Honour of Ongar" (*Essex Arch. Trans.* [N.S.], VII. 144).

[4] See my *Calendar of documents preserved in France*, p. 285.

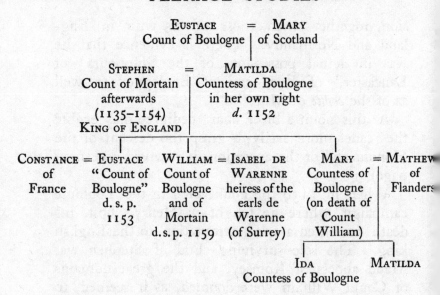

EUSTACE = MARY
Count of Boulogne | of Scotland

STEPHEN = MATILDA
Count of Mortain | Countess of Boulogne
afterwards | in her own right
(1135–1154) | *d.* 1152
KING OF ENGLAND |

CONSTANCE = EUSTACE | WILLIAM = ISABEL DE | MARY = MATHEW
of | "Count of | Count of | WARENNE | Countess of | of
France | Boulogne" | Boulogne | heiress of the | Boulogne | Flanders
d. s. p.	and of	earls de	(on death of
1153	Mortain	Warenne	Count
	d.s.p. 1159	(of Surrey)	William)

IDA   MATILDA
Countess of Boulogne

aunt, " the good queen Molde," had been taken from the same cloister, some half a century before, to become the king's wife—though, unlike her, most unwillingly—the great heiress was restored to the world, by special permission of the Pope, and married to Mathew, a younger son of the count of Flanders. Becket, like Anselm in the previous instance, protested vigorously, but in vain. As for king Henry he was quite willing that the *comté* of Boulogne should pass to a son of the count of Flanders, whose cousin and friend he was ; but the great fiefs, English and Norman, in his own dominions were another matter ; these, it is clear to me, were swept into the royal net.[1]

[1] The vast estates of the Warenne family provided, later, an appanage for his natural brother Hamelin, who received them with the hand of the count's widow.

Mathew, however, was by no means ready to acquiesce in this arrangement. He claimed them all, in right of his wife, and eventually king Henry " promised "—probably in 1166—to give him the then enormous sum of £1,000 in compensation.[1]

But the bribe was insufficient. In 1167 the king's difficulty was the count's opportunity, and the absence of Henry in France inspired him with the daring conception of an armed descent on England in support of his claim. For the mention of this curious episode, which seems to have escaped notice,[2] we are indebted to Gervase of Canterbury, who wrote, of course, with local knowledge. He tells us[3] that the king being busy with the troubles oversea,[4] the count assembled a fleet, it was said, of six hundred ships, which

---

[1] " Ibi enim rex mille libras Matthæo Comiti Boloniæ se daturum spopondit " (*Materials for history of Thomas Becket*, VI. 73-4).

[2] It is not mentioned in the most elaborate and recent history of the reign, that of Miss Norgate.

[3] "Mathæus etiam comes Boloniæ, frater vero Philippi comitis Flandriæ, secentas naves, ut fama fuit, Flandrensibus armavit, juratus in Angliam venire, unde motus magnus in Anglia factus est. Subtraxerat enim ei rex quosdam redditus in Anglia quos dicebat sibi de jure antiquo competere. Quos quia prece non potuit armis conatus est revocare. Sumpsit audaciam suæ præsumptionis eo quod rex Angliæ transmarinis dissentionibus esset occupatus. Verumptamen conatus ejus inanis effectus est, Ricardo de Luci cum Anglicana militia custodiam procurante " (Gervase of Canterbury [Rolls Series], I. 203).

[4] Henry was in Aquitaine, this year, until the spring, was then fighting the French king in the north till August, after which he had to quell an important rising in Britanny (Eyton).

he filled with Flemings, swearing that he would extort his rights by force of arms. Much alarm was caused for the time; but the famous "Richard de Luci the loyal," who had charge of the realm in the king's absence, kept the coast with the English "militia," and the count's attempt came to naught.[1] The story is confirmed, I think, by the Pipe Roll of the year, which shows us that Dover Castle was provisioned, and its defences strengthened,[2] that weapons were sent from London to the coast, precautions taken for the safety of Canterbury, and seven ships despatched from Southampton to Dover "on the king's service."

Instead of revenging himself upon the count, Henry, with the Becket trouble on his hands, and with war and rebellion in prospect, came to terms with Mathew, bought off his claim to his wife's inheritance, and, in 1168, secured his help against the French king.[3] The price he had to pay for

---

[1] Strangely enough, Richard de Luci's own castle of Ongar, the head of his newly-formed Honour, had been part, with its appurtenant manors, of the Boulogne fief, and had been given him by Stephen and his queen (as Count and Countess) and confirmed by their son Count William. (See my paper on "The Honour of Ongar" in *Essex Arch. Trans.* [N.S.], VII. 142–152).

[2] The famous keep was not erected till some years later.

[3] "Rex vero Henricus caute agens cognatum suum Mathæum comitem Boloniæ, sibi pacificavit, spondens ei se daturum per annum maximam partem pecuniæ pro calumnia relaxanda comitatus Moritonii. Habebat enim filiam regis Stephani, qui fuerat comes Moritonii. Cum autem idem Mathæus ad auxilium regis Anglorum, domini et cognati sui, veniret, Johannes comes Pontivi, non permisit eum transire per terram suam, unde, necessitate cogente, navali subvectione ad regem cum multis militibus accessit" (*Robert of Torigni* [Rolls Ed.], p. 238).

this was the gift of a fresh fief in England itself. It can be positively proved from the Pipe Rolls that, although the count did not obtain the Boulogne fief, or even part of it, he received as compensation over three hundred " librates " of other land. The Roll of the 14th year (Michaelmas 1168) shows that the count was then drawing £200 " blanch " a year from Kirton-in-Lindsey, £65 from Ixning, Suffolk, and £61 from Bampton, Oxon. And by Michaelmas 1170 he was drawing, in addition, £60 from Dunham, Nottinghamshire, which had been previously received by his brother the count of Flanders.[1] He did not, however, long retain these English possessions, for, on joining Henry, " the young king," he was treated as having forfeited them all at, or soon after, Easter 1173.[2] The " consideration " by which he had been won to the cause of Henry's rebellious heir was the promise of the coveted *comté* of Mortain, with a confirmation of the important manor of Kirton-in-Lindsey, and a grant of the great Honour of Eye, which had been held by Stephen.[3] Fighting in the cause

---

[1] Pipe Roll, 16 Hen. II. This brought up the total to nearly £400. It is remarkable that we find Count Mathew bestowing the church of St. Nicholas at Droitwich on the abbey of Fontevrault for the local nuns of Westwood (*Monasticon*, VI. 1006–7), and his successor Ida confirming the gift. I should be inclined to connect this with the rights at Droitwich that are entered in Domesday as appurtenant to Bampton (fo. 154*b*).

[2] Pipe Roll, 19 Hen. II.

[3] *Hoveden*, II. 46. But the *Gesta* (I. 44) says that the Honour of Eye was promised to Hugh Bigot.

of "the young king," he was mortally wounded
in Normandy (July 1173), exactly five years, as
the chronicler observes, after he had solemnly
sworn fealty to Henry II.[1]

The hereditary claims of the Countess Mary
passed to her heirs by Count Mathew, their
daughters, Ide and Maud. These, in 1180, were
given in marriage by their uncle Philip, count of
Flanders, Maud, the younger, becoming the wife
of Henry "the Warrior" duke of Lorraine.
Some sort of hereditary claim seems to have been
recognised in her and her husband, for the latter
received from Richard I. the great Honour of Eye,
which had been held by Stephen, and by his son
Count William after him.[2] But the geogra-
phical position of the Boulonnais in the relations
of England, France, and Flanders during the
latter half of the 12th century made the succes-

---

[1] " Quod divino judicio factum esse pro certo cognoscimus. Nam
quia propositis et tactis sacrosanctis reliquiis, inter quas et manus
Sancti Jacobi præsentaliter habebatur, quinquennio jam transacto
in festo Sancti Jacobi fidelitatem patris regis juraverat, et, sicut
modo apparuit, in omnium oculis dejeraverat, in ultionem tanti
sceleris, in die festo Sancti Jacobi letali vulnere percussus est " (*R.
Diceto*, I. 373). This statement gives us the date of their previous reconciliation, namely, 25 July 1168.

[2] " Et tenuit illum honorem iij annis, qui mortuus fuit in servicio
Regis in exercitu de Tulosa [1159] . . . successit Ricardus
Rex et dedit eundem honorem duci Loeringie cum nepte comitis
predicti Willelmi que erat proxima heres. Et Dux Loheringie tenet
illum honorem [1212] sicut hereditatem uxoris sue " (*Testa de
Nevill*, 296). It had then 90½ knight's fees (*Red Book of the
Exchequer*, 477). It was 'restored' to Duke Henry so late as
9 Hen. III. (1224-5).

sion to English lands which had been held by its
counts a matter of policy rather than of right.

The elder sister, to whom was given the *comté*
of Boulogne, brought it eventually to Reginald de
Dammartin, son of a Count Aubrey de Dammartin, who himself had held some land in England.[1]
In conjunction with her he confirmed, in 1201,
to the Hospital of Austin Canons at Cold Norton,
Oxfordshire, the gifts of his predecessors.[2] John,
on 24 April 1200, had sanctioned the arrangement by which the count had charged on Kirton-
in-Lindsey the £5 a year, with which Count
Mathew had endowed St. Mary of Longvillers, in
the Boulonnais, at Norton.[3] Becoming John's ally
against France by the treaty of Château Gaillard
(18 August 1199),[4] Count Reginald had secured
his wife's English inheritance at Kirton, Bampton,
and Dunham ;[5] and nine months later (9 May
1200), at Roche d'Orival (that is at Château Fouet
on the Seine), he obtained from John the curious
grant that if, in the course of the war between
Philip and himself, the strife should reach the
Boulonnais, the count might come to England
with his wife and daughter and reside there
freely, and that, in case of his death, his daughter
and heiress should only be married by her friends'
advice, and " according to the custom of the

---

[1] In East Anglia (*Red Book of the Exchequer*, p. 60 ; cf. p. 128).
[2] *Monasticon Anglicanum*, VI. 421.
[3] *Rot. Chart.*, I. (1) 47. The endowment can be traced at
Kirton in later times.   [4] *Ibid.* p. 30.
[5] Count Mathew had alienated to followers lands at Exning.

PEERAGE STUDIES

Boulonnais."[1] Reginald, it seems, knew his John, and he did not trust him far. The alliance was not of long duration, for the count forfeited his English lands, apparently in 1203, by going over to Philip.

In 1212 there was another sharp change. The *comté* of Boulogne was confiscated by Philip, and the count fled to Otho and Germany, and thence to England. Doing homage to John at Lambeth, 3 May (1212), he received a grant, the next day, of an annuity of £1,000 for three years, during which the rights of his wife and himself in England and Normandy should be ascertained. He also recovered Kirton, Dunham, and Bampton with Norton (Oxon.), and received in addition Norton (Suffolk), Ryhall (Rutland), and Wrestlingworth and Piddington (Beds.).[2] These three last

---

[1] " Quod si occasione nostri vel werre nostre in Buluneys' werratum fuerit, et quod placuerit illi in terram nostram Anglie venire, ipsi et uxori *et filie sue* salvum venire et salvum stare et salvum inde recedere . . . Et ipsum securum . . . per cartam nostram et per barones nostros quod sive tempore pacis vel tempore werre nostre, sicut predictum est, illuc venerint, filiam suam libere . . . et si de eo humaniter contigisset, ad ipsam maritandam *secundum consuetudinem de Buluneis* per consilium amicorum suorum. Si vero . . . quod absit, interim contigisset, barones nostri nichilominus eam libere dimittent ut predictum est " (*Rot. Chart.*, I. (1) p. 58).

[2] "Sciatis quod reddidimus Reginaldo de Dammartin comiti Boloniæ Kirketon', Dunham', et Norton' quod est in comitatu Oxon', [Bampton], et præterea Norton' quod est in comitatu Suff', Ridal', et Wrestlingehal' et Pedint' cum omnibus pertinentiis suis in dominicis feodis et serviciis sicut ea tenuit die qua illa cepimus in manum nostram. Reddidimus eciam eidem comiti Boloniæ Ixning cum pertinentiis suis salvis militibus et libere tenentibus

manors had formed part of the Honour of Huntingdon. A recognition so splendid as this bound the count closely to the cause of John. Next year he is found as one of the commanders of the king's fleet at the naval victory of Damme, and in 1214 he fought for him most gallantly at the famous but disastrous battle of Bouvines. After himself unhorsing Philip, he was taken prisoner by the French, and carried off in fetters to remain captive till his death.

There is something pathetic, when his fate is remembered, in a formal entry on our close rolls, some five years later (15 July, 1219), that the count is to be given Cold Norton and Dunham, as he held them when captured in Flanders, in John's service, and at the outbreak of war between John and the barons.[1]

Thus tragically closed the long but chequered connection of England and the counts of Boulogne. One of those counts had invaded England, by the side of Duke William, in 1066, and had again invaded her, on his own account, in 1067. Another had landed on her shores in 1135, and had mounted, and held, her throne. A third had endeavoured to invade her in 1167, lured by the

feodis et tenementis que Matheus pater Ide comitisse Bolonie uxoris sue eis dedit per servicium quod inde debent et pro defectu aliarum terrarum quas exigit tanquam jus suum et jus uxoris sue predicte Ide dabimus ei annuatim mille libras sterlingorum . . . a Pascha anno regni nostri quatuordecimo usque in tres annos proximo sequentes ut interim jus suum et jus uxoris sue possimus inquirere " (*Rot. Chart.*, I. (1) p. 186).

[1] *Rot. Litt. Claus.*, I. 396.

hope of regaining their great English possessions. A fourth, fighting by sea and land, in the cause of her tyrant king, died a captive and dispossessed, owning nothing but the land which he held within the island realm.

IV

The Family of Ballon and the Conquest of South Wales

AMONG the Norman nobles of the Conquest there is no more striking figure than that of William Fitz Osbern. Son of the loyal guardian of the infant Duke William, that Osbern who had paid for his fidelity with his life (1040), William became, in Mr. Freeman's words, the Duke's " nearest personal friend . . . the Duke's earliest and dearest friend, the son of the man who had saved his life in childhood, the man who had himself been the first to cheer on his master to his great enterprise." [1] In another place Mr. Freeman speaks of him as the duke's " chosen friend . . . the man who had done more than any other man to bring about the invasion of England." Lord of Breteuil, seneschal of Normandy, joint regent for a while of England (1067), earl of Hereford on the morrow of the Conquest, and lord of the Isle of Wight, he was entrusted at one time with the castle at Winchester, at another with the " tower " at York, and yet found time within the four years which covered his English life " to make some fearful inroads " on the Welsh neighbours of his earldom. Mr. Freeman, indeed, went so far as to say that we have in these inroads,—

the beginning, though only the beginning, of that great Norman settlement in South Wales which was a few years later to make Morganwg, above almost every other part of the Isle of Britain, a land of Norman knights and Norman castles ; but this work was to be done by other hands than those of William Fitz Osbern.[1]

I am dealing in another quarter with the traces of this great noble's rule, not only in the Isle of Wight but in Hampshire.[2] Here I can deal only with his rule in his border earldom, where he played the part of a petty sovereign. The position of Herefordshire on the Welsh border was one of such strategic importance that the district had to be organized on a quasi-military system, a system which left its traces for centuries in the exceptional *status* of " the March " and of its lords. Edward the Confessor had led the way by making his French nephew, Ralf, earl of Hereford, and entrusting the borough and the shire to him and to his foreign knights. Under his successor, the same task was taken up anew, and Domesday shows us Herefordshire divided by William Fitz Osbern into castleries, each of which must have had for its centre the moated and palisaded mound which formed the fortress of the time. It was hardly exaggeration on Mr. Freeman's part to speak of Earl William's " reign " in the feudal

[1] *Norman Conquest*, vol. IV.
[2] See Introduction to the Domesday Survey of Hampshire in the Victoria Series of County Histories.

principality thus created. He made, indeed, a special law on behalf of the warrior knights whom his lavish pay attracted, that none of them should pay, for any offence, a higher fine than seven shillings. And this privilege was still in force when William of Malmesbury wrote in the following century. Of more interest, however, was a privilege, to which Mr. Freeman did not allude, bestowed by him on the French burgesses who had settled under him at Hereford. To them he granted that, like their fellows clustered round his castle of Breteuil on the edge of the forest of that name,[1] they should enjoy certain 'customs,' of which the most important was that they should not be fined more than 12 pence for any offence, save three reserved pleas.

As these 'customs' of Breteuil spread from Hereford to other English towns, it seems desirable to explain a matter which, hitherto, has either been overlooked or been misunderstood. In accordance with my standing principle of Domesday interpretation, I here collate the two passages bearing on these 'customs.'

HEREFORD.	RHUDDLAN.
Anglici burgenses ibi manentes habent suas priores consuetudines. Francig[enæ] vero burgenses habent quietas per xii denarios omnes forisfacturas suas preter tres supradictas (pacem [regis] infractam et heinfaram et forestellum)—I. 179.	Ipsis burgensibus annuerunt leges et consuetudines que sunt in Hereford et in Bretuill, scilicet quod per totum annum de aliqua forisfactura non dabunt nisi xii denarios præter homicidium et furtum et Heinfar præcogitata—I. 269.

---

[1] In the south-west of the Department of the Eure.

PEERAGE STUDIES

I cannot find any mention of either of these passages in Professor Maitland's work, *Domesday Book and Beyond*; nor can I find a reference to the Rhuddlan one in the *History of English Law*.[1] Still less can I discover any attempt to collate them, although they, clearly, illustrate one another. The conclusions that I draw from this collation are : (1) that the burgesses of Rhuddlan—which Domesday speaks of as a " new borough " founded by the earl of Chester and Robert of Rhuddlan jointly[2]—were granted the ' customs ' of Breteuil only as used at Hereford, and not directly from Breteuil ; (2) that these ' customs ' had for their chief feature the limitation of fines to 12 pence ; (3) that the Domesday record of such limitation at Hereford represents the ' customs ' of Breteuil ; (4) that this limitation was granted only to its burgesses of 'French' birth ; (5) that three " pleas of the Crown " were excepted, in both cases, from this limitation, and that their names are by no means the same.

The above laws or customs enjoyed by the borough and the shire were by no means the only lasting traces of Earl William's rule. The abbeys he had founded on his Norman lands at Cormeilles and La-Vieille-Lyre[3] were richly endowed from his English fief. In Herefordshire, Hampshire,

---

[1] By Profs. Maitland and Sir F. Pollock, 1895. See vol. II. pp. 452–3.

[2] Orderic writes that " Decreto regis oppidum contra Gallos apud Rodelentum constructum est."

[3] Both now in the Department of the Eure.

Gloucestershire, and Worcestershire, churches, tithes and lands, were theirs by the gift of their pious founder, while even the revenues from the boroughs of Hereford and Southampton were charged by him in their favour. I have urged, in dealing with the Hampshire Domesday, that these endowments have a special value as enabling us to trace those lands which had been held by Earl William and by his son and successor. This value is no less evident in the case of the Herefordshire Domesday, where the frequent mention of the Abbey of Cormeilles[1] points to the previous tenure of royal manors in that shire by Earl William Fitz Osbern, a fact at which Domesday only occasionally hints. Therefore, when Pope Alexander III. is found confirming to the Abbey "decimas reddituum villæ de Munemuta, de Troy,"[2] we may safely infer that Monmouth (with Troy) had been held by William Fitz Osbern. For when Wihenoc and his nephew, William the son of Baderon, were installed there by the Conqueror, they bestowed all the endowments they could on the Abbey of St. Florent de Saumur.[3]

But Earl William's power did not extend only beyond the modern shire to the castled outpost of Monmouth; it extended down the border of South Wales to the very mouth of the Severn. Seizing the great manor of Tidenham, which belonged to

[1] Especially on fo. 179*b*.
[2] In 1168. *Monasticon*, VI. 1076–7.
[3] See Domesday, fo. 180*b*, and the paper on "The Origin or the Stewarts" above.

Bath Abbey, he obtained the important angle of land formed by the Severn and the Wye, while by evicting the holders, royal, clerical, and lay, of the manors of Alvington, Lydney, and Purton, he extended his territory some distance up the right bank of the Severn.[1]   From this district, as a base of operations, he pushed across the Wye into Wales, raising the famous castle of Strigul, now Chepstow, as a fortified *tête de pont* on its right bank.[2] Having thus entered the land of Gwent (the lowlands between the Wye and the Usk) the indefatigable earl soon reduced it to subjection, portioning out some of it in ploughlands for his follower Ralf de Limesi and other Norman knights,[3] while, by permission of king William, he allowed king Gruffyd and the Welsh to hold the rest,[4] on the native system, the grouped *trevs* paying in kind their cows, their pigs, and their honey, with a commutation for the hawks.[5]

All this Earl William had accomplished in the course of his " short reign."   At the close of 1070 he left England for Normandy, having con-

---

[1] See the Gloucestershire Domesday for all this.

[2] "Castellum de Estrighoiel fecit Willelmus comes et ejus tempore reddebat xl solidos tantum de navibus in silvam euntibus. Tempore vero comitis Rogerii, filii ejus, reddidit ipsa villa xvi libras, et medietatem habebat Radulfus de Limesi."—*Domesday*, I. 162.

[3] " In eodem feudo dedit Willelmus comes Radulfo de Limesi l carucatas terræ sicut fit in Normannia."—*Domesday*, I. 162 (and see the entries adjoining).

[4] " Hos misit Willelmus comes ad consuetudinem Grifin regis licentia regis Willelmi."—*Ibid*.

[5] Cf. Seebohm's *English Village Community*, p. 207.

quered within those four years Yorkshiremen in
the north-east and Welsh in the south-west. From
Normandy he soon set out for Flanders, " as
though," says Orderic, " to sport," to join king
Philip in the conquest of Flanders, and to win its
countess as his bride. And there, at the battle of
Cassel, he was slain. So fell one who " had ever
been the man whom William had most trusted,
and whom he had ever chosen for those posts
which called for the highest displays of faithful-
ness, daring, and military skill." [1] Four years
more, and Roger, his son and successor, forfeited
all the great possessions won by his father's sword.
The fatal ' bride-ale ' at the wedding of his sister
with the earl of Norfolk was followed by his
rising, capture, and imprisonment (1074), and the
greatness of his fall proved, we shall find, a text
on which the chronicler could moralize to his
heart's content.

At the time of the Domesday Survey (1086)
changes had followed on his fall. Monmouth was
already in the hands of the father of its Breton
lords ; and in Gwent Ralf de Limesi had been
succeeded in his lands by a new holder, William
de Ou (Eu), himself destined to forfeiture for treason under William Rufus. But the land was still
in the Norman's grip. Caerleon-upon-Usk is
mentioned as theirs,[2] and Caldecote, then or later
' castled,' was in the hands of the king's sheriff.
One Norman lord, on whom we have to keep our

[1] Freeman's *Norman Conquest.*   [2] Domesday, I. 162.

eyes, had penetrated even beyond the Usk into what was then Gwenllwg.

> Turstin the son of Rolf has between Usk and Wye 17 plough-teams. Four and a half of these are on his demesne ; the others are (those) of his men. . . . Of this land, the king's reeves claim five and a half plough[lands], saying that Turstin took them without their being given him.
>
> The same Turstin has 6 carucates of land beyond Usk ; and there his men have 4 plough-teams, etc., etc.[1]

Moreover, I have a strong suspicion that this Turstin was already established at Caerleon-on-Usk itself. For the Herefordshire 'castlery' or William de Scohies is most unexpectedly headed by that of 'Carlion,' where there were eight "carucates of land" (the same measure, be it observed, as in the above entry), together with "three Welshmen living under Welsh law" and a render of honey. And all this was held of him by 'Turstin.'[2]

There is just a doubt as to whether this Turstin Fitz Rolf was the ardent warrior of that name who

---

[1] *Domesday*, I. 162. The land "between Usk and Wye" is now East Monmouthshire ; "beyond Usk" lay what is now the western portion of the shire.

[2] "Willelmus de Scohies tenet viii^to carucatas terræ in Castellaria de Carlion, et Turstin tenet de illo. Ibi habet in dominio unam carucam, et iii Walenses lege Walensi viventes cum iii carucis et ii bordarii cum dimidia caruca, et redd[i]t iiii sextaria mellis."—*Domesday*, I. 185*b*.

It seems to me not improbable that the Herefordshire lands of William de Scohies were given him for the support of this Norman outpost at Caerleon, in which case its acquisition was as early as the days of William Fitz Osbern. But this can only be conjecture.

bore the duke's standard at the battle of Hastings. Genealogists, also, have been baffled hitherto in seeking to trace the descent of his lands in England and South Wales.[1] For when we close Domesday Book, a thick darkness settles down on Gwent and its Norman lords.

It is at Abergavenny that this darkness is first broken by gleams of light. Dugdale begins his account of the family that he terms 'Baalun' with this marvellous passage :—

In the time of King Edward the Confessor Dru de Baladon (or Balon) had issue three sons, viz. Hameline, Wyonoc and Wynebald, as also three daughters, Emme, Ducia, and Beatrix. Which Hameline came into England with William the Conqueror ; and being the first lord of all that territory in Wales called Over-Went, built a strong castle at Bergavenny, where a Gyant called Agros had raised one formerly.

This Hameline also founded the Priory of Bergavenny, and departing the world in 3 *Will. Rufi*, was there buried ; but, having no issue, gave that castle to Briene, son of the earl of the Isle, his nephew (commonly called *Brientius filius Comitis*), viz. son of his sister Lucie.[2]

It would be difficult to pack more errors into so small a space ; and yet Dugdale copied faithfully the story of the Abergavenny monks, who had compiled, after the manner of their kind, one of those "histories of the foundation" which are responsible for more false genealogy than any other medieval documents.

I shall now set myself to prove (1) that Hamelin and Wynebald were two brothers who took their

[1] See p. 194 below.   [2] *Baronage*, I. 453.

name from Ballon (near Le Mans) in Maine, and were benefactors, in England, to the great abbey of St. Vincent at Le Mans ; (2) that they were brought over by William Rufus ; (3) that they were placed in the valley of the Usk, Hamelin at Abergavenny and Wynebald at Caerleon ; (4) that Wynebald at least was provided for from the lands of Turstin Fitz Rou in England and Wales. Lastly, I shall trace the descent of their fiefs and shall reveal the unsuspected origin of the later bearers of their name.

In my *Calendar of Documents preserved in France* (pp. 367–9) I have given abstracts, in English, from the cartulary of the abbey of St. Vincent, of the charters of Hamelin and Winebaud de Ballon (*Baladone*), the former of whom distinctly states that he was born at Ballon, and that his lands in England were given him by William Rufus. Mr. Freeman, although he knew nothing of the tale I am now unfolding, dealt in great detail with the Red King's campaigns in Maine and in Wales,[1] campaigns which must have been responsible, between them, for the settlement in this country of Hamelin and Winebaud de Ballon.

This family must not be confused with that which held, and took its name from, the barony of Bolam in Northumberland. Dugdale treated them, quite properly, as wholly unconnected (vol. I. pp. 453, 680) ; but in the Rolls Series edition of *The Red Book of the Exchequer* the editor (Mr. Hubert Hall) treats the two names as identical and jumbles

---

[1] See his *Reign of William Rufus, passim.*

up the two families (p. 1097). And, by way of further confusing the pedigree, he assumes (one cannot imagine why) that the 'Roger' de Baalun who was still living (if indeed he was) in 1161 is identical with that 'Reginald' de Baalun who occurs 1190–1201.[1]

In a fine passage Mr. Freeman writes as follows of Ballon, when, alone among the fortresses of Maine, it refused to admit the duke of the Normans (1088) :—

The fortress which still held out, one whose name we shall again meet with more than once in the immediate story of the Red King, was a stronghold indeed. About twelve miles north of Le Mans a line of high ground ends to the north in a steep bluff rising above the Cenomannian Orne, the lesser stream of that name which mingles its waters with the Sarthe. . . .[2] The hill forms a prominent feature in the surrounding landscape ; and the view from the height itself, over the wooded plains and gentle hills of Maine, is wide indeed. He who held Ballon against the lord of Normandy, the new lord of Le Mans, might feel how isolated his hill-fort stood in the midst of his enemies. . . . The hill had clearly been a stronghold even from pre-historic times. The neck of the promontory is cut off by a vast ditch, which may have fenced in a Cenomannian fortress in days before Cæsar came. This ditch takes in the little town of Ballon with its church. A second ditch surrounds the castle itself, and is carried fully round it on every side.

Although Duke Robert· succeeded in obtaining

---

[1] It would be unnecessary to refer to the fearful confusion between the lords of Monmouth, descendants of 'Baderon' (see p. 120 above), and the family of 'Balladon,' named "from Baladon a castle in Anjou" (!), in that singular work *The Norman People* (pp. 148, 291), were it not that it is freely cited in the Duchess of Cleveland's excellent *Battle Abbey Roll*, as if an authority.   [2] *William Rufus*, I. 209–211.

possession of Ballon, it was betrayed to William Rufus, ten years later (1098), by the same commander, Payn de Montdoubleau, who had held it against Duke Robert. William placed it in the hands of the famous Robert of Bellême, by whom it was successfully defended on his behalf.

Returning now to this country, we find Hamelin de Ballon giving to the abbey of St. Vincent, not only the endowment for a priory at Abergavenny itself, but " all the tithes of all Wennescoit, both of his own [demesne] and of the lands which he has given or may give [in fee].[1] Here " Wennescoit " appears to stand for " Gwent Iscoed " (lower Gwent) ; but as his territory was upper Gwent, it must represent Gwent Uchcoed. He further gives the churches of 'Capreolum' and 'Luton,' of which we are only told that they were in England. Their identification proved a work of great difficulty, but from later evidence I have satisfied myself that they were Great Cheverel and Great Sutton in Wilts.[2]

As an instance of the difficulties often found in

---

[1] *Calendar of Documents preserved in France*, No. 1046.

[2] These were not held, in 1086, by Turstin Fitz Rou. They are identified by a return in the *Testa de Nevill* (p. 151), where the Honour "de Mortelay" is, we shall find, that of Much Marcle ! From the *Testa* also we learn (pp. 135, 138) that Little Cheverel was held by the earl of Salisbury, which proves, as he was a successor of Ernulf de Hesdin, that the latter's Domesday 'Chevrel' was Little Cheverel. Mr. Jones, in his *Domesday of Wiltshire*, thought that it included both Great and Little Cheverel, but the 'Cheverel' on fo. 64*b*, which he did not identify, may possibly have been Great Cheverel. This would account for its being at the Crown's disposal.

identifying the names in these charters, and of the interesting discoveries to which their solution may lead us, we will now take a gift by Winebaud, the brother of Hamelin, to the same abbey of St. Vincent (? *circ.* 1100).[1] He gives it the churches of 'Torteoda' and 'Augusta' and the tithes of 'Godriton' and 'Pedicovia,' together with the tithes of his lands in Wales. The difficulties here are (1) that there is no clue as to where these places are; (2) that Winebaud is a new-comer, and not the heir of a Domesday tenant, so that Domesday will not help us; (3) that the names, as is so often the case in foreign cartularies, may not be trustworthy. What, for example, can be the places styled 'Augusta' and 'Pedicovia'? The clue is found in 'Torteoda' alone. This was clearly Tortworth, Gloucestershire, which Domesday shows us held by Turstin son of Rou. Following this clue, we discover that 'Pedicovia' is the 'Pidecome'[2] which is found at the head of Turstin's fief in Somerset and is now Pitcombe. But the other two manors can nowhere be found in Turstin's Domesday fiefs. Guided, however, by his name, we discover them in two manors held of the bishop of Worcester by him in Gloucestershire, namely Aust (the 'Austreclive' of Domesday) and Gotherington in Bishop's Cleeve. I would invite special attention to the fact that we here find a newcomer obtaining not merely those manors which Turstin had held *in capite* from the Crown, but also those which he

---

[1] No. 1047.   [2] "vi" having been read for "m."

held from others as a mere under-tenant.[1] One would like to learn by whom Winebaud was placed in the latter capacity in Turstin's shoes.

Keeping, however, to the main point, we find that Winebaud de Ballon was provided for in England out of the fief of Turstin Fitz Rou, which had come, by escheat or forfeiture, into the hands of the Crown. This leads us to the interesting solution of a problem which has hitherto puzzled the experts. Mr. Ellis, an unsurpassed authority on the tenants in Domesday Book, observes that "the fief of Turstin fitz Rou, in 1166, was in the possession of Henry de Newmarch, but in what way it came to him is not apparent."[2] Sir Henry Barkly can only tell us that "Turstin Fitz Rolf's Domesday barony . . . came in some way to the ancestor of the Newmarchs."[3] Here I would observe that Henry de Newmarch held in 1166 two fees from the abbot of Westminster in Worcestershire and Gloucestershire.[4] As Turstin was a tenant of the abbot (1086) in both these counties it is evident that here again his under-tenancies had passed to those who obtained his tenures *in capite*.

The heirship of Newmarch to Winebaud is ex-

---

[1] He was already in possession of them in 1095, for, as Winebald de Balaon, he is found among the tenants of the bishop who were ordered to pay relief in that year (*Feudal England*, p. 309).

[2] "Domesday Tenants of Gloucestershire" (*Bristol and Gloucestershire Arch. Trans.*, vol. IV.

[3] "Testa de Nevill" (*Ibid.* vol. XIV.). 'Newmarch' was the English form of the name 'Neufmarché.'

[4] *Liber Rubeus* (Rolls), p. 188.

THE FAMILY OF BALLON

plained by a charter which Dugdale had seen, but of which the bearing escaped him. He read, in a cartulary of Bermondsey Priory (to which Winebaud de Ballon was a benefactor in 1092) that Henry de Newmarch "ratified all those grants which *Winebald his grandfather*, and likewise Roger and Milo sons of the same Winebald had given."[1] Moreover, a Tewkesbury charter clinches the proof :—

Carta Henrici de Novoforo qua confirmat manerium de Amenel ecclesiæ Theok' quod *Winebaldus de Balun avus suus* ex parte dedit et ex parte vendidit eidem ecclesie primo anno Henrici regis primi, etc.[2]

The place was Amney, Gloucestershire, held as 'Omenie' by Turstin in 1086. These charters are decisive, and give us the following pedigree :—

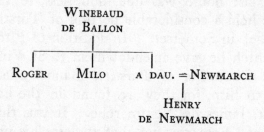

If further confirmation were needed, we should find it in a gift of Winebaud to St. Peter's, Gloucester, with consent of "Roger his son."[3]

The very considerable barony inherited by

---

[1] *Baronage*, I. 435. (The italics are mine.)

[2] *Monasticon*, II. 73, where the charter is followed by a writ of Henry II. in connection with it.

[3] *Cartulary of St. Peter's, Gloucester*, I. 61.

Henry de Newmarch (over 15 knight's fees in
1166) explains his grandfather Winebaud's description of himself as "unus de magnis regis
Henrici post. conquestum primi baronibus" in a
charter of 1126.[1] In spite of this position, Winebaud is scarcely known, while the name of his
brother Hamelin is fairly familiar. This is probably due to the fact that Hamelin founded a
religious house at his stronghold of Abergavenny,
and was consequently commemorated by its monks.
Winebaud, on the contrary, scattered his benefactions. In addition to those to Bermondsey Priory
and to St. Peter's, Gloucester, set out in Dugdale's
Baronage, he bestowed endowments also on St.
Vincent's Abbey at Le Mans [2] and on the Cluniac
Priory of Montacute, Somerset. His patronage
of this last house was due, doubtless, to the fact
that he held a considerable portion of Turstin Fitz
Rou's fief in Somerset.[3] In addition to Pitcombe,
from which he gave an endowment to St. Vincent's,
at least four other of Turstin's manors must have
passed to him, for they are found in the hands of
his heir, James de Neufmarché. It was this possession of a Somerset fief that explains his presence
at the bishop of Bath's court in 1120 or 1121.[4]

---

[1] *Cartulary of St. Peter's, Gloucester*, I. 61.

[2] See above, and my *Calendar of Documents preserved in France*.

[3] Mr. Eyton seems to have been unaware of this (*Domesday
Studies: Somerset*), for he only mentioned that some of Turstin's
manors appear to have gone to his under-tenant, Bernard Pancevolt and his heirs.

[4] *Bath Cartularies* (Somerset Record Society), I. 50. Also
Bigelow's *Placita Anglo-Normannica* (citing Madox's *Exchequer*),

THE FAMILY OF BALLON

His gift to Montacute consisted, according to the cartulary of that house, of "the mill of Cadebiri with the man and the land belonging thereto, and the church of Karion."[1] The mill was at North Cadbury, one of his Somerset manors, but the church of 'Karion' requires interpretation. For that interpretation we must turn to the Book of Llandaff, where we find Pope Honorius (II.) informing Urban bishop of Llandaff that

Winebaldus de Baeluna terram de Cairlion monachis de Monteacuto pro animæ suæ remedio dare disposuit—

and that he is to give them possession accordingly.[2] As this missive is dated from the Lateran 1 June,[3] it cannot be earlier than 1125. The appearance, in this endowment, of Winebaud at Caerleon is of special interest because it is probable, as I said above, that his predecessor Turstin Fitz Rou was there already in 1086.

Winebaud was succeeded by his son Roger, of whom we read under Somerset (where was the *caput* of the barony) in 1161 :—"Rogerius de Baelon debet xxii marcas, sed debet auferri."[4]

p. 114. The document is dated 1121, but the first writ must be previous to the king's son's death in 1120.

[1] Charter of Henry II. (Ed. Somerset Record Society, p. 127).

[2] Register of Llandaff. Book of Llan Dav (1893), pp. 30, 53. See also *Monasticon*, V. 167.

[3] In the text on p. 53 of 'the Book of Llan Dav' it is 'xvi kal. Julii.'

[4] Pipe Roll 7 Hen. II., p. 50. A Roger de Baalon joined with his wife, Hawise (de Gournai) in giving the church of Inglishcombe, Somerset, to Bermondsey Priory. The gift is assigned to 1112, but Hawise belonged to a later generation, so that there seems to be some error.

We have seen above how this barony passed, before 1166, to a branch of the house of Neufmarché, from whom it descended in turn, about the close of John's reign, with the two daughters and co-heirs of James de Neufmarché, of whom one married Ralf Russell of Kingston Russell, thus raising that family to baronial rank,[1] while the other's moiety came to her second husband, Nicholas de Moels, and his heirs.

The statements that Winebaud's brother, Hamelin de Ballon, died "in 3 Will. Rufi" (1089–1090) and that he had "no issue" are alike false. Both brothers are found at the court of Henry I. in 1101, where they witness as "Ego Winebaldus de Baalun, Ego Hamelinus frater ejus."[2] And Hamelin is a witness to a Monmouth charter in 1101 or 1102,[3] and again to one of Henry I., granted between 1103 and 1106.[4] The statement that he died without issue is similarly derived, we saw, from the mendacious narrative of the Abergavenny Priory monks. It is absolutely disproved by his grandson's *carta* in 1166. William son of Reginald, who made his return of knight's fees under Herefordshire, then

---

[1] See below : " The Origin of the Russells."
[2] *Bath Cartularies* (Somerset Record Society), I. 44.   And see on p. 45 their mention in a charter (1100) of Patrick de Sourches, whose origin (like their own) from Maine, together with the true form of his name, I have established in my *Calendar of Documents preserved in France*, p. xlviii.
[3] See the same *Calendar*, p. 408.   [4] *Ibid.* p. 369.

certified that he rendered the service of one knight from his demesne, and that

Hamelinus de Balun, avus suus, feodatus fuit de veteri fefamento ad servitium predicti militis faciendum. Deficit ei Cheverel, quæ est in præcepto domini Regis et honor de Bergeveni, unde deberet servitium suum domino Regi si ei placeret.[1]

The sequel to this return is found, I venture to say, in the following entry on the Fine Roll of 1207 :—

John de Balun dat c marcas et unum palefridum ut finis factus inter Reginaldum de Balun patrem ipsius Johannis et Gaufridum filium Ace et Agnetem uxorem suam de terra que fuit Hamelini de Balun unde cirographum factum fuit inter eos in curia Regis Henrici patris domini Regis teneatur.[2]

The only clue to the locality is that the Roll places it in Wilts. But it was clearly that Great Cheverel, which Hamelin had held as 'Capreolum,' which his grandson stated he had lost possession of, and which John 'de Balon' is found holding under Henry III.[3] It is certain then that what had happened was that Reginald de Ballon, the successor of that William who had made his return in 1166, recovered Cheverel by fine before the death of Henry II. This Reginald was still living in 3 John, when the Pipe Roll shows him, under Herefordshire, holding a knight's fee " quod fuit Willelmi filii Reginaldi.[4]

In the *Testa de Nevill* (p. 151) John ' de Balon '

[1] Black Book text.   [2] Fine Roll, 9 John, m. 11, p. 382.
[3] *Testa de Nevill*, pp. 141, 145, 151.
[4] *Red Book of the Exchequer*, p. 158.₁

is said to hold his Wiltshire fief of the king ' de honore de Mortelay.' The explanation is found on page 68, where we find, under Herefordshire, the " Feoda honoris de Martley," and on page 65, where we finally discover that the place is Much Marcle ('Magna Markele'), where, in 1243, John ' de Balun ' held 15 hides by the service of one knight "de veteri feoffamento." It was for this fief that the return was made in 1166,[1] and it was here, as stated therein, that Hamelin de Ballon had been enfeoffed. We may now, therefore, construct this pedigree.

HAMELIN
DE BALLON
living *temp.* | William II.
and in | 1104

WILLIAM
"son of Reginald "
and grandson of Hamelin
living 1166, 1168
↓
BALLON OF MUCH MARCLE, etc.

At this point, in order to grasp the interest of the genealogical discovery to which we are now coming, we must return to our starting-point, William Fitz Osbern. His great but brief career, and his son's tragic fall, had impressed vividly the world. "Where," cried Orderic Vitalis, " is that William Fitz Osbern, earl of Hereford, and Viceroy [2] (of England), steward of Normandy, and

---

[1] Under Herefordshire.   [2] " Regis vicarius."

leader of knights? Truly he was the first and greatest oppressor of the English. . . . But the just Judge seeth all things. . . . Even as he butchered many with the sword, so hath he himself by the sword perished suddenly." Then, speaking of his son's fall, he tells us of the latter's sons, Reginald and Roger, gallant youths, striving, as he wrote, by arduous service—but striving, as it seemed, in vain—to gain king Henry's favour. "Thus," he added, "William's stock has been so utterly uprooted, that it does not own (unless I am mistaken) a yard of land in England."[1] After this mention, the two brothers disappear so absolutely from view that in a recent genealogical work we read, of Earl Roger, that his "issue was soon extinct."[2]

Let us turn, however, to the cartulary of Godstow, now in the Public Record Office. Under the heading of 'Etona' we find three charters showing how that manor was bestowed on the

---

[1] "Rogerius vero de Britolio comes Herfordensis . . . secundum leges Normannorum judicatus est, et amissa omni hereditate terrena in carcere regis perpetuo damnatus est. . . . Rainaldus et Rogerius filii ejus optimi tirones Henrico regi famulantur, et clementiam ejus (quæ tardissima eis visa est) in duris agonibus præstolantur. . . . Guillelmi progenies eradicata sic est de Anglia ut nec passum pedis (nisi fallor) jam nanciscatur in illa." (Ed. Société de l'histoire de France, II. 264–5.) M. Delisle considers that the 'book' in which this passage occurs was written in 1125, a date of importance for the light it throws on Reginald's age, half a century after his father's fall.

[2] Madan's *Gresleys of Drakelowe* (1899), p. 7. So, too, in the *Complete Peerage* we read that "his issue is said by Ordericus Vitalis to have been (in his time) extinct" (IV. 211).

monastery. Two of them proceed from "Reginald son of Roger earl of Hereford" and Emelina his wife, and the third is a confirmation by "Reginald de Baelun son of Reginald son of the earl"!

(1)

Episcopo Lincolnie et omnibus Sancti Dei ecclesiæ fidelibus, etc. Reginaldus filius Rogeri comitis Herefordiæ et Emelina uxor sua in Christo salutem. Universitati vestræ notum sit me Reginaldum prædicti comitis filium et uxorem meam Emelinam necnon filios et filias meas Willelmum, scilicet, Reginaldum et Hamelinum necnon Agnetem et Julianam, dedisse et concessisse in perpetuam elemosinam sanctimonialibus de Godestow Eatonam manerium meum de p[ropri]o dominio nostro pro salute nostrâ et remedio peccatorum meorum necnon pro animâ Henrici regis etc., et quod teneant et habeant illud bene et in pace sicut nos melius illud habuimus dum in manu nostra fuit, tempore regis Henrici, et postea regis Stephani. Testes : Ricardo de Canvilla, Hugo de Berneriis, Rogerio Britone milites (*sic*) regis.[1]

(2)

Notum sit omnibus me Reginaldum de Baelun Reginaldi filii comitis filium, et Emelinæ de Baelun, concessisse et confirmasse illam donationem quam pater meus et mater mea fecerunt de manerio suo, scilicet Eatona, sanctimonialibus in Godestow in

[1] This and the following charter are printed in the *Monasticon* from Glover's collections only, so that the text is not perfect, while the interesting witnesses and the date are omitted. The third charter in the cartulary is practically the same as the one above with a different address. The charter printed above contains, in the cartulary, this important clause: "cujus [*i.e.* regis Stephani] etiam carta hec nostra donacio confirmata est anno x regni sui, testibus Alexandro episcopo Lincolniensi, et Roberto episcopo Herefordensi, et Roberto priore Oxenfordie, et Waltero archidiacono Oxenfordensi," etc., etc. This gives us a date (1145–6) for the many witnesses named, including Robert (of Cricklade) prior of St. Frideswide's.

perpetuam elemosinam . . . sicut Reginaldus pater meus
melius tenuit dum in manu suâ fuit, et sicut Hamelinus de Baelun
avus meus melius et liberius in vita sua tenuit.   Hiis testibus :
Hugone Brit[one], Hamelino de Baelun, etc.

With this clue we can now identify the mysterious "Raginaldus filius comitis" who was excused
Danegeld on 26 hides in Wilts in 1130,[1] as the son
of Roger earl of Hereford, who held in Great
Cheverel etc. the fief of his father-in-law, Hamelin
de Ballon.[2] The 'Eatona' of these charters is somewhat difficult to identify, as Jones' *Domesday for
Wiltshire* does not help us.   The Record Office, indeed, seems to have been baffled, for, in its recent
Ministers' accounts, it suggests 'Yatton Keynell,' as
the equivalent of ' Etone monialium ' (p. 340 and
Index).   But the Hundred Rolls, together with a
document printed in the *Monasticon*, prove that
the place was Eaton in Stapley Hundred.[3]   Under
the Hundred of Stapley we read in the former (II.
271):—

Item dicunt quod Johannes de Balun tenet 1 feodum militis in
manerio de Eton de Rege in capite pertinens ad baroniam suam.

---

[1] Pipe Roll 31 Hen I., p. 22.
[2] I see no reason to suppose that the earl's son was illegitimate.
Mr. Freeman wrote of him and his brother striving "to merit the
restoration of some part of their father's possessions" (IV. 592), and
Orderic's words imply, surely, that they were his disinherited
children.   The same impression is conveyed by a passage in
Heming's Cartulary (I. 2637) : "filius ejus, paterne hereditatis
parvo tempore dominus, pro traditione quam regi facere voluit
publica custodia mancipatus, omne vite sue explevit tempus ergas-
tulo religatus, *omnisque ejus progenies illa hereditate lege publica pri-
vatus est.*"   [3] In the extreme North-East of Wilts.

Et Abbatissa de Godestouwe tenet dictum manerium de dicto
Johanne in elemosina sed nesciunt quomodo alienat' nec a quo
tempore.[1]

We may now briefly recapitulate what we have
discovered about the fief held by Hamelin de
Ballon.   In addition to Abergavenny and its lordship, he held, in Wiltshire, Great Cheverel, Great
Sutton, and Eaton.   It is this Wiltshire fief which
enables us to trace his heirs for at least two
centuries.   Opposite is the most remarkable pedigree to which that possession leads us.

We saw above (p. 199), that John de Ballon,
living in 1207, was son of a Reginald de Ballon,
who was living under Henry II. ; so that the only
possible question is whether there were two Regi-
nalds, father and son, living under Henry II.
Beyond the fact that the fief was in possession of
a Reginald de Ballon so late as 1201,[2] there is
no reason to presume this, nor would it affect, in
any way, the directness of the descent.[3]   The
head of the Ballons' barony, we have seen, was at
Much Marcle, Herefordshire, and was so at least
as early as 1166.   As it was held of 'the old feoffment,' it must have been given by the Crown
before 1135,[4] but, unfortunately, there is nothing
to show whether it was given, as seems probable,
like the rest of the fief, to Hamelin de Ballon,

[1] His manor of Great Sutton is entered, as half a fee, on p. 277.
[2] As proved by the Pipe Rolls.
[3] When the later Pipe Rolls are in print, they may decide
this point.
[4] See my correction of Mr. Oman, on this most important
date, in *The Commune of London and other studies*, pp. 58-9.

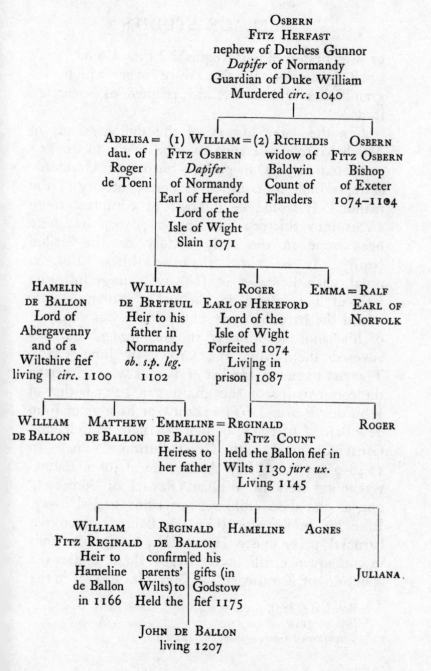

OSBERN
FITZ HERFAST
nephew of Duchess Gunnor
Dapifer of Normandy
Guardian of Duke William
Murdered *circ.* 1040

ADELISA = (1) WILLIAM = (2) RICHILDIS   OSBERN
dau. of   FITZ OSBERN   widow of   FITZ OSBERN
Roger   *Dapifer*   Baldwin   Bishop
de Toeni   of Normandy   Count of   of Exeter
      Earl of Hereford   Flanders   1074–1104
      Lord of the
      Isle of Wight
      Slain 1071

HAMELIN   WILLIAM   ROGER   EMMA = RALF
DE BALLON   DE BRETEUIL   EARL OF HEREFORD   EARL
Lord of   Heir to his   Lord of the   OF
Abergavenny   father in   Isle of Wight   NORFOLK
and of a   Normandy   Forfeited 1074
Wiltshire fief   *ob. s.p. leg.*   Living in
living | *circ.* 1100   1102   prison | 1087

WILLIAM   MATTHEW   EMMELINE = REGINALD   ROGER
DE BALLON   DE BALLON   DE BALLON   FITZ COUNT
              Heiress to   held the Ballon fief in
              her father   Wilts 1130 *jure ux.*
                       Living 1145

WILLIAM   REGINALD   HAMELINE   AGNES
FITZ REGINALD   DE BALLON
Heir to   confirmed his
Hameline   parents'   gifts (in
de Ballon   Wilts) to   Godstow   JULIANA
in 1166   Held the   fief 1175

JOHN DE BALLON
living 1207

PEERAGE STUDIES

or was bestowed on Reginald 'Fitz Count' as a small possession in that shire over which his grandfather and father had reigned as sovereign lords.

For the later history of the Ballons, lords of Much Marcle, reference may be made to Cooke's continuation of Duncombe's history of Hereford-shire,[1] which contains an elaborate history of the manor. It would be difficult to compress more errors into thirteen lines (pp. 2-3) than has here been done in the early history of the Ballon family. It is worse than worthless. But, as usual, with the reign of John we emerge into the light of day. John de 'Balun' of Much Marcle joined the baronial party under John, was deprived of his lands accordingly in July 1216,[2] but re-covered them from the Crown in June 1217.[3] The last name on the list of barons who witnessed the confirmation of the charters in 1225 is that of John de 'Baalun.' The barony or honour of John de 'Balun,' in 1243, included Much Marcle, and Great Cheverel with Great Sutton, Wilts.[4] In 1248-9 (33 Hen. III.), Auda, wife of John 'Balun,' was found heir to William Paynel of Somerset,[5] but, as she died childless, her lands passed away. Like his predecessor John 'de Balun' joined the baronial party under Henry III., losing his lands in consequence, till he recovered them under the 'Dictum' of Kenilworth. This John figures in the

---

[1] Vol. III. (1882), pp. 1 et seq. [2] Close Rolls, II. 278.
[3] *Ibid.* p. 311. [4] *Testa de Nevill.*
[5] *Calendarium Genealogicum*, pp. 22, 23.

THE FAMILY OF BALLON

Hundred Rolls as lord of Much Marcle, etc.,[1] but was succeeded in 1275 by his next brother Walter, who married Isolde daughter of Edmund de Mortimer and wife after his death of Hugh de Audley. Much litigation followed, after Walter's death, between his widow and his next brother and heir, Reginald. There is preserved among the Lansdowne MSS. (No. 905, fos. 80–89b) a series of transcribed deeds relating to Much Marcle in the 13th century, which throw some further light on the Ballons. There are also, at the British Museum, three original charters of some interest. Of these, the first is a feoffment by John de Balon "in manerio meo de Merkelai," which is dated by the name of Maurice de Arundel, archdeacon of Gloucester, as between 1210 and 1245.[2] Another mentions the land of "dominus Walterius de Balun" in Much Marcle,[3] and the third is a charter of "Reginaldus de Balun Dominus de Magna Markeleya," dated 1294.[4] This is of special interest on account of its armorial seal. The official catalogue blazons the coat as " 3 bars dancettées," but I think it is a barry dancetty coat, as indeed it seems to be blazoned on the old Rolls of arms.

It is needless to work out in detail the later pedigree of the family, beyond pointing out that it ended, at Much Marcle, in three brothers, John,

---

[1] See above p. 203. The Inquest for Stapley Hundred was taken in March 1275.
[2] Harl. Cart. 111. D. 18. It has an equestrian seal.
[3] Eg. Cart. 346.   [4] *Ibid.*, 352.

Walter, and Reginald, who were successively its lords. At Michaelmas 1258 John de 'Balun' bestowed an annuity of £10 a year on Reginald de 'Balun' and his heirs,[1] and Walter de 'Balun,' when in possession, leased the manor for three years from 8 September 1285 to Edmund de Mortimer (whose daughter he had married) for £60 a year.[2] How the manor was lost to the Ballons is not quite clear. Edmund de Mortimer, however, did obtain possession of it, and bestowed on his daughter one-third of it (which she was holding in dower), known afterwards as "Purparty Audley," from Audley, her second husband. The remaining two-thirds was known as "Purparty Mortimer." In the *History of Herefordshire*,[3] from which we learn this, it is stated that Reginald de Ballon sold the manor to Mortimer for £500. On the other hand there is an entry which looks as if Reginald, on the contrary, had redeemed the manor for £500 in 1294.[4] But the extraordinary thing is that, nearly two hundred years after they had lost the manor (1490), we find "the manor called 'Audeleys' in Much Marcle, held of John Balom, service unknown."[5] The tendency of the name, on Eng-

---

[1] Lansd. MS. 905, fo. 83*b*.   [2] *Ibid.* fo. 84.

[3] Ed. Cooke *ut supra*.

[4] " Acquietancia Edmundi de Mortuo Mari facta Reginaldo de Babun (*sic*) domino de Magna Markelea pro ccccc libris receptis per ipsum pro redempcione dicti manerii de Markelea " (*Abbreviatio placitorum*, p. 234).

[5] *Calendar of Inquisitions : Henry VII.*, vol. I. p. 46. I have referred to the original, where the words are : " et tenetur de Johanne Balom, sed per quod servicium ignorant."

lish lips, to become corrupted into 'Balom' suggests that, perhaps, through folk-etymology, we may have in some obscure ' Balaam' the heir-male of the body of the great Viceroy of England.

That male descendants of these Ballons, in all probability, exist, is shown by the mention of cadet lines. Apart from a certain John 'de Balun,' a small holder in Much Marcle, who was hanged for felony at the close of Edward I.'s reign,[1] we find there a " dominus Reginaldus de Balun " and John his son in 1290-1 (19 Ed. I.).[2] Now, only three years earlier (16 Ed. I.), a John " filius Reginaldi de Balun" occurs in a good position in Dorset ;[3] and we find that he was an under-tenant of Colbury and Stokk, in Sturminster Newton Castle, Dorset, and that these were held by John ' de Balun' under Edward II.[4] Again, in Hampshire we have Maihel ' de Baalun' occurring as a holder of land in 1168,[5] and Roger 'de Baalun,' its coroner, deceased shortly before 27 Dec. 1225.[6] Here too we have ' John Balom' named in the list of gentry for the county under Henry VI.

But the most interesting younger branch is that which settled in Somerset. In 1166 we meet with Hamelin ' de Baalun' and Mathew ' de Baalun' as tenants by knight-service of Henry de Neufmarché, grandson and heir of Winebald de Ballon in Som-

---

[1] *Calendarium Genealogicum*, and *Calendar of Close Rolls 1307–1313*, p. 110.   [2] Lansd. MS. 905, fo. 86b.
[3] *Abbreviatio rotulorum originalium*, I. 58.
[4] Hutchins' *Dorset*, IV. 340.
[5] Pipe Roll, 14 Henry II., p. 186.   [6] Close Rolls.

erset and elsewhere.[1] In 1199–1200 William de
Neufmarché grants to Hamelin 'de Balun,' in his
court, a mill and land at Cadbury,[2] where Roger
'Balon' seems to have been holding under Henry
III.[3] Their Somerset home, however, was at Dunkerton, some four miles south of Bath, which was
held in Domesday by our old friend Turstin Fitz
Rou.[4] Walter 'de Balun' was installed there in
1256,[5] and Petronilla, his widow, occurs in 1295.[6]
In 1316 John 'Balon' was one of the lords of
'Dunkerton cum Cridelcote' (Credlington),[7]—for
they went together, and so late as 1417–8 (5 Hen.
V.) they were held by John 'Balon.'[8] I have now
given sufficient clues for those who may be interested in the history of the family, after it had sunk
from baronial rank, to follow out its fate by local
research.

We may return, therefore, to the fate of Abergavenny, which, we have seen, did not descend to
the heirs of Hamelin de Ballon. Dugdale's statement that, having no issue, he " gave that castle to
Briene, son to the earl of the Isle, his nephew," is
as erroneous as it can be. The assertion in the
valuable *Complete Peerage*[9] that Hamelin was suc-

---

[1] See p. 195 above.
[2] See p. 197 above. The record is a Somerset fine in the
Somerset Record Society's volume of them, p. 4.
[3] *Calendar of Close Rolls*, 1330–1333, p. 514.
[4] See p. 196 above.
[5] *Bath Cartularies* (Som. Rec. Soc.), I. 71.
[6] Somerset Fines (*Ibid.*), p. 294.   [7] *Nomina villarum.*
[8] Inq. p.m.   [9] Vol. I. p. 12.

ceeded by "Brientius de Insula or de Wallingford,
(his) son and heir," is, if possible, wider of the
mark. Brian—who had nothing to do with the
Isle, but was a natural son of Count Alan of
Britanny—obtained Abergavenny and ' Overwent '
(the appendant district of Upper Gwent) from
Henry I., of whom he was a trusted officer, and
was established there at least as early as 1119,
when we find him named by Pope Calixtus among
the magnates of the diocese of Llandaff.[1] It was
as governor of this district that, as late as 1136,
he escorted Richard (Fitz Gilbert) de Clare on his
way back from England to Cardigan. Giraldus Cam-
brensis, describing his approach to Abergavenny,
from Cardigan, "through that narrow wooded [pass]
known as the evil pass of Coit Wroneu, that is of
the wood of Gronwy," writes :—

Contigit autem paulo post obitum Anglorum regis Henrici
primi, nobilem virum Ricardum Clarensem, qui cum honore de
Clara Kereticam regionem in australi Kambria possidebat ab
Anglia in Walliam hac transire. Et cum provinciæ illius tunc
dominum, Brienum videlicet Gualinfordensem, cum militibus
multis, usque ad passum prædictum socium habuisset et deduc-
torem, tam ipsum invitum [tamen] in ipso silvæ ingressu cum suis
remisit, quam contra ejusdem monita silvam inermis intravit.[2]

Between July 1141 and December 1142 the
empress Maud, to whom Brian was as faithful as
he had been to her father, granted at his request
" and (at that) of Maud de Wallingford his wife,"
that Milo earl of Hereford should hold from them
the castle of Abergavenny, with all its appurtenant

[1] *The Book of Llan Dav*, p. 93.
[2] Ed. Rolls Series, VI. 47–8 (cf. p. 118).

"Honour," by the service of three knights.[1] This Milo had already acquired the lordship of Brecon, adjoining Overwent on the north-west, by his marriage, in 1121, with Sibyl, the daughter of its conqueror, Bernard de Neufmarché.[2]

In the meanwhile, Chepstow, with the lordship of Nether-Gwent, which had passed into the hands of the Crown in 1074,[3] had been bestowed by Henry I. on Walter, a son of Richard de Clare,[4] who there founded Tintern Abbey, and at whose death his possessions passed to his nephew, Gilbert de Clare, first earl of Pembroke or of 'Strigul' (Chepstow). The part taken by the house of Clare in the conquest of South Wales has never yet been worked out, although it was of great importance. In addition to the grant of the present Cardigan to Gilbert the head of the house,[6] a footing was established in Caermarthenshire, under William Rufus, by the Devonshire branch of the family. This most interesting fact seems to have escaped notice. In the *Brut y Tywysogion*[7] we read, under 1096 ('1094'), that—

William, son of Baldwin died, who founded the castle of Rhyd

---

[1] See my *Ancient Charters* (Pipe Roll Society), p. 43, where this charter is fully discussed (pp. 44–5).

[2] *Ibid*. pp. 8–9.   [3] See p. 187 above.

[4] He heads, as 'Walter the son of Richard,' a list of the magnates of the diocese of Llandaff in Oct. 1119, being followed immediately by Brian Fitz Count (*Book of Llan Dav*, p. 93).

[5] See Clare pedigree in my *Feudal England* (facing p. 472), and my *Commune of London* (p. 309), and my article on "The Family of Clare" in *Archæological Journal* (LVI. 221–231).

[6] In 1111, it is said.   [7] Rolls Series.

y Gors by the command of the king of England, and after his death the custodians left the castle empty.

Again, under 1104 (' 1102 '), we find this entry :—

Rickart, son of Baldwin stored the castle of Rhyd y Gors.

Lastly, we are told, under the year 1102 (' 1100'), that Henry I., to gain over the Welsh chieftain Iorweth son of Bleddyn, promised him—

half of Dyved, as the other half had been given to the son of Baldwin.

Mr. Freeman appears to have thought that the important castle of Rhyd-y-Gors, which had successfully resisted a Welsh attack before 1096, was in north-east Wales ; for he wrote that—

Earl Roger meanwhile, from his capital at Shrewsbury and his strong outpost at his new British Montgomery, pushed on his dominion into Powys. The king at least approved if he did not at this stage help in the work ; the castle of Rhyd-y-Gors was built by William son of Baldwin.

[Note]. Was this William son of that Baldwin from whom Montgomery took its Welsh name ? [1]

But in the Brut the castle is associated with the valley of the Towy ('Tywi'), and Sir James Ramsay is doubtless right in placing it " near the town of Caermarthen." [2] Moreover, the noteworthy statement that " half of Dyved " had been given to " the son of Baldwin " must refer to the lord of Rhyd-y-Gors ; and Dyved (Pembrokeshire) adjoined Caermarthenshire.

It is at this point that a knowledge of Norman

---

[1] *William Rufus*, II. 97 (where the marginal heading is " North Wales "). [2] *Foundations of England*, II. 180.

genealogy comes to our help and enables us to identify those sons of Baldwin by whom the above historians were puzzled. It was, as I have elsewhere observed, the habit of the members of the house of Clare to distinguish themselves only by the Christian names of their fathers. The following pedigree will show clearly the connection of this mighty house with the conquest of South Wales.

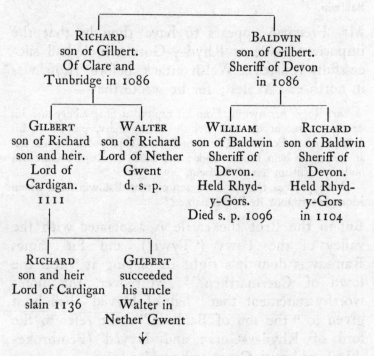

It is possible that Richard son of Baldwin, who was in favour with Henry I in 1102, received from him " half of Dyved " on the forfeiture of Arnulf de Montgomery.

THE FAMILY OF BALLON

We may perhaps find another hint that the Normans invaded Caermarthenshire from Devon in the fact that a small religious house at St. Clears, in the valley of the Taf, was a cell of St. Martin des Champs, which was also the mother house of the priory at Barnstaple opposite. It may be worth noting that the peninsula of Gower, lying to the south of Caermarthenshire, was occupied, according to a Welsh authority, by " Saxons from Somerset " under " Harry Beaumont." It is quite true that this Henry (the first earl of Warwick) did obtain possession of it ; and he founded there the priory of Llangennith as a cell of St. Taurin of Evreux.[1] But I gather from the charter I found at Evreux that he did so earlier than the *Brut* implies, perhaps even before the Conqueror's death.

To complete these notes on the conquest of South Wales, I may point out that " Rickert son of Ponson," who is found in the *Brut y Tywysogion* holding Cantref Bychan, with the castle of Llanymddyvri (Llandovery) in 1115 ('1113'), is no other than the ancestor of the Cliffords, Richard the son of Pons, who held that district—East Caermarthenshire, lying along the east bank of the Towy, between it and Brecon—in 1121 and *circa* 1127.[2]

---

[1] See my *Calendar of Documents preserved in France*, No. 316.

[2] See my *Ancient Charters* (Pipe Roll Society), pp. 8–9, 21. I have proved on the latter page that his wife was a sister of another of the *Conquistadores*, Miles of Gloucester, Lord of Brecknock. His gifts to Malvern of the church of Llandovery (?) and tithes in the district will be found in the *Monasticon*, III. 448.

V

Our English Hapsburgs : a Great Delusion

ROMANTIC in its story, unique in its splendour, the descent of the Feildings, earls of Denbigh, is without a rival in the English Peerage. Their earldom, comparatively ancient (1622) though it be, is, as it were, but a creation of yesterday by the side of that dignity of count of Hapsburg, which they have held for centuries in the male line as members of the proudest and one of the mightiest of the reigning houses of Europe. For it is no mere question of pedigree that is involved in their illustrious descent : the earls, according to *Burke's Peerage*, were counts of Hapsburg, Lauffenburg and Rheinfelden ; an eagle of Austria bears their arms, which are surmounted by the cap of a count of the Empire ; and the name of Rudolph, which the heads of the house have borne now for two generations, keeps before our eyes a descent immortalized by the pen of Gibbon.

Nor is it only in *Burke's Peerage* that this descent was fully recognised.[1] In Dugdale's *Warwickshire*

---

[1] So, in Mr. Shirley's well-known *Noble and Gentlemen of Eng-*

and in his *Baronage* it is accepted as an undoubted fact. It has been recognised, one may say, by the English Crown in the patent of creation for the barony of St. Liz (1664) : it is said to have been always recognised by the emperors of Austria themselves, and is at least, as I am credibly informed, admitted by the reigning sovereign. Indeed, I have seen it stated, on what ought to be good authority, that an earl of Denbigh has been treated by the Imperial Ambassador at Rome " in all respects as a member of the Imperial House," and " as if he was one of the Grand Dukes."

There is no lack of documentary evidence in support of the family claims. In addition to the documents given by Dugdale, many others will be found in the elaborate history of the family, composed for its head in 1670 by the Rev. Nathaniel Wanley, and printed in what is perhaps the best known of our county histories, Nichols' *Leicestershire*.[1]

The story, as I have said, is somewhat romantic. Geoffrey, count of Hapsburg, Laufenburg and Rheinfelden (d. 1271), head of the younger line of

---

land we read :—" The princely extraction of this noble family is well-known ; its ancestor Galfridus, or Geoffrey, came into England in the twelfth year of the reign of Henry III, and received large possessions from that monarch. The name is derived from Rin *felden* in Germany, where, and at Lauffenburg were the patrimonial possessions of the House of Hapsburg."

[1] Vol. IV., Part I., pp. 273-290. It is there stated that there was another similar history of the family executed " before the year 1658," which being sent to London by command of George II., for his inspection, " unfortunately perished by fire."

Hapsburg, is said to have been reduced to comparative poverty by his cousin Rudolph (afterwards the first Hapsburg emperor) and to have sent his son and namesake Geoffrey to England, *temp*. Hen. III. This younger Geoffrey married Maud de Colville over here, took the name of Feilding ("Felden"), and had issue a son and heir Geoffrey, who, by his wife Agnes de Napton, was the direct ancestor of the earls of Denbigh. Geoffrey, the father, returning to Germany, was refused his inheritance for having married Maud de Colville without his family's permission ; and Geoffrey his son, likewise disinherited, eventually (1309) obtained from Count Rudolph, the uncle who had supplanted him, a sum of 7,000 marcs in compensation for his claim on Rheinfelden. The deeds relating to this transaction are carefully preserved by the family.

I have, for some time, been interested in this unique story, because, unless it is wholly false, it must be wholly true, in which case it is difficult to exaggerate the splendour of the claim it involves. A certain John Vincent, of whom we shall hear again, spoke of Feilding's " originall from that greate German family of Hapsburg, that hath produced so many emperors, kings, and great nobility, in many countries of Christendome,"[1] and the worthy Wanley urged their right " to claime alliance with the godds, meaning crowned kings."

But now comes the strange point that first raised my suspicion. I found that although the family

[1] Nichols *ut supra*, 278.

had come here, we are told, under Henry III., their earliest assumption of the German *dignities* seems to have been under Charles II. (1675–1685).[1]

As to the German *descent* it first appears in print, so far as I can find, in Dugdale's *Warwickshire* (1656).[2] In short, as was observed in the *Quarterly Review*,[3] it was only after their lucky rise, through marriage with Buckingham's sister,[4] that, "in due course, the family revealed a fact which they had hitherto kept to themselves, namely that they were not of English origin, but were descended, in the male line, from the mighty house of Hapsburg." Let us turn for proof of this assertion to four sources of information : (1) the family monuments, (2) a glass window put up by the family at their seat, (3) the family pedigrees, (4) the family patents.

On the family monuments and brasses, of which several are recorded, we find neither mention of the Hapsburg descent, nor use of the Hapsburg arms.[5] To the family window of painted glass I attach

---

[1] This is the date of the third earl, in whose time there was executed an engraving of the family seat, on which he was assigned the style of " Comes de Hapsburg, Dom's Loffenburg & Rinfelden in Germania, Baron of Newnham Padox and S^{nt} Liz, Viscount Feilding & Earle of Denbigh in England," etc., etc. It is probably to this that 'Burke' referred when it said that " William, third Earl of Denbigh, resumed the ancient denomination of HAPSBURG, which his descendants still use."

[2] In Burton's *Description of Leicestershire* it had not yet appeared. (See Nichols, p. 251.)   [3] Oct. 1893, p. 390.

[4] See Gardiner's *History of the Civil War* and the *Dictionary of National Biography*, XVIII. 290.

[5] See Dugdale's *Warwickshire* and Nichols' *Leicestershire*.

considerable importance. It may be remembered
that the famous imposture by which the Cambridgeshire Stewarts were derived from the Royal
Stuarts of Scotland was supported by a similar glass
window, which was made to confirm the descent.
The Feilding window was put up (or at least com-
pleted), it would seem, about the close of the
sixteenth century, for the first Lord Denbigh's
parents are the last members of the family that it
depicts. Erected *ad majorem gloriam gentis*, we
might fairly expect it to make the most of their
pedigree, especially at a period, in these matters, so
unscrupulous. Yet it only begins with Geoffrey
Feilding, who married Agnes de Napton, an heiress,
under Ed. II. or Ed. III. Coming now to our
third source—the pedigrees, we find the Visitation
Pedigree of 1563 [1] beginning in the same way with
this Geoffrey and Agnes. The Visitation of 1619
raises a difficult question. The copy of this Visitation among the Harleian MSS. is in the actual
handwriting of Sampson Lennard, Bluemantle, and
bears his arms upon the cover, as we learn from
the official catalogue. Now he was one of the
deputies who actually took this Visitation for Camden. We may therefore claim this MS. as the
very best authority. Humphrey Wanley, to whom,
I believe, we owe the long note on it in the official
catalogue, discusses its relation to the College copy
(C. 7), which is less full, and, in that sense, imperfect. This discussion is worth reading by all who
are interested in the genesis and *modus operandi* of

[1] Coll. Arm. G. xi., fo. 46 ; H. xii., fo. 31.

Visitations. Now the Feilding pedigree, which is duly found in Bluemantle's own copy,[1] is here carried back for two generations to a "John Feldinge," but an alternative descent is also entered as "out of Mr. Feilding's pedigree." This carries back the descent from Geoffrey and Agnes for *nine* generations (!), and is one of those familiar concoctions that nobody nowadays accepts. Its only value lies in its witness that the family were already trying to get beyond Geoffrey, though the glorious vision of Hapsburg had not yet burst upon their view.

Turning next to our fourth source, a comparison of the family patents of creation leads us to the same conclusion. The original patent for the barony (30 Dec. 1620) recites that "Willelmus Feilding miles genere et nomine clarus et illustris ex antiquâ Willingtoniorum quondam baronum hujus regni familiâ per multas baronum et equitum auratorum successiones oriundus est."[2] This claim can scarcely be said to err on the side of modesty, for according even to Dugdale, the panegyrist of the family, the new peer's ancestor was William Willington, "a wealthy merchant of the staple," who bought a property at Barcheston, Warwickshire, 14 Sept. 23 Hen. VII., "depopulated the town" in the following year, and died in 1555.[3]

---

[1] See the Harl. Soc. edition of the *Warwickshire Visitation* (1619).   [2] Nichols, 289.

[3] See, for details of the depopulation (in 1509), Mr. Leadam's *Domesday of Enclosures*, II. 416–7 :—"quasi totum hamelettum de Barcheston desolatur et adnichilatur . . . et 24 persone de suis mansionibus expelluntur et lacrimose de victu et opere evitantur et sic in miseria perducuntur."

According to Dugdale, he was

son to John Willington of Todnam in Gloucestershire, and he
of William Willington of the same place, son of another John ;
descended, *as 'tis probable*, from that Ralph de Wylinton, who
lived in E. 1 time, of which line *I conceive that* John de Wylinton
and Ralph de Wylinton were, who in the times of King Edward 3
and Ric. 2 had successively summons to Parliament amongst the
Barons of this Realm. [1]

So much for the long succession of barons and
equites aurati from whom, according to this vera-
cious patent, Lord Feilding derived his descent.
But even in this patent there is, we see, no trace
of the Hapsburg claim. Nor is it found two years
later, when the earldom was created (1622). But
when we come to the St. Liz patent of 1664, we
read :—

> Cum Basilius comes Denbigh a celeberrima et antiquissima
> prosapia comitum de Hapsburg in Germania, per Galfridum
> quondam comitem de Hapsburg oriundus, etc., etc. [2]

Having thus made good my point that, in England, this splendid descent was not revealed till
about the middle of the seventeenth century, I
shall now show that on the *German* side the alleged
descent has not been recognised by historical or
antiquarian authorities, nor even by the House of
Austria itself, as alleged, in the past.

I select for this purpose three typical authorities
from the seventeenth, the eighteenth, and the nineteenth centuries. The first of these is Francis
Guilliman, whose *Habsburgica* dedicated to the
then emperor Rudolf, was published in 1609. I

---

[1] *Warwickshire* (1730), 601.   [2] Nichols, 291.

have quoted from the revised edition of 1696.
The title runs :—

Francisci Guillimanni Habsburgisca
sive de antiqua et vera origine domus Austriæ
*   *   *   *
Ad Rudolfum II
Habsburgi—Austriacum Imperatorem semper Augustum (Editio
nova, a plurimis mendis purgata).
Ratisbonæ . . . 1696.

The subject was taken up where Guilliman left
it by a writer of unimpeachable, because official
authority. I allude to the great work of Herrgot,
the Imperial Historiographer, based on original
documents throughout. It was executed for and
dedicated to the emperor Charles.

Genealogia Diplomatica Augustæ gentis Hapsburgicæ, quâ
continentur vera gentis hujus exordia, antiquitates, propagationes,
possessiones, et prærogativæ, chartis ac diplomatibus maxima
parte ineditis asserta . . . opera et studio R. P. Marquardi
Herrgot . . . sacræ Cæsareæ Regiæquæ Catholicæ Majestatis
Consiliarii et Historiographi . . . Viennæ . . . 1737.
[Dedication]
Augusto Cæsari Carolo Hapsburgensi D. Leopoldi F. patriæ
patri optimo maximo.

Guilliman devotes his seventh book to the counts
of Hapsburg of the Laufenburg line, and, combining his work with that of Herrgot, the pedigree
runs as shown on the next page :—
The scene of our story, it is needful to explain,
is on the south or Swiss bank of the Rhine from
Basle on the west to Constance on the east.
Ascending the river eastwards from Basle, we first
pass the town of Rheinfelden—of which more

PEERAGE STUDIES

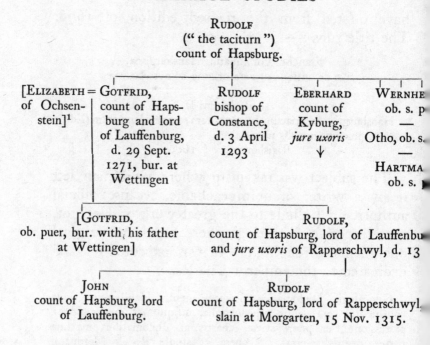

RUDOLF
("the taciturn")
count of Hapsburg.

[ELIZABETH = GOTFRID,   RUDOLF   EBERHARD   WERNHE
of Ochsen-   count of Haps-   bishop of   count of   ob. s. p
stein][1]   burg and lord   Constance,   Kyburg,   —
    of Lauffenburg,   d. 3 April   *jure uxoris*   Otho, ob. s.
    d. 29 Sept.   1293   ↓   —
    1271, bur. at   HARTMA
    Wettingen   ob. s.

[GOTFRID,   RUDOLF,
ob. puer, bur. with his father   count of Hapsburg, lord of Lauffenbu
at Wettingen]   and *jure uxoris* of Rapperschwyl, d. 13

JOHN   RUDOLF
count of Hapsburg, lord   count of Hapsburg, lord of Rapperschwyl
of Lauffenburg.   slain at Morgarten, 15 Nov. 1315.

anon—then Säckingen, the site of an abbey, with
which the Hapsburgs were connected, and lastly
Laufenburg, the "castle of the rapids," the pic-
turesque and ancestral home of our counts.

Their line was founded by Rudolf, "the Taciturn" (d. 1249), from whose elder brother descended the Hapsburg emperors of Austria. With
Gotfrid, his son and heir, our story begins. This
Gotfrid was lord of Laufenburg, which he held of
the abbey of Säckingen. In one document he
occurs as "comes de Laufenburg" (1258); in all
others as "dominus Lauffenburgi," or count of
Hapsburg only. Guilliman assigns him Elizabeth

[1] In Guilliman only.

224

Ochsenstein as a wife : Herrgot says the fact rests
on Guilliman's authority alone. By the latter he
is assigned two sons, Gotfrid (the Feildings' alleged
ancestor), who, dying shortly after his father, was
buried at Wettingen in the same grave, and
Rudolf,—both of them left in ward to their uncle,
Bishop Rudolf.[1] Herrgot ignores Gotfrid altogether (p. 236)—probably from his dying too
young to be mentioned in any documents. That,
in any case, he cannot long have survived his
father is shown by an important deed of 1274,
printed by Herrgot,[2] from the archives of Wettingen,[3] which runs : " per legitimum. tutorem aut
tutores *Ruodolfi* domicelli nostri, filii videlicet bonæ
memoriæ Comitis Goetfridi."

Herrgot lays special stress on the fact that this
Rudolf alone continued the line :—

> totam progeniem lineæ Lauffenburgo—Habsburgicæ, absque
> controversiâ, Rudolpho ejus [Gotfridi] filio, de quo hic agimus,
> esse adscribendam.

Rudolf remained in ward till 1288,[4] and we
have accordingly a deed, of 5 June 1287, printed
by Herrgot " ex Archivo Wettingensi,"[5] in which
the bishop, his uncle and namesake, styles himself—

---

[1] " Uxor fuit Elisabetha Ochsensteinia. Ex quâ filii Gotfridus, qui paullo post patrem excedens, eodem tumulo insertus
est, et Rudolfus : uterque sub tutelâ Rudolfi præpositi et post
episcopi, patrui," p. 549.   [2] p. 447.

[3] The great abbey of Wettingen, the burying-place of the
family, is situated on the line from Basle to Zurich, considerably
south of the Rhine.

[4] *Allgemeine Deutsche Biographie.*   [5] DCXLII., p. 533.

R. dei gratia Constantiensis episcopus, tutor pupilli R[udolfi] Comitis de Hapsburg.

and refers " prædicto R[udolfo] Comiti nostro nepoti." This long minority, Herrgot observes, greatly improved the family estate.

I now pass to my third authority, representing the results of the latest German research on the subject (1879). This is the article on the house of " Hapsburg-Laufenburg " in the *Allgemeine Deutsche Biographie* (vol. X. p. 284), which is based on the monographs of Münch in *Argovia*, the local historical organ, supplementing Herrgot's work. The pedigree there given is as follows :—

RUDOLF
the Taciturn, of Laufenburg,
d. 6 July, 1249
|
GOTTFRIED
of Laufenburg,
d. 1271
|

RUDOLF, of Laufenburg (and afterwards = Elizabeth, heiress of of Rapperschwyl, *jure uxoris*), b. 15 July Rapperschwyl, widow 1270, in ward to his uncles till 1288. of Ludwig von Homberg, mar. 1296.

It is here positively stated that Rudolf was the *only* son (" der name H[apsburg] L[aufenburg] blieb jetzt dem *einzigen* am 15 July 1270 geborenen, *Sohne* Graf Gottfrieds I, Rudolf III "). The Feildings' alleged ancestor is wholly ignored ; and Rheinfelden is not included in the possessions assigned to the house. The date of Rudolf's birth, which this article gives us, explains his long

minority from 1271 to 1288. Had the original
concoctor of the pedigree known of these dates,
he would have hesitated to make Rudolf's *brother*
come to England under Henry III. (1216–72).

Now, bearing in mind the true pedigree, as
given by the German authorities, let us see how
the original concoctor of the Feildings' spurious
pedigree set to work. He had to affiliate their
undoubted ancestor and founder of their house,
Geoffrey Feilding, husband of the Napton heiress,
who must have lived under Edward II. and Edward
III. For this purpose he boldly pitched upon
Gotfried,[1] the son of Count Gotfried, who died,
according to Guilliman, just after his father.
Probably, as I have said, he was unaware that Gotfried was an infant at his father's death (1271) and
that his brother, as we know now, was only born
in 1270. Wanley had read, it is true, in Bucel-
linus :—" Gotfridus secundus obiit in juventute " ;
but he got over this difficulty by holding that this
" *juventus*, in the gradations of the yeares of man,
may be extended to the period of fourty yeares " !
This enabled him to assign to Gotfried a career of
which, on the German side, there is no trace.
Bringing him to England, in his father's lifetime,
at some unspecified date in the reign of Henry III.
(1216–1272), he made him there marry Matilda
de Colville and have children. Then, at a date
equally unspecified, he made him return to Germany, to satisfy the authorities who say that he
was buried at Wettingen. A difficulty faced him,

[1] See pedigree, *supra* p. 224.

of course, in the fact that in *all* the English documents the Christian name is " *Gal*fridus," and in *all* the German ones " *Got*fridus." The two names might occasionally be confused, but such unanimity as this cannot be explained away. He got over it, however, by simply converting every "Gotfridus" of the house of Hapsburg into "Galfridus."[1]

But the chief obstacle, of course, in his way was the utter absence of any evidence for his story, combined with the utter ignoring of it by every German authority. Now I shall not profess to state each step in the growth and development of the legend. I can only take the alleged proofs as they stand. First, then, in an evil hour for himself, the concoctor endeavoured thus to explain the name of Feilding :—

> Memorandum quod Galfridus Comes Hapsburgicus propter oppressiones sibi illatas a Comite Rodolpho, qui postea electus erat Imperator, ad summam paupertatem redactus, unus ex filiis suis, nomine Galfridus militavit in Anglia sub Rege Henrico tertio. Et quia pater ejus Galfridus Comes habuit pretensiones ad certa dominia in Lauffenburg & Rinfelden, *retinuit sibi nomen de felden*, *Anglice Filding.*

Dugdale, who printed this " Memorandum " in his *History of Warwickshire*,[2] declared the MS. to be " written about K. Edward 4 time," but, even if genuine, the style of the handwriting, it will be found, is of the time of Henry VIII. We shall see that this unlucky derivation has

---

[1] Compare the similar conversion of the Scottish Stewarts into Stywards on p. 140 above.   [2] (2nd Ed.) I. 86.

proved fatal to the whole imposture. In the meanwhile, we may note that the excellent Wanley was somewhat puzzled by the occurrence of a "Feilding" at Lutterworth (their abode) before the arrival of the mysterious German, the alleged founder of the family ;[1] but he suggested that perhaps the exile adopted Feilding as " by a double reflection the fittest surname for this family " !

Let me now enumerate the deeds and documents on which rests the alleged descent :—

(a) Six German deeds, namely, two of 1307, two of 1309, and two of 1365.[2]

(b) Eleven English deeds (as I reckon them) of the fourteenth century.

(c) Several English documents or memoranda (printed in Dugdale's *Warwickshire* and Nichols' *Leicestershire*).[3]

Taking these in order, I begin with the German deeds. The first point to strike the expert is a strange air of unreality, a sense of there being " something wrong " ; the expressions are strange, the language unusual. The next point is that their concoctor has overdone his part : in his extreme anxiety to introduce the story of Count Geoffrey's settlement in England, in his eagerness to connect the name of Feilding, through Felden, with Rheinfelden, he has shown his hand too plainly and only raised our strong suspicions. The

---

[1] Nichols, pp. 278–9
[2] All in Nichols (pp. 280, 281, 286).
[3] Two in Dugdale (p. 86), the rest in Nichols.

third point is that " Germania " is used throughout for Germany, whereas the right name, in deeds
and documents of the time, is, of course, " Ale-
mania." I may add that, as we might expect,
"family" is rendered " familia " !

Let us, however, examine in detail the first two
charters. Wanley describes them as being "jointly
in one deed," but the first is dated at Säckingen
" primo kalend' Junii" (!) 1307, and the second at
Rheinfelden " decimo kalend' Decembris," 1307.
In the first of these documents, John " de Rot-
bery," as " procurator specialiter delegatus " for
the abbey of Säckingen, testifies that John
" Steine," the " servus familiaris " of the exiled
noble's son and heir, has come to claim on his behalf "omnia dominia, feoda, et servitia tam in
comitatu de Rhynfelden quam in diversis aliis locis
in Germania," and that the Abbess and Convent
can only pray to God " et omni curie celestium
animarum " (!)

ut exaltent illum ad dignitates non indignas viro tam alti san-
guinis, ut qui a longa serie comitum et principum de Hapsburg,
tandem a primis Francorum regibus genus suum deducens, mereatur
honorem et estimationem in illo glorioso regno Angliæ, sicut justum
et decorum esse videatur.

This extract may serve as a sample of these
ridiculous documents, of which the dog-Latin is
at times exquisitely funny. But their concoctor
might at least have avoided introducing into those
of 1307 the clause " regnante domino *Adolpho*
Imperatore," considering that the Emperor Adolph
had died in 1298—nine years before !

The hand of the forger stands revealed.

After this it is useless to waste time over the deeds of 1309, of which the first has the seal, alas ! "broken off from the label." This reminds us that the abbess of Säckingen had, we are told, reasons of her own for not affixing her seal to the first of these deeds, so that her proctor used his own by her orders (" ex ordine suo "). So with the two deeds of 1365, of the first of which we read that " the bishop's seal was, by the motions of several journeys broken off, but exactly copied out before." The last of these documents has, indeed, the seal of " Sir George Hirschorn, knight," still " entire " ; but this proves to be only a fancy rebus on his name, which anyone could invent. It is singular that an English deed (2 Ed. III.) of considerable importance for the descent " had the seal of the eagle affixed to it, but by accident broke off" (p. 284). Another English deed (28 Ed. III.) was " so defaced as not thought fit to be made use of amongst other evidences whose originals remain so clear and entire[1] especially since the seal, which had the impression of a lion rampant, in its passage from London into Warwickshire, was unfortunately thrown into the water with the sumpter-horse, wherein it was (as also by the motion of the horse) broken off and mouldered to nothing ; the type of which seal was taken long before, and remains yet in the earl of Denbigh's Book of Evidences." How provoking these seals were !

[1] No doubt !

There was a deed of 3 Ric. II. which " had affixed to it the seal of an eagle," which is what we want, but—" by often removals broken off, though before entered into the earl of Denbigh's Book of Evidences " (p. 285). How prescient it was to enter these seals, and how invaluable are the entries now !

But to return to the German deeds or " 1365," which are respectively dated " tertio die mensis Martii " and " tertio Calend' Martii "—rather an awkward combination (p. 286). I must explain at the outset that though they are composed in the same queer Latin as the others, they ought to be in old German. Herrgot prints, in his great work, some seventy charters for the period 1360–1390 ; they relate to the same parties as these two documents, the duke of Austria, bishop of Basle, counts of Hapsburg, etc., etc., and, *without one exception*, they are all in old German. But doubt-less old German was more than the forger could attempt. The story these deeds tell is really rather a clever one. They relate to " William Filding, Esq., of Lutterworth," whom they trans-form into " Willielmus de Hapsburg, natione Anglus vocatus autem in Angliâ *Felden*, ex antiquâ prosapiâ comitum et principum de Hapsburg in Germania oriundus." According to them, " post multas devastationes ab Anglicis commissas in Alsatiâ et aliis partibus Germaniæ," this William " in illo exercitu[1] prefectus equitum," was taken prisoner, " fortiter dimicans," near the Rhine, by

---

[1] " in exercitu Anglorum," in the other deed.

the bishop of Basle's men. His alleged kinsman, Duke Leopold of Austria, heard that he was undergoing greater hardships " quam convenire poterit dignitate (*sic*) Germanicæ gentis, vel nataliis ipsius Willielmi, qui ab antiquis comitibus de Hapsburg originem suam deducit." He intervened, therefore, to help him in his distress (" in tempore distressus sui " !), and procure his liberation at the hands of the bishop. Now, what, it may be asked, could an English army be doing at this time in Alsace ? Well, a celebrated leader of the time, Enguerrand de Coucy, Earl of Bedford, and Knight of the Garter, son-in-law of Edward III., maternal grandson of Duke Leopold of Austria, and son of the proudest baron in Europe, raised an army to enforce his claims, through his mother, on Austria, in which was comprised a picked force of 6,000 Englishmen. Hence this army was known as the " English " bands, and the scene of its defeat between Basle and Lucerne is still known as " the English Barrow." Moreover, it actually did march to the banks of the Rhine, and—through Alsace— into Switzerland. But, alas, all this took place, not in 1365, but in 1375, and the ingenious forger has clearly confused it with the raid of Cernola's French freebooters in 1365 ! This is sad, for had he only made his document quite accurate, it would have gone far to support the Hapsburg claim.

Passing to the English deeds and documents, I select, as the simplest test, their mention, among the family dignities, of Rheinfelden. The best known, probably, of these evidences is that letter of attorney of 1316 (9 Ed. II.), in which Geoffrey Feilding (the real ancestor, as I term him) styles his grandfather " Comes de Hapsburg et Dominus in Laufenburg et Rinfilding in Germania." For, Dugdale having selected it for insertion in his *Warwickshire* and his *Baronage*, it found its way into Collins' *Peerage*, etc., etc. The attempt to make the name of the place approximate to that of the family will, of course, be observed. The same form recurs in a deed assigned to Geoffrey, his alleged father (the one who came to England *temp.* Hen. III.).[1] There are several other of these documents in which the name is found ; and in two of them at least the style runs, not " dominus," but " *Comes* de Hapsburg, Laffenberg & Rinfelden "—which is that used by the Feilding family. If it can be shown that the Hapsburgs of Laufenburg were neither lords nor counts of Rheinfelden, and did not so style themselves, these documents are, obviously, forgeries. I turn, therefore, to the German authorities for information on the subject.

In his chapter " de dominio et burggraviatu Rhinfeldensi,"[2] Herrgot, who elsewhere tersely says : " in nostris monumentis nullus occurrit Comes Rhinfeldensis," discusses the early history of Rheinfelden, and shows that the town, at an early period, belonged directly to the Emperor. An imperial charter of 1225 guaranteed this

[1] Nichols, 277.   [2] Lib. I. cap. xi.

position, and promised that the town should not be severed from the imperial domain.[1] Accordingly in June 1243 we find it administered by Ulric de Liebenburg " Sacri Imperii Ministerialis et Burgravius in Rinfelden."[2] So again we find the emperor Rudolf granting liberties to " omnes nostros de Rinvelden " (31 July 1276).[3] It would, therefore, he observes, be waste of time to discuss the supposition that the Laufenburg counts had any connection with Rheinfelden. And indeed in his vast collection of charters relating to the family, there is not one to be found in which they occur as lords of it, or claim any rights over it. Guilliman had written no less positively:—

De Hapsburgi Comitibus qui ad avitum præter Lauffenberg dominium nihil tituli addiderunt . . . Hapsburgi comitum nomen retinuerunt, neque ad id adjunxerunt aliud, quam ex Lauffenbergo oppido Rheni denominationem."

Lastly, the *Allgemeine Deutsche Biographie* (1879), enumerating the possessions of these Hapsburg counts, wholly omits Rheinfelden, and gives Laufenburg as their residence, till their marriage with the heiress of Rapperschwyl made them occasionally reside there also. This point is the more important because the second, third and fourth of the spurious *German* deeds are all dated from Rheinfelden, an obvious attempt to introduce the name which has merely increased the evidence against them.[4]

[1] Vol. II. p. 231.   [2] *Ibid*. p. 269.   [3] p. 269.
[4] I mean the deeds professing to be German in origin, not in language.

But how, it may be asked, did the daring concoctor come to make Rheinfelden the keystone of his story ? This raises the difficult question whether Rheinfelden was merely introduced to patch together a connection between Feilding and Hapsburg, or was itself the origin of the whole story by the tempting termination Rhein*felden*. In either case he had clearly got hold of some foreign work which assigned Rheinfelden, in error, to the Laufenburg Hapsburgs. Exactly such a work is found in the *Basilikon* of Elias Reusnerus, of which the first edition was published in 1592, and which is actually referred to throughout by Wanley.[1]

Now this writer gives us (p. 26) the following pedigree (see next page) :—

But, indeed, even Wanley tacitly rejects this erroneous pedigree, and points out that Reusnerus had confused Gotfrid [d. 1271], who fought against Berne, with his son. Yet it is to such untrustworthy writers that we are referred throughout, and when appeal is made to the *Annales Murenses* for confirmation,[2] we find they do not include Rheinfelden among the family possessions.

We may therefore safely reject every Feilding deed or document in which Rheinfelden occurs ; and difficult—almost impossible—though it be to

[1] His general reference at the end is to " Hemminges, Reusnerus, Albicius, Bucelinus, and all the German writers on this subject as well ancient as modern " (Nichols, 290) !

[2] Nichols, 265.

RODOLPHUS TACITURNUS Comes Habsburgius, facta divisione cum fratre, Lauffenburgi et *Rhynfeldæ* sortitus est comitatus, cum Advocatia Seckingensi . . . tandem a fratruelo Rudolpho Cesare [1] . . . proscriptus, obiit in exilio.

EBERHARDUS, etc., etc.	GOTOFRIDUS Comes Hapsburgius Dynasta Lauffenburgi & *Rhynfeldæ*. Naturæ concessit 1271. Tumulatus Wettingæ.	RUDOLPHUS Episcopus Constantensis, etc., etc.

JOANNES I. Comes Hapsburgius et Lauffenburgius in cænobio Wettingensi prope fratrem sepultus. Uxor N. Comitissa á Niddar.	GOTOFRIDUS II. Comes Lauffenburgius et *Rhynfeldensis* Bernates . . . bello aggresus aliquamdiu quidem afflixit, sed . . . arma vertit in Rudolphum Augustum . . . In quo sane bello occubuit. Sepultus in cænobio Wettingensi.
JOANNES II. Comes Hapsburgi et Kiburgi. ↓	RUDOLPHUS II. Comes Lauffenburgi, Palatinus Burgundiæ . . . [ob.] 1314.

[To show how wildly erroneous is this pedigree, I need only print its outline by the side of the true one :—]

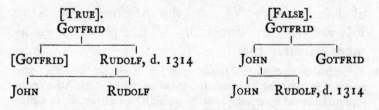

[TRUE]. GOTFRID	[FALSE]. GOTFRID
[GOTFRID] RUDOLF, d. 1314	JOHN GOTFRID
JOHN RUDOLF	JOHN RUDOLF, d. 1314

---

[1] Rudolph, of course, was not emperor till many years after the count's death.

believe that all these evidences were forged to prove the pedigree, the facts leave us no alternative to this astounding conclusion.

I now pass from the pedigree to the arms.

Strenuous efforts were made by those who were responsible for the Hapsburg descent to connect the arms of Fielding with those of Hapsburg. The former are " Arg. on a fess Az. three lozenges Or," the latter, " Or a lion rampant Gu." (now " ducally crowned Az."). The attempt to prove the user of the latter having virtually failed, another line was adopted. The arms of Austria—which are quite distinct from those of Hapsburg and are now borne, separate, by their side on the emperor's shield—were pressed into the service. These are Gu. a fess Arg. It is needful to remember that the *Laufenburg* Hapsburgs had nothing to do with Austria, and of course (as their seals prove), did not use its arms. Undaunted, however, the bold concoctor produced a document " Extract' ex antiquis historicis et evidenciis comitum de Hapsburg,"[1] of which " the handwriting cannot be of lesser antiquity than the latter end of King Henry VI., or the beginning of King Edward IV. of England." This precious document narrates that :—

Galfridus comes de Hapsburg filius Rodulphi comitis, cum ambiret in uxorem Margaretam viduam et hæredem Austriæ, in signum amorosi obsequii [!] sæpe in hidis equestribus et in sigillis usitare solitus erat tramitem cum tribus cuneis ornatum, postpositis armis suis gentilitiis, scilicet leone.[2]

---

[1] Nichols, 276.
[2] It will be observed that this story is curiously parallel to that

Then it goes on to say how he sent his son Geoffrey, "tunc exutum patrimonio in comitatu *Rinfeldensi*," to England, *temp*. Hen. III. A variant (in English) of this document is quoted by Nichols (p. 251) "from a MS. written about the middle of the seventeenth century"—a significant date. Wanley follows it by some sapient remarks, with which should be compared those he makes on p. 286. As to the palm tree crest now used by the family, he opines (p. 275) that it may refer to a tournament " in the time of Frederick the Second," at which their ancestor was " said to carry away the palme " !

I do not undertake to identify positively the original culprit (or culprits) in this colossal imposture. According, indeed, to Dugdale, the belief is of great antiquity : but where the whole evidence is so tainted with forgery, one cannot be blamed for looking on every document with suspicion. I cannot at present find that the claim was advanced even by the first earl of Denbigh ; but when we come to his son, the second earl (1643–1675), we find him identified with it at every point. It was by his command that Nathaniel Wanley drew up the family history ; it was in his time that Dugdale was induced to publish the claim for the first time, in his *Warwickshire* and *Baronage* ; it was he who obtained the St. Liz Patent, in 1664, containing a formal re-

which was concocted by the Cambridgeshire Stywards to account for their bearing a lion coat instead of the fess of their alleged ancestors, the "royal Stewarts" (see pp. 138–141).

cognition of the claim ;[1] it was he who put up, at his family seat, a window, introducing for the first time, as it seems, the palm tree crest ;[2] it was he who corresponded, we shall find, with Ashmole (1670) about the Hapsburg claim ; it was he (*I am told*) who subscribed to rebuilding the College of Arms, and thus secured the entry in the book of " benefactors " of his Hapsburg descent ; and it was he who employed John Vincent, that " needy, seedy " man, as I have heard him described, in connection with it. For we find an entry by Vincent in Lord Denbigh's *Book of Evidences*, concerning a chimney-piece he had seen at Lutterworth in 1665, " having some relation to the renowned family of Hapsburg, from whence the right eminent family of Feildings thereabouts (most truly and clearly deriving their discent) doe very frequently use a lyon rampant crowned in theire seales."[3]

Now this clue is worth following up, for John

---

[1] *Ante*, p. 195. This title represented his claim to descend from St. Liz, earl of Northampton, through the Seytons (who were alleged to be "*alias* St. Liz "). As G. E. C. points out, under Denbigh, he held already a barony of earlier date (1620), which renders strange his desire for this one. But besides gratifying his evident craving for ancient descent, it gave him (as a friend has pointed out to me) the opportunity of introducing the Hapsburg claim into the patent.

[2] He also introduced an eagle crest. Dugdale asserts (*Warwickshire*, I. 87) that they had used " for their crest sometime an *Eagle*, and at other a *Palm Tree*, though of later times alterned." But the old glass window and the Visitation pedigrees show only the true crest, a nuthatch with a fructed bough.

[3] Nichols, 278. This makes an important addition to the memoir of Vincent by Nicholas, in which it is stated (p. 100) that " no trace has been found " of him after 1653.

was the son of Augustine Vincent, and inherited his heraldic collections. According to Noble,—

John Vincent was . . . a good genealogist, herald, and antiquary; but so ill an economist and so fond of liquor that he frequently pawned some of his father's literary labours to pay tavern expences.[1]

This character may be derived from a remark by Anthony à Wood, in a letter of 14 October 1685, on the Sheldon MSS. (now among the treasures of the College of Arms):—[2]

John Vincent, the sometime owner of them, had pawned several of them in alehouses before he died.[3]

A further statement of Anthony à Wood serves to clinch the connection :—

You must know that John Vincent was a boone companion and a great company keeper with noblemen, *especially with Basil Earl of Denbigh*, and being always inquisitive and happy in a good manner might learn these things.[4]

Have we then in John Vincent the clever forger, who—as Meschini in *Sant' Ilario* forged the documents for Prince Montevarchi—supplied the too ambitious Earl with the evidences he required We cannot say, as yet, for certain; but if Marlowe died in a tavern brawl, there is nothing, perhaps, derogatory in the thought that the Hapsburg evidences may have been concocted to pay for pots of ale.

[1] *History of the College of Arms*, p. 241.
[2] Nicolas terms it " that unrivalled collection."
[3] Nicolas, *Memoir of Augustine Vincent*, p. 99.
[4] *Harl. MS.* 1056, fo. 44 (Nicolas, p. 94).

Now that we have so closely identified the second earl with the Hapsburg claim, we can approach the very remarkable letter he wrote to Ashmole, 26 June 1670 :—

. . . The other day, ransacking among my papers, I found three letters from Prince Thomas of Savoy ; one of them I send you inclosed to be restored at our next meetings, wherein hee stiles me his cosen. This putt me in minde of the curious serche Duke Vittorio Amadeo, the eldest Prince of that family, made after my armes and descent both in my private travells and when I was the late Kings amb^r of glorious memory with his highnesse, who asking me which were the cristen names of my ancestors, I replied Jeffrey, John, Everard, Basill, and hee presently declared by my armes, sirname, and these christian names, I must descind from the howse of Hapsburg, with whom, espetially the Earles Geffrey and Everard, his ancestors had bene engaged against in the warrs and att other times in treaties of correspondence, upon wch occasion, joynd to the dignity of a viscount in England, hee treated me ever in his letters with the stile of his cousen, an honor not given to any, as I was told, under the degree of a duke and peer of France. That Prince's letters I cannot yet finde, but I am certaine they are amongst my papers. Upon the same account Monsieur Bernegger of Strasburg, a great historian and antiquary of Germany, gave me those lights wch beefore ware not so cleerely discovered to mee, nor indeed ware my studies and inclinations att that time taken upp with notions of this kinde. For that reason did the city of Basill treat me with great honor and respect in my private travells, and my brother-in-law, Duke Hamilton, beeing entered into Germany with a great army (1631) to second the King of Swedes attempts and designs, the Emperor, then Ferdinand II., att Ratisbone thought my honor a sufficient tye to separate me from all other interests but his owne if I would have accepted of those great advantagious offers he made me, etc., etc.[1]

It is not pleasant to be obliged to say what one thinks of this letter. In the first place, the names

[1] *Fourth Report on Historical MSS.*, I. 262.

of the writer's ancestors[1] were Geoffrey (*one*), John (*one*), Everard (*one*), Basil (*two*), and *William* (*five*). It is odd that he should have omitted the chief one, which happens not to suit his theory. More serious, however, is the statement that the Prince " declared by my armes, sirname, and those christian names, I must descend from the house of Hapsburg." The arms of Feilding are totally distinct, we have seen, from those of Hapsburg : the sirname of " Feilding " cannot possibly have suggested that of Hapsburg. As to the christian names, there was nothing in " Basil " to suggest the Hapsburgs, while Geoffrey, John, and Everard were common names enough. It is thus absolutely certain that the writer must here have been romancing. We must therefore doubt what he tells us about " the city of Basill " (the spelling suggests that he connected its name with his own) ; nor can we believe that the emperor's offers were connected with his alleged Hapsburg descent, when we find it so completely ignored in Herrgot's great work. And, for my part, I doubt " Duke Vittorio," in the seventeenth century, recollecting and taking so keen an interest in the Hapsburg cadets of the thirteenth. The letter is, throughout, that of a man trying to make out a case for the descent on which he has set his heart.

But when we come to " Monsieur Bernegger," I must confess that it looks to me as if we may have in him the ingenious antiquary who supplied

---

[1] Visitation of 1563, and the glass window.

(or gave the " local colour " for) what I term the
" German " deeds. The name of " Stein," for
instance, savours of a local knowledge which
even the " inquisitive " Vincent is scarcely likely
to have acquired. And the story told in the deeds
of " 1365 " might well have occurred to a Strasburg man. Still, they are rather poor imitations,
and " a great historian and antiquary " would,
perhaps, have done better.

Strange to say, such a man as was required was
actually engaged on a similar task, in the same part
of the world, perhaps at the very time when the
Feilding story was concocted. Even as Basil, Lord
Denbigh, claimed, on the strength of these deeds,
a Hapsburg origin for his house, so did Jérôme
Vignier, an Oratorian priest, who was a year or
two his senior, claim for the Hapsburgs themselves a new and Alsatian origin on the strength of
a manuscript fragment which he had discovered in
Lorraine. This discovery he published in his *La
veritable origine des tres-illustres maisons a'Alsace, de
Lorraine, d'Austriche* (1649). His ' find ' proved as
immediately ¦successful as Bertram's manuscript
" Richard of Cirencester." Even as Stukeley
accepted and gave its vogue to the latter,[1] so
Chiflet, who had written on the Hapsburgs,
promptly retracted his conclusions and accepted
Vignier's new theory in his *Stemma Austriacum
annis abhinc millenis* (1650). Wanley alludes to
this in his history of the Feilding family (1670) :—

[1] See a letter of Stukeley in my Calendar of the Round MSS.
(14th Report Hist. MSS. IX. 293–4).

The last derivation comes from the princes and lantgraves or
Alsatia, which chevalier Chiffletius (a worthy and gentile writer)
seems to fix upon in his last volume, though in his former he
fell upon King Sigebert. This latter opinion is so backed with
authority and proofes that I refer you to them for satisfaction.[1]

Eccard also adopted the results of Vignier's
discovery in his work on the Hapsburg family
(1721). At last a brilliant French scholar, whose
untimely death was much deplored, I mean M.
Julien Havet, pointed out that Jérôme Vignier
had successfully imposed upon the world. It was,
he observed, " a remarkable circumstance" that
his manuscript fragment " was full of genealogical
details, that is to say, exactly what he wanted in
order to prove his theory." This, we have seen,
was also a feature of those convenient Feilding
deeds. M. Havet tersely inferred that

Il est clair que nous avons là simplement un faux de plus à
enregistrer, et que celui qui l'a commis est le même auquel on
doit imputer le faux testament de Perpétue, la fausse donation de
Micy et les autres falsifications dont il a été question.[2]

As in the case of the Shipway pedigree, only the
other day, Father Vignier had discovered just
what he went to find. There is nothing, however,
to connect him directly with Basil Lord Denbigh.

It will have been seen that two questions are
raised by this paper. That the Hapsburg descent
is an absurd fiction has been abundantly demonstrated, but its actual author and the date of its
origin cannot be so surely decided. Everything
points to Basil, second earl of Denbigh (1643–

[1] Nichols' *Leicestershire*, IV. (1), p. 273.
[2] *Bibliothèque de l'Ecole des Chartes*, XLVI. 267–8.

1675) ; but if all the documents were concocted
for him, it is difficult to see how Dugdale could
speak of those known to him[1] as " authentique
evidences" in the middle of the seventeenth century. Either his honesty or his critical power is
thereby gravely impugned. If on the other hand
some of these " evidences" were, as alleged, of
earlier date, they could not have been concocted
till the error about Rheinfelden found its way into
England about the beginning of the seventeenth or
end of the sixteenth century. Thus in no case
should they have seemed in Dugdale's days " authentique." Perhaps the great Herald looked
with partial eyes on documents produced by a
peer of the realm, who was also a Warwickshire
man.

As to the recognition, whatever it may be, that
this claim has now obtained abroad, it is sufficiently explained by the natural belief that a
descent recognised by the English Crown and
admitted by the most famous of all our officers of
arms, could not be a sheer invention, and must
therefore be true.[2] The evidence of the deeds
proves the descent, and no one could suppose that
a noble family would rely for its pedigree on a
pack of forgeries. The strange thing is that this

---

[1] Wanley seems to have had access in 1670 to many more
than Dugdale.

[2] In vol. XXV. of " Johannes von Müller sämmtliche Werke,
herausgegeben von Johann Georg Müller" (Tübingen, 1817), we
find it recognised on Dugdale's authority only " Wenn Dugdale's
Briefe . . . wen diese Schriften ihre Richtigkeit haben."

pretended descent should be coveted by such a family as that of Feilding. For whether the antiquity of their earldom be considered, or that of their position as county gentry, they must rank high among what in England is deemed *ancienne noblesse*. It is, however, only right to add that the family do but inherit this claim from their ancestors, and, though it has been, no doubt, accentuated by the introduction of the name Rudolph, they are wholly guiltless of its original concoction, and could scarcely, indeed, be expected to abandon it, till it was, as now, disproved.

This article, when first published, ended here. Its results remain to be told. The first, naturally enough, was that I was vehemently assailed; indeed, I am told that the British Museum contains a reply to my criticism almost libellous in its virulence. The question, however, had to be faced by the author of *Armorial Families*, for its avowed object is to make it clear "which coats-of-arms are lawfully and legally borne," and which are "bogus." The way he dealt with it was this. In his first edition (1895) he ignored the claim, with the arms and titles based upon it, in the case of Lord Denbigh himself and of one of his uncles; but in the cases of another uncle and a cousin he recognised the claim, without question, by assigning to each "the cap of his rank as Count of the Holy Roman Empire." But in one of these cases he ignored the 'quarters' borne in right of the above claim, and gave only the impossible coat

"Quarterly 1 and 4"—which is a description as absurd as that of a square with only two sides. In the other case he blazoned the four "quarters" in full, and placed the whole on an Austrian eagle, of which he gave a gorgeous engraving. But he added this curious note:—

> The right to the second and third quarterings and to the Austrian eagle has not been formally established in the College of Arms, and the engraving was executed under the mistaken supposition that it was, though the Editor understands it is capable of proof.

One might suppose that in his third edition (1899) Mr. Fox-Davies would have tried to put matters right, or, at least, to have made his statements consistent. But this is not so. The impossible coat of two quarters again makes its appearance, and the engraving, admittedly executed by mistake, is now more conspicuous than ever, that "fearful wild fowl," the Austrian eagle, being here transferred to the text itself, while the same note as before is appended with the trivial addition of a 'yet.'[1] On what possible ground does he blazon in Roman type armorial bearings and a crest which, he admits, are still not "formally established," and which, accordingly, in other cases, he would print in italics as "bogus"? This exposure of his methods and of his self-contradictions should, of itself, be sufficient to destroy any semblance of authority in his work.

Turning to Debrett, now probably the most accurate of the peerage books, we find that the

---

[1] "not yet been formally established."

whole Hapsburg claim silently disappeared some time ago. The absence of its recognition in continental books has always been so marked that one is not surprised to find the *Gothaisches Taschenbuch der Gräflichen Häuser* (1899) ignoring it altogether, although the well-known countship of the Empire held by Lord Arundel of Wardour is duly recognised in that work. But *Burke's Peerage* hardened its heart, and continued to insert every year the German titles, the Hapsburg arms, the Austrian eagle, and the Count's cap. It is only a few weeks ago that my conclusions were accepted even there; in *Burke's Peerage* for 1900 the whole story has disappeared, lock, stock, and barrel. The inevitable surrender has come at last: *Magna est veritas et prævalebit.*

VI

The Origin of the Russells

It would be at once impertinent and superfluous
to insist on the position of the house of Russell
among "the great governing families" of English
political life. Whether as leaders of the Whig
party, or as holders, for more than two centuries,
of the highest rank in the peerage, its chiefs
have occupied a foremost place in the eyes of their
fellow-countrymen.

As is matter of common knowledge, the Russells belong to that group of families which rose
to wealth and power on the ruin of the monastic
houses. But this "new nobility" of the Tudor
reigns was by no means all of *parvenu* character.
If Paget, Petre, "Wriothesley," and, we probably
may add, Thynne, were of humble origin, the
Paulets and Seymours were knightly houses, and
the Cavendishes and Russells were, at least, already
country gentlemen. Yet the sudden access of
wealth and rank was accompanied, in these as in
other cases, by that desire for a longer pedigree
which rarely remains unfulfilled. It would certainly not so remain in those halcyon Tudor days,

when the reigning house itself had provided a gorgeous example, and when heralds were always ready to give reins to a brilliant imagination. The real difficulty, however, is to learn when and where the Russell pedigree first makes its appearance. I have spent much time and toil in the effort to ascertain this; but, although I can find no trace of it in the volumes of Visitations at the British Museum, it is hardly likely that the earls of Bedford waited till the reign of Charles I. to provide themselves with this appendage. It is, however, we shall find, at about the beginning of that reign, that the fully developed pedigree was compiled. This is the "authentic pedigree" of which Jacob speaks, and which must also have been seen by Mr. Wiffen, who styles it the "genealogy in the Bedford Office."[1] It is to this last writer that we owe the clue to its origin and date. He wrote that, in the eleventh century, "Hugh du Rozel," patriarch of the house,—

in variation of the Bertrand arms, bore *argent*, the lion rampant *gules*, uncrowned, with the addition of a chief *sable*; which arms we find ascribed to him in a descent drawn out by William Le Neve, York Herald, preserved with the other archives of the Russells, dukes of Bedford.[2]

It is quite clear that this, which I shall call the 'authentic' pedigree, was adorned throughout with coats of arms.[3]

---

[1] *Memoirs of the House of Russell*, I. 86, 153, 155, 156 (*notes*).
[2] *Ibid.* p. 28.
[3] There is also, Mr. Wiffen states, "a pedigree in the Herald's Office," from which we learn "that the shells (on the

Unfortunately, this pedigree has never been published exactly as it stands. So, at least, I gather. It has been tinkered here and there by those who have used it as the basis of their accounts, so that one never knows with what one is actually dealing. In fact, the attempt to pour, as it were, new wine into old bottles has proved as disastrous as usual. And it affords us a really excellent example of how a pedigree should *not* be constructed. When a statement in a herald's pedigree is actually disproved by records, it is useless to tinker the production by altering it here and there; we have to face the fact that all its statements are, when unsupported, thenceforth unreliable.

The "authentic" pedigree was the work, as I have said, of William Le Neve, York Herald, and must, therefore, have been compiled between 1625 and 1633.[1] I cannot think (see above) that this was the first attempt. Indeed, the monument to the first earl (d. 14 March 1554–5) implies that it was not. This monument was erected by the second earl (1555–1585), whose own monument is also at Chenies, and should be carefully compared with it. According to Lipscomb's *Bucks*, the first earl's monument bears the following coats: (1) Russell; (2) a tower machicolated and embattled; (3) 3 barrulets, a crescent for

chief) were borne by Robert de Rosel, the son of Hugh the Second, so early as the tenth year of King Henry I." (*Ibid.* p. 43, *note*.)

[1] See Mr. Walter Rye's "Preface to Le Neve Correspondence" (1895), p. xviii.

difference; (4) 3 lucies hauriant in pale; (5) a griffin segreant; (6) 3 chevronels ermine. These coats appear to represent: (1) Russell; (2) De la Tour; (3) Muschamp; (4) Herring; (5) Godfrey; (6) Wyse. When we turn to the monument of the second earl (d. 1585), we find *eight* coats in his shield. But the first six of these coats are identical with those in his father's shield, with one significant exception: the fifth coat, instead of a simple griffin segreant, shows us "a griffin segreant, arg., between 3 cross-crosslets fitché of the second." Now this was the coat of the first earl's grandmother, a Froxmere; and it comes here in its right place between that of his mother, who was a Wyse, and of his great grandmother, who, we shall find, was a Herring. I suspect, therefore, that the Godfrey coat in the first earl's shield was merely a mistake for that of Froxmere. It will have, however, to be borne in mind, because we shall meet with it again.[1]

The two really important coats, however, on these monuments are those of De la Tour and Muschamp. The whole pedigree will be found to hang on a marriage with a De la Tour heiress; and if the conclusion I have reached is right, the coats both of Muschamp and of De la Tour indi-

---

[1] The monument to the second earl's son, Lord Russell of Thornhaugh, at Thornhaugh, Northants, is described in Bridges' *Northamptonshire* (II. 598). Here the De la Tour coat is given as "Sable, three towers argent"; and the "griffin segreiant argent" has no cross-crosslets in the field.

:ate that heralds had already found a baseless descent for the family.

Working back from the first earl we come to his father, James Russell of Berwick (or Barwick) in Swyre (co. Dorset), Esq., who married Alice Wyse of the Wyses of Sydenham, Devon. There is no reason to doubt that the first earl's grandfather was the John Russell Esq. who died in 1505 and was buried in Swyre church.[1] Moreover, we can now prove this John Russell's tenure of Berwick as early as 1485.[2] It is beyond this that the difficulty begins. We must now, therefore, turn to the family's "authentic" pedigree and see what its statements are.

As this pedigree extends from the Conquest to the days of Henry VII., it will be convenient to divide it into three distinct sections. The middle section is that which deals with the "baronial" Russells, and extends from the reign of John to about 1340. This section need not be questioned. The first section is that which connects the "baronial" Russells with the Conquest; and the third is that which connects them with the owners of Berwick. These are the two questionable sections, and they can be considered separately.

In default of access to the authentic pedigree, I append the early section from Lipscomb's *Bucks* (III. 248), which seems to represent it.

---

[1] "beneath a plain stone inlaid with brass, which bears above a shield of arms, Russell impaling Frocksmere," etc., etc. (Wiffen, I. 174).

[2] See *Calendar of Inquisitions post mortem : Henry VII.*, vol. I.

THE ORIGIN OF THE RUSSELLS

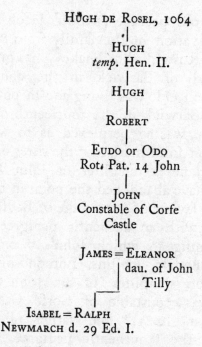

HUGH DE ROSEL, 1064

HUGH
temp. Hen. II.

HUGH

ROBERT

EUDO or ODO
Rot. Pat. 14 John

JOHN
Constable of Corfe
Castle

JAMES = ELEANOR
dau. of John
Tilly

ISABEL = RALPH
NEWMARCH d. 29 Ed. I.

This, it will be seen, almost tallies, down to John, with the version in a little work published under the patronage of the family :—

On the invasion of England by William the Norman, in 1086, Hugh de Russell, or Rossel, (who took that name from his estate in Normandy,) was one of his attendant barons. . . . The portion of this baron was in Dorsetshire, from whence he and his successors assumed the title of Russells of Barwick. His two immediate successors were of the same name. To them succeeded Odo, whose son and heir, Sir John Russell, married the daughter of Lord Bardolph. . . . Nothing very remarkable is recorded of his descendants for upwards of 100 years, although one of them, Sir John Russell, was twice Speaker of the House of Commons during the reign of Henry VI.[1]

---

[1] " The origin and genealogy of the Russell family " in Dodd's

In his cumbrous peerage (1766)[1] Jacob had repeated this derivation of the family from " Hugh de Rossel or Russel," but makes his grandson " Robert Russell of Barwick in the county of Dorset, whose son Odo was living and in possession of the estate at Barwick in the fourteenth of King John." But he was so perplexed as to whether Odo's alleged son John married " the sister of Doun Bardoffe" or " Jane, a daughter of John Tilley," that he would have abandoned the point in despair, when, " by the favour of" the duke of Bedford, he was "furnished with an authentic pedigree of the Russels," according to which John's " son James (omitted by Dugdale, Collins, Edmondson, etc.) married Eleanor, daughter of Sir John Tilley, knight, and was constable of Corfe Castle, in Dorsetshire, A.D. 1221," and father of Ralph Russell. Here the " authentic pedigree" is demonstrably quite wrong. James and his wife are sheer inventions. Ralph was certainly the son of John.

Jacob then gives us the later pedigree (see next page), presumably from the " authorized pedigree." It is to Jacob's credit that, though the second John was " said to have been speaker of the house of Commons " in 2 and 10 Hen. VI., " there is not," he observes, " sufficient authority to clear this point against those who insist that the speaker at that time, although named John Russel, was of another family " (p. 216).

History of Woburn (1818), pp. 72–3. This work was dedicated to the duke and duchess of Bedford. [1] Vol. I. p. 215.

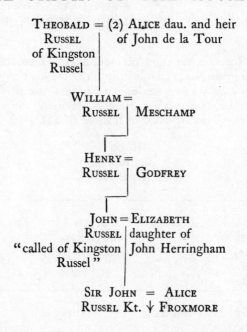

THEOBALD = (2) ALICE dau. and heir
RUSSEL | of John de la Tour
of Kingston
Russel

WILLIAM = MESCHAMP
RUSSEL |

HENRY = GODFREY
RUSSEL |

JOHN = ELIZABETH
RUSSEL | daughter of
"called of Kingston | John Herringham
Russel"

SIR JOHN = ALICE
RUSSEL Kt. ⅄ FROXMORE

But we must keep for the present to the early pedigree, and see what Mr. Wiffen had to say about it, enjoying access as he did to all the available materials, including the "authentic" pedigree. His version, though somewhat difficult to follow, works out as given on the next page. Mr. Wiffen's own contribution to the early history of the family, namely, that the first Hugh du Rozel was a son of "William, baron of Briquebec,"[1] of the house of Bertrand, need not detain us, for it is really only a guess, and, as Hutchins observed, " he adduces no evidence in support of this statement, which seems to rest merely upon

[1] Vol. I. p. 18, and chart pedigree facing p. 1.

conjecture." [1]   It is amusing, however, to learn that

Hugh du Rozel, in variation of the Bertrand arms, bore *argent* the lion rampant *gules*, uncrowned, with the addition of a chief *sable*, which arms we find ascribed to him in a descent drawn out by William Le Neve, York Herald, preserved with the other archives of the Russells, dukes of Bedford (I. 28).

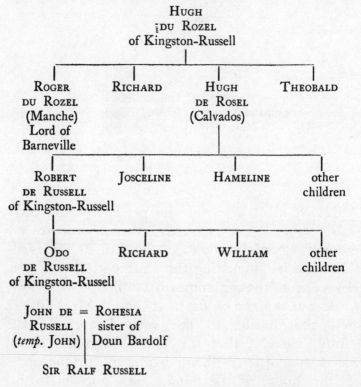

HUGH
ɪDU ROZEL
of Kingston-Russell

| ROGER DU ROZEL (Manche) Lord of Barneville | RICHARD | HUGH DE ROSEL (Calvados) | THEOBALD |

| ROBERT DE RUSSELL of Kingston-Russell | JOSCELINE | HAMELINE | other children |

| ODO DE RUSSELL of Kingston-Russell | RICHARD | WILLIAM | other children |

JOHN DE = ROHESIA
RUSSELL | sister of
(*temp.* JOHN) | Doun Bardolf

SIR RALF RUSSELL

Now John Russell, *temp.* John, is a man whose existence is well established. He held Kingston-Russell, co. Dorset, by serjeanty, and the tenure

is said, in a *Testa* entry, to be as old as the reign of
the Conqueror. But John's parentage cannot, so
far as I know, be proved. This seems to be
admitted, now, in *Burke's Peerage*, where we read
that

the first whose name is mentioned is RICHARD RUSSELL, who
held a knight's fee in Dorset 12 Hen. II., and who was living in
the 31st of that reign. He was succeeded by John Russell, Constable of Corfe Castle.[1]

There was a *Robert* Russell who held a fee in 12
Hen. II., but no 'Richard.' The narrative in
'Burke,' therefore, starts with a fiction.

To me the interesting thing is to discover how
the pedigree was concocted down to John Russell;
for it serves to illustrate the methods of a herald
at that date. Such pedigrees were by no means the
fruit of mere invention. As in the great genealogy of the Westons drawn up about the same time
(1632) by Garter himself (Segar),[2] records, public
and private, were adduced in support of the statements made. Unfortunately, as was sometimes the
case with a well-known genealogist of our own
time, if the evidences themselves were true, the
pedigree based on them was not. In the case of
the Russells, York Herald first provided John with
a father, by identifying him with a John son of Odo
Russell, who occurs on the Patent Roll of 14 John.
Then, deeming it a point of honour to carry

---

[1] A footnote adds: "For the early history of the Russells and
their presumed descent from the Du Rozels of Normandy refer to
Wiffins' (*sic*) *Memoirs of the House of Russell*."

[2] Now in the British Museum (Add. MS. 31,890).

back his patrons to the Conquest, he gave them for a patriarch Hugh de Rosel, whom he found as a witness in a charter of the Abbaye des Dames, Caen, about the time of the Conquest. To bridge the gap between him and Odo, he had only a rather suspicious charter to Cannington Priory, Somerset ("from the original with Mr. Robert Treswell"), which gave him a "Robert de Russell," *temp*. Stephen, apparently.[1] This Robert, however, he made father to Odo ; and then he duplicated (or triplicated) the family patriarch, Hugh, so as to "let him down" till he should reach Robert. And that is how the trick was done.

It was left for the too ingenious Mr. Wiffen to clothe this skeleton with flesh. "Hugh de Rosel" blossomed out into "Hugh Bertrand, lord of Le Rozel" ; from "love of adventure" only, for he was "neither greedy nor necessitous," he "sailed with his prince and fellow-barons to Pevensey, and pitched his tent (!) upon the celebrated field of Hastings." It is "a little singular," Mr. Wiffen admits, that this potent baron cannot be found anywhere in Domesday Book ; but this, of course, he explained away. A more serious difficulty remained. "It is difficult," Mr. Wiffen tells us, "to account for the entire obscurity that hangs over the life of Odo de (*sic*) Russell. Not a single act of his has come to light, either by the evidence of public records or by reflection from domestic or monastic grants." But the truth is that John son

---

[1] Wiffen, I. 85–6.

of Odo Russell, who occurs on the Patent Roll of 14 John, is found there only as the presentee to a living then in the king's hands ! He was, therefore, most certainly not the John Russell who flourished during that reign at Kingston Russell. This was "nasty" for Mr. Wiffen, but he glozed it over by writing that the king conferred on John "the advowson (!) of a church in Gloucestershire." [1] Odo, therefore, like all before him, must be swept away from the pedigree of the house, which, however, perpetuated his memory in the late Lord Odo Russell, first Lord Ampthill.

There is a grim irony in the fact that Dugdale himself bluntly ignored everything before John Russell's appearance on the Pipe Roll of 3 John (1201). If he knew of the gorgeous pedigree constructed by York Herald, he did not believe a word of it.

With the evidence before us there is no reason to suppose that the surname Russell was territorial at all. There were persons styled " de Rosel," from Rosel now in the Calvados (which had nothing to do with Le Rozel, Manche, from which Mr. Wiffen derived the race) ; but the name " Rossellus," or " Russellus," was common enough, and represented simply " Roussel "—the little redhaired man. Mr. Wiffen scraped together all who bore that name, interpolated freely a " de " before it, seized upon every genuine " de Rosel," and joined the whole menagerie in one connected pedigree.

[1] Vol. I. p. 100.

Let us now pass to the third section, the most important of the whole pedigree ; namely the links connecting the earl of Bedford's grandfather with the Russells of Derham and Kingston Russell.

It will be remembered that the " authorized pedigree " was, according to Jacob, this :—

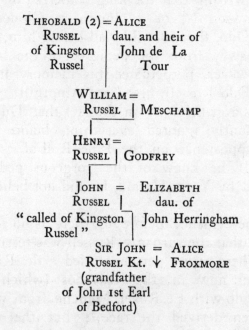

THEOBALD (2) = ALICE
RUSSEL | dau. and heir of
of Kingston | John de La
Russel | Tour

WILLIAM =
RUSSEL | MESCHAMP

HENRY =
RUSSEL | GODFREY

JOHN = ELIZABETH
RUSSEL | dau. of
" called of Kingston | John Herringham
Russel "

SIR JOHN = ALICE
RUSSEL Kt. ↓ FROXMORE
(grandfather
of John 1st Earl
of Bedford)

The only subsequent alteration of importance that has been made in this pedigree has been the substitution of Eleanor (or Alianore) for " Alice " as the name of the De La Tour heiress, in deference to records which prove that the former was the name of Theobald Russell's widow. With the exception of this alteration and of the name 'Meschamp,' which has been variously given, Jacob's pedigree appeared so recently as 1887 in Worthy's *Devonshire Parishes* :[1]

> Upon the death of Eleanor Gorges, Theobald Russell took to wife Eleanor, daughter and heir of John de la Tour, and by her he had William, who married the daughter and heir of Mustian, and had issue Henry, whose son John, by Elizabeth, his wife dau. and heir of John Heringham, was the father of Sir John Russell, Kt., who was Speaker of the House of Commons in the second and tenth years of king Henry VI., and who married Alice, daughter of Freuxmere. . . .
>
> James Russell, son and heir of the Speaker, "married Alice, daughter of John Wyse." . . . His son John, mentioned in the will, is stated to have been born at Kingston Russell, the ancient seat of the family, etc., etc.

Mr. Wiffen, however, here as elsewhere, bestowed upon the bare pedigree much artistic decoration. He knighted William ; he knighted Henry, and made him serve with distinction in France ; and then he knighted the first John, and made him Speaker of the House of Commons. The second John he reduced to an Esquire, for the inscription on his tomb, unfortunately, so describes him.

The difficulty of identifying this John, who died in 1505, with a Speaker of the House of Commons in 1423, has been always felt to be serious. Mr. Wiffen solved it by transferring the Speakership (of which he, obviously, could not deprive the family) from the younger to the elder John. Jacob, we have seen (p. 256), had admitted (1766) that the Speaker probably belonged to

---

[1] Vol. II. pp. 260–1. Mr. Worthy spoke of " the noble House of Russell, descended from the Du Rozels of Normandy."

another family ; and, in *Great Governing Families*,[1] it is questioned whether the Bedford Russells can claim him as an ancestor. But in *Burke's Peerage* the younger of the two Johns in the pedigree is annually recognised as the Speaker ; and, stranger still, the whole story, as concocted by Mr. Wiffen, has now found its way into the *Dictionary of National Biography*, where the elder of the two Johns is identified as the Speaker :

> Sir John Russell, Speaker of the House of Commons, was son of Sir Henry Russell, a west of England knight who had fought in France in the hundred years' war, and who was several times M.P. for Dorchester and once for Dorset, and who married a lady of the family of Godfrey of Hampshire. John was a member of Parliament in 1423, when he was chosen Speaker of the House of Commons. . . . The Speaker is doubtfully said to have had two sons, John and Thomas. John . . . left . . . a son James . . . father of John Russell, first earl of Bedford.[2]

Mr. Archbold, the writer of this article, is also responsible for that on the first earl of Bedford,[3] who, we read, was probably born in 1486. Further,—

> He occupied some position at the court in 1497, and Andrea Trevisan, the ambassador, says that when he made his entry into London in 1497, Russell and the Dean of Windsor, 'men of great repute,' met him some way from the city.

How Russell could have become a 'man of great repute' at the age of eleven I do not profess to understand.

But keeping to the Speaker, no question as to

---

[1] By Sanford and Townsend, 1865.
[2] Vol. XLIX. (1897), pp. 441–2. [3] *Ibid.* p. 444.

his identity can arise. He was clearly the John Russell who was knight of the shire for co. Hereford in seven consecutive Parliaments, 1417–1423, and again in five consecutive Parliaments, 1426–1433. He was Speaker in that which met in October 1423, and again in that which met in May 1432. John Russell of Dorset was not even born at the former of these dates.

Having thus deprived the family of its Speaker, I shall further show that there was but one John Russell of Dorset, the grandfather of the first earl of Bedford. The pedigree-makers have converted him into two; they have made the first half of him a knight, and assigned him his own mother as wife; and then they have discovered that he filled the post of Speaker of the House of Commons several years before he was born. And all this is reproduced, year by year, in *Burke's Peerage*.

From John I turn to his father Henry, the alleged warrior knight.[1] Henry Russell really existed, and he did, as Mr. Wiffen states, endow a foundation at Weymouth; but he was not a warrior, nor even a knight.

With this Henry Russell of Weymouth we are at last on sure ground. It was he who in 1445 was part owner of a " barge " called the " James of Weymouth ";[2] it was he who was returned as burgess for Weymouth in 1425, 1428, 1433, and 1442; it was probably he whose name occurs, with that of Stephen Russell, in a list of Dorset men in 12 Henry VI. who were able to spend

[1] Wiffen, I. 159–162. [2] Hutchins' *Dorset* (1863), II. 421.

PEERAGE STUDIES

£12 a year and upwards; and it was he who
endowed the chantry priest of the gild of St.
George, Weymouth, with seventeen messuages,
etc., in Weymouth, (West) Knighton, Wootton
Glanville, Portland, and Wyke Regis. I have
examined the return of the *Inq. quod damnum,*[1]
together with the writ commanding it, 24 February 1454–5, and find the name given as Henry
Russell "de Weymouth." No relatives, unfortunately, are named; but among those to be commemorated are Adam Moleyns, "lately dean of
Sarum" (who, as bishop of Chichester, had been
murdered at Portsmouth five years before), and
Henry Shelford, late parson of the church of
Wyke Regis (the mother church of Weymouth).
It is clear that Henry Russell had his home at
Weymouth, where he was doubtless a wealthy
townsman. He married in the neighbourhood,
his bride being a woman of good family, Elisa-
beth, daughter and co-heir of John Herring of
Chaldon Herring (East Chaldon).

This marriage is of great importance, not only
as helping us to the true pedigree, but also as
demolishing the false one. In the latter, Henry
Russell is made to marry a Godfrey, while Elisabeth, daughter of John "Herringham," is made
the wife of his son John! This wild blunder has
been steadily repeated by Jacob, Collins, Wiffen,
etc., and duly figures in *Burke's Peerage* for 1899.
The strange thing is that, in Hutchins' *History of
Dorset* the Herring pedigree correctly gives Henry

[1] Thursday after 24 June 1455.

and John Russell as respectively the husband and
the son of Elisabeth Herring.[1] The true pedigree,
in short, is this:

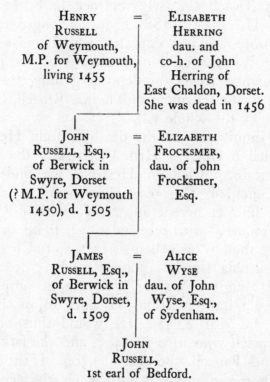

HENRY   =   ELISABETH
RUSSELL   HERRING
of Weymouth,   dau. and
M.P. for Weymouth,   co-h. of John
living 1455   Herring of
East Chaldon, Dorset.
She was dead in 1456

JOHN   =   ELIZABETH
RUSSELL, Esq.,   FROCKSMER,
of Berwick in   dau. of John
Swyre, Dorset   Frocksmer,
(? M.P. for Weymouth   Esq.
1450), d. 1505

JAMES   =   ALICE
RUSSELL, Esq.,   WYSE
of Berwick in   dau. of John
Swyre, Dorset,   Wyse, Esq.,
d. 1509   of Sydenham.

JOHN
RUSSELL,
1st earl of Bedford.

At present the pedigree cannot be carried beyond
Henry Russell, nor is it probable that it ever will
be. But there is at least a fair presumption that
he was descended from, or related to, Stephen
Russell, a bailiff of Weymouth in September and
October 1388,[2] and M.P. for the borough in

---

[1] Ed. 1862, vol. II. p. 520.
[2] *Ancient Deeds* (P.R.O.), C. 144 and C. 2375.

1395. It is also probable that William Russell, returned as burgess for the adjacent borough of Melcombe Regis in 14 Ed. III. (1340), and Thomas Russell similarly returned in 8, 11, and 13 Ric. II. (1384, 1388, 1390), belonged to the same family. It was doubtless this Thomas who, in 1397, was one of those presented by the jurors of Melcombe Regis for depositing dung "at the east end of the tenement of Thomas Russell, to the nuisance of the whole vill." [1]

The Inquisition on the death of John Herring (who died 6 Oct. 34 Hen. VI.) makes the pedigree certain.[2] Chaldon Herring, we find, was strictly entailed, the remainder being "Johanni Russell, filio et heredi apparenti Henrici Russell de Waymouth," with remainder over to his brother William, then to Joan their sister, then to Christian, then to Isolda Lynde. John Russell is described as aged "viginti quatuor annorum et amplius." This would imply that he was born in, or shortly before, the year 1432. He would thus be the John Russell who died in 1505, and the father of that James Russell who died in 1509. If the latter date is borne in mind, it will be clearly seen that there is no room for more than one John Russell.

It must be explained that there is no authority for the form Herring*ham*. Mr. Wiffen found it in the "authentic pedigree," and consequently gave what he termed the "Lineage of Harange or

[1] Borough Records of Weymouth.
[2] The writ was issued 4 Feb. 34 Hen. VI., and the Inquisition taken 25 Oct. 35 Hen. VI.

Heringham " (I. 163–166), although, on his own showing, the family name was Herring (in its various forms).

At this point we may pause to consider how the pedigree was here concocted. York Herald—if, as it would seem, he was the guilty party—must have faced the problem thus: " I have to connect the genuine ancestor, Henry Russell of Weymouth, who was living under Henry VI., with the baronial Russells. Now I find there was a William Russell returned for Melcombe Regis, which adjoins Weymouth, in 14 Ed. III. I shall claim him therefore as father of Henry ; but as he lived too early for the purpose, I shall throw back Henry a generation by making two John Russells out of one. Keeping the Herring(ham) heiress in her place, I must now find respectable wives for the two men at the head of my tree. I find on the monument of the first earl[1] a coat which looks to me like that of the Godfreys of Hampshire,[2] after that of Herring ; so I shall say that Henry married one of that family. I also find, before Herring, a coat which I take to be Muschamp ; this will give me a wife for William. In neither case shall I venture on particulars. I shall then have provided a pedigree comprising all the coats on that monument." [3]

---

[1] See p. 252.

[2] This is the coat which I hold to be intended for Froxmere.

[3] But, as I pointed out above (p. 253), the 'Godfrey' coat *follows* Herring, and must be intended for Froxmere, which should appear in that position.

All this, however, turns on the question I raised at the outset, namely, whether the coats on the monument erected by the second earl (d. 1585) do not imply that the whole of this section of the pedigree was concocted at an earlier date. And this question is specially raised by the coat of De La Tour which figures on that monument. For the masterstroke of the whole pedigree was to make the above William a cadet of the Derham Russells, and to make him inherit Berwick, the seat of his alleged descendants, from his mother, an heiress of the De La Tours, to whom it had previously belonged. As the wives of the Derham Russells were known, and none of them was a De La Tour, the heiress was assigned as a *second* wife to Theobald Russell of Derham, who was probably selected as her husband because the house of De La Tour disappears from view at about the time he lived. By this ingenious arrangement the inheritance of Berwick by a younger son of the Russells was accounted for.

The most critical link in the whole pedigree is this, which connects the alleged ancestor of the Bedford Russells' branch with the parent house of Russell seated at Kingston Russell, and afterwards at Derham. It needs, therefore, close scrutiny. Now " the authorised version " originally was that given by Jacob, namely that William the founder of the Bedford Russells' line was the son of a Theobald Russell by his second wife, " Alice, dau. and heir of John de la Tour." But then the tinkering began. As the name of this Theobald's widow is proved by records to have been, not Alice, but Alianore, the pedigree was altered accordingly. But she was still represented as heiress of Berwick, which "became the fixed residence of the branch" of the Russells descended from her.[1] Two difficulties, it is true, arose; for her brother John is described as "co-heir with" herself[2] to the De la Tour estates, an obvious impossibility; and the statement that "the greater portion" of the De la Tour estates came ultimately to her heirs[3] is not true. She cannot, therefore, have been, as alleged, the heiress of her house. But this is by no means all.

Let us see how the pedigree here works out on Mr. Wiffen's own showing.

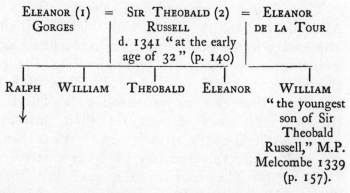

ELEANOR (1) GORGES = SIR THEOBALD (2) RUSSELL d. 1341 "at the early age of 32" (p. 140) = ELEANOR DE LA TOUR

RALPH   WILLIAM   THEOBALD   ELEANOR   WILLIAM "the youngest son of Sir Theobald Russell," M.P. Melcombe 1339 (p. 157).

That is to say, William "the youngest son of Sir Theobald" (by a second wife) was returned to Parliament when *his father* was only thirty years old![4]

---

[1] Wiffen, I. 157.   [2] *Ibid.* 156.   [3] *Ibid.*

[4] Sir Theobald, as a fact, seems to have been 37 (not 32) at his death, but this makes little difference.

Let us take another test. According to Mr. Wiffen, Sir Theobald was born in 1304, for he was " but seven years of age " in 1311 (p. 133), and his minority terminated in 1325 (p. 135). Yet we read that " Sir " John de la Tour, father of Eleanor his second wife, " died so early as 1272 " (p. 155). She must therefore have been, at least, more than thirty years older than her husband, and scarcely less than sixty when she married him, as above, and became the mother of William the duke of Bedford's ancestor!

Having now discovered the difficulties that here surround the pedigree, let us boldly examine the alleged link and ask not merely whether it is true, but whether it cannot be proved to be false.

The alleged marriage of Theobald Russel to Alice de la Tour, as his second wife, is of vital importance to the pedigree. For, in the first place, it is from this match that the Bedford Russells claim descent ; and, in the second place, it is as heirs of Alice, heiress of the De la Tours of Berwick, that they account for their ancestors' possession of Berwick as their seat. What then is the evidence for this marriage ? None whatever is vouchsafed. The facts of the case are these. Theobald, it is admitted, married Alianore Gorges. It is certain that his widow was named Alianore, and it is no less certain that she bore, on her own seal, the Gorges arms. Who then could she be but Alianore Gorges, Theobald's so-called 'first' wife ? In that case, his 'second' wife is a sheer, deliberate invention.

But let me prove the seal. Mr. Wiffen actually described and depicted it,[1] and admitted that its arms were Russell of Derham impaling Morville or Gorges.[2] But as he had 'dodged' the difficulty of 'Alianore' instead of 'Alice,' so he did with her use of the arms of Gorges instead of De la Tour. His feeble suggestion that these arms were "perhaps considered more appropriate to a deed relative to lands which she held in dowry of the lords of Derham, than her own ancestral arms" will be found in his note upon the seal. I have myself examined the seal and deed,[3] which is granted by "Alianora que fuit uxor Theobaldi Russel," and in which we read : "in cujus rei testimonium presentibus sigillum meum apposui." As for the seal, I had better quote from the official *Catalogue of Seals* (III. 461), British Museum :—

"Alianora widow of Theobald Russel of co. Somers. (dau. of Ralph de Gorges).

"13,167 [A.D. 1356] . . . originally fine . . . [*Cott. Chart.*, XXIX. 37].

"A shield of arms : per pale dex., on a chief three bezants[4] *Russell* ; sin. lozengy *Gorges*. Betw. four small lozenge-shaped shields of arms : the two at the sides (l. h. side wanting) *Russell*, the two at top and bottom, *Gorges*."

I claim, therefore, to have now shown that the

---

[1] p. 156 and plate V.

[2] Gorges, he thought, had adopted the Morville arms, having married an heiress of that house (*Ibid.* pp. 136-7). But the assumption of "lozengy, or and az." by the father of Alianore Gorges seems to be unconnected with the Morville coat.

[3] *Cotton Chart.*, XXIX. 37.   [4] Misprinted 'lozants.'

match on which the pedigree depends is a sheer invention.

But the seal takes us further. Mr. Wiffen asserted of Ralf, Theobald's eldest son, that—

> By way of distinction from the old ancestral arms that continued to be borne by his half brother, the son of Eleanor de la Tour, he assumed a new coat, viz. *argent*, on a chief *gules*, 3 bezants *or* " (p. 142).

But this most improbable story is at once disposed of by our seal, which shows that these were the arms of his father, that is of Russell of Kingston Russell. Nor do we stop even here. "Planché's Roll of Arms," which the late Mr. James Greenstreet published in the *Genealogist*, can, according to him, " be pretty safely assigned to the close of the reign of king Henry III." [1] In this roll we find " Raufe Russell " assigned " Arg., on a chief Gu. three roundles Or." [2] Now it was precisely at the close of the reign of Henry III. that Ralph Russell of Kingston Russell flourished.[3]

The arms, therefore, of the Bedford Russells, with their rampant lion *gules* and their escallop shells *argent* on a chief *sable*, are *not* " the old ancestral arms," but, on the contrary, a new coat, evidently granted to distinguish them from the house from which they claim descent.

Mr. Wiffen held that the Russell lion was originally that of Bertrand (p. 13 and plate II.), and that—

---

[1] *Genealogist* (N.S.), III. 149.   [2] *Ibid.* V. 176.
[3] He died early in the reign of Edward I. (Wiffen, I. 117). He was *jure uxoris* of baronial rank.

THE ORIGIN OF THE RUSSELLS

Hugh [Bertrand] du Rozel, in variation of the Bertrand arms, bore *argent*, the lion rampant *gules*, uncrowned, with the addition of a chief *sable* ; which arms we find ascribed to him in a descent drawn out by William Le Neve, York Herald, preserved with the other archives of the Russells, dukes of Bedford (p. 28).

This patriarch first appears, he held, in 1066, and was father of " Hugh II. de Rosel," who, " probably in token of his return as a victorious palmer from Jerusalem . . . added to the lion of his father's shield the three escallop-shells which are borne by his descendants " (I. 42–3). In proof that this was so, we read :—

It appears, by a pedigree in the Herald's Office, that the shells were borne by Robert de Rosel, the son of Hugh the Second, so early as the tenth year of King Henry I. (I. 43, *note*).

If so, one can only say, 'so much the worse for the Heralds' College ' !

The 'variation' of "*or* a lion rampant *vert*, langued and unguled *gules*, crowned *argent*" (p. 13) into "*argent*, a lion rampant *gules*, on a chief *sable*, three escallops of the first," is, indeed, a curiosity of heraldry, apart from the fact that it all took place before armorial bearings were even in existence.

Of all those who have been concerned in this egregious imposture, Mr. Wiffen was, I fear, the worst. For, though living in an age of greater enlightenment and of freer access to authorities, he deliberately and largely added to the fictions previously existing ; he set himself to explain away the flaws he could not but perceive ; and he then

ultroneously proclaimed that his researches were
" based always upon authentic records," and had
enabled him "to complete, in an unbroken line, the
chain of family descent, and to ascertain the pre-
cise spot whence the House derived its surname."
On his own showing (p. xi.), the initiative was
his ; and it was not till he had spent two years
upon the work that the then duke was approached
by him, and fell, not unnaturally, a victim. His
Grace's "liberality," we read, charged him with
a mission to Normandy ; nor do we read with any
surprise : " I went upon a tour of four weeks—I
stayed as many months." This is by no means, I
believe, an uncommon experience with those who
charge these gentlemen with similar missions.
Mr. Wiffen, indeed, was so loth to leave the
pleasant Norman land that his grief broke forth
in verse, which the ducal liberality enabled him
to embalm in print :—

> But, hark—the snorting steeds that prance
>   To whirl me on my homeward way !
> Farewell to Fancy's musing trance—
>   Adieu each loved and lorn Abbaye.
>
>   .   .   .   .   .
>
> Now break the cup ! the spell is past—
>   The guest gone by—the banquet o'er ;
> 'Tis vain ! 'tis vain ! the fragments cast
>   Yet brighter lights than beam'd before. [1]

Poor Mr. Wiffen ! He had at least served his
ducal patron with ' butter in a lordly dish.' Even
the enterprising gentleman who discovered Colonel
Shipway's ancestors would not have ventured to

---

[1] Appendix to vol. I.

begin the pedigree, about the year 600, with "Olaf the sharp-eyed, king of Rerik."

When an author sends forth his work "to undergo the same frank ordeal of opinion, which I myself have exercised," and to be received with his own "candour," he compels the critic to observe that the evidence is 'doctored' throughout with the very reverse of candour. The territorial "de" is interpolated where it is not found; fancy knighthoods are bestowed on those who did not enjoy the honour; and, at every step, the evidence is distorted *ad majorem gloriam gentis*. Thus, for instance, an entry on the Rolls which is vouched for the statement that "John Russell Esquire" took part "in public affairs" as "keeper of the royal artillery in Carisbrook Castle,"[1] proves, on verification, to refer to an ordinary soldier, whose wages were threepence a day.

But I have now sufficiently exposed the true character of the work. It is, perhaps, the strangest part of the story, and not the least instructive, that the present century should have brought to perfection a legend on which Dugdale himself remained ominously silent. Though giving his pedigree of the later family "ex relatione Willelmi comitis Bedf.," he stopped short with William Russel of Kingston Russell *temp*. Edw. I. and guardedly proceeded :—

Touching the descendants of this William, considering they stood not in the ranks of peers of this realm, I have no more to say until I come to John Russel Esq. whose residence was at Barwick.[2]

---

[1] Vol. I. p. 170.　　[2] *Baronage*, II. 377–8.

He then takes up his tale anew with the first earl of Bedford.

Shirley in his famous *Noble and Gentle men*,[1] followed Wiffen and 'Brydges' Collins,' writing :—

> Although this family may be said to have made their fortune in the reign of Henry VIII. . . . yet there is no reason to doubt that the Russells are sprung from a younger branch of an ancient baronial family of whom the elder line . . . were barons of Parliament in the time of Edward III.

But, in their *Great Governing Families* (1865), Sanford and Townsend dismissed the story with these sceptical words :—

> They may possibly have an old pedigree. Immense labour has been expended in tracing it by genealogists dependent on the family, and it now lacks nothing except historic proof (II. 25).

It was, however, hardly fair to assert that, beyond 1509, "all is genealogical, *i.e.* more or less plausible guesswork." There is no reason to doubt the pedigree up to Henry Russell, returned, as we have seen, for Weymouth, under Henry VI. The association, therefore, of the Russells with the House of Commons, can be carried back at least four and a half centuries, while it is quite possible that men of their race represented in Parliament their fellow-burgesses five hundred years ago. It was thus appropriate enough that this great Whig name should have been so closely connected with the passing of the first Reform bill, which placed the balance of political power in the hands of that very class from which the Russells originally sprang.

[1] 3rd Ed., 1866.

VII

The Rise of the Spencers

THAT quaint old work Lloyd's *State Worthies* is responsible for this sketch of the first Lord Spencer :—

He was the fifth knight of his family, in an immediate succession, well allied and extracted, being descended from the Spencers, earls of Gloucester and Winchester. In the first year of the reign of king James [1603], being a moneyed man, he was created baron of Wormeleiton in the county of Warwick. He had such a ready and quick wit, that once speaking in parliament of the valour of their English ancestors in defending the liberty of the nation, returned this answer to the earl of Arundel, who said unto him : "Your ancestors were then keeping of sheep"; "If they kept sheep, yours were then plotting of treason."

This 'scene,' which made, at the time, no small stir, took place on 8 May 1621. It is somewhat differently recorded by Dr. Gardiner, on the authority of a State Paper. According to him it was Lord Spencer who first reminded Arundel that two of his ancestors had been condemned to death, upon which Arundel, "stung by the retort . . . replied, with all the haughty insolence of his nature" :—

I do acknowledge that my ancestors have suffered, and it may be for doing the king and the country good service, and in such time as when, perhaps, the lord's ancestors that last spoke, were keeping sheep.

An interesting biography of this, the first Lord Spencer, is contained in Colvile's *Warwickshire Worthies* (pp. 712–721), the information being brought together from a number of sources. From Arthur Wilson's *Life of James* is quoted the panegyric :—

Like the old Roman dictator from the farm, he made the country a virtuous court, where his fields and flocks brought him more happy contentment than the various and mutable dispensations of a court can contribute ; and when he was called to the Senate he was more vigilant to keep the people's liberties from being a prey to the encroaching power of monarchy, than his harmless and tender lambs from foxes and ravenous creatures.[1]

The wealth, the hospitality, and the high character of this Lord Spencer were spoken to by divers writers, Camden terming him " a worthy encourager of virtue and learning."[2]   He seems to have inherited the tastes of his ancestors, with whom Lord Arundel taunted him, and, like ' Coke of Holkham,' in later times, to have devoted himself to farming and breeding stock.   Thus it was that Fuller, himself a Northamptonshire man, tells us, writing about the middle of the seventeenth century, that Warwickshire was famous for its sheep, to which the Spencers had owed their rise.   They were

   . . .   most large for bone, flesh, and wool about Worm-

---

[1] This passage is also quoted in *Collins' Peerage* (1779), I. 357.   [2] *Ibid.*

leighton [the Spencers' seat]. In this shire the complaint of J. Rous [d. 1491] continueth and increaseth that sheep turn cannibals, eating up men, horses, and towns ; their pastures make such depopulation.[1]

The first lord's grandfather and namesake, who died in 1586, had "employed his thoughts on husbandry as of most skill and profit to his country; for at his death he had numerous flocks of sheep and other cattle in his grounds and parks of Althorp and Wormleighton."[2]

The haughty words of the head of the Howards referred to a fact of much interest, which was then, probably, notorious. Alone, perhaps, among the English nobility, the Spencers owed their riches and their rise, neither to the favour of a court, nor to the spoils of monasteries, nor to a fortune made in trade, but to successful farming. That a fortune

[1] Fuller's *Worthies*. Compare the testimony of Dugdale below, p. 285. Fuller seems to be referring to Rous' *Historia Regum Anglie* (Ed. Hearne, 1745), pp. 120–137, where the writer denounces to Henry VII. the destruction of townships in East Warwickshire. It is interesting to note that Hodnell and Radbourne are among those he names.

[2] Collins *ut supra*. Harrison had complained about this time of the "enormity" of the aristocracy dealing with "such like affairs as belong not to men of honour, but rather to farmers or graziers ; for which such, if there be any, may well be noted (and not unjustly) to degenerate from true nobility, and betake themselves to husbandry." A case in point is that of Thomas Lord Berkeley (1523–1533), styled by Smyth, the historian of his house, "Thomas the Sheepmaster." This bearer of a famous title is described by him as "living a kind of grazier's life, having his flocks of sheep sommering in one place and wintering in other places as hee observed the fields and pastures to bee found and could bargaine best cheape."

could then be made by a pursuit which now spells ruin, may seem at first sight strange ; but there was a time in England, under the early Tudors, when sheep-farming meant a road to fortune, as it did, in our own time, for Australia's "shepherd kings." Those were days when a sheep's wool proved indeed a " golden fleece." [1]

The trend of historical study, of late, towards economics and social evolution, has caused much attention to be given to the great development of pasture, at the cost of arable, resulting from the large profits derived from the growth of wool.[2] For more than a century the face of the country was undergoing a vast change, and its economic conditions being profoundly modified, by the depopulation of the rural districts, where the highly profitable growth of wool was ousting the labours of the plough. In vain did Henry VII. and Henry VIII. alike endeavour to check this great movement by acts of parliament and other measures, backed though they were, in Mr. Corbett's words, " by all the preachers and thinkers of the day." John Spencer was one of those ordered by Wolsey to destroy his enclosures, and restore his land to tillage, in 1518 or 1519, but we find an act of parliament in 1534 still denouncing

. . . "divers persons to whom God in His goodness hath disposed great plenty," studying " how they might accumulate into few

---

[1] Harrison (*circ.* 1580) wrote, of "our great sheepmasters," that sometimes one owned 20,000 sheep.

[2] See, for instance, Mr. Leadam's *Domesday of Inclosures* (2 vols.), published by the Royal Historical Society.

THE RISE OF THE SPENCERS

hands, as well great multitude of farms as great plenty of cattle, and in especial sheep, putting such land to pasture and not tillage, whereby they have not only pulled down churches and towns,[1] . . . but enhanced the prices of all manner of agricultural commodities almost double . . . by reason whereof a marvellous number of the people of this realm . . . be so discouraged with misery and poverty that they . . . pitifully die for hunger and cold."

Indeed some fifty years later, in the lifetime of his grandson, Sir John Spencer (p. 281 above), the complaints were as loud as ever.

> *Husbandman.* . . . where threescore persons or upwards had their livings, now one man with his cattle has all, which is not the least cause of former uproars. . . . Ye raise the price of your lands, and ye take farms also, and pastures to your hands, which was wont to be poor Men's livings, such as I am.
> *Merchant.* On my soul ye say truth.
> *Husbandman.* Yea, those sheep is the cause of all these mischiefs.[2]

It was, as ever, useless to fight by legislative enactment against land being put to the most profitable use, however unpopular the change might be. The grazing farms of Connaught, at the present time, are denounced by the small tenants, who would have them parcelled out; but they have

[1] As villages were then termed.

[2] *A compendium and brief examination of certain ordinary complaints of divers of our countrymen in these our days.* By W. S., 1581. Harrison observes, about the same time, that "where in times past many large and wealthy occupiers were dwelling within the compass of some one park. . . . some owners, still desirous to enlarge those grounds, as either for the breed and feeding of cattle, do not let daily to take in more, not sparing the very commons, whereupon many townships now and then do live."

proved to be the best use to which that land can be put. It is, however, doubtless true that, like all great economic changes, the conversion of arable into pasture dislocated rural life, and involved suffering and loss to individuals if not to classes. And therefore, although wholly consistent with the *laissez faire* principles of the old Liberal party, it figures among the sins in English history with which the owners of land are so often charged by the present Radical factions.[1] But the founder of the Spencers was shrewd enough to seize the opportunities of his time. As he is stated to have been, maternally, a nephew of Richard Empson, the famous (or infamous) official employed by Henry VII. to fill his treasury, his evidently rapid acquisition of wealth may not have been unconnected with the fact that Empson was in power at the time.[2] But, so far as the known evidence takes us, it was by stock farming that he made, as he said, " his lyvyng." [3]

[1] By the irony of fate we have lately witnessed exactly the same phenomena, namely, the conversion of arable into pasture (or now, sometimes, into waste), ruined and deserted farmsteads, and rural depopulation,—as the direct result of that policy of which Cobden secured the adoption by the false assurance that such result could not possibly follow it. And the Radicals, in their hatred of the landed interest, rejoice in its present result.

[2] *i.e.* till 1509.

[3] It may seem strange that a ' grazier ' could acquire sufficient wealth to purchase Wormleighton and Althorpe, and could even become high sheriff of his county. But we learn from Harrison (p. 324 below), in this century, that such men " live wealthily, and with grazing . . . do come to great wealth," and buy gentlemen's estates. Nor was a rapid social rise any strange

THE RISE OF THE SPENCERS

In this paper, however, the subject I propose to discuss is that of the Spencer pedigree and arms. For theirs, it will be found, is a typical case of the Heralds' College providing a family, when it has acquired wealth, with arms to which it is not entitled, on the strength of a pedigree concocted for the purpose. I lay the guilt at the heralds' door, not at that of the family itself, because its founder, John Spencer, the purchaser of Althorpe and Wormleighton, made, we shall see, no claim to any other than his true origin; while its first peer,—although "for his skill in antiquities, arms, alliances it was singular,"—desired, in his will, to be buried "not in the pompous traine of Heraulds and glorious Ensignes, nor in dumbe ceremonies, and superfluous shewes, but in a decent and Christian manner, without pomp or superfluities."

It was at the beginning of the sixteenth century that this family of Spencer first emerged from obscurity; and it is quite evident that they were then wealthy graziers, living in the south-east of Warwickshire, on the Northamptonshire border. Their true pedigree was as given on the next page. Hodnell and Radbourne lay together just to the north of Wormleighton. When Dugdale wrote (1640), Hodnell, which had "been antiently well

phenomenon in the days of the Tudor kings. But, indeed, grazing could still lead to it two centuries later; for Nash writes of Tredington, in S.E. Worcestershire: "Here lived Mr. Snow, an eminent butcher and grazier, who by extensive dealing and great integrity raised a very considerable fortune: he was high sheriff of the county" in 9 George II. (*Worcestershire*, II. 427).

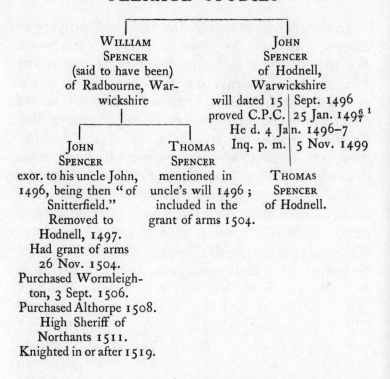

WILLIAM SPENCER (said to have been) of Radbourne, Warwickshire

JOHN SPENCER of Hodnell, Warwickshire will dated 15 | Sept. 1496 proved C.P.C. | 25 Jan. 149$\frac{6}{7}$ [1] He d. 4 Jan. 1496–7 Inq. p. m. | 5 Nov. 1499

JOHN SPENCER exor. to his uncle John, 1496, being then " of Snitterfield." Removed to Hodnell, 1497. Had grant of arms 26 Nov. 1504. Purchased Wormleighton, 3 Sept. 1506. Purchased Althorpe 1508. High Sheriff of Northants 1511. Knighted in or after 1519.

THOMAS SPENCER mentioned in uncle's will 1496 ; included in the grant of arms 1504.

THOMAS SPENCER of Hodnell.

inhabited, and had a church, whereof, now, the ruines are scarce to be seen," had shrunk to insignificance, as had Radbourne, which, " from a village of divers inhabitants, and having a church, is now by depopulation shrunk into one dwelling." It was the fate of such villages as these that had stirred Sir Thomas More to his outburst against " the noblemen and gentlemen, yea, and certain abbots, that lease no ground for tillage ; that enclose all into pasture, and throw down houses ; that pluck down towns, and leave nothing standing, but only the church, to be made into a sheep house." [1]

The social position of John Spencer, the future purchaser of Althorpe, when living at Hodnell after his uncle's death, is proved by a deed now preserved among the British Museum manuscripts, [2] which is dated 26 Nov. 1497. This deed is also of interest from its mention of his neighbour, William Graunte, "husbondman"; [3] for he himself, according to his monument, had married a daughter of Walter Graunt, of Snitterfield, as had his uncle also.

Noverint universi per presentes nos Johannem Spenser de Hodenhill in Com. Warr. Grasier, Willelmum Graunte de Priours Herdewyk in Com. Warr. husbondman, Rogerium Belcher de Gyldesburgh in Com. Northt. husbondman, et Thomam Lawney de Maydeford in Com. Northt. husbondman, teneri et firmiter obligari Thome Haselwode armigero in decem libris sterlingorum. . . . Dat' vicesimo sexto die mensis Novembris anno regni Regis Henrici Septimi tercio decimo.

---

[1] Compare the words of Fuller above, p. 280, and those of Harrison (*circ.* 1580) :—"It is an easy matter to prove that England was never less furnished with people than at this present ; for if the old records of every manor be sought, . . . it will soon appear that, in some one manor, 17, 18, or 20 houses are shrunk. I know what I say by my own experience . . . of towns pulled down for sheep-walks, and no more but the lordships now standing in them. . . . I could say somewhat ; . . . Certes, this kind of cattle is more cherished in England than standeth well with the commodity of the commons or prosperity of divers towns, whereof some are wholly converted to their feeding."   [2] Add. Chart. 21,448.

[3] As William Graunt 'de Haidewyke' he entered, with Alice his wife, in 1493, the Knowle Guild, which was joined by his neighbour John Spencer in 1495.

It need hardly be said that the seals affixed by
the parties to this deed are not armorial. On the
death of John Spencer, his uncle and namesake,
the future purchaser of Althorpe went to reside at
Hodnell, doubtless to carry on the grazing business
as his uncle's executor. When his cousin came of
age, he had to leave Hodnell, and he had bought
Wormleighton, according to his own account, to
provide himself with a home.

All this we learn from his own interesting
petition to Henry VIII., against being forced to
restore to tillage his pastures at Wormleighton.
We owe the text of this document to the industry
of Mr. Leadam, who has printed it from the
original, among Lord Spencer's MSS., in his *Domesday of Inclosures*.[1]

John Spencer of Wormeleighton . . . bought the seid
lordship of the seid William Coope . . . wherupon he
made hym a dwelling place, where he had noon to inhabit hym-
self in his countrey where he was borne, for at Hodnell where
he dwelt byfore he had yt no longer but during the nanage of his
unkyls son, which now there dwellith and hathe doone this iij
yeeris, and so this iij yeris the seid John Spencer hathe be in
bylding in Wormeleighton to his great cost and charge.[2]

Mr. Leadam assigns this petition to 1519. In
it John Spencer goes on to plead that to restore
the land to tillage would be " to his uttour un-
doyng "—

for his lyvyng ys and hathe byn by the brede of cattell in his
pastures, for he ys neythir byer nor seller in comon markettes as
other grasyers byn, but lyvyth by his own brede of the same

---

[1] Issued by the Royal Historical Society.   [2] Vol. I. pp. 485–6.

pastures, and sold yt when it was fatt to the citie of London and other places yerely as good chepe in all this v or vj yeris past as he dyd in other yeres when they were best chepe within ijs. in a beste and ijd. in a shepe.[1]

In 1512 the same energetic man had acquired, by exchange, Wicken, in Northamptonshire, and had promptly extended its park and turned arable into pasture.[2] Even before his purchase of Wormleighton—which had cost him, he claimed, first and last, two thousand pounds—John Spencer had felt himself in sufficiently good circumstances to aspire to a grant of arms. Accordingly, on 26 Nov. 1504, "Richemount, otherwise Clarencieux," granted to John and Thomas Spencer, sons of William Spencer of the county of Warwick, *az. a fess erm. between six sea-mews' heads erasea arg.*, as a coat.

There seems to have prevailed a doubt among those who have written on the family as to whom this coat was granted to. Sir Egerton Brydges did not know, and Baker guessed that it must have been obtained by the father of the actual grantees, William Spencer. It was granted, however, as above. One could hardly conceive a coat differing more widely from that of the baronial Despencers;[3] and it is equally to the credit of John Spencer and of the herald who made the grant that this should

[1] Vol. I. p. 487.

[2] "et quatuor persone que ibidem nuper manentes et laborantes (*sic*) abinde penitus in magnum suum dampnum recesserunt et vagarunt" (*Ibid.* pp. 285, 286).

[3] *Quarterly arg. and gu. in the 2nd and 3rd quarters a fret or, over all a bend sable.*

have been so. The coat, also, of the Bedford Russells differed widely, we saw, from that of the baronial Russells. In both cases the practice of the heralds at this period of their history appears to very great advantage by the side of that which they adopted later and which prevails at the present day. I propose to return to this subject below.

The grant of this coat in 1504 is obviously hostile to the claim that the family was already entitled to the arms of the baronial Despencers. For if it had been, John Spencer was hardly likely to apply for new ones before the Heralds' Visitations, with their coercive powers, had begun; and he was even less likely to change, as has been suggested, the coat to which he was entitled for a new one pointedly implying that he was not of the Despencer stock. When the Heralds' Visitations began, the Spencers were satisfied with this coat and with John, who obtained it, as their ancestor. Nay, they were using it at least as late as 1576; for Sir John Spencer of Althorpe and his son Thomas were parties, in that year, to a deed to which they affixed their seals, bearing only the coat granted in 1504.[1]

Moreover, the head of their other house, Thomas Spencer of Everdon, obtained a fresh grant of arms so late as *circ.* 1560. Descended as

[1] Add. Chart. 21,996 (in British Museum). The official catalogue of the Museum seals describes the coat as "a fess between six pigeons' heads erased"; but the heads, even to the naked eye, are clearly those of seamews.

he was from an uncle of John, the purchaser of Althorpe, he did not come within the limitation of the 1504 grant. The coat assigned him, in the language of the day, was " Sables, on a fece golde betw. 3 bezantes 3 lions heads razid of the field " —with a very complicated crest. He evidently made no claim to be entitled to a Despencer coat, or, for the matter of that, to any arms at all.[1]

Baker indeed asserts, of the first Spencer of Althorpe, that—

The arms of his great grandfather, Henry Spencer, which had been disused for several generations, were resumed by Sir John Spencer,[2] as is evident from their being blazoned on his monument, and that they were not deemed "a late assumption where the want of authority is fatal to the right," needs no other proof than the simple fact of their having been uninterruptedly borne by his noble descendants under the sanction of the college of arms.[3]

With the value of this " sanction " I shall deal in due course ; for the present I have to point out that the above monument has been " faked." Whether it was erected on Sir John Spencer's death (1522), or somewhat later,[4] this effigy displays on its tabard no other coat than that which was granted in 1504. The first effigy on which is found the differenced coat of the baronial

[1] This is not mentioned by Baker, and seems to be a new fact.

[2] To whom, on the contrary, the new coat had been granted in 1504. [3] *History of Northamptonshire*, I. 106.

[4] It speaks of his eldest son as a knight ; and *Collins' Peerage* states (on the authority of Cotton MS. Claud. C. 3), that he was not knighted till 1529. But Mr. Metcalfe's book gives Sir *James* Spencer as then knighted.

Despencers is that of the Sir John Spencer who died in 1586.[1] As we found this Sir John, in 1576, using the coat granted in 1504, we might suppose that the change was made between 1576 and 1586.

But was this monument erected at the time of his death? It was not. This I can prove from the evidence of the inscription itself. It speaks of one of his daughters as "married to George Lord Hunsden" (who did not succeed to that barony till 1596). The monument, therefore, cannot have been erected before 1596.

At this point of the enquiry we may turn to the invaluable testimony of one who was himself a member of the College, Mr. Townsend, Windsor Herald. From him we learn the true genesis of the pedigree deriving the Althorpe house from the famous baronial Despencers.[2]

The family of Spencer of Wormleighton and Althorpe recorded its pedigree at the Heralds' Visitation of the County of Northampton in 1564 (H. IV. in Coll. Arms) beginning with Sir John Spencer of Hodnell, in the County of Warwick Kt who died in 1521. At that time no pretension was made to a descent from the Despencers or of any relationship to the earls of Winchester and Gloucester, nor was there the least similitude in the arms.

Clarencieux Lee in 1595 made a pedigree for the then Sir John Spencer or Wormleighton and Althorpe, in which he drew the descent nearly in the manner in which Dugdale has given it; he professes to have compiled it from divers records, registers,

---

[1] These effigies and all the monuments are fully described in Baker's *Northamptonshire*, and are beautifully depicted in colours in a British Museum MS. (Add. MS. 16,965).

[2] See *Collectanea Topographica et Genealogica*, vol. V. p. 6, *note*.

wills, and other good and sufficient proofs which he had diligently and carefully perused, and in his character of Clarencieux King of Arms he confirms and allows it officially. Whatever the proofs which he saw and examined, I confess that I cannot give implicit credit to his work.

So it was Clarencieux King of Arms who foisted this pedigree on Sir John Spencer in 1595. The family had, by that time, largely increased its wealth, for Sir John's mother was a daughter of the well-known Sir Thomas Kytson, who had acquired a great fortune as a mercer in London. Lee, to whom queen Elizabeth said that " if he proved no better " than his predecessor Cooke, Clarencieux, " yt made no matter yf hee were hanged," [1] must have felt that it was Sir John's duty to "pay, pay, pay" for a new pedigree and coat. For a hungry King of Arms he was a marked man. Now we understand how it was that the monument erected in or after 1596 displays the 'Despencer' coat, while those already existing in the interesting Spencer chapel were bedecked, right and left, with the fruits of Lee's discovery. When the heralds next "visited " the county (1617–8), the new baronial pedigree was entered in all its splendour.[2] The shepherd peer was now of the stock of " ye Earles of Winchester and Glocester." A year later he had soared higher;

[1] So, at least, Segar (afterwards Garter) asserted.
[2] It will be found in Harl. MS. 1,187 (a copy of the Visitation) with the alleged proofs. Baker prints it from this source, and it is also printed in Lipscomb's *Bucks* and set forth in *Collins' Peerage*, with references to " Visitat. Com. Northampton in Coll. Arm., anno 1617."

he was in direct male descent from " Ivon Viscount
de Constantine," who had married, even before the
Conquest, a sister of the "earl of Britanny." [1]   Can
we wonder that 'the noble lord' took a leading part
in the petition to the king, in 1621, against those
Irish and Scottish creations " by which all the
Nobility in this realm " were injured in "their
birthrights " ?   Did not a peer of Hebrew extraction and very recent creation sign the petition
against erecting the statue to Oliver Cromwell,
who abolished the House ot Lords—and gave us,
instead, the Jews ?

The pedigree to which Mr. Townsend refers [2] is
headed :

The pedegree or S[r] John Spencer Kt. of Althrope and
Wormleighton in the Countyes of Northampton and Warr.
being a branche issueing from the ancient familly and chieffe of
the Spencers, of which sometymes were y[e] Earles of Winchester
and Glocester and Barons of Glamorgan and Morgannocke.

It begins with " Thurstanus pater Americi et
Walterii," and at its foot we read :

This pedegre and discent of S[r] John Spencer of Althroppe
and Wormleighton in y[e] countyes of Northampton and Warr.

---

[1] Baker's *Northamptonshire*, I. 108, from Harl. MS. 6,135.
But the real authority for this descent is the Heralds' Visitation
of Warwickshire, in 1619, as found in Harl. MS. 1,563. See
the paper on "Our English Hapsburgs " (p. 220) for the authority
of this, as Bluemantle's own copy. It is, however, only right to
add that the college copy of this Visitation (C. 7) begins the pedigree, I believe, only with Henry Spencer of Badby (on whom see
p. 326 below).
[2] It is incorporated in the Visitation pedigree of ' 1617 ' in MS.
Harl. 1,187.

Kt. issueing from the auncient family of the Spensers herein set downe together wth the armes and coates thereunto belonginge collected out of divers records, registers, evidences, ancient seales of Armes, sundry willes and Testamentes with other good and sufficient proofes of ye truth haueinge beene diligently and carefully seene and perused, is allowed of and confirmed by me Richard Lee als. Clarencieux Kinge of Armes, of the East, West, and South parts of England at my office 8 May 1595.

[Signature follows].

This pedigree proves, for the early period, to be little more than a skeleton. Eighty-six years later it was brought down, by a certain J. T., to 1679, and, though the early portion remained unchanged (save for the alteration of 'Thurstan' to 'Tristram'), an addition was made by carrying it back, as in the Harl. MS. 1563 Visitation, four generations (through the lords of Dutton !) to "Ivo Viscount of Constance in Normandy," who married "Emme sister to Alane Earl of Brittaine." [1]

It is desirable to print a portion of Clarencieux Lee's pedigree (see next page), as it has proved the foundation of all after it. We shall see below that this descent, on which the whole pedigree hangs, can be absolutely proved to be false. For the present we need only note that Clarencieux, having made one Geoffrey into two (to eke out his pedigree),[2] threw back, as even his own dates sug-

[1] Harl. MS. 6,135. This, as the cookery books say, is "another way" of serving up the pedigree, and figures accordingly among Baker's three alternatives (*Northamptonshire*, I. 108).

[2] Cf. pp. 265, 269, above. The pedigree here given must be kept in mind throughout; and it must be grasped that the elder Geoffrey is a mere invention of the heralds.

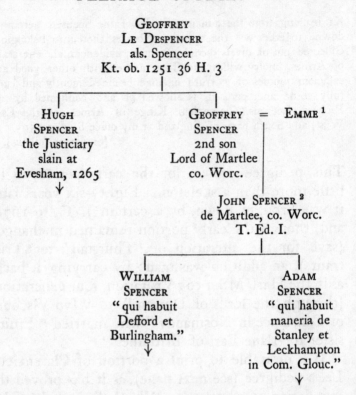

GEOFFREY
LE DESPENCER
als. Spencer
Kt. ob. 1251 36 H. 3

HUGH
SPENCER
the Justiciary
slain at
Evesham, 1265

GEOFFREY = EMME[1]
SPENCER
2nd son
Lord of Martlee
co. Worc.

JOHN SPENCER[2]
de Martlee, co. Worc.
T. Ed. I.

WILLIAM
SPENCER
"qui habuit
Defford et
Burlingham."

ADAM
SPENCER
"qui habuit
maneria de
Stanley et
Leckhampton
in Com. Glouc."

gest, the death of the husband of Emma (1251) to that of his imaginary father!

It may have been observed that Mr. Townsend, though expressing suspicion of the pedigree, left its truth undecided. Shirley, in the same way, wrote, in his *Noble and Gentle Men*, that—

[1] The authority cited is: "Emma que fuit uxor Galfridi le Despenser habuit custodiam Johannis filii et heredis ipsius Galfridi A° 35 Hen. III."

[2] The authority given is "Johannes le Despenser tenuit manerium de Marthlee in Com. Wigorn Ao 1 Ed. I."

THE RISE OF THE SPENCERS

The Spencers claim a collateral descent from the ancient baronial house of Le Despencer, which without being irreconcilable perhaps with the early pedigrees of that family, admits of very grave doubts, and considerable difficulties.

Instead, however, of investigating that claim, he included the family without question, although it had not, we have now seen, his qualification for admission, namely, that of " being regularly established either as *knightly* or *gentle* houses before the commencement of the sixteenth century." Brydges, again, in his *Collins' Peerage*, expressed his doubts in a running commentary on the Spencer pedigree as recorded ; but he did not attempt disproof. Baker, somewhat petulantly, complains of Brydges' criticisms that

the glaring discrepancies in the leading line of Despenser have escaped his animadversions, whilst he has minutely scrutinised every step of the descent from Geoffrey to Sir John Spencer.[1]

And yet Brydges was right. For there is no occasion to discuss the early Despencer pedigree, until the fact has been established that the Spencers are descended from them. If the links connecting the two families will not bear investigation, the historian of the Spencers need not discuss the origin of the baronial house.

Let us first take the version published in 1764 in the ' Baronagium Genealogicum . . . originally compiled from the publick records and most authentic evidences by Sir William Segar Knt. Garter Principal King of Arms and continued to

---

[1] *History of Northamptonshire*, I. 106.

the present time by Joseph Edmondson Esqr. Mowbray Herald Extraordinary ' :—[1]

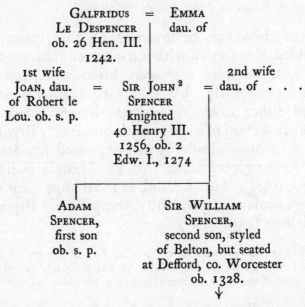

GALFRIDUS = EMMA
LE DESPENCER   dau. of
ob. 26 Hen. III.
1242.

1st wife   2nd wife
JOAN, dau. = SIR JOHN [2] = dau. of . . .
of Robert le   SPENCER
Lou. ob. s. p.   knighted
40 Henry III.
1256, ob. 2
Edw. I., 1274

ADAM   SIR WILLIAM
SPENCER,   SPENCER,
first son   second son, styled
ob. s. p.   of Belton, but seated
at Defford, co. Worcester
ob. 1328.

This descent had been greatly elaborated by 1779, when it appeared in *Collins' Peerage* fortified by ample proofs.[3] The odd blunder of the two Geoffreys was still retained, on the authority of the Visitation in the College of Arms, which was also the authority vouched for the fact that " Sir John Despencer had two sons, Adam who died young and William Le Despencer his heir." But an Inq. p. m. of 3 Ed. III. (1329) is cited in that work as proof that this Sir William " resided at

[1] Vol. I., plates 39, 40.
[2] The authority here vouched is ' Visit. com. Northant. in coll. Arm. Ao. 1617.'   [3] Vol. I. pp. 348–9.

Defford, in com. Wigorn, and died possessed thereof." Lee had recorded him (see above, p. 296)
as "qui habuit Defford et Burlingham."

Baker (1822) gave virtually, at this point, the
same pedigree :

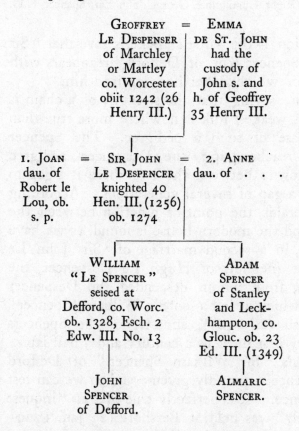

GEOFFREY = EMMA
LE DESPENSER | DE ST. JOHN
of Marchley | had the
or Martley | custody of
co. Worcester | John s. and
obiit 1242 (26 | h. of Geoffrey
Henry III.) | 35 Henry III.

1. JOAN = SIR JOHN = 2. ANNE
dau. of | LE DESPENCER | dau. of . . .
Robert le | knighted 40 |
Lou, ob. | Hen. III. (1256) |
s. p. | ob. 1274 |

WILLIAM | ADAM
"LE SPENCER" | SPENCER
seised at | of Stanley
Defford, co. Worc. | and Leck-
ob. 1328, Esch. 2 | hampton, co.
Edw. III. No. 13 | Glouc. ob. 23
| Ed. III. (1349)

JOHN | ALMARIC
SPENCER | SPENCER.
of Defford.

In Lipscomb's *History of Buckinghamshire* (1847),[1]
there is a pedigree of the family

[1] Vol. I. p. 565.

From the most authentic sources, collated with the Family evidences of his Grace the Duke of Marlborough and Earl Spencer with extracts from a Book in the Althorpe Collection, containing the Genealogical Descents, collected and certified by Sir Isaac Heard, Knt. Garter King of Arms, dated 3 June 1803, and compared with the Original, as farther certified under the hand of the Right Honourable George John Earl Spencer K.G. 21 Feb. 1827.

This version is the same as Baker's save that " Sir William Spencer Knt. of Defford " reappears with his title, of which Baker had deprived him.

Now the saying that the strength of a chain is that of its weakest link is nowhere more true than in the case of such a pedigree. The Spencer pedigree reaches up ; the Despencer pedigree reaches down : between the two there is a gap to be filled, a gap of several generations. According to the heralds, the point of junction between the ancient and the modern house is found, as we have just seen, in a second marriage of ' Sir ' John Le Despencer (nephew of Hugh Le Despencer, the Justiciary,[1] from whom descended the Despencer earls), by which he left a son ' Sir ' William " Spencer " of Defford (d. 1328), ancestor of the Spencers when they first meet us a century and a half later.

For this " Sir William Spencer " of Defford the reference is proudly given ; and so we can test his existence. It is perfectly true that an "inquest after death " was held at Pershore (23 Jan. 1329–30), but, unfortunately, William " Le Spencer " turns out to have been only a socage tenant of Geoffrey Dabitot, holding of him a messuage, four

---

[1] See pedigree on p. 296 above.

virgates of land, and two acres of meadow in Defford.[1]

But the heralds not only knighted this William " Le Spencer"; they also, we have seen, made him the son of " Sir John le Despencer " who died in 1274. And here at last we " have " them. For the inquests taken after the death of this John Le Despencer are not only quite decisive, but must have been examined by the heralds when constructing this pedigree. In two separate returns (11 June 1275) we read that " Hugo filius Hugonis le Dispenser est propinquior heres predicti Johannis le Dispencer et fuit ætatis quatuordecim annorum primo die Martii ultimo præterito." It is, therefore, absolutely certain that this John le Despencer left no issue. I can, further, identify his heir as the son of Hugh le Despencer, the Justiciar, who was slain at the battle of Evesham (1265), and as the Hugh who himself afterwards became famous as the favourite of Edward II. and earl of Winchester. For his age in 1275 proves the fact.[3]

---

[1] " dicunt quod Willelmus le Spencer die quo clausit extremum non tenuit aliquas terras ut tenens de domino Rege in capite. Dicunt etiam quod tenuit apud Defford de Galfrido Dabitot unum mesuagium, quatuor virgatas terre, duas acras prati, cum pertinentiis, in liberum socagium per servicium octodecim solidorum redditus," etc., etc. (Chancery Inquisitions 3 Edw. III., No. 13.)

[2] Chancery Inquisitions 3 Edw. I., No. 2. The returns relate to manors in Leicestershire.

[3] Compare the Inquest 9 Ed. I., No. 9, returning him as heir to his mother, and then aged 20 ; also, his proof of age.

It is needless, after this exposure, to pursue the pedigree further. We are, once more, simply dealing with one of those lying concoctions hatched within the walls of the Heralds' College, certified by its Kings of Arms, and still " on record " among its archives. This, be it observed, is no case of a tradition rashly or credulously accepted. Clarencieux compiled the pedigree, as he said he had done, from records ; but, with these records before him, he deliberately and fraudulently invented a descent which their evidence proves to be false. He knew, therefore, perfectly well that what he officially certified to be true was a lie of his own invention. Recorded by Vincent at the Visitation of 1617, accepted by Garter Segar, and certified by Garter Heard—even in the present century, this impudent concoction is indeed an instance of what we owe to the College of Arms.

The pedigrees with which it is hardest to deal are those in which fact and fiction are cunningly intertwined. Here, for instance, it is perfectly true that John le Despencer married Joan, daughter (and heiress) of Robert le Lou (*Lupus*), who brought him the manor of Castle-Carlton, co. Linc. This we learn from the Lincolnshire Inquest taken after his death, which proves that Joan died without surviving issue, and that John held the manor, by the courtesy of England, till his death. John himself had inherited the manor of Martley, co. Worc., which had been granted to his father by Henry III.[1] The heralds must have seen the

[1] See Inq. p. m. The Inquests on the death of this John are

difficulty caused by its not descending to his alleged sons, but being, on the contrary, afterwards found in the hands of the Hugh Despencers. For they " doctored " the pedigree accordingly. But their real crime was providing John with a wholly fictitious second wife, in order to make him the father of men with whom he had nothing to do.

The resemblance of the *modus operandi* here to that employed in the Russell pedigree is so close as to tempt one to suggest that there was a " Compleat Herauld " for the use of the College of Arms. In both cases a modern family had to be derived from a baronial house ; in both, the entries in genuine records were fraudulently used and connected; and in both, the worst *crux* was surmounted by the same device, namely, that of providing one of the baronial house with a wholly imaginary second wife, by whom he could be made the ancestor of the artful herald's dupes.[1]

Although, as I have said, we are not called upon to investigate the origin of the baronial Despencers, they played, in the history of their time, so conspicuous a part that one may be pardoned a brief digression on a problem that is deemed obscure. All the three origins set forth in Baker's *Northamptonshire* (I. 108) are wrong alike. The clue has to be sought in the descent of the manor of Arnesby,[2] which was held in two

fully abstracted in *Collins' Peerage*, but the fatal finding as to the heir is of course ignored.   [1] See p. 272.
  [2] In the Hundred of Guthlaxton, co. Leic.

moieties by the above John le Despencer, according to the Inquisition of 1275. Arnesby having escheated to the Crown with the rest of the fief of 'Peverel of Nottingham,' Henry II. bestowed it on Hugh de Beauchamp, and Hugh proceeded to enfeoff there " Elyas Dispensator, Radulphus de la Mare, Hugo de Alneto." These three feoffees were represented in or about 1212 by "Thomas Dispensator et Jacobus de Mara et Hugo de Alneto," who then held " in Ernesby " of Hugh de Beauchamp. The two first held by the service of a quarter of a knight each, and the third by that of a tenth, " of the honour of Peverel." [3] Thomas was succeeded in this quarter-fee at " Erendebi " by his younger brother Hugh, who was accordingly charged 25 shillings for relief on it in 1218,[4] this being the regular rate on fees held " ut de honore." But this sum was remitted to him in 1225, he being then in the king's service. He and his heirs continued to hold this estate *in capite* (the overlordship of Beauchamp

---

[1] This is set forth in the *Testa de Nevill* (p. 88), the description there of Henry II. as *proavus* of Henry III. being clearly a mistake. Nichols, in his *History of Leicestershire* (VII. 9–10), gives the facts very imperfectly.

[2] *Red Book of the Exchequer*, p. 586.

[3] *Ibid.* p. 180. This accords exactly with their respective holdings there, 15 virgates, 15 virgates, and 6 virgates (*Testa de Nevill*).

[4] " Pro relevio suo de quarta parte feodi unius militis in Erendebi que ei excidit per mortem Thome Dispensarii fratris sui primogeniti cujus heres ipse est " (Excerpts from the Fine Rolls, vol. I. p. 18).

[5] Rot. Claus. 9 Hen. III., No. 12.

having been eliminated), but by 1235 Geoffrey Despencer had been subenfeoffed in this quarter-fee.[1] Thus it was that the latter's heir, the above John le Despencer, was found by the Inquisition of 1275 to hold the manor of Arnesby in two moieties,[2] one of them from Hugh le Despencer as a quarter-fee, the other from Wigan "de La-mare" (representing the original feoffee of that portion, Ralph 'de la Mare'). We must therefore trace the origin of the family to Elyas 'Dis-pensator' of Arnesby (who was a benefactor there to Sulby Abbey), though neither he nor his successor Thomas is even mentioned in any one of the three versions of the pedigree.[3]

Hugh le Despencer the first prospered in the service of Henry III.[4] He was given Ryhall, with Belmethorpe, Rutland, in the 8th year of the reign, and Loughborough in the 11th year, while Freeby and Hugglescote, also in Leicestershire, increased his possessions, which passed to his namesake, the Justiciar Hugh le Despencer, as his heir. We have thus a house which rose to wealth in the service of Henry III., which then (in the person of the Justiciar) joined the barons against him, and which finally became obnoxious for the favour it received from his grandson.

In the meanwhile, Geoffrey, its cadet, who was

---

[1] " De quarta parte militis quam Galfridus Dispensator tenet in Hernesbi" (*Testa de Nevill*, p. 92). The exact relationship of this Geoffrey seems to be undetermined.

[2] Chancery Inquisition 3 Edw. I., No. 2.   [3] Baker, I., 108.

[4] He acted as a sheriff and governor of castles.

given the royal manor of Martley (co. Worc.), seems to have speculated in wardships. In January, 1230, he bought for £100 the heir of John de St. John (of Stanton St. John), and his marriage; and ten years later he bought, in like manner, the 'wardship' of the heir and lands of Robert Musard for 500 marcs, being pardoned, 9 May 1243, 50 marcs of that amount. Lastly, in 1247, he secured for 80 marcs the custody of Robert le Lou's manor, during the minority of his heiress, who was herself secured as a wife for his son John. This John was himself under age at his father's death, his wardship being bought by his mother Emma (June 1251) for 400 marcs. It was this John whom we found, above, dying without surviving issue in 1275, and succeeded by his relative Hugh le Despencer, son of the Justiciar.

Having now traced, for the first time, as it seems, the rise of the Despencers, I return to the Spencer family.

The proved falsehood of the alleged link connecting the 'Spencers' with the 'Despencers' does not merely shatter the pedigree; it is absolutely fatal to the *bona fides* of the herald by whom it was concocted. Consequently, when we find him citing evidences that are not now forthcoming, it is impossible to accept his statements as valid evidence. He asserts, for instance, that Henry Spencer, the alleged great grandfather of John (the purchaser of Althorpe), sealed his will with a coat-of-arms identical with that differenced Despencer coat now borne by the family in 1476 (16 Edw. IV.); and he further asserts that John, Henry's son, used, in 1473–4 and 1479–80, a seal bearing the arms of his mother (a Lincoln) quartered with those of his wife (a Warsted)! This most amazing heraldry is actually given as the reason why the family ceased to use their own illustrious coat till their right to it was rediscovered by the too ingenious Lee in 1595! It is obvious that these alleged facts were intended to explain away the family's application for a fresh grant in 1504, and the no less awkward fact, which seems to have escaped notice, of the Everdon branch obtaining yet another fresh coat.

It was difficult to know how to deal with the 1504 coat after the "resumption" of the ancestral arms in 1595 by the Althorpe branch. But the heralds overcame the difficulty by placing it in the second quarter, where, marshalled with the arms of Lincoln, Warsted, Graunt, and Ruding, it figures in endless shields adorning the Spencer monuments.

And now let me once more insist on the *modus operandi* of Clarencieux Lee, the original rascal, and the "onlie begetter" of this precious pedigree. He took from the records Spencers and Despencers wherever he could lay hands on them, fitted them together in one pedigree at his own sweet will, rammed into his composition several distinct families,[1] and then boldly certified the whole as

[1] For instance, the Despencers of Stanley Regis, Gloucestershire, an entirely different family, who had received that estate

gospel truth. To him enter Vincent (1617), beloved of the College still, but ready to swallow, as a loyal herald, whatever had been certified as true by a " Clarencieux Roy d'Armes." Vincent's Visitation pedigree, of course, was evidence enough for Segar, Garter King of Arms, who indeed had himself certified for the Westons, with all formal solemnity, a little concoction of his own (1632).[1] Lastly comes Sir Isaac Heard, Garter in the present century, ready, as we learn from Lipscomb, to certify the pedigree anew,—and doubtless to pocket his fees like a herald and a man. One seems to understand why a King of Arms bears around his crown the suggestive words " Miserere mei Deus."

It was at a great time that the Spencer pedigree was forged. Four years earlier (1591) the then Lancaster herald had endowed the Mauleverer family with a no less spurious descent ; and only

from the Crown as early as the 12th century. Lee got from them his Almerics and his Thurstans (see pp. 295, 299 above, and compare my article on " the Red Book of the Exchequer " in *Genealogist*, XIV. 4). It is doubtless from this imaginary descent that the Spencer Churchill branch have taken the Christian name of ' Almeric.'

[1] Segar, who was Garter 1607–1633, traced their pedigree in a direct line from " Haylerick de Weston Saxonicus " to Sir Richard Weston of Sutton, and signed it as ' Garter principal King of Arms ' throughout. It is worth while quoting, for comparison with Lee's certificate of the Spencer pedigree, Segar's certificate of this Weston one as compiled :—" Ex publicis regni Archivis et privatis ejusdem Familiæ archetypis, ecclesiis, monumentis, historiis, monasteriorum registris, et rotulis armorum vetustissimis, aliisque reverendæ antiquitatis et indubitatæ rebus maximo labore ac fide oculata."

two years later (1597) the earl of Kent brought an action against Garter King of Arms for wronging him in a peerage case, and the Commissioners who tried the charge " determined that part of the pedigree made by Garter to be unlawful," and the arms dependent on it, therefore, to be unlawfully borne.[1] This case would seem to be exactly parallel with that of the arms assigned to the Spencers on the strength of a spurious descent.

But, it may be said, all this happened long ago. Why revive it ? The answer is that it has become absolutely necessary to insist upon these facts since the appearance of the present attempts to exalt the paramount authority of the officers of arms and of their records.

In an article on " the Pedigree of the Fane and Vane Family," [2] Mr. W. V. R. Fane set himself " to test the authenticity of the Fane pedigree as given in the Heralds' Visitations of Kent, preserved at the College of Arms, by the light of contemporary records." Of this he wrote that—

when we refer to generations twelve to sixteen of that pedigree, which can be tested by such contemporaneous evidence, we find them constantly incorrect, while the various copies of the pedigree in the Heralds' Visitations do not even agree in all points among themselves. If this is so even in the 120 years immediately preceding the first appearance of the pedigree, how much less probable does the authenticity of the first eleven generations appear.[3]

---

[1] See "Arms and the Gentleman" in *Cont. Review*, August, 1899.   [2] *Genealogist* [N.S.], XIII. 81.

[3] I am merely concerned here with the reliance on ' Visitation ' authority as against Mr. Fane's case.

Mr. Keith Murray, replying on behalf of the College of Arms, and supplied by York Herald with the necessary information from its records, seemed to be shocked at any one rashly daring to question " the genuineness of the pedigree registered by a Herald acting under Royal Commission." [1] The writer who masquerades under the pseudonym of ' X,' exalts in the same manner the authority of Heralds' Visitations. Dealing with " the right to bear arms," he assures us that a fair copy was made when the herald returned to London, and then—

the pedigrees and arms were checked by the records contained in the College. The whole was carefully corrected, and the corrected and authoritative copy was delivered into the custody of the College of Arms in conformity with the requirements of the Royal Commission. [2]

So also the latest edition (1898) of Burke's *Landed Gentry* appeals in the preface to " the Heralds' visitations, documents of high authority and value . . . invaluable documents," and insists upon " the royal commission under which the Visitations were held." To appraise the value of this ' Royal Commission,' we need not appeal to the Spencer pedigree ; we have only to cite the words, written in his official capacity, of a present member of the College. Windsor Herald (Mr. Lindsay, Q.C.) drew up a formal memorandum at

---

[1] *Genealogist* [N.S.], XIII., p. 209. The pedigree appears in Visitations of 1574 and 1592 (*Ibid.* p. 212).

[2] *Genealogical Magazine*, II. 24. And compare the same writer's book on *The Right to Bear Arms*, p. 105.

the College, 27 August 1896, in which he thus exposed a single generation of the pedigree of the Pepys family, recorded at a 1684 Visitation by Clarencieux St. George : [1]

> The following corrections require to be made in the Visitation pedigree :—
>
> Robert did not die unmarried ; Thomas called Black did not die unmarried, nor without issue ; Thomas called Red did not die unmarried, nor without issue ; no daughter married Sir Gilbert Pickering ; there were two daughters not mentioned in the Visitation pedigree—Elizabeth, who married an Alcocke, and Edith, who lived to be 28, but died unmarried.   There are other inaccuracies.
>
> Truly a fine collection of blunders for one generation of a pedigree which, being reported under a Royal Commission, is *ipso facto* evidence and *primâ facie* proof in a court of law ! [2]

After this specimen of what was done even at the last Visitation, it is difficult to repress a smile at the sorrowful lament of ' X ' that these precious Visitations were discontinued :

> That no further Visitation has since been made is infinitely to be regretted.   It is the saddest thing one can find to chronicle in the history of British armory.[3]

I desire to call attention to the fact that a fresh pedigree of Pepys, for the period, has now been ' recorded ' at the College in the place of that which Mr. Lindsay has demolished.   This is one

---

[1] It is in the previous Cambridgeshire Visitations that the spurious Stuart pedigree is recorded (pp. 132, 144 above).

[2] ' Pepysiana ' Volume (in Mr. Wheatley's edition of Pepys), pp. 5–6.   Mr. Lindsay points out that it was even in the life-time of the famous diarist that his grandfather was ' recorded ' as dying childless, and indeed unmarried !

[3] *Genealogical Magazine*, II. 25.

of the little ways that the Heralds' College has. Their ' recorded ' pedigrees are sacrosanct—until they are found out ; and then—well, they alter them.

In the same spirit they allow it to be proclaimed in the works of ' X ' and Mr. Fox-Davies,—the latter avowing his dependence on the help of one of their number,[2]—that arms are ' bogus ' or illegally borne unless they are ' on record ' at the College of Arms.[3] And yet so perfectly conscious are the heralds of the grave deficiencies in their records that they had—it is no secret—to go to Oxford, not long ago, for the particulars of grants of arms of which they had no record. It will be interesting to see whether Mr. Fox-Davies will venture to deny a fact which demolishes his whole case. For unless every grant of arms was duly recorded at the College, the absence there of a record of any given coat being granted is no proof whatever that the coat is ' bogus.'

A good test of the heraldic value of ' Visitation ' evidence is found in the case of the pedigree and arms of the Yorkshire family of Stapleton. About 1530 a member of that family compiled for it a gorgeous pedigree,[4] tracing its descent from " Sir Myles Stapelton Knight, one of the founders of

---

[1] Compare *Cont. Review* (Aug. 1899), Vol. 76, p. 258.

[2] " Without his help I could have done but little."—*Armorial Families.*

[3] " Arms are good or bad as they are recorded or unrecorded."— *The Right to Bear Arms*, p. 108.

[4] Now in the Harleian MSS.

the Garter, by the dau. and one of the heires of John de Bretagne Earl of Richmond by his wife Beatrice dau. of King Henry III." This story was accepted by the great Dugdale himself when he made his Visitation of Yorkshire (1666); and, on the strength of it, he allowed the family to quarter " Checky or and azure within a bordure gu. a canton Ermine,"[1] as the coat of Britanny and Richmond. It is now known, and fully admitted, that it was not Sir Miles who made this match, but his uncle Sir Nicholas,[2] and that the family, consequently, are not descended from this alleged heiress, and have, therefore, no right to this illustrious quartering. And yet they can claim it as allowed by Dugdale and thus on record at the College, and this they do. Mr. Chetwynd-Stapylton, the historian of the family, writes as follows :

The Earl's arms have always been quartered on the shield of Stapelton. They are represented in Christopher Stapelton's pedigree *circ.* 1530, and Dugdale places them among the quarterings of the family in 1665. Numerous monuments and painted windows at Carlton and Wighill and Myton, also prove that successive generations have always maintained their connection with the Earl's family, though being descended from Sir Gilbert, the younger brother of this Sir Nicholas, none of them can actually claim Plantagenet blood.[3]

The author omits to mention that Dugdale only allowed the quartering in the belief that the family

---

[1] *Genealogist* [N.S.], XII. 129 ; *The Stapeltons of Yorkshire*, pp. 58, 241.
[2] *Ibid*. pp. 4, 58, 307–8.   [3] *Ibid*. (1897), p. 58.

were lineally descended from the Earl, a descent which he himself denies.

But in spite of monuments, glass, and ' Visitation,' the arms as well as the descent are, if I may use the graceful term of Mr. Fox-Davies, " bogus." Not only have the Stapletons no descent from this alleged heiress ; but even if they had, she was not, as they allege, a daughter of the earl of Richmond. She is now, indeed, made a daughter, not of the son-in-law of Henry III., but of Earl John ' de Bretagne,' his son ; but this does not mend matters, for this latter earl died unmarried ! [1] Indeed, Mr. Chetwynd - Stapylton, in despair, is driven to describe her in the strange terms " daughter, it may be illegitimate, but at least one of the heirs of John de Bretagne Earl of Richmond." [2] His sole evidence consists of his belief that she brought her husband an estate at Kirkby Fleetham, which estate, it can be shown from his own book, the Stapletons had held before.[3]

I need not labour the point further. When ' the veiled prophet ' of the College of Arms adjures the public to place its faith in the College records, and in no others, it ought to be sufficient

[1] See *Complete Peerage*, VI. 353.
[2] *The Stapeltons of Yorkshire*, p. 58.
[3] I emphasize this point because the author has no right to consider that he has disproved the conclusion of that eminent genealogist Mr. Thomas Stapleton that she was not a daughter of the earl of Richmond. The point here, it should be observed, is that a quartering wrongfully assumed—one of the abuses complained of by Mr. Fox-Davies and his friends—has the authority of the Heralds' College on the strength of its absurd " records."

to quote the words written by the great Blackstone
even in the last century.

> The marshalling of coat-armour, which was formerly the pride
> and study of all the best families in the kingdom, is now greatly
> disregarded, and has fallen into the hands of certain officers and
> attendants upon this court called heralds, who consider it only as
> a matter of lucre, and not of justice, whereby such falsity and
> confusion have crept into their records (which ought to be the
> standing evidence of families, descents, and coat-armour) that,
> though formerly some credit has been paid to their testimony,
> now even their common seal will not be received as evidence in
> any court of justice in the kingdom.[1]

" Who consider it only as a matter of lucre " :
that is, unhappily, the point. The deplorable
system by which the heralds, when they were
needy or greedy men, were dependent for their
income on the fees they could obtain, lies at
the root of the evil. In the old days, they were
ready to construct such pedigrees as those I have
discussed ; in later times they have had to look to
their profits from grants of arms. The history of
the College in the past is smirched by the sordid
squabbles of its members—squabbles originating,
as is well known, in the rivalry for fees thus
obtained.[2] Nor can one imagine any system

---

[1] See article on "Arms and the Gentleman" in *Cont. Rev.*,
August, 1899.

[2] Cooke, Clarencieux King of Arms, was accused by Segar
(afterwards Garter) of having given "Armes and Creasts without
number to base and unworthy persons for his private gayne
onlye " ; and by Dethick, another famous herald, of having
"prostituted his office in the vilest manner for money "
(Noble's *History of the College of Arms*). See also the outspoken letter from Peter Le Neve, Norroy King of Arms

better calculated to bring about the degradation
of coat-armour than that which made all concerned, from the King of Arms to the herald's
tout, gainers in proportion to the number of
coats for which the members of the British
public could be induced, by cajolery or by
terrorism, to apply.[1] Happily there are, in the
present day, among the members of the College,
gentlemen of social distinction and of independent
means, who could never act in the spirit of trades-
men with wares to push. It is, therefore, greatly
to be hoped that they will soon publicly repudiate
that beating of drums and clashing of cymbals—in
front, metaphorically speaking, of their grave and
sober walls—with which they are not in any way
connected, and which can only arouse their pro-
found disgust.

If the self-appointed champions of the College
would heap their indignation on the real abuse by
which the arms belonging to an old family are

(1704–1729), to Sir John Vanbrugh, Clarencieux King of Arms
(1704–1726), asking him "how it came to pass" that Sir
John had bagged the £15 fee on a grant to one of the family
of Smith "when in my province" (*Calendar of Le Neve Correspondence*, by F. Rye, edited by Walter Rye, p. 193).

[1] In the *Morning Post* of 20 January 1899 an advertisement
from "Two Single Clergymen," who desired "Good social
introductions to Persons of means," was followed by one inti-
mating that "A Gentleman, moving in good Suburban Society,
can, by introducing an historical subject, benefit his income.
Apply, *Herald*," etc. It is, of course, impossible to suppose
that anyone connected with the Heralds' College can have been
responsible for this attempt to add to the existing horrors of
"good Suburban Society."

pirated by any *nouveau riche* who happens to possess the same name, they would have a strong case. But when they denounce with equal fervour those who are guiltless of such piracy, and make no pretence to belong to any family but their own, one sees that, for them, the real crime is not to have paid heralds' fees. As a matter of fact, the College itself is virtually the worst offender in the above piracy of arms. Instead of distinguishing pointedly, as it should, the new family from the old, it will grant the former—if the fees are paid—as near an imitation as it dares of the old coat. Just as it confirmed to the modern Spencers a form of the old Despencer coat, so, when still more modern Spencers required armorial bearings, they were granted so close an imitation of the coat granted to Lord Spencer's ancestor in 1504 as to be absolutely undistinguishable in a seal or engraving, and virtually so even in colour.[1] Surely such devices are worthy only of a tradesman who should try to make his margarine look like butter.[2]

A very apposite case in point is afforded by the

[1] I refer to the coat of Spencer of Cannon Hall, Yorks., as now borne, quarterly with Stanhope, by Mr. Spencer-Stanhope and blazoned by Mr. Fox-Davies as *az. a fess erm. between six seamews' heads erased ppr.* The Spencer coat granted in 1504 was *az. a fess erm. between six seamews' heads erased arg.*

[2] So obviously wrong is this system that even the champion of the College himself has to admit that "there is much to be said in favour of the contention" of its opponents, and indeed that this contention has his "thorough sympathy" (*The Right to Bear Arms*, 1899, pp. 172-3).

arms of Buxton. The Derbyshire Buxton gave
name to a family which held land there, and which
is entered as of "yeoman" rank in 1431.[1] When
it came to bear arms, its coat was " Sa. two bars
ar., on a canton of the second a buck of the first
attired or."[2] Removing to Brassington in the
same county, this family had a cadet branch, descending from a second son, *temp*. Elizabeth,[3]
which resided in the adjoining parish of Brad-
bourne, and entered its pedigree at the Derbyshire
Visitation of 1662–3, when it bore the arms given
above, differenced by the addition of 3 mullets
argent between the bars.[4]

But there is, in Norfolk, another Buxton, and
this place must have given name to a Norfolk
family of Buxton, which emerged towards the
close of the 15th century, at Tibenham, and,
under Elizabeth, acquired Shadwell, which place
is still its seat. This family, most properly, bore
a coat entirely distinct from that of the Derbyshire Buxtons, viz.: "ar., a lion rampant sa., tail
elevated and raised over the head." The crests,
also, of the two families were entirely different in
character. So far, so good. But now comes the
amazing development sanctioned by the Heralds'
College.[5] The Shadwell Buxtons were actually

---

[1] *Feudal Aids*, I. 281.   [2] Papworth's *Ordinary*.
[3] Burke's *Armory*.
[4] Lysons' *Derbyshire*, p. lxxx.; and *Genealogist*, III. 123.
Compare the cases below of differencing a cadet coat by adding
3 mullets.
[5] See Mr. Fox-Davies' *Armorial Families*, Ed. 1895, 1899.

allowed to *quarter* the coat of the Derbyshire Buxtons[1] and to use the latter's crest in addition to their own (as if they had married their heiress), although they had nothing in the world to do with them ! This absolutely crazy heraldry is, if possible, even worse than allowing the Norfolk family to annex the Derbyshire coat in the place of its own.

But the real chance of the College of Arms came when a third family of the name required to be fitted with a coat. The well-known brewing family of Buxton,—nonconformist clothiers, in the last century, at Coggeshall, Essex, where they had lived since the latter part of the 16th century,—were, as usual, granted the arms of the Buxtons of Shadwell, with the addition only, for difference, of two mullets to the shield, almost the very addition employed by the Derbyshire Buxtons to difference the arms of their cadet branch. Can one wonder that such grants as these encourage the belief—which indeed they

---

[1] In *Burke's Peerage* for 1886 we read : "A second coat is stated to have been granted by Charles II., viz. Sa., two bars arg. ; on a canton of the second, a buck of the first attired or." But the engraving of the family arms had previously shown this latter coat in the *first* quarter. When the above sentence was inserted (between 1880 and 1883), the coat disappeared altogether from the engraving. In *Armorial Families* (1899) it is placed in the second quarter.

Apart from the above coat there was one with two bucks in it used, earlier, in connection with their own by the Tibenham Buxtons. It is styled "the ancient coat of the family" in Farrer's *Church Heraldry of Norfolk*, I. 51, 210. Compare Blomefield's *Norfolk* [1806], V. 276.

imply, it heraldry means anything,—that the grantee is a cadet of a house which declines to recognise him as such, but which cannot prevent the College from assigning him a 'colourable imitation' of its own arms ?[1]

We have already seen that the Bedford Russells were assigned a coat of which the 'lion rampant' rendered it quite distinct from that of the 'baronial' Russells, while the ancient Worcestershire house of Russell of Strensham bore a coat charged with a chevron between three crosslets. Thanks to this sound heraldry, there was no possibility of confusing the families although they bore the same name. The modern heralds, on the contrary, in accordance with their vicious system, have assigned to Lord Russell of Killowen's house the arms of the Bedford Russells (with whom it is wholly unconnected) differenced only by a bordure. The coat which follows it in *Burke's Peerage* completes the case against them. It is that of Russell of Swallowfield, and its origin is thus accounted for:

---

[1] Indeed, even after the modern family had received this new grant, Mr. Charles Buxton, in his Life (1848) of his distinguished father—a work which passed through thirteen editions—wrote that " William Buxton, his lineal ancestor, died in 1624 ; Thomas, the son of William Buxton, claimed and received from the Heralds' College in 1634 the arms borne by the family of the same name settled before 1478 at Tybenham, Norfolk, and now represented by Sir Robert Buxton, Bart." This was an entire misapprehension, as the fact of a new grant being necessary proves. But the nature of the arms granted encouraged the belief.

THE RISE OF THE SPENCERS

This family came originally from Worcestershire, and their arms, until slightly altered on the creation of the first baronet, were the same as those of the Russells of Strensham in that county, of whom the last baronet died in 1705.

To those who can read between the lines it is obvious that the real story is that this family of Russell, which appears to have emerged at Dover in the 18th century, had assumed the arms of Russell of Strensham, and that, when the first baronet was created (1812), these arms were disallowed and a fresh coat granted. But, to gratify the family, this coat was based on that of Russell of Strensham, and is now adduced, as we see above, even in *Burke's Peerage*, to support a descent which must have been rejected in 1812. Such is the natural result of this deplorable system.

But indeed one could go further. When the heralds' champions furiously denounce, as on pp. 145–6 above, the "contemptibly snobbish" use of arms belonging to "some noble family of your name" when you cannot trace descent from it, what have they to say to the case of the Howards, earls of Wicklow, who use, with full heraldic sanction,[1] the famous arms of the 'Norfolk' Howards (as borne by that family before the battle of Flodden, and as they ought to be borne by it now),[2] although, according even to *Burke's Peerage* itself, they do not claim descent from that house, and cannot trace their ancestry beyond the father of a Dublin physician who died in 1710?

---

[1] See Mr. Fox-Davies' *Armorial Families*.
[2] See pp. 39–41 above.

It is a pleasure to turn from the heralds and their ways to the family of Spencer itself. Precisely as its ancestor was content to trace, in 1564, his pedigree to the purchaser of Althorpe, so are his descendants in the Peerage books to-day. As Egerton Brydges well observed :

> The present family of Spencer are sufficiently great, and have too long enjoyed vast wealth and high honours, to require the decoration of feathers in their cap which are not their own.

Baker, who set an example to all county historians by the thoroughness, the patience, and the skill displayed in his great work on Northamptonshire, protested, it is true, indignantly against the remarks of Brydges, urging that "in the absence of *positive*, there is all the *circumstantial* evidence which the nature of the case will admit."[1] This somewhat "impotent conclusion" was due, perhaps, to the fact that Baker had examined the records for himself, when constructing his great pedigree,[2] and had thereby become conscious of the fatal flaw that they revealed. But his position was most difficult ; he had not only received assistance, locally, from Lord Spencer, but had dedicated to him his volume in terms of humble gratitude. Dugdale, on the other hand, though he would not be likely to offend a Warwickshire magnate, treated the records of his own College with the silent contempt that they deserved. *Il les connaissait si bien.* In his *Baronage* he began the

---

[1] *History of Northamptonshire*, I. 106.   [2] *Ibid.* p. 108.

pedigree with John, the purchaser of Althorpe, of whose origin he was so careless that he made him the son of his uncle.[1]

There is no reason even to suppose that the name of Spencer suggests descent from the great house of Despencer. It is found, at a comparatively early period, scattered about the country, in counties, for instance, so far apart as Somerset and Norfolk, while in Warwickshire itself, to my own knowledge, there were Spencers at Rowington at least as early as the middle or the 15th century.[2] Mr. Skeat, in his *Etymological Dictionary*, explains that the " Middle English " word *spensere* or *spencere* is equivalent to *cellerarius* in the " Promptorium parvulorum." The family, therefore, we may safely say, has derived its name from the buttery or the cellar, and has bestowed it, in turn, on an overcoat and a wig.

The time, happily, has come at last for honest genealogy and for truth. Those responsible for the new histories of our counties and their county families have resolved to seek the truth only, without favour and without fear.

Every effort will be made to secure accuracy of statement,

---

[1] " Son to John Spenser of Hodenhull, as it seems " (II. 418). He says indeed that the Spencers " do derive their descent from a younger branch of the antient Barons Spenser," but, under ' Despencer,' he ignores them.

[2] A Richard ' Spenser ' occurs a few years later, at Halesowen, in a Hagley charter.

and to avoid the insertion of those legendary pedigrees which have in the past brought discredit on the whole subject.[1]

And facts will be found to possess an interest that no fiction, however elaborate, can in these days claim to arouse.

Nor is the new genealogy a work of destruction only. It will show that the Spencers were substantial yeomen, members of a class famous in our history, when the House of Tudor obtained the throne.[2] John Spenser "de Snytfylde,"[3] I find, was already styled 'Master' when he joined the great Warwickshire Guild of Knowle in 1495. The writers on the family, strangely enough, have ignored the important Inquest after death of John Spencer of Hodnell, taken 5 Nov. 1499 (15 Hen. VII.). It not only gives us the date of his death (4 Jan. 1496–7) and recites the provisions of his will, but contains the particulars of a deed of feoffment of some of his lands (including

---

[1] Prospectus of the *Victoria History of the Counties of England* (Archibald Constable & Company).

[2] Harrison wrote of the yeomen, in the days of Queen Elizabeth, that "This sort of people . . . live wealthily, keep good houses . . . and with grazing . . . do come to great wealth, insomuch that many of them are able and do buy the lands of unthrifty gentlemen," and leaving their sons "sufficient lands, whereupon they may live without labour, do make them by those means to become gentlemen. These were they that in times past made all France afraid." He elsewhere observed that "some such graziers are reported to ride with velvet coats and chains of gold about them," and that, owing to their "cunning" and their large profits, "the poor butcher . . . can seldom be rich or wealthy by his trade." The tables are turned now.

[3] He is styled of "Snitterfield" in his uncle's will (1496).

those in Wormleighton), so far back as 15 Jan.
1491–2. As the first of the feoffees was Sir Edward Raleigh (of Farnborough)—himself charged
with devastation for pasture in that very year
(1492)[1]—we gather that John's position was
good, and obtain, further, some probability for
the statement in Lee's pedigree that John Spencer
' of Wormleighton and Hodnell '[2] had joined " in
divers deeds of feoffment with Sir Edward Rau-
leighe of Farneborowe Kt. and others" in 13
and 19 Ed. IV. (1473–4 and 1479–80). But
it is precisely this mixture of genuine evidences
with false genealogy that makes the pedigree so
deceitful. John Spencer, for instance, is assigned
only the wife mentioned in his will (1496), who
is made the mother of his three children, although
Baker subsequently found that he had been married before, and that his eldest child was by his
first wife. Moreover, when we read that his
"*grand*father" Henry had made his will[3] only
twenty years (1476) before his own, we cannot
but suspect that there may be some fearful confusion, and that two entire generations were made
by Lee out of one. If so, his composition becomes
more worthless than ever.[4]

---

[1] *Domesday of Enclosures*, p. 413. Farnborough adjoins Wormleighton.

[2] Hodnell is close to Wormleighton, but the latter estate did
not belong to this John Spencer the elder. It was only bought
by his nephew and namesake many years later (see p. 288 above).

[3] This is the will alleged to have been sealed with the present
arms of the family.

[4] One must repeat that Lee's deeds and persons may be

PEERAGE STUDIES

The above Inquest states that Thomas, son of John Spencer of Hodnell, was six years old when it was taken (1499). This date is of some interest, because it proves that John, the purchaser of Althorpe and Wormleighton, resided at Hodnell, his uncle's house, till his cousin came of age in 1514.[1] According, therefore, to this evidence, the date of his petition (p. 288 above) would be 1517, i.e. a little earlier than Mr. Leadam thought. It is recorded on the monument of this, the first Spencer of Althorpe (d. 1522), that his wife was

one of the daughters and coheirs of Walter Graunt of Snitterfield in the countie of Warwick Esquire; her mother was the daughter and heir of Humphrey Rudinge of the Wich in the county of Worcester Esquire.

And her mantle of arms displays Graunt quartering Rudinge. But the inscription seems of doubtful accuracy. Walter Graunt was a bailiff of Droitwich ('the Wich') in 1494,[2] and a parishioner of Salwarp, close to Droitwich, in 1496.[3] Snitterfield is a long way off. There has always, also, been

genuine, but that he connected and combined them at his own sweet will (compare my article on "The Origin of the Thynnes" in *Genealogist* [N.S.], XI. 193). It is, for instance, quite possible that he found a Henry Spencer obtaining a lease of tithes at Badby in 20 Hen. VI. (1441–1442), and that his wife's name was Isabel; for, although it has been supposed that there is now no evidence for this Henry, I have found Henry Spencer 'of Badby,' with Isabel his wife, occurring in 1468.

[1] I find that his cousin joined the Knowle guild in 1514 as "Mr. Thomas Spensar de Hodnell."
[2] Calendar of Inquisitions: Henry VII., I. 380.
[3] Nash's *Worcestershire*, II. 340.

some difficulty about the Rudinge match.[1] Lee, as a matter of fact, gave Walter's wife as " Elizabeth dau. and heir of Edmund Rudinge de Wiche" [Droitwich], but adds, as a note : " Sir Robert sayth she was daughter of Humfrey Rudinge, and hath a deed to prove it." This ' Sir Robert ' can be no other than the first Lord Spencer, then (1595), clearly, a youthful knight ; and we thus learn that he assisted Lee with his " singular skill" in alliances and arms.[2]

And now I will close this paper with a suggesttion about the origin of the arms allowed by Lee to the Spencers. These were no mere colourable imitation of an old coat in a new grant ; they were the actual arms of the Despencers, with a recognised cadet ' difference,' allowed them in right of their alleged descent from a cadet branch of that house. And all their descendants to this day, Spencers and Spencer-Churchills, are thus heraldically proclaimed a branch of the baronial Despencers. The placing of *three escallops argent* on the bend of the Despencer coat was, I have said, a recognised difference. The armorial bearings of the Claverings are an instance specially to the point. In the excellent *History of Northumberland* now in course of publication, there is a "genealogy of the lords of Warkworth and Clavering," whose coat was *quarterly or and gules ; a bend sable*. It is there pointed out that—

---

[1] See Grazebrook's *Heraldry of Worcestershire*.
[2] See p. 285 above.

Sir John de Clavering bore (during his father's lifetime) a *label vert* Caerlaverock, 1300 ; Sir Alexander charged the bend with *three mullets argent*, as did Sir Alan with *three mullets or*.

Sir Hugh de Eure [1] and his descendants bore *three escallops argent* on the bend.[2]

The Clavering difference, it should be observed, originated about the very time when we find Geoffrey a cadet of the Despencers, holding Arnesby and Martley.[3] It would have been, therefore, in accordance with the practice that he should adopt such a coat as is now borne by the Spencers as his alleged descendants.[4]

It is, perhaps, a little rash to go even further. But now that heraldry is beginning to be rescued from the heralds' hands, and to be intelligently studied in the true historical spirit, it is worth while making the suggestion that the original Despencer coat itself may have been based on that of 'Beauchamp of Bedford' (both coats were quarterly with a bend), even as the latter was directly derived from those of Mandeville and De Vere. For, as I have shown above (p. 304), the ancestors of the Lords Despencer first appear as feudal tenants of the Beauchamps of Bedford. In that case we should start with the coat of

---

[1] A younger son of the lord of Clavering, living *circa* 1274.

[2] Vol. V. (1899) pp. 25–6. Compare also Dallaway's *Heraldry*, 129, and the instances there given, and Woodward's *Heraldry*, II. 49. [3] See p. 306 above.

[4] In his important work on Heraldry Mr. Woodward observes, of the Despencer coat, that "This coat Sir Hugh le Despencer, in the reign of Edward II., differences by charging the bend with 3 mullets arg. ; for which in 1476 Henry Spencer substitutes 3 escallops arg." (II. 50).

THE RISE OF THE SPENCERS

Mandeville, *Quarterly or and gules*, which Beauchamp of Bedford adopted, as a relative, with the addition of a bend.[1] Then Despencer, as a tenant of Beauchamp, would adapt the coat by altering the tincture of the first and fourth quarters, and adding a fret in the second and third.[2] And lastly, a Despencer cadet would add yet another 'difference' by placing *three escallops argent* on the bend. If this view should be accepted, the evolution of the coat in question would be one of peculiar interest for the student of feudal arms, of heraldry as a living science. There is reason to believe that this branch of archæological research is about to receive worthy treatment at the hands of competent scholars.[3] We may then learn, at length, what armory once meant before the days of its decline and fall in the hands of the Heralds' College.

[1] See my *Geoffrey de Mandeville*, p. 392. The Clavering coat, referred to above, was derived from the same source (*Ibid.*).

[2] 'Frets' and 'fretty' seem to have been sometimes used for differencing.

[3] Mr. St. John Hope and Mr. Oswald Barron have in hand what ought to prove the standard work upon the subject.

VIII

Henry VIII. and the Peers

SUMMARIZING the labours of the Parliament which sat from 1529 to 1536, Mr. Froude, in his *History*, has extolled its importance as " the first great Parliament of the Reformation, . . . which had commenced and concluded a revolution which had reversed the foundations of the State." But the House of Commons was, for him, the Parliament ; he saw but " an ornament " in the House of Lords. It is difficult to reconcile this treatment of the Upper House as a cipher with his own description of the opening session (3 Nov. to 17 Dec. 1529) of this seven years' Parliament. He describes the situation, at that time, as follows :

It seemed likely for a time that an effective opposition might be raised in the Upper House. The clergy commanded indeed an actual majority in that house from their own body, which they might employ if they dared. . . . " In result," says Hall, " the acts were sore debated ; the Lords spiritual would in no wise consent, and committees of the two houses sate continually for discussion."

At length the obnoxious bills were passed, " to the great rejoicing," says Hall, " of the lay people and the great displeasure of the spiritual persons."

HENRY VIII. AND THE PEERS

I propose to ask in this paper whether we may not be able to trace a special creation of peers by the king, in accordance with the modern constitutional theory, at the very time of this clerical obstruction in the Upper House.[1]

Although the reign of Henry VIII. admittedly witnessed a vast change in the composition of the House of Lords—substituting, as it did, a decided lay for a decided clerical majority—I have never seen the process worked out in detail. When we compare the summonses to Parliament in 1529 with those in 1523 we find that the lay peers summoned numbered 44 as against 28, the estate of the clergy, of course, remaining the same (*i.e.* about 48 or 49).[2] The details are as follows :—

	1523[3]	1529[4]
Dukes	2	3
Marquises	0	2
Earls	7	9
Viscounts	1	3
Barons	18	27
	28	44

[1] Mr. Wakeman observes, in his *History of the Church of England* (1897), that, for " the legislation against the pope " in this parliament, " the only danger of serious opposition came from the spiritual lords and the clerical estate," and that the anti-clerical statutes of its first session were passed " in spite of the opposition of the clergy " (p. 212).

[2] See below. Dr. Stubbs reckons them, in these years, at 51.

[3] Dugdale's *Summons of Nobility* (from Roll in College of Arms), pp. 492-3. This appears to be the only authority available.

[4] *Ibid.* pp. 494-5 (from Roll in Petty Bag Office). This

But the forty-four lay peers summoned to the Parliament which met in November 1529 were soon substantially reinforced. The lamentable gaps, at this period, in the Lords' Journals— 22 Dec. 1515 (I. 57) to 15 Jan. 1534 (I. 58) —leave us dependent on other sources, including a MS. in the College of Arms (H. 13), which has not, hitherto, it seems to me, received scientific treatment. From this MS. are printed by Dugdale, in his 'Summonses,' two passages, fo. 398*b* (p. 500) and fo. 403*a* (p. 496). The first of these, which is of great importance, is thus headed by him in his book :

> The names of the Barons as they sate and entred in the Parliament in order, *in the xxviij year of the Reign of King Henry the Eighth* [*i.e.* 1536–1537].

It may seem scarcely credible that he has actually interpolated, himself, the words I have here italicized, which are not, I discovered on collation, found in the MS. ! As Mr. Gairdner, in his official *Calendar* (No. 104) reproduces this list from Dugdale, assigning it (in accordance with the interpolated words) to 18 July 1536, it becomes of interest to enquire whether this important list was actually drawn up in the summer of 1536. The name of the very first baron, George Lord Abergavenny, is decisive. He cannot have " sat " in this Parliament, because he had died the year before (1535). "John Lord Berners," also, had died in 1533. "The Lord Tail-

proves on collation to be virtually accurate. Rymer printed the list from the Close Roll.

boys of Kyme" was not summoned in 1536; and lastly, the entry "Lord Hastings, George, after created Earl of Huntingdon," is proof, from its form, that it deals with a sitting before the creation of the earldom of Huntingdon, 8 Dec 1529, and therefore quite at the beginning of the seven years' Parliament.[1]

On the other hand, the last two entries relating to Lord Hungerford of Heytesbury, admitted "8 June" 1536, and Lord Cromwell "of Wimbleton," admitted "by writ and patent the last day of the Parliament, *scil.* 18 July" 1536, prove that this list, which is written in one hand, must have been so written after the latter date. But it does not describe, as Dugdale, by his heading, makes it do, the state of things in the summer of 1536. It represents a list of the barons, according to their precedence in the Parliament of 1529, brought up to date, with two additional barons added from the Parliament of 1536. All this has been fused together in the list, as now existing in the MS., which was actually written not earlier than 18 July 1536

But Dugdale has not only erred in making a wrongful addition to the heading. He could not even print the text accurately. George Boleyn Lord Rochford was "admitted," not "anno xxvij" but "anno xxiiij."[2] Lord Bray was ad-

---

[1] At any later date there need only have been mentioned the precedence of the earldom, and the dignity would not have appeared at all in this list of "barons."

[2] This grave error is reproduced by Mr. Gairdner in his *Calendar*.

mitted, not " the xxiiij day," but " the iiij day "
of December ; Lord Conyers the 16th, not the
17th of January.

Leaving for the present this list, I turn to that
on fo. 403*a* (pp. 496–7). This is a Garter's list
of 25 peers who "made their first entry into
the Parliament Chamber" in the Parliament of
1529.[1] The last seven were barons created after
it had met ; the others, except the prior of St.
John and Lord Lumley (an anomalous case),[2] had
succeeded to their dignities since the previous
Parliament. It is not, however, easy to say why
Garter does not claim from such barons as Montague, Rochford, and Vaux, who cannot have sat
before.

As I shall have to rely largely on the former of
these lists, I may mention that (when explained
as above) it seems to me deserving of credit,
though its legal status appears to have been left
somewhat hazy by the House of Lords. It evidently divides the barons into sets : (1) those who
had been created before the Parliament of 1529,
ending with Lord Sandys and Lord Vaux ;[3] (2)
those created by writ or patent, after it had met.
But while Montague, Rochford, Maltravers, and
Talbot are treated as pre-existing dignities, Burgh
("Borough") of "Gaynesborough," which the

---

[1] " A Reward " being claimed by him " for their said entries."

[2] *John* Lord Lumley, as rightly given in the summons. Dugdale's *Summonses* gives " Thomas " in error.

[3] These dignities are alleged to have been created together
27 April 1523 (see below).

peerage writers assign to 1487, is here ranked as a new creation in December 1529, as indeed it continued to be.[1]

I shall now, in the light of Dugdale's lists, his " Summonses " for 1529 and 1534, and the Lords' Journals for the latter year, endeavour to trace the changes, between these dates, in the composition of the House.

A very careful collation of the lists leads to the conclusion that no fewer than twelve barons were added, in the course of this Parliament, to the twenty-seven summoned to its opening session. These may be classed as follows :

ELDEST SONS SUMMONED.

(1) George Boleyn, son of the earl of Wiltshire and Ormond[2] } Lord Rochford.

(2) Henry Fitz-Alan, son of the earl of Arundel } Lord Maltravers.

(3) Francis Talbot, son of the earl of Shrewsbury } Lord Talbot.

[1] This is a point of some importance in view of the fact that the last summons had been to Lord Burgh's grandfather more than thirty years before (1495).

[2] Strictly this was a new creation, as his father was only a co-heir of the Barony of Rochford ; but it was ranked above the two next and several ancient baronies, higher, it seems, than the old barony of 1495. This was probably, however, believed to be the precedence to which the old barony was entitled.

RESTORATION.

(4) Henry Pole, son of the countess of Salisbury } Lord Montague.[1]

NEW CREATIONS.

(5) John Hussey   Lord Hussey of Sleaford.
(6) Andrew Windsor   Lord Windsor of Stanwell.
(7) Gilbert Tailboys   Lord Tailboys of Kyme.
(8) Thomas Wentworth   Lord Wentworth.
(9) Thomas Burgh   Lord Burgh of Gainsborough.[2]
(10) Edmund Bray   Lord Bray.
(11) John Mordaunt   Lord Mordaunt.

PEER PREVIOUSLY OMITTED.

(12) Thomas Vaux[3]   Lord Vaux of Harrowden.

If we now arrange these additions to the barons in chronological order, we have :

---

[1] This is styled a restoration, but the barony, if extant, was in his mother at the time, and I should therefore consider it a summons like the three preceding. He was allowed precedence above Lord Rochford. This would seem to have been a much higher precedence than was enjoyed by the old barony, but no holder of it had sat as Lord Montacute since 1336.

[2] See Note 1 on p. 335.

[3] I cannot but think that his omission was due to his being under age when Parliament was summoned. The date of his subsequent summons seems to have been that of his majority.

1st Dec. 1529	Lord Montague.
„ „	Lord Hussey.
„ „	Lord Windsor.
„ „	Lord Tailboys.
2nd Dec. 1529	Lord Wentworth.
„ „	Lord Burgh.
4th Dec. 1529	Lord Bray.
19th Jan. 1531	Lord Vaux.[2]
7th Feb. 1533	Lord Rochford.
„ „	Lord Maltravers.[3]
(?) Feb. 1533	Lord Talbot.[4]
4th May 1533	Lord Mordaunt.[3]

{ [1]

Of the twelve barons stated above to have been admitted to the House of Lords before the Prorogation of May 1533, eleven are found members of the House in the session which opened 15 January 1534. Lord Tailboys alone was omitted, being dead.[5]

On the other hand, of the twenty-seven originally summoned to that Parliament, the

---

[1] " Admitted " on these dates (H. 13).

[2] " Entered " on this date (H. 13).

[3] " Admitted " on this date (H. 13).

[4] The Henry VIII. " Calendar " has brought to light the very interesting fact that fiants for writs of summons were issued to Lord Rochford and Lord Maltravers on 5 Feb. 1533, and to Lord Talbot twelve days later. This strikingly confirms the accuracy of H. 13, which states that the two former were 'admitted' 7 Feb. (1533), while it gives us the date, hitherto unknown, of Lord Talbot's summons. Lord Rochford's summons, as I have explained (*Athenæum*, 25 June 1898) is exactly parallel, in its anomalous character, to that of Lord Mowbray in 1640 (see p. 335, note 2).   [5] See below, p. 350.

names of three are not found among the Barons
in January 1534. Hastings had become earl of
Huntingdon ; Sutton, Lord Dudley, had died;[1]
and Lord Ogle was not summoned.[2] Deducting
these three, together with Lord Tailboys (four
in all), from the barons, who had been increased
by twelve, we obtain a net increase of eight.
Accordingly 35 barons were on the roll for 1534
as against the 27 summoned in 1529.[3]

The alleged summonses to Parliament for the
session of 1534 gave me extreme trouble. They
will be found in Dugdale's *Summonses* (pp. 497–8)
from which they have duly found their way into
the Record Office *Calendar* for 1534 (No. 55),[4]
Mr. Gairdner citing Dugdale's list as his authority.
But not only did these writs of summons issued in
the midst of a Parliament strike me as singular ; I
also wanted to know Dugdale's authority. He
himself prints in the margin, " Ex diario domus
Procerum in Parliamento " ; but no such list is
found in any volume of the kind. At last, the
explanation was discovered. This list, which has
been gravely cited as if an original authority, is
an absolute concoction by Dugdale himself, who

---

[1] In Jan. 1532. His successor, " being a weak man of understanding," had begun at once to alienate his estates, and having
to subsist "on the charity of his friends," was "commonly called
the *Lord Quondam* " (Dugdale).

[2] There seem to have been no summonses to the Ogles
between 1529 and 1554.

[3] Berners, however, must be deducted, being inserted in error
(see below, p. 340).

[4] There entered as " Writs or summons to the Parliament."

has simply taken the Lords' Journals, where they recommence, and constructed from them writs of summons in what he thought would be their form![1]   Nor is even this the extent of his offence. He overlooked the earl of Sussex, who appears at the opening of the session, to say nothing of the earl of Oxford and the Lords Sandys and Mountjoy, who are found on the roll two days later (17 Jan.), thus bringing up the total of the lay peers to 54, as against the 50 given by Dugdale as "summoned" to this session.[2]

While on the subject of this unintentional, but splendidly successful hoax, I may explain that writers on the historic peerage have been so completely imposed upon by Dugdale, that they have even quoted as genuine his concocted Latin writs. Courthope stated that George Boleyn was summoned to Parliament by writ 5 Jan. 1533[3] as "Georgio Bullen de Rochford" (p. 402), and is followed in this by the editor of *The Complete Peerage* (VI. 382).   Nay, this valuable work, now our standard authority, has even gone further than Courthope in inventing a new peerage dignity—"Bullen de Ormond and Bullen de Rochford"—on the strength of Dugdale's work.   For on p. 492 of the *Summonses*, in a list similarly constructed

---

[1] His remark in the closing paragraph of his Preface would hardly lead one to suspect he had gone so far as this.

[2] Dr. Stubbs reckons the maximum for the reign as 51 (in 1536).

[3] This date is Dugdale's error for 15 Jan. 1533-4 (the date, moreover, not of a writ, but of Parliament reassembling).

from the Lords' Journals (though no authority is cited), Dugdale constructed from the word "Ormond" an imaginary writ "*Thomæ Bullen de Ormond*" in 1515 ! Evidently what had really happened was that the writ (apparently lost) had been issued to Thomas earl of Ormond (and Lord Rochford), who had died about the time of its issue. Dugdale, knowing he was dead, had coolly assumed that the writ was issued to Sir Thomas Boleyn, who was not, as a matter of fact, raised to the peerage till several years later.[1] Of his concocted writs for Jan. 1534 one more instance must be noted. The Barons' roll in the Lords' Journals includes on the opening day (15 Jan.) the name of Lord "Barnes." Dugdale concocted, on the strength of this, a writ of summons "Humphrido Bourchier de Berners, chel'r," which has sorely puzzled the peerage writers. For the only possible Lord Berners was named John, and had died some ten months before. Courthope, in his *Historic Peerage*, repeated the speculations of Nicolas as to who this Humphrey could be, and they are now copied into the *Complete Peerage* (I. 345).

Before leaving the above Parliament of 1515, I would note that Mr. Brewer, like his successor in the editorship of the Henry VIII. *Calendar*, was imposed upon by a list, not indeed constructed, but actually copied, from the Lords' Journals, 12 Nov.

---

[1] This instance may serve to illustrate the liberties Dugdale took with his names. In other cases, such as those of Lumley and Grey de Powis, he erred in the Christian name.

1515. It is calendared as a "modern copy."[1] One is really tempted to copy a page from the printed Journals of the House of Lords, and to leave it about in the Public Record Office, in the hope that one's manuscript may be calendared among the treasures of the nation.

Having compared the numbers of the lay peers summoned in 1523 and 1529,[2] we will now compare the numbers summoned at the latter date with those upon the roll for the session which opened on 15 Jan. 1533-4.[3]

	1529.	1534.
Dukes . . .	3	3
Marquises . .	2	2
Earls . . .	9	13
Viscounts . .	3	1
Barons . . .	27	35
	44	54

The total increase of ten may not seem large; but it was sufficient to convert the lay peers from a minority to a majority. The composition of the House, according to the Lords' Journals (15 Jan.), was now as follows:

---

[1] *Calendar* 1515–1518, No. 1131.
[2] p. 331 above.
[3] By an unlucky slip (p. 497) Dugdale prints the date "quinto [instead of 'quintodecimo'] die Januarii."

Spiritual peers	.	.	.	.	.	48
Lay peers	.	.	.	.	.	51 [1]
Prior of St. John	.	.	.	.		1 [2]

100

The addition of the earl of Oxford and Lords Sandys and Mountjoy raised the number of lay peers to 54 at the very outset of the session (17 Jan.), while the spiritual peers, simultaneously, shrink on the Journals to 37.

The importance of these figures lies in the fact that the spiritual peers are supposed to have retained their majority till the Dissolution of the Monasteries (1540). Hallam was emphatic on the subject :

> The fall of the mitred abbots changed the proportions of the two estates which constitute the upper house of parliament. Though the number of abbots and priors to whom writs of summons were directed varied considerably in different parliaments they always, joined to the twenty-one bishops, preponderated over the temporal peers. It was [now] no longer possible for the prelacy to offer an efficacious opposition to the reformation they abhorred.[3]

Mr. Pike would seem to take the same view, for he writes that—

> The most important of all permanent changes ever effected at any one time in the constituent parts of the House of Lords was

---

[1] I. 58–9. One more than Dugdale's total, because he omits the earl of Sussex. As the lists tally in all else, the omission is obviously an error.

[2] Sat at the head of the barons.

[3] *Const. Hist.* (Ed. 1832), I. 99.

that which befel when the greater monasteries were dissolved.
. . . The Lords Spiritual, reduced now only to archbishops
and bishops, could never again command alone a majority in the
House of Lords.[1]

Mr. Taswell-Langmead, again, was quite positive
on the subject :

The dissolution of the monasteries . . . reduced from a
majority to a minority the Spiritual Peerage, who alone were
likely to be sufficiently independent to offer a serious opposition.[2]

Mr. Lecky also appears to hold the same view :

The Reformation had a capital influence on the constitution of
the House. By removing the mitred abbots it made the temporal
peers a clear majority.[3]

Lastly, Mr. Amos, in his monograph on the
Reformation Parliament,[4] took only the numbers
summoned at its outset (44 lay lords, 48 spiritual
lords), and observed that " The Spiritual Peers did
not, in fact, avail themselves of their numerical
strength to oppose Henry's measures against the
Pope and the Anglican Church " (p. 4).

Dr. Stubbs, I find, has a paragraph on the subject in a monograph on " Parliament under Henry
VIII." [5] He holds that—

The number of lay peers varied little, for there were few new

---

[1] *Constitutional History of the House of Lords* (1894), pp. 349,
351. [2] *Constitutional History of England* (Ed. 1890), p. 399.
[3] *Democracy and Liberty* (1896), I. 302.
[4] *Observations on the Statutes of the Reformation Parliament*. By
A. Amos (1859).
[5] *Lectures on Mediæval and Modern History* (1886), pp. 269–
270.

creations except where an old peerage had been extinguished. The minimum number was called in 1523, being only 28, several of the peers being that year employed in military affairs abroad ; the maximum was in 1536, in the parliament called to approve of the destruction of Anne Boleyn, and the number was 51. In the other parliaments it varied between 36 and 46. It will be thus observed that until the dissolution of the monasteries, the spiritual lords were always in a numerical majority.

But he guards himself by adding that—

the tendency was decided towards an equalisation, a tendency which is ocularly perceptible in the journals where, in the list of attendances which from 1515 onwards are marked daily, the two bodies are arranged in parallel columns.[1]

And he proceeds to urge that as the lay peers attended much more regularly than the spiritual lords, the former may have had more voting power, unless the spiritual lords had given proxies, which they may often have omitted doing. He admits, however, on the next page that proxies were largely used by them.

To those who have followed my narrative above there can be little question that so far back even as the close of 1529 the king's creations had deliberately given the lay peers a majority by raising their number to 51. And the Lords' Journals, extant for the last part of the Parliament (1534–1536), show at a glance the substantial majority possessed throughout that period by the lay peers.

To the summer Parliament of 1536 (8 June,

[1] But there is a serious gap in the Journals (1515–1534), as I observed above (p. 332).

28 H. VIII.) there were summoned, according to Dugdale, 51 peers, divided as follows :

Dukes	3
Marquises . . .	2
Earls	13
Viscount . . .	1
Barons . . .	32
	___
	51

But this is another of Dugdale's concocted lists,[1] and is distinctly unreliable. It cannot be identified, I think, with any particular list in the Lords' Journals ; and it omits Lords Conyers and Mountjoy, who, as we know from the Journals, were on the Roll. In the case of this parliament there is record evidence for the writs (27 April), namely the Close Roll of 28 H. VIII., m. 43*d*., from which the list of summonses is printed in Rymer's *Fœdera*. From this authentic list we find that Dugdale omitted no less than three peers who on this occasion received writs of summons. These were Arthur Viscount Lisle, Christopher Lord Conyers, and Charles Blount Lord Mountjoy. On the other hand, he added an imaginary writ, " Thomæ Cromwell (de Wimbleton) Chivaler "

---

[1] He describes it as " Adhuc ex dicto diario [Procerum]." In this case he has successfully imposed, it is clear, on Dr. Stubbs, who, in his monograph on the subject, asserts of the lay peers that " the maximum was in 1536 . . . and the number was 51."

(p. 499). He further made George Lord Cobham
into Thomas, and Edward Lord Grey de Powys
into John.   The net result of substituting the correct figures from Rymer is that 53 lay peers were
summoned.   The exact constitution of the House,
as summoned, was this :

Lay peers . . .	53
Prelates . . .	17
Keepers of spiritualities .	4
Abbots . . .	27
Prior	1
Prior of St. John . .	1
	103

But on June 13 there are only 40 spiritual peers
and the prior of St. John on the roll as against 52
lay peers.

A new lay peerage was created on this occasion
in Lord Hungerford of Heytesbury, who was
admitted to the House 13 June,[1] and a further one
by the admission of Thomas Cromwell as a baron
on the last day of the Parliament (18 July) " by
writ and patent," says H. 13, but, according to
the Lords' Journals, under the writ.   The date of
his patent was 9 July.

Lastly, if we take the Parliament which opened
28 April 1539 (31 Hen. VIII.), we find that the

---

[1] Lords' Journals, I. 86.   Not " the eighth day of June," as
in Dugdale's *Summonses* (p. 500).   He produced his writ, which,
according to Rymer, had been issued with the others on 27 April.

summonses, according to Dugdale, give these totals :

Prelates	.	.	20 ⎫ 39
Abbots	.	.	19 ⎭
Dukes	.	.	2 ⎫
Marquis	.	.	1 ⎪
Earls	.	.	15 ⎬ 48
Viscount	.	.	1 ⎪
Barons	.	.	29 ⎭

87 [1]

But the Lords' Journals (I. 104) give us on the opening day :

Spiritual peers	.	. 40
Lay peers [2]	.	. 50

90

For ten years before the Dissolution, it seems clear to me, the king had systematically secured a majority of lay peers ; and this majority, as the crisis approached, he made decisive. At the same time, it is notable that the Parliament of 1539 presents the opposite tendency to that of the sessions 1534–1536. For, instead of the lay majority increasing, it now diminished, though continuing to exist. On the last day that the abbots sat (28 June) the Lords' Journals show us the lay peers in a majority of only six.

[1] *Summonses*, p. 501.
[2] They omit Viscount Lisle (who is given by Dugdale), but have three more barons.

And now, from this historical enquiry, I would pass to a more antiquarian subject, namely, the fate of the seven baronies created, as we have seen, in the Parliament of 1529. My reason for doing so is that our dependence on a single MS. (H. 13, Coll. Arm.) for their first appearance has led, not only to much confusion among peerage writers on the subject, but also to conflicting action in the treatment of these dignities. The question is not one of mere academic interest, for it may actually arise at any moment before the Committee for Privileges.

If we take these peers in order, we find the first three are Hussey, Windsor, and Tailboys, all admitted alike 1 Dec. (1529) :

(1) John Hussey, rightly stated in *Complete Peerage* to have taken his seat as above.

(2) Andrew Windsor, wrongly there stated to have been summoned by writ 3 Nov. 1529.[1] There is no such writ.

(3) Gilbert Tailboys, there stated " to have been summoned to Parliament as a baron in or before 1529."

The next two are Wentworth and Burgh, both alike admitted the day following (2 Dec. 1529) :

(4) Thomas Wentworth, stated in *Complete Peerage* to have been summoned to Parliament by writ from 2 Dec. 1529.[2] There is no such writ.

---

[1] This simply repeats Courthope's statement.
[2] This, again, repeats Courthope.

(5) John Burgh, wrongly there stated to have been summoned to Parliament 3 Nov. 1529.[1] There is no such summons.

Sixth is Bray, admitted 4 Dec. (1529) :

(6) Edmund Bray, stated in *Complete Peerage* to have been " summoned as a baron from 3 Nov. 1529."[1] A footnote adds that " the reasoning in support of such summons was deemed conclusive, in 1839, by the House of Lords, though neither the original writ nor the enrolment thereof could be found." But this is a misconception.[2]

Seventh and last is John Mordaunt, admitted 4 May 1533 :

(7) John Mordaunt, stated in *Complete Peerage* to have been " summoned to Parliament as a baron from 4 May 1529.[1] This date is four years too early, and impossible to boot.

Now the sole authority for the dates of all seven creations is H. 13, and Dugdale's book containing its list was before the editors of both works. Yet only for the first of the seven has its evidence been rightly reproduced, and this only in the *Complete Peerage*.

---

[1] This, again, repeats Courthorpe.

[2] It was only " Resolved that it appears to this Committee that Edmund Lord Bray was summoned to Parliament and sat in the House in the Twenty-First year of the reign of King Henry the Eighth." The sole evidence adduced for his doing so was H. 13, which merely records his admission (4 Dec.) as above.

PEERAGE STUDIES

The fate of these seven baronies has varied widely. It may be summarized thus :

(1) Hussey. Forfeited 1537.
(2) Windsor. Fell into abeyance 1641. Called out 1660. Abeyance again 1833. Called out 1855. Extant.
(3) Tailboys. Seems to disappear (in Parliament) after 1529.[1]

---

[1] The peerage writers are all wrong about this interesting barony. The *Complete Peerage*, following Courthope, states that Gilbert Lord Tailboys (who had doubtless received the barony as the husband of the king's mistress) died 15 April 1539. But the inscription on his monument states that he died 15 April 1530 (*Genealogist* [O.S.], vol. II.) ; that is, within a few months of his becoming a baron. This is confirmed by entries in the Henry VIII. "Calendar," which show that his wife was a widow before 24 May 1532 (No. 1,049). Their son George is regularly termed Lord Tailbois. He is still spoken of as a minor in 1538, but in April or May 1539 he married Margaret daughter of Sir William Skipwith. He was among the peers in attendance upon Anne of Cleves on her arrival, Dec. 1539. There is an entry in the Lords' Journals, 17 May 1539 :— ' quædam allata est billa concernens stabilimentum quarundam terrarum *Domino Tailboys* et Domine Anne uxoris ejus," but it is clear from the Calendar that his wife's name was Margaret. He is named in a Lincolnshire commission of Sept. 1540, but had been succeeded by his brother before 15 Feb. 1541, when "Robert Lord Talboys," a minor, occurs in a royal grant. His name is an addition to the peerage. He was dead 19 May, 1542.

The above account, it will be found, differs widely from that in the *Complete Peerage*, according to which the father died 15 April, and the son 6 Sept. 1539, the latter being unmarried. The father's death in 1530, and the fact that his sons were minors, explain the absence of the name in Parliament ; but the barony was fully recognised.

It became the subject of an important decision, as to a husband's right to be styled a baron *jure uxoris*, on a Mr. Wimbish,

(4) Wentworth.　Fell　into　abeyance　1815.
　　　Emerged 1850.　Merged in Lovelace, 1893.
(5) Burgh.　Fell into abeyance 1601 (?).
(6) Bray.　Fell into abeyance 1557.　Called out
　　　1839.　Extant.
(7) Mordaunt.　Fell into abeyance 1836.

Thus Wentworth alone is inherited by the sole
heir of the original grantee ; Mordaunt was so
inherited down to 1836 ; and Windsor, though
falling twice into abeyance, has only remained in
that condition some forty years in all.　Compared
with these three dignities the barony of Braye has
been the subject of what is rightly deemed very
peculiar treatment.　After remaining in abeyance
for no less than 282 years, it was "called out"
(1839) in favour of one of several junior co-heirs.[1]

　At this point it may be well to observe that
there is confirmatory evidence *aliunde* for the
creation of all these baronies in the Parliament of
1529.　It is not a little remarkable that the first
four of the barons "admitted" in December (1529)
had been returned to this Parliament as knights of
the shire.[2]　The new peers, probably, are first

who had married the sister and eventual heiress (in 1542) of the
above George, claiming (unsuccessfully) to be styled Lord
Tailboys in her right.　　[1] See also pp. 30–31 above.
　[2] "Sir John Husee, now Lord Husee," and "Sir Gilbert
Tailboys, now Lord Tailbois" for Linc. ; "Thos. Wentworth, now
Lord Wentworth," for Suff. ; and "Sir And., now Lord Wyndesore" for another county.　It is clear from these entries and that
of "Sir John Neville, now Lord Latymer" (Yorks), that this
Record Office list, as printed, is not earlier than 1530 (see Calendar, 1529, No. 6,043[2]).

found collectively in a curious copy of their auto-
graph signatures appended to a draft act.[1] Mr.
Gairdner dates this interesting list, " Nov. 1529," [2]
which is certainly too early, for the earls of Wiltshire and Sussex were not so created till 8 Dec.
The signatures run thus :

Henry R.—Thomas More, cancellarius—T. Norfolk—Charlys
Suffolk—Thomas Dorset—H. Exeter—W. Arrundell—John
Oxynford—E. Derby—H. Worcester—Thomas Rutland—T.
Wylsher—Robt. Sussex—Arthur Lysle—G. Bergevenny—Aude-
lay—T. Berkeley—Henry Montagu—Willm. Dacre [3]—Harry
Morley—Edward Grey [4]—William Graye [5]—John Berners—
W. Mountjoy—Henry Daubney (?)—T. Darcy—T. Mountegle
—John Husey—A. Wyndesore—T. Wentworth—Thomas
Burgh—Edmond Bray.

It is obvious that the list must be previous to
the resignation of Sir Thomas More (May 1532),
and indeed to the Marquis of Dorset's death,
10 Oct. 1530. It is therefore much earlier than
Lord Mordaunt's creation. But as Lord Tailboys'
name alone is absent among those of the newly
created barons, I am disposed to associate his
absence with his death in 1530 (15 April) ; and
therefore to date this list as later than 1529. We
have, at any rate, for extreme limits, 8 Dec. 1529
—10 Oct. 1530.[6]

[1] Cott. MS. Titus B. IV. 114.
[2] Calendar, Vol. IV., No. 6,044.
[3] Of Gillesland.   [4] Of Powys.   [5] Of Wilton.
[6] This investigation has a further bearing. The object of
these " Articles condescended and agreed by the king's highness
and the noblemen of this his realm of England being assembled in
this present Parliament," etc., was to secure the full rights of the
Crown in wardships, which was the motive for the Statute of

I would specially call attention to the fact that the barons' precedence in this list is precisely the precedence assigned them in H. 13,[1] with the sole exception that Lord Morley and Lord Dacre change places. Of the newly-created barons the precedence is the same in both : Hussey, Windsor, Wentworth, Burgh, Bray.

The next list in which we find them is that of 13 July 1530, when the peers sign an address to the Pope.[2] Here again the junior barons are : (1) 'John Husey,' (2) 'Andrew Wyndesor,' (3) 'Thomas Wentworth,' (4) 'Thomas Burgh.' Tailboys, as I said, was dead : Bray is unaccounted for. Sir John Mordaunt (the last creation) was still so styled in March 1532 ; but is " John Lord Mordaunt " 16 May 1532,[3] twelve days after his admission (according to H. 13) to the House of Lords.

Before dealing with the treatment of these baronies by the Crown or the House of Lords, we must glance at one of the difficulties created by the want of evidence, namely, the question whether we should hold them to have been created by

---

Uses. Consequently, it proves that this legislation was initiated by Henry from the earliest days of this Parliament, and not, as historians have held, introduced towards its close. Hall states that the king sent down the Bill to the Commons, as approved by the Lords and himself, in his 24th year [1532–1533].

[1] Fo. 398*b* (see p. 332 above).

[2] Calendar, No. 6,513. The appearance of " George Rocheford " as the second baron on the list, at this early date, is difficult to account for, as his first known summons was in Feb. 1533.

[3] Calendar, No. 1,023.

patent or by writ of summons.   It is difficult to
say what, if any, should be the presumption on
this point in the reign of Henry VIII.   It is now,
I believe, recognised that Eure and Wharton were
baronies created by patent (1544).   Yet in the
absence of evidence on the point, the House of
Lords treated the latter, in 1845, as a barony by
writ, and actually recognised a right to co-heirship
to that dignity accordingly.[1]   In this, indeed, it
did but follow the precedent of 1836, when the
Committee for Privileges accepted the strenuous
contention of the Vaux and Bray claimants that
the non-enrolment of a patent of creation, and the
failure to discover one, constitute a sufficient presumption that the creation was by writ.   The
creation of Eure and Wharton by patent (1544)
seems to be well established;[2] and the fact that
this is so, though the patents are not enrolled, has
a grave bearing on the doctrine of presumption in
cases of future occurrence.

The strange uncertainty of practice at the time
is shown by the curious fact that the Cromwells,
father and son, were apparently created barons

---

[1] Resolution of 28 July 1845 (repeating that of the Committee
for Privileges) : "That the Barony of Wharton is a Barony
created by Writ and Sitting on the 26th of Nov. 2nd Edw. VI.,
in the year 1548, and is descendible to heirs general." The
Resolution further asserts that this barony fell into abeyance in
1731.

We know now that the barony was created by patent four
years earlier (1544), though efforts have been made to dispute this.
(*Notes and Queries* [1899], 9th S. IV. 459).

[2] See *Complete Peerage*.

both by writ and by patent. Thomas, summoned (it would seem) by writ to the Parliament of 1536, was created Lord Cromwell by patent on the 9th of July. He took his seat on the 18th, " by writ and patent," says H. 13, but, according to the Lords' Journals, under the writ.[1] Gregory, his son, summoned by writ to the Parliament of (28 April) 1539,[2] was created Lord Cromwell by patent, 18 Dec. 1540.

I believe that there was a change of practice about the year 1536. In that year Thomas Cromwell, summoned to Parliament by writ, was also, we have seen, created a baron by patent (9 July). In 1539 Lords Russell, St. John, and Parr were all created barons by patent (9 March).[3] Gregory Cromwell, indeed, was summoned by writ to the Parliament of 28 April 1539,[4] but was created baron by patent 18 Dec. 1540. Lord Wriothesley was created by patent 1 Jan. 1544, as also (we now know) were Lords Eure and Wharton (? 24 Feb.) 1544.

The immediate precedents for the baronies I am discussing are the creations in the opening days of the Parliament preceding (15 April 1523).

[1] Compare p. 346 above.
[2] There is much confusion on this subject in the *Complete Peerage* (I. 119, II. 433), due to the erroneous supposition that this was a summons in his father's barony.
[3] There is some doubt about the date of Parr's creation, but, as he sat below Russell and St. John in 1532, he cannot have been created before them.
[4] According to Dugdale's *Summonses*, p. 501 (from original record).

These were the Viscountcy of Lisle and the baronies of Berkeley, Sandys, and Vaux. Nothing could be more unsatisfactory than the authorities vouched for these creations in the pages of the *Complete Peerage*. None whatever is cited for Vaux ; " Dugdale " alone is quoted for Sandys ; while, for Berkeley, we read that " Fitz James' letter and this (contemporary) account in the ' Chronicle of Calais ' are the only proofs of the alleged summonses " (*rectius* summons). The evidence for all four creations is as follows :

(1)   " In the month of Aprell [1523], a parliament being holden at Westmynstar, ser Arthur Plantagenet was made vicounte Lile and ser Morreis Barkley, lyvetenaunte of Calleis, was made lorde Barkley, ser William Sands was made lorde Sands, ser Nicholas Vauxe was made lorde Vauxe." [1]

(2)   "The 27th of April was Sir Arthur Plantagenet, a bastard son to King Edward the Fourth, at Bridewell, created Viscount Lisle in the right of his wife, which was some time wife to Edward Dudley, beheaded ; Sir Maurice Berkeley, lieutenant of Calais, was made Lord Berkeley ; Sir William Sandys, Lord Sands, and Sir Nicholas Vaux, Lord Vaux." [2]

(3)   " In parliament Sir Arthur Plantagenet has been created Viscount Lisle. Sir Thomas Boleyn,[3] Sir William Sandys, Sir Morres

[1] *Chronicle of Calais* (Camden Soc.), pp. 32–3.
[2] *Stow's Chronicle*, Ed. Howes, II. 520.
[3] This name is inserted by error.

Barkeley, and Sir Nicholas Vaux have been made barons, and summoned by writ of the Parliament. No acts have yet passed the Lords or the Commons." [1]

Of these three witnesses, the first could not be better. Lord Berkeley was lieutenant of Calais, Lord Vaux, lieutenant of Guînes, and Lord Sandys, treasurer of Calais.

There is abundance of concurrent testimony from independent sources. A letter to Surrey, 14 May 1523, speaks of "Lord Vaux" (he is said to have died that day) as "sick and in great danger." [2] Two days later Sir W. Fitzwilliam is appointed governor of Guînes, "as held by Nicholas Lord Vaux"; [3] and the latter's Inq. p. m. styles him late "Lord Harrowden." [4] Moreover, his son, as "Lord Harrewden," landed at Calais with Wolsey 11 July 1529 [5] (being then about 18).

Berkeley did not long survive; but a letter of Wolsey to Henry VIII., 20 Aug. 1523, speaks of "letters to Lords Sandes and Berkeley," [6] and eight days later there "landyd at Caleis 100 soldiers sent to the Lord Barkley." [7] He died 12 Sept. 1523, and the writ to make Inquisition for his lands as " Maurice Lord Berkeley " followed on October

---

[1] Letter of 28 April 1523 from Richard Lyster to Lord Darcy (Calendar of Henry VIII. documents 1519–1523, p. 1,260). [2] *Ibid.* p. 1,272. [3] *Ibid.* p. 1,273.
[4] See Vaux case (Minutes of Evidence) for this and some other proofs. [5] *Calais Chronicle*, p. 38.
[6] Calendar (*ut supra*), p. 1,352. [7] *Calais Chronicle*, p. 33.

24.[1] We have also the important letter of 6 May (1523) from his counsel Fitz James, touching his precedence as a peer.[2]

Sandys presents no difficulty, as the new peer lived on till 1542.[3]

Given the above evidence, we ask whether these baronies were created by writ or patent? Fitz James, who as a lawyer understood the subject, wrote to Lord Berkeley of the honour "which the king's grace by his write hath late callid yowe to." And this expression harmonizes well with that in Lyster's letter.[4] The statement of Banks that Lord Vaux was created by patent, and that this patent was wilfully destroyed by the infamous Lady Banbury in the next century,[5] seems to be unsupported. Moreover, her alleged object—to prevent her husband's brother succeeding—is absurd, for he would have been the heir to the dignity whether created by writ or by patent. As to the subsequent decision of the question by the House of Lords, the *Complete Peerage* assigns to 1838 [6] (the Vaux case) the " rather rash " assumption that the creation was by writ. But the House had decided the point so far back as 1660–1661, when an heir-general obtained the barony of Sandys,[7] which was on all fours with that of Vaux.

---

[1] Calendar (*ut supra*), p. 1,453.

[2] Smyth's *Lives of Berkeleys*, II. 208 ; and *Complete Peerage*, I. 332. It was cited in the Vaux case.

[3] " The xxij of Auguste Landyd at Caleis 100 men to go into France with lorde Sands." *Calais Chronicle*, p. 33.

[4] p. 357 above.   [5] *Complete Peerage*, VIII. 18.

[6] *Rectius* 1836.   [7] *Ibid.* VII. 57.

HENRY VIII. AND THE PEERS

Let us now return to the baronies created in the parliament of 1529, and ask whether their creation was by writ or by patent. The answer must be sought in the case of the barony of Tailboys, the bearing of which has been imperfectly realized. In this case attention has been concentrated on the claim of a husband to the style of his wife's dignity.[1] But for our purpose the point is that the Crown accepted, without a question, its inheritance by a female within some fifteen years of its creation. Now as Tailboys was one of several baronies which all appear simultaneously,[2] we must presume them all alike to have been created by writ and descendible to heirs-general. The question arose in the case of another of these baronies, that of Braye, and was argued at length in the Vaux case, which came on, oddly enough, about the same time.[3]

But the question had arisen long before in the case of another of these dignities, the barony of Windsor. Although unnoticed, it would seem, in Cruise's Treatise on Dignities, the Windsor case (1660) has been held to be the earliest certain

---

[1] Cruise on *Dignities*, pp. 106–7.   [2] See p. 337 above.

[3] See Mrs. Cave's claim to the barony of Braye, pp. 5–8, where the argument is very full, and Mr. Bourchier Hartopp's claim to that of Vaux, pp. 8–11, and p. 15. The evidence collected in the Vaux case certainly creates a very strong presumption in favour of a writ. A petition from the Vaux claimant that his case might be heard before the committee came to any decision as to the creation or limitation of the barony of Braye was read in the House 29 Feb. 1836. In his case the object was to assign the creation to the summons of 1536, in order to prove that Vaux was a barony by writ and not by patent.

instance of the determination of an abeyance by the Crown,[1] the method then adopted being a declaratory patent. Mr. Pike, in his *Constitutional History of the House of Lords* (1894), has given great attention to this case (pp. 133–135, 138) as "the earliest case in which anything like the doctrine of abeyance was recognised." But neither he nor any one else (though Dugdale alludes to it) seems to have known of the singular "grant" of Feb. 1645–6, which I here transcribe from the Signet Office Docquet Book 1644–1660.

A graunt whereby (reciting that Henry sometime Baron Windsor of Bradenham in the County of Bucks to him and his heires dyed and left issue Thomas his only sonn and heire who was Baron Windsor to him and his heires now deceased without issue and two daughters, Elizabeth the elder married to Dixey Hickman Esq. and now also deceased and another daughter. And that Thomas Windsore Windsore als. Hickman Esq. is sonn and heire of the said Elizabeth and Dixey) his Majestie is hereby pleased to dispose conferre and confirme the said Barony and honour to the said Thomas Windsore and the heires males of his body, and to declare, accept, elect, and ratify him and his heires males to bee Barons Windsore. And if this declaracion bee ineffectuall in Law, his Majestie hereby erecteth, confirmeth and establisheth to him and his heires males the said dignity with all priviledges and immunities thereunto belonging. And declareth, approveth, confirmeth, restoreth and establisheth to him and his heires males the same place degree and Precedency in Parliament and elsewhere, and the same priviledges and immunities as the said Henry or Thomas Barons Windsore enjoyed. Subscribed by Mr. Attorney General upon signification of his Majesty's pleasure and his signe manuall procured by Mr. Secretary Nicholas.

The immediate point of this document is the

---

[1] Courthope's *Historic Peerage*, p. xxxiv.

bearing on the 1529 creations of its recital that the late Lord Windsor held the dignity " to him and his *heires*," thereby making it a barony by writ. But still greater is the interest of this effort on the part of the grantee to hold the dignity, when thus " disposed " of in his favour to him " and the heires *males* of his body." The Crown's doubt of its power in the matter is very significant ; and the effort was completely abandoned at the Restoration, when the dignity was simply confirmed to the same grantee " and his heirs." [1]

The question of these baronies and their origin arose next in the Wentworth case 1. April 1702, when Martha, wife of Sir Henry Johnson, claimed, before the House of Lords, to be Baroness Wentworth.[2] The Minute Book containing notes of the evidence produced on this occasion was discovered in time to be adduced in the Braye case, 22 March 1836. They ran thus :

They produced the Heralds' proofs. Sir Henry St. George : He says—This Book hath been in my office ever since his Time, and looked upon to be very good.[3]

" This Book " was clearly H. 13,[4] and on its

[1] Pike, p. 134 ; from Signet Office Docquet Book, June 1660. Henry VIII. did, indeed, create Sir William Paulett, Kt. of Basing, who was similarly a co-heir of the lords St. John of Basing, in 1539, lord St. John with limitation to his heirs *male*, but this was a new creation, and the barony was ranked accordingly.

[2] Lords' Journals, XVII. 91.

[3] Braye case : Minutes of Evidence, pp. 34–5.

[4] This is evident from " Brief of case of the Barony of Wentworth " in the Heralds' College. (See Mrs. Cave's Braye claim, p. 7.)

decidedly flimsy (till corroborated) evidence the House clearly accepted Wentworth as a creation of 1529.

The whole question, however, was investigated much more thoroughly in the Braye case ; but the procedure, on that occasion, was very strange. H. 13 and the Wentworth minute book of evidence were put in for the claimant, but "the Counsel were informed that they could not be used as Evidence." Nevertheless, although the committee had no other evidence before it to prove that Edmond Bray was summoned to Parliament or sat in it before 25 Hen. VIII., it was

Resolved that it appears to this committee that Edmund Lord Braye was summoned to Parliament and sat in the House in the Twenty First year of the Reign of King Henry the Eighth.[1]

This resolution, it will be found, simply accepts the opening words of Mrs. Cave's original petition (1836):

Sir Edmond Braye of Braye in the County of Bedford Kt. was summoned to Parliament as a Baron of the Realm, by Writ, in the 21st year of the reign of King Henry the Eighth, anno 1529, and sat in Parliament in pursuance of such writ.

This was an assertion based on nothing but H. 13, and its acceptance, therefore, as valid, was an acceptance of that MS. as equivalent to legal evidence.

Nevertheless the Crown, when determining the abeyance, did not specify the year of the reign in which the barony was created. Here are the

---

[1] Lords' Journals, 1839, p. 647.

letters patent from the *London Gazette* of 10 Sept. 1839 (p. 1,740).[1]

Whitehall, Sept. 7, 1839.

The Queen has been pleased to direct Letters Patent to be passed under the Great Seal, declaring Sarah Otway Cave . . . Baroness Braye, she being one of the co-heirs of John the last Lord Braye, and as such one of the co-heirs of the Barony of Braye originating by writ of summons granted to Sir Edmund Bray in the reign of King Henry the Eighth; and that she, the said Sarah Otway Cave, shall be Baroness Braye, and have, hold, and enjoy the said Barony of Braye, together with all the rights, titles, privileges, pre-eminences, immunities and advantages, and the precedency thereunto belonging, to hold to her and the heirs of her body, in as full and ample manner as John the last Lord Braye held and enjoyed the same.

The barony was ranked, quite properly, after that of Wentworth, as, we have seen, it was from its earliest days. The relative precedence of Windsor was not then in question, that barony having been, since 1682, merged in the earldom of Plymouth, and being, moreover, actually in abeyance since 10 July 1833. When that abeyance was terminated (1855), the Braye precedent ought to have been strictly followed, the evidence for the origin of the two dignities being absolutely the same. But, instead of that, it will be seen, the proof of sitting in 25 Hen. VIII. was now treated as the earliest evidence for the existence of the dignity.

[1] The precedent here followed, as to date, seems to have been that of Vaux, in which the House (following the committee) resolved, 2 March 1837, "That the Barony of Vaux of Harrowden was a Barony created by writ *in the reign of King Henry the Eighth* and therefore descendible to Heirs General." (The italics are mine.)

PEERAGE STUDIES

Whitehall, October 15, 1855.

The Queen has been pleased to direct letters patent to be passed under the Great Seal declaring Harriet Clive (commonly called Lady Harriet Clive), Widow, Baroness Windsor, she being one of the coheirs of Other Archer, last Baron Windsor (sixth Earl of Plymouth), deceased, and as such one of the coheirs of the Barony of Windsor, originating by writ of summons to Parliament, granted to Sir Andrew Windsor, in *the twenty-fifth year of* [1] the reign of King Henry the Eighth, and that she . . . shall be Baroness Windsor, and have, hold, and enjoy the said Barony of Windsor, together with all the rights, titles, privileges, pre-eminences, immunities, and advantages, and with the precedency belonging, to hold to her and the heirs of her body in as full and ample manner as Other Archer . . . or any of his ancestors, Barons Windsor held and enjoyed the same.[2]

The importance of this action by the Crown is that it virtually ignores the evidence of H. 13, although, as I have now shown, that evidence is strikingly confirmed by what has elsewhere been brought to light.

But in abandoning H. 13 as evidence for the creation of the dignity in 1529, the Crown has only increased the confusion. For the alleged writ of summons granted "in the twenty-fifth year" is wholly imaginary! It is actually found only in Dugdale's deliberate concoction.[3] The result of the whole muddle is that no one can tell what is really held by the Committee for Privileges, the House, or the Crown. What, for instance, is the origin to be assigned to Vaux of Harrowden? It is historically certain that its creation belongs to 1523; but there is no legal evidence that the first

[1] The italics are mine.
[2] *London Gazette*, 16 Oct. 1855 (p. 3,797).
[3] See p. 339 above.

peer either received a writ of summons or ever sat
in the House, and Mr. Hartopp's elaborate claim
seemed to treat the general summons in 1536 as
the origin desired (in order to reject a creation by
patent).[1]   In the Windsor case, the letters patent
(1855) deduce, we have seen, the issue of a writ
from the fact of a proved sitting ; in the Braye
case, and apparently in that of Wentworth, no
legal proof for either writ or sitting was produced
as evidence of creation, for which H. 13 seems to
have been deemed sufficient by the Committee for
Privileges and the House.

It is one of my objects in this paper to call
attention to the unsatisfactory, because unsystematic,
practice of the Committee for Privileges and the
House of Lords.   In the Mowbray case, (1877),
as I have elsewhere shown,[2] the modern doctrine
of abeyance was carried back centuries *per saltum.*
But even more important, though apparently overlooked, was the startling acceptance without question of writs of summons to the " parliaments "
of 1283, 1294, and 1297.   For the validity of
the writs to the meeting at Shrewsbury in 1283
affects of itself a hundred baronies, and the

[1] The Lords, we have seen, evaded the difficulty by resolving
that the barony had been created " in the reign of Henry VIII."
The *Complete Peerage* holds, somewhat strangely, that this in-
dicates " the date 1529, being that in which there is the first
notice of a sitting in this Barony" (VIII. 18).   But there is no
such notice in 1529, or indeed till 1534, though H. 13 places the
young lord's entry into the House in Jan. 1531.

[2] " The Determination of the Mowbray Abeyance " (*Law
Quarterly Review*, X. 68–77) and in this work below.

Mowbray decision, as I have observed, thus effects a revolution in peerage law.[1]

The position, at present, of the Tudor baronies specially discussed in this paper is somewhat analogous to that which has been caused by conflicting decisions on Simon de Montfort's Parliament. De Ros and Despencer are ranked as dating from that Parliament, while its summons has not been deemed valid in the case of other baronies.

It is, in any case, quite clear that the present ranking of these baronies—Wentworth, Braye, Windsor—is altogether wrong. In the Parliament beginning June 1536, the precedence found both in the enrolment of summonses and in the Lords' Journals is precisely that which we have found in H. 13 and elsewhere : (1) Hussey, (2) Vaulx,[2] (3) Windsor, (4) Wentworth, (5) Burgh, (6) Braye, (7) Mordaunt.[3] This being so, Lord Windsor is certainly entitled to claim a higher precedence ; and the closing words of the letters patent of 15 Oct. 1855 undoubtedly enable him to do so.

[1] See p. 10 above ; and cf. Stubbs' *Constitutional History* (1875), II. 116, 131, 184, 223, 225.

[2] Vaux is not one of the baronies in question. Its ranking here seems anomalous (see p. 365 *note* 1). In H. 13 (fo. 398*b*) it is ranked with Sandys *above* Hussey in the Parliament of 1529–1536 ; and it is so ranked in the Lords' Journals where they recommence in Jan. 1534. This would seem to be the right ranking.

[3] Journals, 12 June 1536 (28 Hen. VIII.).

IX

Charles I. and Lord Glamorgan

PART I

GLAMORGAN'S DUKEDOM

FOR some two hundred and fifty years—indeed, ever since their creation or alleged creation—the dukedom of Somerset and earldom of Glamorgan, bestowed on Lord Herbert, the son of the marquis of Worcester, have been surrounded by a baffling haze of mystery and doubt. But while the dukedom has long been so forgotten that it is not even mentioned by modern writers on the Peerage, the earldom has continued to vex the souls not only of antiquaries, but of historians. For on the authenticity of these dignities and of the documents affecting them there hangs, to some extent, the solution of a great problem. This problem is that of Glamorgan's secret treaty (1645), of which his biographer observes that—

The genuineness of the commissions and of the patents on the authority of which he acted—a question involving the character of Charles I., has since been one of the most intricate and fiercely debated points in English history.[1]

[1] *Dictionary of National Biography*, LIII. 233. It may be as

I have dealt elsewhere with the earldom of Glamorgan, and shown that, save in two documents which I reject as forged, we can find no mention of it earlier than the month of January, 1645.[2] A bill for its creation reached the signet office in the following April, but, as Mr. Gardiner observes, " nothing further was done in it." [1]   Lord Herbert, however, styled himself ' Glamorgan,' and was so addressed by the king in 1645 and 1646, till he succeeded to his father's marquisate. It was my suggestion that Charles may have purposely kept back the patent in order that the prospect of securing it might serve as a hold on the grantee and as an incitement to success.

We may now turn from the earldom of Glamorgan to the dukedom of " Somerset and Beaufort."   The peerage writers seem to have generally

well to give the references for the previous steps in the discussion between Mr. Gardiner and myself.   In " The True Story of the Somerset Patent 1644 " (*Academy*, 8 Dec. 1883), I showed how strong was the belief after the Restoration that Glamorgan's patents were forged.   In the *English Historical Review*, October 1887, Mr. Gardiner dismissed my criticisms, and in " Charles I. and the Earl of Glamorgan " (pp. 687–704) upheld the validity of all the documents.   In the *Athenæum*, 15 Jan. 1898, I published a paper on " Charles I. and Lord Glamorgan," urging that the latter's letter to Clarendon in 1660, on which Mr. Gardiner relied, did not refer, as he had assumed, to events in 1644, and was too confused in its statements to afford reliable evidence.   To this Mr. Gardiner replied, 26 Feb. 1898, frankly admitting that he had " built on too unstable a foundation in regard to this letter."   Lastly, I contributed to the *Genealogist* for April 1898 an article on " The Earldom of Glamorgan."

[1] *E. H. R.*, II. 694, *note*.

[2] *Genealogist*, April 1898 (N.S. XIV. 213–5).

assumed[1] that the patent produced, at the Restoration, by the marquis of · Worcester, as granting him a dukedom was the curious quasi-patent of April 1, 1644, in which *inter alia* occurs this relative passage :

> We give and allow you henceforward . . . the title of Duke of Somerset to you and your heirs male for ever, and from henceforward to give (*sic*) the Garter to your arms, and, at your pleasure, to put on the George and blue ribbon.[2]

But this most "casual" clause, inserted in the middle of a commission, was not the document upon which he relied.[3] Dugdale, in the private letter to which I originally drew attention, writes :

> The Marquis of Worcester did exhibit a patent under the Great Seal pretended to be granted to him by the late king at Oxford for creating [him] Duke of Somerset and Beaufort ; but this being in truth suspected to be forged, there appearing no vestige of it at the signet or privy seal, nor any other probable way, and my Lord of Hartford being prepared to make such objections against it as might have tended much to the dishonour of my Lord of Worcester before a committee of Lords, about three days since the Marquis of Worcester was pleased to tell the Lords that he must confess that there were certain private considerations upon which that patent was granted to him by the late king, which he performing not on his part, he would not insist thereon, but render it to his Majesty to cancel if he so pleased.[4]

---

[1] This idea originated with Birch, author of the *Inquiry* in the middle of the last century.   [2] See *Collins' Peerage.*

[3] It was supposed to be so by Birch (1756) in his *Inquiry* (p. 23), by Sir C. Young, and by Courthope, etc., afterwards.

[4] Dugdale to John Langley 25 Aug. 1660. (Hist. MSS. Commission, 5th Report, App., p. 178.

From the phrase "duke of Somerset *and Beaufort*," it is certain that the patent in question must have been that which contains that title, and which alone contains it. This patent, of which, as I have said, the existence is ignored by the peerage writers, is still preserved at Badminton, where it was examined by Mr. Gardiner. As it has never, I believe, been printed,—except a portion of the preamble by Dircks,—it may be of interest to give here the words of creation, and those of the limitation which Mr. Madan, of the Bodleian Library, has most kindly copied for me from the Carte MSS., which contain a transcript of it.[1]

Passing over, for the present, the preamble, we come to the actual creation.

His igitur perspectis, Sciatis quod nos de gratia nostra speciali ac ex certa scientia et mero motu nostris præfatum Consanguineum nostrum Edvardum Comitem Comitatus nostri Glamorgan ad statum, gradum, stilum, dignitatem, titulum, et honorem Ducis de Somerset et Beaufort ereximus, præficimus (*sic*), insignivimus, constituimus et creavimus, ipsumque Edvardum Comitem Comitatus Glamorgan Ducem de Somerset et Beaufort tenore presentium erigimus, præficimus, insignimus, constituimus et creamus, eidemque Edvardo nomen, statum, gradum, stilum, dignitatem, titulum, et honorem Ducis de Somerset et Beaufort imposuimus, dedimus et præbuimus, et per præsentes imponinimus (*sic*) damus et præbemus, ac ipsum Edvardum hujusmodi statu, gradu, stilo, titulo, dignitate, nomine et honore Ducis de Somerset et Beaufort per gladii cincturam capæ honoris et circuli aurei impositionem insignimus, investimus, et realiter nobilitamus per præsentes, habendum et tenendum, etc.

The limitation is as follows :

[1] Bodleian MS. Carte 129, fo. 349 (Carte's foliation 228). This is transcribed by Carte from Anstis' copy.

præfato Edvardo et hæredibus suis masculis legitime procreatis et procreandis in perpetuum, volentes et per præsentes concedentes pro nobis hæredibus et successoribus nostris quod prædictus Evardus (*sic*) et hæredes sui prædicti prædictum nomen, statum, gradum, stilum, titulum, dignitatem et honorem Ducis de Somerset et Beaufort successive gerant et habeant et eorum quilibet gerat et habeat.

The first point to arrest attention, here, is the double title found only in this patent and in Dugdale's letter referring to it. The great aim of the family—or at least of Glamorgan himself—was to revive the title of Somerset, borne by the Beauforts, from whom they were illegitimately descended. The double title (suspicious in itself) must have been adopted to distinguish this dukedom from that which had been held by the house of Seymour.

The next point is the limitation, of which the language is important ; for Mr. Gardiner observes that it " was not as usual to the heirs of Glamorgan's body, but to his heirs male, implying that in case of his own sons predeceasing him the title was to go to his father or his brother." [1] If, as Mr. Gardiner has observed, such problems as those of the Glamorgan documents " are not to be solved even by the most impartial person who approaches the subject from a purely antiquarian point of view," [2] it is no less true that they cannot be solved without antiquarian knowledge. We here find him, for instance, accepting a limitation to " heirs male " as equivalent to a limitation to heirs male collateral—in spite of the doubt notori-

[1] *E. H. R.*, II. p. 693.   [2] *Ibid.* p. 687.

ously surrounding that construction,[1] and, in the second place, restricting the parties to whom the dukedom was limited to the grantee's "father or his brother," a construction which, on any hypothesis, is obviously inadmissible. But this is not all. It will have been observed that the words of the patent are :

> hæredibus suis masculis *legitime procreatis et procreandis* in perpetuum.

This anomalous formula, which here replaces the normal " de corpore suo exeuntibus," must be construed (I am assured by a well-known peerage counsel) as a limitation to the heirs male of the grantee's body.

From this limitation I now pass to the date at which the dukedom was granted. The patent gives this as " quarto die Maij anno regni nostri vicessimo primo " (*i.e.* 4 May 1645). Anstis had pointed out that the word " primo " had been added, and Mr. Gardiner, accepting this as indisputable, held that Glamorgan had added the word " to gain easier credence for what was otherwise a true tale." This was, he urged, " the full extent of Glamorgan's forgery." [2] And this conclusion he applied in the case of Glamorgan's negotiations, urging that " just as in 1660 he did not scruple to add *primo* to the date of his patent," so did he treat his powers when he made his secret treaty.[3] And again, in a later proposal of his,

---

[1] See *Complete Peerage*, III. 107–109.
[2] *E. H. R.*, II. 689, 694–5.   [3] *Ibid.* p. 705.

Mr. Gardiner sees "the work of the man who subsequently added the word *primo* to a patent."[1] But, in the next volume, Mr. Gardiner withdrew his conclusions, and suggested that Glamorgan had forged nothing, but that when a warrant for a dukedom of Somerset was sent to his father the marquis of Worcester (Jan. 1645), the date of the son's patent was formally altered by the Crown to avoid a question of precedence.[2] The suggestion is as plausible as it is ingenious.

Mr. Gardiner found the precedence difficulty in the singularly conflicting evidence on the grant of this dukedom. For, according to him, we have :

(1) 1 April 1644. The anomalous grant to "Glamorgan" of "the title of Duke of Somerset."

(2) 4 May 1644. The patent creating him duke of Somerset and Beaufort.

(3) 6 Jan. 1645. The warrant for a signed bill creating his father, Worcester, duke of Somerset[3] (enclosed in a letter of 10 Jan. to Lord Worcester from the king).

(4) 12 Feb. 1645. A letter from Charles to Glamorgan himself, mentioning that he sends him "a warrant for the title of Duke of Somerset."[4]

---

[1] *E. H. R.*, II. p. 707.   [2] *E. H. R.*, III. 125.

[3] Hist. MSS. 12th Report, IX. p. 14 ; Dircks, p. 104.

[4] Dircks, p. 74. "And yet," says Mr. Gardiner, "Glamorgan subsequently informed Rinuccini that the dukedom was to be his father's" (*E. H. R.*, II. 694).

It is no wonder that Mr. Gardiner finds this last letter " not very easy to understand." But that is only because of his belief in the earlier documents as genuine.

The difficulty, it will be seen, is that (1) Glamorgan is made a duke by patent ; then (2) his father, Worcester, is sent a warrant for the dukedom ; and (3) only a month later, Glamorgan is sent a warrant for it himself. Now, bearing in mind the above evidence, as given in Mr. Gardiner's article, we turn to his *History*, where we read : [1]

> The informal patent conferring a dukedom on Glamorgan was allowed to fall asleep. There is reason to believe that his father was displeased that his son should be a duke whilst he himself remained a marquis, and though the steps of the process cannot be distinctly traced, it is plain that the intention was already formed of making the old man a duke instead of the son. In February (*sic*) a warrant to that effect was actually sent to Worcester ; but, as in the case of his son's earldom, complete secrecy was both enjoined and observed, no attempt being made to carry the grant beyond the initial stage. [2]

The marginal heading to this passage is " February 12. Worcester to be a duke." It is scarcely credible, yet a fact, that, referring to his own article, Mr. Gardiner has so confused its evidence that he mistakes the warrant sent to *Glamorgan* on February 12 for the warrant sent to Worcester on

---

[1] *History of the Civil War* (Ed. 1894), II. 166–7.
[2] Mr. Gardiner adduces no proof that secrecy was either enjoined or observed in the case of the earldom of Glamorgan. Indeed he cites " a catalogue of lords," published in 1645 as proof that it was " a matter of public notoriety " (*E. H. R.*, II. 694).

January 10 (more than a month before), and by leaving out the former, ignores the main difficulty.

Indeed, he seems quite to have forgotten the letter to Glamorgan of Feb. 12 (1645), with its fresh warrant for the dukedom, when he holds that his patent of 4 May 1644 had its date altered to 4 May 1645, that it might not take precedence of his father's warrant.[1] For this implies that it was still valid in 1645.

Mr. Gardiner's theory, therefore, is that Glamorgan could not make use of his patent till his father was dead, and that—as this did not happen till Dec. 1646—his first opportunity of doing so came at the Restoration.[2] But what would become of this theory if we found that, long before the latter date, he was trying to obtain the coveted dukedom? Now among the MSS. at Badminton is a letter to him (as marquis of Worcester) from Charles II., so early as Oct. 1649, which can only be a reply to an application for a dukedom :

I feare that in this conjuncture of tyme it will not be seasonable for me to graunt, nor for you to receyve *the addition of honour you desire*, neyther can I at this tyme send the order you mention concerning the garter, but be confident that I will in due tyme

---

[1] *E. H. R.*, III. 125 :—"If Worcester lived to produce his warrant and to have the patent made out, his son, whose patent was now dated 4 May 1645, could not come before him; whereas, if Worcester died before sending his warrant to the signet office, Glamorgan could show his own patent, and it would not be of much consequence to him whether it was dated in 1644 or in 1645."   [2] *E. H. R.*, II. 693.

give you such satisfaction in these particulars, and in all other things that you can reasonably expect from me, as shall lett you see with how much trueth and kindness I am

Your affectionate friend,

CHARLES R.[1]

Here we have the two things on which the marquis had set his heart : (1) the dukedom ; (2) the garter. Fortunately, it does not matter whether the letter is genuine (there is no reason to suspect it), for, in any case, it alters the whole problem. The marquis here makes (or represents himself as making) a request for a dukedom, although, in Mr. Gardiner's belief, he was actually in possession of a genuine patent (to say nothing of a subsequent warrant) conferring one on him. This request is refused, and a most guarded prospect of future reward held out. What we naturally ask is whether such a letter is consistent with the applicant's possession of a patent from Charles I. granting him a dukedom. At the Restoration, he produced such a patent, instead of asking the king to grant him a new one, as, from this evidence, he clearly did in 1649.

The king's letter, I maintain, is an answer to a new application ; from which we must infer that the applicant did not at the time possess, or even believe himself to possess, a patent granting him a dukedom. Baffled in this attempt to obtain such a patent from Charles II., he must have fallen back on that document which he produced at the

---

[1] Charles II. to the Marquis of Worcester (12th Report on Historical MSS., IX. p. 47 ; Dircks, p. 190).

Restoration as a valid patent of dukedom from
Charles I.

I have said above that the two objects on which
he had set his heart were a dukedom of Somerset
and the garter. Throughout, the two are found
together; and it is singular that the story of the
one is no less a puzzle than the story of the other.
How does the matter of the ' Garter ' stand ?

(1) 1 April 1644.   In the preposterous document bearing this appropriate date, Charles
empowers Glamorgan " from henceforward
to give (!) the garter to your arms, and at
your pleasure to put on the George and blue
ribbon."

(2) 4 May 1644.   In the patent of dukedom
assigned by Mr. Gardiner to this date, Glamorgan is formally styled " Knight of the
Garter."

(3) 12 Feb. 1645.   Charles writes to Glamorgan saying that he sends him " the Blue
Ribbon and a warrant for the title of Duke
of Somerset, both which accept and make
use of at your discretion " (Glamorgan's discretion !).

(4) 13–21 Oct. 1649.   Charles II. declines
Glamorgan's (Worcester's) application for the
Garter.[1]

---

[1] " neyther can I at this tyme send the order you mention
concerning the garter " (Hist. MSS. Report, *ut supra*, p. 47).   It
should be observed that Lord Ormonde had been given the Garter
a month before (18 Sept.), which may account for Worcester's
application.

Remembering that all the first three are accepted as genuine by Mr. Gardiner, it would be interesting to learn how he reconciles their evidence, and, still more, how he reconciles it with that of the fourth.

We have now discovered the suspicious and contradictory character of the evidence for Glamorgan's dukedom and for his 'Garter' as well. Especially should it be observed that a warrant is sent him for the dignity on 12 Feb. 1645, although he was already in possession, on Mr. Gardiner's hypothesis, of an actual patent of it.

From this external evidence I turn to the document itself.

So strangely careless was Mr. Gardiner here that his views must be received with caution. He first tells us that an opinion of Anstis "decidedly unfriendly to the dukedom patent follows the copy of it in the Carte MSS.,"[1] and then that—

As to the dukedom patent . . . Anstis, *who does not say there was any fault with it*,[2] allows that Willis, who countersigned it, was the proper person to do so.[3]

I am compelled to give further evidence of Mr. Gardiner's singular inaccuracy, or carelessness, in this minute and full enquiry. While thus contradicting himself over the dukedom patent, he tells us that " a hostile opinion " of the 1644 (April 1) document, " which is not now to be found at Badminton, by Anstis garter king of arms in the

[1] *E. H. R.*, II. p. 688.   [2] The italics are mine.
[3] *Ibid.* p. 692.

middle of the eighteenth century, is embodied in the ' Case of the Royal Martyr ' (p. 141)."[1] Now, on referring to the work cited, we find Anstis quoted as follows :

> As they [Anstis and Carte] often talked together of the Earl of Glamorgan's unaccountable conduct, so Mr. Anstis as often answered him (Carte) "that *all* the pretended Patents of that Nobleman were forged ; that some of them he had seen and considered with great exactness ; that, observing the Matrix of the Great Seal in *all* of them to be considerably thicker than he had ever observed before, he had the curiosity to examine one of them, and found the Great Seal to be formed of two Great Seals, clapped together, so as to inclose the Label fixed to the Patent." In the year 1737, October 3, he shewed me, says Mr. Carte, two of these patents which he had been curious enough to copy. One of them was the same which was afterwards published by Mr. Collins in 1741[2] . . . The other . . . is the very same which Mr. Anstis, upon the nicest Examination, found to be an arrant forgery. "This," says Mr. Anstis, "is a copy of the very Patent which I examined so curiously, and found the Seal to be composed of two Great Seals, clapped together, so as to inclose the Label " (pp. 141–3).[3]

Yet Mr. Gardiner, actually citing (p. 692) " the Case of the Royal Martyr, pp. 142, 143," from which the latter part of the above passage is taken, tells us that it was the " commission patent " of 1 April of which " Carte reports from Anstis " that " it is composed of two great seals clapped together so as to inclose the label." [4] It was, on the contrary, the *dukedom* patent of which Anstis so reported [5] (pp. 142–6).

[1] *E. H. R.*, II. 688.
[2] This is the document of April 1, 1644.
[3] This, as the writer goes on to explain, is the *dukedom* patent.
[4] *E. H. R.*, II. 692.
[5] It will be found that Mr. Gardiner carried his confusion so

The document itself, therefore, was as unsatisfactory to Anstis, a well-qualified expert, as is the external evidence concerning its grant.

With the anomalous and blundered limitation in this patent I have already dealt,[1] so that we have only its preamble left. Its inflated description of the grantee's services ought to be compared with his own description of them in the wild speech he composed for delivery, under Charles II., in the House of Lords.[2] For our present purpose, we need only consider the words I have italicized below : [3]

Whereas our right trusty and well-beloved cousin Edward Somerset, alias Plantagenet, Knight of the most noble Order of the Garter, Earl of our county of Glamorgan, son and heir apparent of our right trusty and well-beloved cousin Henry, Earl and Marquess of Worcester, Baron of the Honours of the Castles of Raglan, Chepstow, and Gower, a man eminent for the nobleness of his blood, . . . illustrious by a long train of noble ancestors, and by the high nobility transmitted by paternal succession—from John of Gaunt Duke of Lancaster, and his son John Plantagenet Duke of Somerset, from the place of his nativity surnamed Beaufort—and by other connections of blood with the Royal Houses of Lancaster and York, etc., etc.

With what courage and successful conduct did he take Goodridge Castle, the Forest of Dean, and the city of Hereford ? In short, with what remarkable good fortune, with what unhoped-for success he made himself master of the strongly fortified town of Monmouth ? And not content with the confined limits of one

---

far as to connect this report of Anstis on the *dukedom* patent with a passage in Worcester's letter to Clarendon referring (he held) " to the commission patent " (*Ibid.*).   [1] p. 371 above.

[2] Hist. MSS. Report, *ut supra*, pp. 56–63.

[3] In the text they run :—" et unius regni finibus non contentus in ultimas trans oceanum oras per medios hostes et naufragia tendit."

kingdom, *go to the most distant places beyond the seas, through the midst of hostile forces and the dangers of shipwreck*, . . . that he might raise succours for the support of the tottering crown of his King.[1]

Really, one need only quote Mr. Gardiner's unconscious comment :

On the 25th [March 1645] he sailed from Carnarvon on this hopeful enterprise. A storm drove him northward, and on the 28th he was wrecked on the Lancashire coast, whence, slipping past the Parliamentary forces in the neighbourhood, he made his way to the safe refuge of Skipton Castle.

But to this may be added Digby's words, 21 May 1645, in a letter to Ormond :

As to my Lord Herbert he made a dangerous escape, but I hope is now well on his way towards you from Skipton Castle.[2]

How perfect a confirmation do these passages afford of the statement in the patent that the earl is striving to cross the seas " per medios hostes et *naufragia* "—if that patent was granted in the spring of 1645. But Mr. Gardiner has burnt his ships ; " to the later investigator " he writes, " to myself even more than to Anstis, 1645 is an impossible date."[3]

The patent, therefore, can only, he holds, have been granted in 1644—nearly a year before the earl's shipwreck, to which it so magniloquently alludes ! For my part I prefer to believe that the

---

[1] Dircks (translation), pp. 162–3. It should be observed that this allusion to his dangerous journey refers, like those preceding it, to a definite achievement. Glamorgan himself (as Worcester) refers to the incident in his letter to the duke of Albemarle, 29 Dec. 1665 : " besides hazard by sea, even of shipwreck."

[2] Carte's *Ormond*, III., No. 388.   [3] *E. H. R.*, II. 694.

artist by whom it was concocted intended to assign it to May 1645, but omitted by error the word *primo*, which was inserted at a subsequent time, to correct his error.

It has been shown above that the documents which are used by Mr. Gardiner himself are enough, when placed side by side, to make the grant of this dukedom a matter of inextricable confusion. He has, unfortunately, increased that confusion by mistaking, as we saw, one of them for another, by misquoting the testimony of Anstis, and by misunderstanding the patent. When he writes anew— as he doubtless will—this portion of his history, he will examine, I trust, the preamble in the light of the suggestion I have made, and will come, I venture to think, to the same conclusion as myself.

I can scarcely suppose that any one who has followed the evidence with care will henceforth accept as genuine this patent of dukedom. Regarded as a forgery at the Restoration, and criticised, in the next century, by such an expert as Anstis, it is further discredited, for ourselves, by all the external evidence now available to the student. Therefore, with even greater confidence than in 1883, I can now repeat Dugdale's words :

The Marquis of Worcester did exhibit a patent under the Great Seal, pretended to be granted to him by the late King at Oxford for creating [him] Duke of Somerset and Beaufort ; but this being in truth suspected to be forged, there appearing no vestige of it at the signet or privy seal, nor any other probable way, and my Lord of Hartford being prepared to make such objections against it as might have tended much to the dishonour of my Lord of Worcester before a committee of Lords, about three days since the Marquis of Worcester was pleased to tell the Lords that he must confess that there were certain private considerations upon which that patent was granted to him by the late King, which he performing not on his part, he would not insist thereon, but render it to His Majesty to cancel if he so pleased.[1]

The lameness of this excuse for withdrawal is obvious from the fact that, if valid, it ought to have precluded the claim being brought forward at all. It seems to have been only remembered by the marquis when his patent was denounced as a fraud.

Let us now return to Mr. Gardiner's case :

In itself the question of the irregularity of this dukedom patent would only indirectly concern an inquirer into the Glamorgan treaty ; but it is closely connected with another patent granting to Glamorgan a commission conferring on him very extraordinary powers to command an army in chief, and embodying the "certain private considerations" referred to by Dugdale, and paving the way for his subsequent employment in Ireland.[2]

The close connection between the two documents (for which Mr. Gardiner accepts the dates of 1 April and 4 May 1644) is indisputable. Anstis believed them both to be frauds, and this was also, we shall now see, the belief at the Restoration.

---

[1] Dugdale to Langley, 25 Aug. 1660 (Hist. MSS. Commission, App. to Fifth Report, p. 178). Mr. Gardiner, repeating the above quotation, erroneously treated it as a mere expression of Dugdale's personal opinion, and refused to follow him "in the inference which he drew" (*E. H. R.*, II. 688). It will be seen that Dugdale is speaking of the current belief.

[2] *E. H. R.*, II. 688.

As touching the King's declaration upon his father's grant of the title of Duchess to the old lady you mention, with place and precedency to her daughter, this is the account which I can give you thereof, viz., that Sir Edward Walker did draw a petition for this now Duchess to the King, and being assisted by Secretary Nicholas, moved His Majesty in it, but could not prevail ; for he told me in private that the King had no great opinion of the truth of the pretended grant from his father, *which they showed under the Great Seal*, but *deemed it to be one of those counterfeits which the now Marquis of Worcester is shrewdly suspected to be guilty of (there being one for himself, which creates him Duke of Somerset and a Knight of the Garter, nay, which gives him power to create any degree of honour under an Earl, now in question before the Parliament of which you will hear more perhaps very shortly).* But not[withstan]ding that Sir Edw. Walker and the secretary could not set the whole agoing, one doctor B—— (one of the King's physicians), and one Thomas Killegrew (an old courtier) as I am credibly [in pri]vate informed, did the business, not without good reward you may be sure. Mr. William —— told me it was £500 . . . I hope you will keep this letter private, for it [is] not fit that any but yourself should be acquainted therewith, nor would I impart so much to [any] one but an entire friend as I know you to be.[1]

I explained the references in this letter to the 'Duchess Dudley' patent on a previous occasion,[2] so need only mention here, in further illustration, that Worcester, two days before writing formally to the Lord Chancellor (Clarendon) in defence of the genuineness of his " commission," at " the amplitude " of which, he admitted, " your Lordship may well wonder, and the king too," wrote to him (9 June 1660) ; in strict privacy, offering him his mansion, Worcester House, rent free, so long as he himself lived, if he would be his " friend."[3]

[1] Dugdale to Langley, 30 Aug. 1660.
[2] *Academy*, Dec. 8, 1883, p. 383.
[3] Dircks, pp. 235–7 (from Clarendon).

As to the really preposterous document—" the commission patent" Mr. Gardiner terms it—of 1 April 1644, one could hardly treat it seriously, did he not insist on doing so. What it was, what it professed to do, and why it was given, must all be mysteries alike to any student of documents.

Was it a patent? Its own description of itself is as follows :

> And for your greater honour, and in testimony of our reality, we have with our own hand affixed our great seal of England unto these our commission and letters making them patents.

I pass over the absurd phraseology ; I pass over the pertinent enquiry how, when the great seal was in the due keeping of Lyttelton, it came to be in Charles' hands, for this irregular purpose ; and I pass straight to Mr. Gardiner's explanation :

> Not only was the English of the commission patent very unofficial in its character, but its seal was everything that it ought not to have been. As Carte reports from Anstis, it is composed of two great seals clapped together so as to inclose the label[1] . . . This is, however, no more than Glamorgan himself acknowledged with respect to the commission patent.

> "In like manner" (he writes to Clarendon) "did I not stick upon having this commission inrolled or assented to by the king's counsel, nor indeed the seal to be put unto it in an ordinary manner, but as Mr. Endymion Porter and I could perform it, with rollers and no screw-press."[2]

But how could Glamorgan and Endymion Porter have sealed this "commission patent," when,

---

[1] I have shown above (p. 379) that Mr. Gardiner here confuses the two patents discussed by Carte and Anstis.

[2] *E. H. R.*, II. 692.

according to itself, the king "with our own hand
affixed our great seal"? Yet even this is not
all. Mr. Gardiner now, admitting the force of
my criticism that, in his letter to Clarendon,
Glamorgan was not describing this amazing Commission,[1] suggests that it may have been another
which was thus irregularly sealed :

> What then is the commission which was irregularly sealed
> by Glamorgan and Porter ? Was it the commission mentioned
> some time before, or is it a synonym for the powers given to
> Glamorgan to treat with the Pope and Catholic princes men-
> tioned much more recently ? If the latter interpretation is right,
> then we need not be troubled by the mention that 'it' con-
> ferred powers to create a mint. The first-mentioned commission
> may have been that of April 1st, 1644, the second commission
> that for treating with the Pope and erecting a mint.[2]

But what becomes of his original explanation,
if he is thus ready to abandon the identity of the
document referred to in the letter to Clarendon ?
While thus oscillating between hypotheses,
which, as he himself admits, are "plausible but
. . . no more,"[3] Mr. Gardiner proceeds to
suggest "the following sequence of events" :

> On April 1st, 1644, when there was a chance of getting an
> Irish army from the Irish agents at Oxford, Charles gives Gla-

---

[1] Mr. Gardiner had assumed that the document referred to in
Worcester's letter to Clarendon was what he terms the 'commission patent' of 1 April 1644 ; but I pointed out that Worcester's letter spoke of a commission giving him power "to erect
a mint anywhere and to dispose of . . . delinquents' estates," which power was given him expressly by other documents
that he produced, but not by the 'commission patent' (*Athenæum*,
15 Jan. 1898).

[2] *Athenæum*, 26 Feb. 1898, p. 279.   [3] *Ibid.*

morgan a wide commission, and, *either then, or a few days later, another empowering him to treat with the Pope and other princes for money*.[1]

But the words I have italicized are a counsel of despair : they are the first mention that has ever been made of such a commission being granted in April 1644. Indeed, Mr. Gardiner himself had written that he felt " little doubt that the powers of 12 Jan." 1645 (nine months later) were those referred to in the letter to Clarendon as authorizing " financial arrangements with the pope and catholic princes."[2] Can he have forgotten his own words ?

The point is of such importance that I venture to drive it home. Alike in his original article and in his *History*, based upon it, Mr. Gardiner had strongly urged that Glamorgan was commissioned by Charles, in the year 1645 (1) to raise troops abroad, (2) to negotiate with the Pope and Catholic princes for money with which to pay them. This, he held, was the right explanation of the warrant of 12 Jan. 1645. Here are his own words :

That these words are perilously wide is beyond question ; but is there any reason to believe that they had anything to do with the Irish peace ? Not only do they seem much more appropriate to the negotiations which Glamorgan *would* these words . . . are more appropriate to the other negotiation with which Glamorgan was entrusted, the negotiation with the Pope and the Catholic powers for money to pay the armies which were to be brought from the Continent in support of the troops from Ireland.

---

[1] *Athenæum*, 26 Feb. 1898, p. 279.   [2] *E. H. R.*, II. 697–8.

have to carry on[1] with foreign powers for the money with which the foreign levies were to be paid (*E. H. R.*, II. 697–8).

'The maintenance of this army of foreigners,' wrote Glamorgan in explanation many years afterwards, 'was to have come from the Pope and such Catholic princes as he should draw into it. . . . And for this purpose had I power to treat with the Pope and Catholic princes,' etc., etc. . . . In all probability the powers referred to in this explanation are the warrants mentioned by Charles (12 Jan. 1645). . . .

This interpretation of the meaning of Charles' warrant of the 12th is the more probable as that warrant followed closely on a commission granted on the 6th under the great seal . . . by which Glamorgan was empowered to levy troops not only in Ireland but on the Continent as well (*History*, II. 167–8).

Yet, having thus emphatically urged that Charles commissioned Glamorgan to negotiate, in 1645, for men and money on the Continent, Mr. Gardiner, hard pressed, argues, in the *Athenæum*, that that is just what Charles would not, and did not do! He there urges:

Another point in my favour is that in April, 1644, the arrangements for foreign succours were directly in the hands of the king, whereas in 1645 they were in the hands of the queen, and instead of sending Glamorgan to the Pope, she then employed Sir Kenelm Digby . . . he (Charles) leaves this negotiation to the queen in the first months of 1645, leaving Glamorgan to carry out his

---

[1] The italics are mine.

instructions in Ireland, and to take military command of Irish and foreign forces invading England.[1]

The sole cause of all this trouble is Mr. Gardiner's resolve to believe in the document of 1 April 1644, and to connect it with the statements in Worcester's letter (11 June 1660), of which he has to confess, after my criticism, that—

his statement appears to me on re-examination to be too confused to build with certainty upon it.[2]

No doubt his history would be gravely affected, should he be driven from both positions.

When we next ask what it is that this ridiculous document professes to do, we find at its tail this addition :

We give and allow you henceforward . . . the title of Duke of Somerset to you and your heirs male for ever ; and from henceforward to give (sic) the Garter to your arms and at your pleasure to put on the George and blue ribbon.

Is this a creation of a dukedom, or is it not ? If it is, why was it necessary to create it, on Mr. Gardiner's hypothesis, by a later patent (4 May 1644), de novo ? If it was not, what was the use of it ?

And the Garter ? Mr. Gardiner writes:

On 2 Aug. 1644, Charles writes to Worcester that he is to have the first vacant garter ; the garter, it will be remembered, having before been promised to the son.[3]

But the Garter is not " promised " by the above

---

[1] *Athenæum*, 26 Feb. 1898, p. 279. The other point in Mr. Gardiner's favour is left obscure.

[2] *Athenæum*, as above.   [3] *E. H. R.*, II. p. 693.

document : it is *given*, and "from henceforward." Indeed, in the patent of dukedom, which Mr. Gardiner accepts as genuine, and assigns to 4 May 1644, the son is already styled "Knight of the Garter."

In both these documents, admittedly "closely connected," we find Lord Herbert styled "Earl of Glamorgan," although, as I have shown, he has nowhere else been found so described before 1645.[1] In both he is described as "Edward Somerset *alias* Plantaginet" as he again describes himself in his formal ratification to the nuncio, 18 Feb. 1645–6.[2] He was as eager to become a "Plantagenet" and a duke as was his contemporary, Lord Denbigh, to become a "Hapsburg" and a German count.[3] They both, at about the same time, appear to have been playing the same game.

"Your son Plantaginet" is, in this document, the unintelligible style applied to the grantee's boy. Among its "startling concessions," as Mr.

---

[1] I attach considerable importance to this point. For even so late as 27 Aug. 1644 the alleged earl of Glamorgan, writing privately to his father, signs himself only "Ed. Herbert" (see facsimile of his signature in Dircks, p. 77). In 1645 he uses the title openly. Mr. Gardiner (*History*, II. 158) asserts that in or about March 1644 Charles "conferred on him the title of Earl of Glamorgan by warrant," which warrant was "presented at the Signet Office." But in his own article he rightly states that the "signed bill" was only "received at the signet office in April 1645," *i.e.* a year later (*E. H. R.*, II. 694).

[2] Nuncio's Memoirs, fo. 1,087 (*Inquiry*, p. 177).

[3] They succeeded, respectively, to their fathers' honours in 1646 and 1643, so were virtually contemporaries.

Gardiner terms them (although they do not shake his faith), is the " promise of our dear daughter Elizabeth " as a wife for this boy with £300,000 in dower. This, Mr. Gardiner does admit, is " very startling indeed " ; yet he deems the statement corroborated by a letter from the king to Worcester, in which occurs the passage :

As by a matche propounded for your grandchilde you will easily judge. The particulars I leave to your son Glamorgan his relation.

But it turns out that this letter was written on Jan. 10, 1645 (a likely time), that is, more than nine months after the date of the alleged patent assuring (not propounding) that " matche " under the Great Seal.

As to the instructions of 2 Jan. 1645, which Mr. Gardiner deems so " singularly confirmatory of the genuineness of the commission of 1 April 1644,"[1] from their containing certain similar clauses, I should, on the contrary, draw the inference that Glamorgan " faked " the earlier document out of some genuine instructions etc. of 1645,[2] adding to their language what he wished to add, and, in short, " flavouring to taste."

And this (to anticipate), in my belief, was also

---

[1] *E. H. R.*, II. 697.

[2] Even these instructions, unfortunately, are known to us only from Dircks (pp. 72–4), being unmentioned in the Report to the Historical MSS. Commission. Mr. Gardiner accepts them without question, but we do not know the nature of the document or even whether it exists.

how he produced the warrant alleged to have been granted on 12 March 1645.[1]

To the historical side of the "commission patent" I have scarcely the space to do justice. As for the grantee's military achievements, he had, early in 1643, received a local command in South Wales, where he had raised a little "mushroom army," as Clarendon terms it, which was routed at the first blow. His "judgement," moreover, we shall find, was frankly distrusted by Charles. Yet we here find him suddenly appointed " Generalissimo of three armies, English, Irish, and foreign, and Admiral of a fleet at sea"; he is even to exercise his own judgment whether he will obey the king's orders.[2] To all this farrago of nonsense the answer is plain and brief. Mr. Gardiner has failed to produce one scrap of evidence that there was the slightest intention of employing "Glamorgan" in any such capacity in the spring of. 1644.

When, at the close of the year, the king decided to employ him, it was, admittedly, as a negotiator, to act as intermediary between Ormond and the Catholics.[3] And when Ormond, in the following spring, "was quite ready to take up the negotiation on Charles' terms, there was

---

[1] I mean, of course, that he adapted the language, not the document itself.

[2] " And lest through distance of time or place we may be misinformed, we will and command you to reply to us, if any of our orders should thwart or hinder any of your designs for our service."   [3] *E. H. R.*, II. 695–6.

LORD GLAMORGAN'S DUKEDOM

no immediate necessity for Glamorgan's presence
in Dublin."[1] It would, then, have been equally
unnecessary, had the treaty been carried through,
at Oxford, a year before.

I have not the slightest doubt that Glamorgan's
references to the "army of foreigners" and its
payment by the Pope and Catholic princes, in
his letter to Clarendon (11 June 1660), apply to
the royal schemes in the winter of 1644–5, as
indeed Mr. Gardiner himself held,[2] and cannot
possibly be forced into confirmation of the "commission patent" as part of "a plan for raising half
Europe to take arms on behalf of Charles and the
Catholic cause,"[3] in April 1644.

As Mr. Gardiner has, here, now shifted his
ground, I will briefly contrast the schemes on foot
in the spring of 1644 and in January 1645. It is
rightly observed in his *History* that, only after the
Irish treaty had broken down at Oxford (1644),
did Charles turn to the Continent for help. It was
not till May 30 that he requested the prince of
Orange to find transport for troops whom he hoped
(but, as yet, merely hoped) to obtain from France.[4]
The foreign army was intended to be a substitute
for the army hoped for from Ireland, not part of
the same scheme. But, in 1645, the Irish and

[1] *E. H. R.*, II. 700.   [2] See p. 387 above.
[3] *History*, II. 158–160, and *Athenæum*, 15 Jan. 1898, p. 86.
[4] Groen van Prinsterer, 2nd Ser., IV. 100, 103; *History*, I.
348 : "Mazarin, it is true, had hitherto made no promise to
allow Charles the benefit of this little army (4,000 French foot
and 2,000 French horse)."

the foreign armies were both hoped for.¹ And the foreign army was to be partly composed of a contingent from the Low Countries.

This latter occasion (1645), therefore, must be that to which Glamorgan (Worcester) alludes in his letter to Clarendon. He there says that there was to be an Irish and a foreign army, the latter comprising " 2,000 men," drawn out of Flanders and Holland.² And yet Mr. Gardiner, quoting this letter and both the requests to the prince of Orange, would persuade us of the very opposite.³

It is a striking coincidence that the instructions (as above) of 2/12 Jan. 1645 were issued on the very same day as those to Glamorgan himself. Mr. Gardiner dates them correctly in his *History*, but now strangely speaks of them as "given to Goffe in February or the end of January, 1645"⁴

¹ *Ibid.* pp. 123, 126. Also *History* (Ed. 1893), II. 171, where we read that the queen "on January 2 instructed Dr. Goffe, her agent at the Hague, to urge the Prince of Orange . . . to lend 3,000 soldiers for service in England and to supply vessels in sufficient numbers, not only to transport this contingent, but also to convoy across the sea such forces as might be obtained from France or Ireland."

² The actual number, we see, was 3,000.

³ *Athenæum*, 26 Feb. 1898, p. 279.

⁴ *Athenæum*, 26 Feb. 1898, p. 279. The same strange looseness of statement, where dates are concerned, is seen in Mr. Gardiner's contention that Glamorgan, in his letter to Clarendon, "could not possibly refer to a commission granted in 1645, because, as everybody then knew, Sir Henry Gage was killed in January, 1644/5" (*E. H. R.*, II. 690). I pointed out (*Athenæum*, 15 Jan. 1898) that "so far from being dead, Gage was at the height of his reputation" in the first week of January, 1645, the date required (see p. 397).

—an absolutely impossible date; for Goffe had actually arrived in Holland and communicated his instructions in January.[1] Indeed Mr. Gardiner himself, in his *History* (II. 172) holds that these instructions were superseded so early as 17 January in consequence of the duke of Lorraine's promises reaching the queen.[2]

Mr. Gardiner, in fact, has found himself driven from conjecture to conjecture, and plunged, as I have shown above, into even greater confusion, solely because of his resolve to uphold, at all costs, the impossible document of 1 April 1644. This document and the dukedom patent with which, as he rightly says, it was so closely connected, must be frankly and absolutely recognised by him as forgeries before he can extricate himself from the bog into which they have plunged him. And with them there will go by the board all that he has written on the great scheme, based upon their evidence, for 1644. Nor can he stop even here. For, as he himself wrote (1887):

It is necessary to come to some understanding on the history of both these patents before proceeding to that of the later documents which Glamorgan produced in Ireland. As Mr. Round says, if both or either of these were forged in 1660,[3] there is an end of Glamorgan's credit, and the warrants which he produced to justify his conduct in Ireland must be regarded with grave suspicion.[4]

[1] Zuylichem to Jermyn, 6 Feb. 1645 (N.S.); Groen van Prinsterer, 2nd Ser., vol. IV. p. 127.   [2] *Ibid.* p. 125.
[3] I am not responsible for this date.
[4] *E. H. R.*, II. 688.

PART II

GLAMORGAN'S TREATY

To the historian, Glamorgan's dukedom and the
documents connected with it are of interest only
for their bearing on " the main question at issue,"
as Mr. Gardiner terms it, " Glamorgan's actual
mission to Ireland in 1645." To quote his own
summary of the case :

> It is well known that in the course of that year he signed a
> peace with the Irish, the particulars of which he did not com-
> municate to the Lord Lieutenant, and that he produced to them
> certain documents signed by Charles which, as he contended,
> authorized him to enter upon a secret negotiation.[1]

It will be desirable to commence by setting forth
in order the letters, instructions, and powers proceeding from the king, when he had resolved on
despatching Glamorgan to Ireland. Their dates
are of importance, and still more so are the authorities upon which the documents rest. For these
latter differ widely in character.

(I)

(1) 27 Dec. 1644. Letter from Charles to
Ormond announcing that Glamorgan (" Lord
Herbert ") was coming.[2]

[1] *English Historical Review*, p. 695 (pp. 695–708 of Mr.
Gardiner's article relate to the Irish negotiations).
[2] Letter in Carte's *Ormond*.

(2) 2 Jan. 1645. Instructions to Glamorgan, giving him powers.[1]

(3) 5 Jan. 1645. Warrant granting to Glamorgan (as Lord Herbert) lands to the value of £40,000.[2]

(4) 6 Jan. 1645. Warrant for preparing signed bill creating the marquis of Worcester duke of Somerset.[3]

(5) 6 Jan. 1645. Commission to Glamorgan to levy troops "vel in nostro Iberniæ regno, aut aliis quibusvis partibus transmarinis."[4]

(6) 10 Jan. 1645. Letter from Charles to Worcester, referring gratefully to his " sonnes endeavours."[5]

(7) 12 Jan. 1645. Wide powers to Glamorgan[6] (for his Continental schemes, according to Mr. Gardiner).

This group of 2–12 January stands by itself. It is here collected, I believe, for the first time ; but even now it may not be complete. The earldom of Glamorgan, for which the signed bill

---

[1] Dircks, p. 73 (nature of the document itself not stated).

[2] Signet Office Docquet Book (March 1663–4), fo. 293.

[3] Now in possession of the duke of Beaufort (Historical MSS. Report, XII. 9, p. 14 ; Dircks, p. 104).

[4] Only known from the Nuncio's Memoirs (Lord Leicester's MS., fo. 713).

[5] Report *ut supra* (from duke of Beaufort's MSS.), p. 14 ; Dircks, p. 103 (undated).

[6] " Dircks, p. 79," is the authority cited by Mr. Gardiner ; but Dircks merely copied the text from " Birch and others " ! Birch (*Inquiry*, p. 48) cites for it "Nuncio's memoirs, fo. 715, and Carte, vol. I. p. 554."

reached the signet office so mysteriously in the following April, was, according to my own suggestion,[1] probably granted (though not certified) at this very time.

We have next a further group of documents, of which the existence is only known to us from subsequent allusion :

(II)

(1) "A commission to coin money anywhere in the king's dominions,[2] and to impower others to do the same ; to name one Secretary of State, a Treasurer, either the Attorney or Solicitor-General, and two of the Privy Council in England ;[3] and to make concessions in point of religion in Ireland, by way of supplement to the Lord Lieutenant's authority."

(2) "Among other patents and commissions signed by the King and brought by the Earl of Glamorgan from England, there is one appointing him Lord Lieutenant of Ireland upon the expiration of the Marquis of Ormonde's term of holding that post, or in case the Marquis should, by any fault, deserve to be removed from it."[4]

---

[1] *Genealogist*, April 1898.

[2] This is referred to by Glamorgan (then Worcester) in his letter of 11 June 1660, as *part of* his Commission—the Commission, as Mr. Gardiner imagined (until the appearance of my criticism in the *Athenæum*) of 1 April 1644—in which Commission, however, no such power is found.

[3] It would be interesting to learn if Mr. Gardiner believes even this to be genuine.

[4] Nuncio to Pamphili 21 Sept. 1646, in Nuncio's Memoirs,

LORD GLAMORGAN'S TREATY

It should be observed that the first of these (which may, from the text, be one or more) is known to us only from "a paper in Italian," presented by Glamorgan to the Nuncio, and headed :

Patents and Commissions granted to me by the King my Master, with which I desire to serve the Catholic religion, the Apostolic see," etc., etc.[1]

He had already communicated to the Nuncio the famous warrant of 12 March and the king's letter of 30 April, which, we shall find, he treated as his powers.[2] The above " paper " was only intended to display to the Nuncio his influence with the king.[3]

To the above second group we cannot assign a date.

It will be best to treat as a third group these two letters from Charles to Glamorgan :

fo. 1,376 (*Inquiry*, pp. 253-4). This is fully accepted by Mr. Gardiner in his *History*, where he adds the gloss that the fault meant "in the event of his persisting in his refusal to carry on the negotiation on the lines indicated by his last instructions " (II. 165). Writing to Ormond, 29 Sept. 1646, when this pretension had leaked out, Glamorgan evasively claimed only " a promise from the king " to that effect. Digby, who was in the confidence of the king, queen, and prince, wrote that " the fool " had certainly " forged new powers from his Majesty to take upon him the command at least of Munster, if not of Ireland " (Digby to Ormond, 18 Oct. 1646).

[1] Nuncio's Memoirs, fo. 1,004 (*Inquiry*, p. 79).
[2] *Ibid.* fos. 998–1,002 (*Inquiry*, p. 77).
[3] According to Birch, it " particularly mentions the patent of 1 April 1644 " (impugned by me) but not (unless the *Inquiry* omits it) the Lord Lieutenancy.

(III)

(1) 12 Feb. 1645. Letter to Glamorgan from Oxford, urging him to hasten his departure, and sending him " the blue ribbon and a warrant for the title of duke of Somerset." [1]

(2) 12 March 1645. Letter to Glamorgan from Oxford, expressing surprise that he has not started. [2]

Last of all is a fourth group, containing the special powers to which Glamorgan referred the Nuncio as his authority for the Irish Catholics :

(IV)

(1) 12 March 1645. Warrant pledging Charles to ratify and perform " whatsoever " Glamorgan should promise them.

(2) 30 April 1645. Letter to the Nuncio pledging Charles " a perfectioner ce que a quoy il [Glamorgan] s'obligera en nostre nom." [3]

The question we have now to consider is : what were the powers really granted by Charles to Glamorgan, either in written documents or, secretly, by word of mouth ?

[1] Dircks, p. 74.

[2] Dircks, p. 75. Both these letters (with others printed by Dircks) are strangely omitted in the Report to the Historical MSS. Commission, as if they were no longer to be found at Badminton.

[3] The authority for these two documents, which are of the utmost importance in the matter, will be fully discussed below.

LORD GLAMORGAN'S TREATY

The issue in this famous controversy was, at first, crude enough. Did Glamorgan forge all the documents he produced, or were they all genuine ? Did Charles I. intend to make concessions to the Catholics, or did he not ? Such were the questions that men asked, and undertook to answer. But the historian of to-day replies *Distinguo.* If Glamorgan forged one or more of his documents, the rest may yet be genuine : Charles, again, may never have intended to offer what Glamorgan promised, and yet he may have intended to make certain concessions.

It is here that Mr. Gardiner has rendered an inestimable service to the student by narrowing the controversy to certain points and clearing the ground of others. On the one hand, he has shown that, of all the warrants and commissions granted to Glamorgan, only that of 12 March 1645 was really cited by him as the power for his famous treaty ; on the other, he has shown (conclusively, I think) that " the two concessions " which Ormond refused, and which Glamorgan granted in his Treaty [1] (25 August 1645) were concessions which Charles cannot possibly have authorized him verbally to make, since the king had strenuously objected to them throughout.[2]

Mr. Gardiner himself put forward an avowedly novel explanation of the whole difficulty :

[1] Mr. Gardiner describes them as "(1) the surrender to the catholics of the churches in their possession, and (2) the abandonment of the jurisdiction of the protestant clergy over the catholics." [2] *E. H. R.,* II. pp. 699–700, 702, 703–4, 707–8.

On one side it has been held that these documents were forged by Glamorgan, but the prevailing opinion has been that Charles really authorized him to make the secret treaty, and mendaciously disavowed him when the truth lurked [1] out. I now propose to show that neither of these views is correct, and that all the evidence consistently points to an explanation of a different character from either.[2]

That explanation is that Charles

merely meant him to assist the lord lieutenant, and to use his own zeal and opportunities as a catholic with the confederates whilst he was guided by Ormond's judgment.[3]

The earl, in fact, was merely to be a go-between ; " Ormond might, as he desired [to do], keep in the background and guide Glamorgan with that judgment in which Charles acknowledged his new emissary to be deficient." [4]

Of this explanation I will only say that, to me as to Mr. Gardiner, all the evidence seems to point in that direction. But I think that Mr. Gardiner might have made his case at once clearer and stronger. To understand clearly the part Glamorgan was intended to play, we must remember that, in all this business, the difficulty was to persuade the Catholics that concessions which Ormond was only privately empowered to grant would be subsequently ratified by the king. Therefore, apart from Ormond's reluctance to mix himself up in the matter at all (the point on which Mr. Gardiner dwells), we have the Catholics' anxiety to make sure of the concessions, intensified by the

---

[1] (?) leaked.   [2] *E. H. R.*, II. p. 695.
[3] *Ibid.* p. 696.   [4] *Ibid.*

fact that Ormond was a sturdy Protestant.[1] If
Glamorgan, a zealous Catholic (" ter Catholicus ")
and a man high in the king's favour, could personally pledge himself that Charles would ratify
what Ormond did, his co-religionists would more
willingly believe the concessions real. And this is
what the king commissioned him to do.[2]

Again, Mr. Gardiner might fairly have appealed
to the letter from Charles to Ormond, when the
secret treaty was discovered, and to the important
letter (if genuine) from Charles to Glamorgan[3]
(12 March 1645), distinctly treating the earl not
as a plenipotentiary, but as subordinate to Ormond.
From first to last, on this at least, Charles is absolutely consistent : he never authorized Glamorgan,
he says, " to treat independently of Ormond."[4]

What then, I ask, was the state of affairs ?
Glamorgan, arriving in Ireland,[5] finds negotiations

[1] Rinuccini's words on this point are very interesting. He
denies that the hope of Ormond's conversion, entertained at
Rome, "has any foundation, as the dogmas taught by the archbishop of Canterbury are firmly implanted in his mind, and I
know that he has several times declared in private *the impossibility
of believing* two articles in the Catholic creed, viz. : *the presence
of Christ in the sacrament*, and the authority of the Roman
pontiff" (*Embassy*, p. 136 ; *Nunziatura*, p. 106). The italics are
mine. The said archbishop must be Laud.

[2] "First, you may engage your estate, interest, and credit, that
we will most really and punctually perform any our promises to
the Irish," etc., etc. (*E. H. R.*, p. 697).

[3] Mr. Gardiner, I find, does quote this letter in his *History*.
He may have overlooked it when he wrote his article.

[4] The actual words are Mr. Gardiner's (*E. H. R.*, p. 697).

[5] Mr. Gardiner writes that he "arrived at Dublin in August"
(1645) ; but so early as 23 June Charles wrote to the earl

403

at a standstill, because " Ormond refused to grant "
the confederates' " request for the abolition of the
jurisdiction of the king or of the clergy, and for
the retention of the churches." [1] Glamorgan thereupon leaves Ormond, follows the confederate
delegates who had withdrawn to Kilkenny, and,
on August 25, makes a secret treaty with their
Supreme Council, conceding both the points
which, as he and they knew, Ormond refused to
concede.

Now what, under these circumstances, would be
the first question that the confederates would ask
him ? They would ask to see his powers for treating independently of Ormond. Glamorgan, thereupon, produced precisely what was wanted, the
famous warrant of 12 March ; and this was incorporated in the treaty as his authority for making
it. That he himself appealed to it as empowering
him to act independently is certain.[2] Nor can I
conceive it possible that any one would read it
otherwise.

But, in that case, what becomes of Mr. Gardiner's
theory ? There are two ways of meeting the
difficulty, assuming that theory to be sound. Mr.
Gardiner, on the one hand, urged that " these

expressing his pleasure that he " was gone for Ireland " (*E. H. R.*,
p. 701). He may therefore have arrived somewhat earlier.

[1] *E. H. R.*, p. 703.

[2] " Est mihi potestas in Iberniâ faciendi concessiones (in
Proregis supplementum) Catholicorum gratiâ, . . . idque
sine relatione ad ullum alium" (Nuncio's Memoirs, fo. 1,004).
" This evidently refers," Mr. Gardiner writes, " to the powers of
12 March."

powers do not contemplate any action independent of the lord lieutenant."[1]   I, on the contrary, shall hold that they do, but that they were forged by Glamorgan for that express purpose.

Although Mr. Gardiner has done so much to clear the issue by fixing our attention on the warrant of 12 March, as the document in virtue of which Glamorgan made his treaty, it is necessary to observe that Glamorgan himself, when insisting on his powers to the Nuncio, placed on a level with that warrant the king's letter of 30 April, sent through himself to the Nuncio.   Writing on 6 Feb. 1645–6 he proposed to the latter to send

the articles agreed on between his Holiness and Sir Kenelm Digby to the King my master, in the form of an agreement made between your Lordship and me, by virtue of *the authority given me by his Majesty* and of the security given your Lordship by *the King's own letter*.[2]

Again, in another letter, very shortly afterwards, he urges the Nuncio thus :

whom I beseech to consider the authority granted your Lordship by his Holiness, and to recall to your memory *the letter written by the King my master to your Lordship* and *my powers* for treating with your Lordship.[3]

Glamorgan would, most naturally, lay stress upon this letter, for it afforded precisely that independent confirmation of his warrant of 12 March of which he found the need in dealing with the cautious Nuncio.   Its reference to himself ran thus :

[1] *E. H. R.*, p. 699.   [2] *Inquiry*, p. 157.   [3] *Ibid*. p. 175.

avec qui ce que vous resolvez, nous nous y tiendrons obligéz, et l'acheverons a son retour. Ses grandes merites nous obligent a la confidence que sur tous nous avons en luy . . . rien ne manquera de nostre costé a perfectionner ce que a quoy il s'obligera en nostre nom, au prix des faveurs receues par vos moyens. Fiez vous doncques a luy.[1]

Nothing could be more sweeping than this. Glamorgan is treated as a plenipotentiary, and Ormond absolutely ignored. There can be no question that the Nuncio would attach great importance to this private letter of Charles, if it indeed was what it professed to be.[2] But was it ? He himself had his doubts. He writes to Rome (27 Dec. 1645) that—

The Earl of Glamorgan, after having showed me two patents in which the King gives him secret but full powers to conclude a peace with the Irish . . . presented to me a letter directed to myself from his Majesty, in the ordinary form sealed with a small seal in two places with the superscription in French and dated 30th of April last. . . .[3]

This letter has raised a variety of doubts in my mind, as I cannot understand why in the month of April, when the King was as yet not much cast down, he should have shown such a desire for peace and assistance from Ireland or why he should have given such full powers to Glamorgan.[4]

---

[1] *Rinuccini's Embassy*, p. 104. Also *Inquiry*, p. 29.

[2] Glamorgan appealed to it as "propriam regis epistolam" (Nuncio's Memoirs, fo. 1,069 ; *E. H. R.*, p. 707. The author of the Nuncio's Memoirs observes that Glamorgan "nedum facultates superius positas, quibus ad pacem contrahendam munitus esset, ostendit, sed etiam literas eidem a Rege Gallice scriptas . . . quibus Regem manu propria subscripsisse video." Fo. 998 (*Inquiry*, p. 27).

[3] "literas a sua Majestate ad me ipsum directas ; . . . datas præterito Aprilis die 30" (Memoirs, fo. 1,002).

[4] *Embassy*, pp. 103, 105 ; *Nunziatura*, pp. 81–83.

Apart from its contents, the date arouses grave misgivings as to this letter. Glamorgan had been wrecked on the Lancashire coast 25 March, and, says Mr. Gardiner,—

Here arises a fresh question, which has often been asked, but never answered. Why is it that if Glamorgan was trusted with a secret mission of such tremendous importance, he was allowed to stay in England for three months after his shipwreck, apparently without the slightest attempt being made to hasten his departure? I, at all events, find no difficulty. As soon as Charles became aware that Ormond did not insist on resigning, and was quite ready to take up the negotiation on Charles's terms, there was no immediate necessity for Glamorgan's presence in Dublin. I must leave it to those who think that Glamorgan was to have given a secret consent to much more than this to explain his delay as best they can.[1]

Mr. Gardiner holds that the whole negotiation was now left to Ormond, and that the first intimation of any hitch is found in his letter of 8 May.[2] And yet it was during these very weeks, when Charles believed (in Mr. Gardiner's view) that the negotiation could be carried through without Glamorgan's help, that he is represented as writing this letter (30 April) referring the Nuncio, when he should arrive, to Glamorgan alone as his plenipotentiary authorized to negotiate secretly!

So much for the date. But indeed it is waste of time to discuss this letter seriously. For Mr. Gardiner does not attempt to defend its authenticity. He dismisses it in a footnote so amazing that it must be quoted *verbatim*:

I have taken no notice of a letter from the king presented by

---

[1] *E. H. R.*, p. 700.   [2] *Ibid.* p. 701.

Glamorgan to the nuncio. It has been correctly said that its language and its date are inconsistent with the supposition that it proceeded from Charles himself. The obvious explanation is that it was written by Glamorgan's secretary on a blank signed by the king. Some criticisms on this and other documents connected with this affair would lead one to suppose that those who make them imagine that Charles wrote formal documents with his own hand. The flowery language of the patents is no doubt traceable to Glamorgan ; but that is only what is to be expected.[1]

It is difficult to comment on this note in language that would not be indecorous in dealing with so pre-eminent an authority. In spite of its almost contemptuous allusion to those who have criticised this letter, we must remember what the Nuncio received from Glamorgan's hands. It was no formal document, but a strictly secret letter,[2] ending

Vostre Amis
CHARLES R.

De nostre Cour d'Oxford
Le 30esme d'Avril 1645.[3]

Of what it professed to be, there is no question whatever. And Glamorgan, we have seen, more than once, referred the Nuncio to it as of equal consequence with his warrant. Yet Mr. Gardiner calmly tells us that, date and all, it was concocted by Glamorgan's secretary, and implies that this was quite regular and not in any way a fraud !

To the Nuncio it could only be one of two things, a private letter to himself from the king,

---

[1] *E. H. R.*, p. 705.

[2] " combien il importe que se tient secret, il n'y a pas besoign de vous persuader, ny plus de recommander," etc., etc.

[3] I take the text from Rinuccini's *Embassy*.

written from Oxford on 30 April,—or, as he anxiously suspected, a mere fraud.

The obvious inference from this document was duly drawn in the last century :

> If his Majesty had wrote his name in a blank in England, the letter itself was certainly wrote in Ireland. This undoubted forgery proves plainly that the person who was guilty of it would not probably have scrupled any other.[1]

Certainly the secretary who concocted on a blank (as the Nuncio feared and Mr. Gardiner admits) the Oxford letter of 30 April might equally well have concocted on a blank the Oxford warrant of 12 March. The effect of the two documents was the same : they, and they alone, pledged the king to perform anything that Glamorgan might concede.

But, before proceeding to the warrant, it may be well to speak of that mysterious letter to the Pope, concerning which the Nuncio writes, in the same despatch as above (27 Dec. 1645) :

> The Earl . . . allowed me to see a letter from the King consisting of a quarter of a sheet, folded in the smallest possible compass, and directed to his Holiness thus : "Beatissimo Patri Innocentio Decimo," but he neither explained its contents nor when it was to be sent.[2]

The reason for mentioning this letter is that there exists at Badminton a mysterious letter "in a formal clerk's hand," beginning "Beatissime Domine" and ending impossibly :

[1] See *Inquiry*, p. 330. [2] Rinuccini's *Embassy*, p. 103.

PEERAGE STUDIES

Datum apud curiam nostram pene carcerem in Insula de Wight, 20 Aprilis 1649.

Sanctitatis Vestræ
devinctissimus CHARLES R.

Three months after his head was cut off, Charles here urges " His Holiness " to place faith in (Glamorgan now) the marquis of Worcester, "omnium subditorum nostrorum optime merito."[1] On the document some one has written : " It is perhaps a forgery."   For us, it is chiefly of interest for its blundered date, suggestive, as this is, of the earlier patents.

And now at length we come to the warrant, " the famous Warrant of 12 March."

When I was at Balliol, I once attended a lecture on Thucydides by Jowett, where he had to deal with a famous *crux* on which we hoped for disquisition.   But in this we were disappointed, " This passage," the Master piped, " should be taken thus."   It is somewhat in the same spirit that Mr. Gardiner treats the warrant :

" That this document was genuine there can be no reasonable doubt " (*E. H. R.*, p. 698).

But that is precisely the question that we have to discuss.

Mr. Gardiner, unfortunately, could not say what had become of the original.[2] As a matter of fact, it is now preserved in the library of

[1] Hist. MSS. Report, XII. 9, p. 33.
[2] " What became of it afterwards I have been unable to discover, but I have in my possession a photograph taken of it by Mr. Bruce whilst it was in Canon Tierney's possession. . . . Unfortunately the photograph itself is now too faded to admit of

Ushaw College.[1] The superscribed "Charles R." is doubtless written by the king, and Mr. Gardiner adds : " The only question is whether the body of the document is not also in Charles' handwriting."[2] Well, this is a point on which any one can satisfy himself by examining the facsimile prefixed to Mr. Gardiner's article. One has only to compare the king's signature with the " Charles " written below it to see that the two handwritings are frankly and glaringly distinct. But this, of course, merely proves that the body of the document *may* have been written, without the king's knowledge, on a blank having his signature.

We have, therefore, to ask ourselves whether it was so written ; for if so, it can only be described as a deliberate and wilful fraud. Now Glamorgan comes before us as a man under grave suspicion. The king's letter produced by him in connection with this warrant was, we have seen, admittedly fabricated by this very process. And his two patents of the previous year have been shown by me, I hope, to have been sheer forgeries. It is, then, antecedently probable that he would concoct this warrant if he found it essential for his purpose.

reproduction by photography, but a facsimile prepared by the ordinary process is published with the present article " (pp. 698–9).

[1] First Report on Historical MSS. (1874), p. 92 : "It is signed by the king at the top, the Royal Signet is affixed, and it is endorsed, 'the Earl of Glamorgan's especial Warrant for Ireland.' There is here also the draft of a somewhat similar document in a different form, not executed." This last remark is suggestive.

[2] *E. H. R.*, pp. 698–9.

I have argued above that it was essential, for without it he had no power to treat independently of Ormond. Mr. Gardiner urges that

powers are limited by instructions, and that, however enormous is the authority conveyed, Glamorgan would be bound only to use them in assisting Ormond, as he was there directed to do." [1]

It is here that I definitely join issue. If this warrant of 12 March represents his powers under the Instructions (2 Jan.), it ought to have been given him at the same time, in the first group of documents. Had it been given him at that date, Mr. Gardiner's argument might have been urged with at least some force. But it does not make its belated appearance till fully two months afterwards, at a date when Glamorgan ought to have been gone, for some time, on his mission. But this incomprehensible delay is at once explained if the earl forged it as a subsequent enlargement, by the king, of his powers, intended to override the instructions of January 2.

Let us place the two side by side :

DOCUMENT OF 2 JAN.	DOCUMENT OF 12 MARCH.
you may engage your estate, interest, and credit, that we will most readily and punctuelly perform any *our* promises to the Irish, and as it is necessary to conclude a peace suddenly, *whatsoever shall be con-*	. . . Authorise and give you power to treat *and conclude* with the Confederat Romaine Catholikes in our Kingdome of Ireland if upon necessity any thing be to be condescended unto wherein our Lieutenant

---

[1] *E. H. R.*, p. 699. By "there" is meant the instructions of 2 January, though, by an unlucky slip of the pen, Mr. Gardiner describes them as "of 12 Jan.," the date of quite another document.

LORD GLAMORGAN'S TREATY

sented unto by our lieutenant, the marquis of Ormond, we will die a thousand deaths rather than disannul or break it ; and if upon necessity anything to be condiscended unto and yet the lord marquis not willing to be seen therein, or nott fit for us at the present publicly to own, do you endeavour to supply the same.

can not so well be seene in as not fitt for us at the present publikely to owne and therefore we charge you to proceede according to this our warrant with all possible secresie, and *for whatsoever you shall engage your selfe* upon such valuable considerations *as you in your iudgement* [1] *shall deeme fitt,* we promise in (*sic*) the worde of a Kinge and a Christian to ratifie and performe *the same that shall be graunted by you and under your hand and seale,* etc. etc.

Now the point I wish to emphasize, to the very utmost of my power, is that the warrant of 12 March is so far from being governed, as Mr. Gardiner holds, by the Instructions of 2 January, that its very object is, on the contrary, to supplant and supersede them. It will be seen that both the above extracts refer to absolutely the same matter, namely the concessions to be made to the Irish. But while the first document pledges the king to grant only " whatsoever shall be consented unto " by Ormond, the second wholly ignores Ormond,[2] treats Glamorgan as a plenipotentiary, and solemnly pledges the king to " ratifie and performe " anything whatsoever that the earl may grant.[3]

[1] Of which Charles had said in his famous postcript to Ormond : "I will not answer for his judgement " (*E. H. R.*, p. 695).

[2] By which I mean that it wholly ignores the necessity of any consent of his.

[3] I draw the same inference from the words " power to treat

413

This, as we have seen, was Glamorgan's view of his warrant; and it certainly is mine. But I go further. If Mr. Gardiner is right in holding that the document is genuine, and that Glamorgan offended only in making undue concessions and acting independently of Ormond, why did not the king adopt this defence when the secret treaty was discovered? Why did he command Nicholas, when writing to Ormond and the Council, to impugn the document itself, if, as Mr. Gardiner holds, it was not the document that was to blame, but the use which Glamorgan made of it? Is not this letter an admission that the warrant would, if genuine, have given Glamorgan, as he claimed, independent powers?

Let me now explain my theory, and show on what I agree with Mr. Gardiner and on what we differ. We are absolutely agreed in holding that the earl was not empowered to make the two concessions which he did, and that he knew he was doing wrong. As Nicholas wrote to Ormond and the Council:

> The Lord Herbert did not acquaint the Lord Lieutenant with any part of it before he concluded[1] with the said Roman Catholics nor ever advertised his Majesty, the Lord Lieutenant or any of his Council here or there what he had done in an affair of so great moment and consequence four months before, till it was discovered by accident. This doth not sound like good meaning, and I am sure is not fair dealing.[2]

---

and conclude." It is significant, perhaps, that this phrase is also found in Glamorgan's letter of 1660: "my powers to treat and conclude" (*E. H. R.*, II. 698). [1] Note again the use of this word.

[2] Carte's *Ormond*, III. p. 446 (No. 426).

To this I may add that the very man who had drawn up the secret treaty was instructed to deny its existence to the Nuncio, till the latter could reach Ireland and be urged to secrecy, in the matter, by the earl.[1] Mr. Gardiner draws the same conclusion from the " defeasance " which accompanied the treaty.[2] Glamorgan knew that he had done wrong, but was sanguine that he would be forgiven, if he only revealed what he had done after he had brought the Irish army to the king's help :

When once there was an Irish army in England, and perhaps an army of continental catholics as well, Charles would forget his scruples.[3]

Where we differ is that I believe the earl's offence to have consisted in forging the warrant by which alone he could claim to make the treaty. It seems clear that he possessed " blanks " bearing the king's sign manual and the impression of his pocket signet.[4] There was nothing to prevent his

---

[1] " This same gentleman (Barron) tells me that in the General Assembly nothing had been concluded about a peace ; the truce only was tacitly continued, and that no more will be done before my arrival. In proof of this he brought me a letter from the Earl of Glamorgan," etc.   Letter from Nuncio 5 Oct. 1645 (*Embassy*, p. 74).   [2] *E. H. R.*, p. 704.   [3] *Ibid.* p. 705.

[4] "facultas Glamorgano concessa, quæ tota consistebat in foliis albis et concessionibus sigillo Regis cubiculario et privato signatis, quibus sua Majestas non poterat legitime obligari" (Nuncio's Memoirs; *Inquiry*, p. 334).   An interesting illustration of this practice of giving " blanks," ready signed, is afforded by fourteen being sent, in March, 1646–7, to Ormond himself by the Queen and Prince.   The fact is cited in *Inquiry*, pp. 336–7, on the authority of Father Leyburn.

secretary writing the warrant on one of these, without having actually "counterfeited" the king's hand. Digby and Nicholas, secretaries themselves, naturally seized on the suspicious fact that the warrant describes itself as given "under our *signet* and royal signature." As a matter of fact, it only bears the impression of the pocket or private signet, which was quite devoid of such authority as *the* signet. Digby, in his letter to Nicholas (4 Jan. 1646), writes :

I believe you will be as much startled as I was to find *the signet* mentioned in my Lord of Glamorgan's transactions. But it seems that was mistaken, and that he now pretends to some kind of authority under the king's *pocket signet*, which I certainly believe to be as false as I know the other.[1]

Nicholas, writing to Ormond and the Council (31 Jan. 1646), observes that—

The warrant, whereby his Lordship pretends to be authorized to treat with the Roman Catholics there, is not sealed with *the signet*, as it mentions.

To Ormond himself he points out that—

his Lordship's pretended warrant and power is alledged to be (confirmed to him under the signet), though there be no signet to it.

That their criticism was sound is seen when we compare the warrant of March 12 with that of Jan. 12.[2]

---

[1] *Inquiry*, p. 105.
[2] Printed opposite one another in *Inquiry*, pp. 20, 21.

12 Jan.	12 March.
. . . your sufficient warrant. Given at our court at Oxford under our sign manual and *private signet*.[1]	. . . a sufficient warrant. Given at our court at Oxford under our *signet* and royal signature.

I do not undertake to say that even the earlier document is genuine, but at least it illustrates the difference between the private and the official " signet."[2]

There is another point which has, I believe, escaped notice hitherto. The unhappy school of thought to which Charles belonged led him, if he wished to be believed, to make a statement in writing, as in his letter to Ormond, "upon the faith of a Christian."[3] This, at least, he regarded as binding. Now in the warrant of 12 March Mr. Gardiner's own facsimile makes him " promise *in* the worde of a King and a Christian."[4] Is it credible that Charles himself, or even an English secretary, could perpetrate this blunder ? But if the warrant was written by " a Romish Priest " for Glamorgan,[5] he might have easily made a slip suggested by a Latin idiom.[6]

[1] This is from the text as given by Carte and Birch.

[2] The Nuncio, as we have seen above, fully realized that the earl's documents were only sealed with the private signet, which was not binding on the king.

[3] Letter of 30 Jan. 1645–46 (Carte's *Ormond*).

[4] Mr. Gardiner escapes the difficulty by printing it (doubtless from oversight) " *on* the word " (p. 698).

[5] Cf. *Inquiry*, pp. 330, 333.

[6] " in verbo veritatis," which Ducange describes as a " sacramenti formulam " specially used by princes. In the letter from

It can hardly be necessary to labour the point further. What remains to be done is to consider how the conclusion I have drawn affects the characters of Glamorgan and of Charles.

Fantastic, ardent, "feather-brained," the earl is a fascinating study. He has a "scheme" for reducing the Rock of Cashel, if he is but allowed £100 "and four or five barrels of gunpowder"; [1] he has a "method" for enabling Charles to employ him, even after the great exposure; [2] and "when first with his corporall eyes he did see finished a perfect tryall of his water-commanding-engine," he records an "ejaculatory" prayer "that he may not be puffed up by this and many more unheard-of and unparalleled inventions."[3] He is at all times ready to promise money, artillery, ships, and men, till Digby cynically exclaims, "Lord, increase our faith!" And yet with all his rash assurance, his colossal but *naïve* vanity, he was filled with a chivalrous devotion to the causes of his church and of his king. It will not, I hope, be deemed unfair to suggest that his Catholic and foreign training may have imbued him with the faith that "the end justifies the means," and that he may have applied that maxim in the case of his

Charles to Glamorgan, 12 March 1645, alleged by Dircks (p. 75) to exist at Badminton, the king pledges himself "on (*sic*) the word of a king and a Christian" (compare the formula in the warrant); but Mr. Gardiner, misquoting Dircks, omits the words "and a Christian" (*History*, II. 175).

[1] *Inquiry*, p. 221.   [2] 29 March 1646 (*Ibid.* p. 189).
[3] Hist. MSS. Report, *ut supra*, p. 49.

secret treaty. As Ormond finely phrased it, in a stately and dignified rebuke :

> I understand not what your Lordship's authorities from his Majesty are, or what ways you mean to take to serve him ; and therefore can give no judgment of either. . . . In the mean time, I must take the freedom of a better subject than most your Lordship meets with there, and of one that wishes you happiness, to advise you to be careful how you affirm your desires to serve the King to be powers from him.[1]

The paramount necessity of obtaining an Irish army for the king must have overridden, in his mind, every other thought, while his optimism, doubtless, led him to believe that, in gratitude, his master would confirm the concessions he had made to his church. Only success, in short, was needed. As Dr. Jameson exclaimed, to Sir William Harcourt's horror, he knew that, had he succeeded, he would have been forgiven.

As for Charles, on whose character this famous question has always been held to have so grave a bearing, Mr. Gardiner has, at least, rejected the *gravamen* of the charge against him, namely that he gave instructions to Glamorgan to make the concessions in the secret treaty behind Ormond's back.[2] He does, however, charge him with shuffling in his disavowal.

In one document, and in one only, does Charles seem to shuffle in the matter of Glamorgan's

---

[1] Ormond to Glamorgan, 6 Oct. 1646 (at a later stage in the negotiations).

[2] "That Glamorgan had secret instructions from Charles, empowering him to act as he did, is a notion which may be promptly dismissed" (*History*, III. 34).

powers. In his formal despatch to Ormond and the Council, he explains with what object Glamorgan was sent :

and ¹withal knowing his interest with the Roman Catholic party to be very considerable, we thought it not unlikely that you might make good use of him by employing that interest in persuading them to a moderation, and to rest satisfied, upon his engagement also, with those above mentioned concessions, of which, in the condition of our affairs, you could give them no other than a private assurance. To this end (and with the strictest limitations that we could enjoin him merely to those particulars concerning which we had given you secret instructions, as also even in that to do nothing but by your especial directions) *it is possible we might* have thought fit to have given unto the said Earl of Glamorgan such a credential as might give him credit with the Roman Catholics, in case you should find occasion to make use of him, either as a further assurance unto them of what you should privately promise, or in case you should judge it necessary to manage those matters, for their greater confidence, apart by him, of whom, in regard of his religion and interest, they might be the less jealous. This is all and the very bottom of what *we might have possibly* intrusted unto the said Earl of Glamorgan in this affair, etc., etc. . . . he was bound up by our positive commands from doing anything but what you should particularly and precisely direct him to do, both in the matter and manner of his negotiation.¹

The words I have italicized, no doubt, have a very ugly sound. But do they apply to the famous warrant of 12 March ? From the great care with which, throughout, Charles insists on having made his envoy a mere subordinate to Ormond, it is clear to me that they cannot. Mr. Gardiner, however, has jumped at the conclusion that they do,² but that this is not a necessary inference is

¹ Despatch of 31 Jan. 1645.
² "In a public despatch to the Irish Council he allowed himself

proved by two letters from the Nuncio. On Dec. 23, 1645, he writes that Glamorgan made his treaty—

in virtue of *two* most ample but secret powers . . . given by his Majesty to the Earl.[1]

And four days later he writes that the earl

showed me *two* patents in which the king gives him secret but full powers to conclude a peace with the Irish on whatsoever terms he thinks advisable.[2]

But, whatever the Nuncio may here refer to, my own suggestion is that, in the above despatch, Charles refers to the instructions of 2 January, entitled " Several heads whereupon you our right trusty and right well-beloved earl of Glamorgan may securely proceed in execution of our commands." These, if carefully studied, would be certainly " a credential," and for such a purpose as the king describes. And if it be asked why Charles should thus grudgingly own them, it must be

to cast doubts upon the genuineness of his warrant to Glamorgan [the one of March 12 is always intended] by speaking of it as a credential which he might possibly have given, whilst he permitted Nicholas at the same time to call attention to its defects as an official document " (*History*, III. 47).

Is it probable that Charles would thus " give himself away " by admitting that " he might possibly have given " the warrant of 12 March, while instructing Nicholas to assail its genuineness from its internal evidence ? As I have argued above, if the document itself was blameless, what occasion was there to assail its genuineness ?

[1] *Embassy*, p. 95.

[2] *Ibid.* p. 103. These were irrespective of the king's (alleged) letter to the Nuncio (which Siri describes as " credenza ").

PEERAGE STUDIES

remembered that Ormond's Council were so opposed to the Catholic demands that Ormond had had to keep them in the dark as to Charles' letter of 27 February (1645) to himself, enlarging his concessions. That Charles had given any "credential" at all to a Catholic envoy in the matter was a fact that he grudged confessing to a Council of alarmed Protestants.

In the preceding paper, dealing with Glamorgan's dukedom, I suggested that the document of 1 April, '1644', was developed by him from genuine documents of 1645, and that this might be also how he produced the warrant of 12 March.[1] Since doing so, I have found that a precisely similar conclusion had been reached by Mr. Gardiner, independently, on another great contested document, the "commission" from Charles I., bearing a Great Seal, which Sir Phelim O'Neill produced in Ireland 25 Nov. 1641.

That this document was forged there can be no doubt whatever,[2] but it does not follow that it was not forged upon the lines of a real document, sent from Edinburgh by the King to the Catholic Lords.[3]

It is necessary to distinguish the motives by which Glamorgan was inspired, and to remember the policy of the men with whom he had to deal. Rinuccini and the Protestant Ormond represented the two extremes. Between them stood the Supreme Council (of the Confederate Catholics),

[1] p. 391 above.
[2] Compare the equally confident verdict on p. 410 above.
[3] Ed. 1884, vol. X. p. 92.

far too ready, in the Nuncio's view, to come to terms with Ormond and with Charles. From the time of his reaching Ireland (1645), he openly and stubbornly strove, on the one hand, to extort, for the Catholics, more extensive concessions, on the other to obtain greater security for the fulfilment of those concessions. In less than a year the situation had developed into his arrest, at Kilkenny, of the leaders of the Supreme Council (19 Sept. 1646), for making peace with Ormond, while Glamorgan, who had soon become a mere puppet in his hands, had sworn " before the most holy sacrament " that he would adhere to his party "against the marquis of Ormonde and all his relations and favourers." [1]

In dealing, therefore, with the Nuncio, Glamorgan found the need of producing more evidence than the Catholic leaders had required. And this evidence assumed the form of documents and letters intended to prove the absolute confidence reposed in him by Charles and the almost unlimited extent of his powers. We must consequently look with grave suspicion on such evidence as this when found in the Nuncio's Memoirs alone.

Glamorgan's own champions unconsciously reveal his ways. We are shown him writing to the Nuncio, 6 Feb. 1646, urging the necessity of sending, "without the least delay, 3,000 men to succour " Chester, while " the other seven thousand soldiers" (of the 10,000) need not be sent till they

---

[1] 19 Feb. 1646 (*Inquiry*, p. 182, from Nuncio's Memoirs).

had communicated with the king.[1]   Two days later
(8 Feb.) he writes to Ormond :

> Myself alone having, by the interest and goodwill of the
> Nuncio, gained this point, that three thousand soldiers are designed
> to be sent to the relief of Chester ; and to-morrow or next day
> he is to have the chief management of that proposal in the
> General Assembly.[2]

This was either false or a strange delusion ; the
Nuncio, so far from supporting this proposal, held
out stubbornly at the meeting on the 9th.   It was
only after Glamorgan's abject submissions to the
Nuncio on the 16th and 19th February that " the
Nuncio being satisfied with this, went two days
after to the Assembly, exhorting them . . . to
hasten the three thousand soldiers to the relief of
Chester." [3]   Moreover, having instantly hurried to
Waterford " to attend the transportation of those
troops," [4] he wrote only two days later to the king
(23 Feb.):

> I am now at Waterford, providing shipping immediately to
> transport 6,000 (sic) foot ; and 4,000 foot are by May to follow
> them.[5]

And on 28 Feb. he similarly wrote to Lord Hop-
ton, " that the ten thousand men are designed for

[1] Memoirs, fos. 1,066–9 (Inquiry, pp. 157–8).
[2] Ibid. p. 162.   [3] Ibid. p. 183.   [4] Ibid.
[5] Ibid. p. 184 (from Rushworth).   Mr. Gardiner cites the
Carte MSS. for yet another letter in which " on February 24
Glamorgan was able to assure Ormond that not 3,000 but 6,000
men would be sent, and that he was himself starting for Waterford to expedite their embarkation " (History, III. 153).   Yet his
bargain with the Nuncio was only that 3,000 should be sent and
7,000 kept back.

his Majesty's service, six (*sic*) thousand of which are ready for transportation." [1]

There is something, in these instances, more than sanguine imagination : there is that incorrigible bombast, that vainglorious exaggeration, which seems inseparable from everything he writes or (in his forgeries) makes others write about himself and his performances. The glowing recital of his military services in the patent alleged to create his dukedom was repeated by him in his letter to Albemarle (29 Dec. 1665),[2] and in the speech he proposed to deliver in the House of Lords (1666–7).[3] Yet even Dircks, his own most ardent panegyrist, dismisses these achievements in no sparing terms.[4] It must have been, however, on the strength of these performances that this amazing man caused himself to be depicted "as a Roman general, seated by his lady attired in a modern costume of pale blue satin."

[1] *Ibid.* p. 187.   [2] Dircks, p. 279.

[3] "Soe immediately and in eight dayes tyme I raysed six regiments, fortified Monmouth, Chepstow, and Ragland, . . . Garrisoned likewise Cardiffe, Brecknock, Hereford, Goodridge Castle, and the Forest of Dean, after I had taken them from the enemie" (12th Report Hist. MSS., IX. 62).

[4] "The achievements, as thus recorded, are sufficiently high-sounding, but no contemporary historian seems to have considered them of sufficient importance to put on record. Neither his own letters, nor those of his numerous family and connexions, neither political nor religious partizans nor opponents give us a glimpse of our general's skill, bravery, and final successes ; while the few particulars actually recorded leave but a faint impression as regards facts, and a most unfavourable one as regards results. In short, in his military capacity he bears a most mythical character" (pp. 66–7).

His Lordship presents a singular appearance in a toga and tight-fitting hose of deep scarlet, an ornamented. leather jerkin, and wearing a wig [?] streaming over his breast and shoulders . . . while his left (hand) hangs negligently over the arm of the chair in proximity with a mighty sheathed sword.

His lordship's expression, one may add, is that of fatuous complacency.[1]

But more serious is the painful question whether the earl " ran straight," whether his statements, when unsupported, should always obtain credit. Glamorgan, Mr. Gardiner holds, had been instructed by Charles to act in loyal co-operation with Ormond, and to be guided by his judgment. Yet, having made the secret treaty (25 Aug.) behind Ormond's back, he wrote to him (9 Sept.) a letter in which—

To prevent Ormond from becoming aware of the real state of the case, Glamorgan professed entire ignorance of the requests which would now be made by the agents of the Supreme Council.[2]

And again, on November 28—

In writing to Ormond Glamorgan not only gave no hint of this secret negotiation, but assured him with the most fulsome expressions of devotion that he was but carrying out the directions which he had received at Dublin.[3]

It is no wonder that Nicholas wrote, in his indignant letter to Ormond and the Council (31 Jan. 1646) :

[1] See the frontispiece to Dircks' volume and his description on pp. 30, 31.   But, from the child's age, I should date the picture as not earlier than 1643 or 1644.

[2] Gardiner, *History*, III. 37.

[3] *Ibid.* p. 38.

This doth not sound like good meaning ; and I am sure is not fair dealing.

We again find him, a year later, playing the same double game. He writes to Ormond (11 Sept. 1646) as " Your Excellency's most really affectionate kinsman and devoted servant," to assure him that he is about to leave Ireland, unless Ormond persuades him to remain and prove " my affection to your person, to whom my professions have been ever real."[1] Yet, at this very time, he was scheming with his foe the Nuncio to supplant him as Lord-Lieutenant, and " being desirous of advancing himself to the Marquis' post," was soliciting the support, for that purpose, of the Catholic generals and clergy, who had it " in their view to transport the Holy Faith into England by their arms,"[2] and who were actually in the field against Ormond ! Is this the sort of man whose statements should command credit ?

Now that we have seen the startling frauds of which the earl was capable, every document with which he had to do is tainted in an expert's eyes. It is a singular circumstance that Mr. J. A. Bennett, in his report on the duke of Beaufort's MSS. to the Historical MSS. Commission,[3] prints hardly any of the documents given by Dircks as existing among the Badminton MSS. What has become of the others ? Where, for instance, are the let-

[1] Dircks, p. 179, from Carte MSS.
[2] See Nuncio's letter of 21 Sept. 1646 in *Inquiry*, pp. 253-6 (from the Memoirs, fos. 1,376-9).
[3] 12th Report, IX. pp. 1-115 (1891).

ters of 12 Feb. and 12 March 1645 ? I do not
say that they are not genuine, but we ought to see
them, if they exist, before deciding the question.
Mr. Gardiner, although he has visited Badminton,[1]
quotes his documents from Dircks alone, as if that
writer, though admittedly not qualified for their
treatment, were an original authority.[2]

It is, however, on the documents quoted from
the Nuncio's Memoirs alone that the gravest doubt
must rest. And these are of great importance for
the attitude assumed by Charles, after the exposure
of the treaty, towards Glamorgan and his conduct.

Charles, we must remember, would not be harsh
to one who had erred from zeal for his cause, who
had supported him eagerly in the past, and might
yet help him in his need. But did he, to take a
definite instance, write to Glamorgan, from Newcastle (20 July 1646), the extraordinary letter
that Mr. Gardiner quotes ? Moved by its contents to the sarcastic comment that "Charles'
notions of bad faith were all his own,"[3] he quotes
from it this passage :

> If you can raise a large sum of money by pawning my king-
> doms for that purpose, I am content you should do it ; and if I

---

[1] *E. H. R.*, II. 688.

[2] See p. 397 above, and compare *E. H. R.*, II. 708, and
History, III. 48, where he cites 'Dircks' for an important letter
of Charles in Harl. MSS. 6,988 (fo. 191), where I found it to be
of singular character.

[3] *History*, III. 154. Mr. Gardiner again appeals to it on
p. 160 as " the enthusiastic letter in which Charles had expressed
his eagerness to place himself in the hands of Glamorgan and
Rinuccini."

recover them, I will fully repay that money. And tell the Nuncio that if once I can come into his and your hands, which ought to be extremely wished for by you both, as well for the sake of England as Ireland, since all the rest, as I see, despise me, I will do it (Dircks, 174).

One would certainly imagine, from the reference to " Dircks," that the letter was at Badminton. It is not a little surprising to find that Dircks merely quotes it from Birch's *Inquiry* (p. 245), where it is, in turn, translated from the Latin text in the Nuncio's Memoirs (fo. 1,373) ! Although he enjoyed the great advantage of access to these memoirs, Mr. Gardiner cites this letter from 'Dircks' alone. Such treatment of authorities, surely, is somewhat out of date.

But when we turn to the contents of this epistle, what are we to say ? We see the king suggesting to Glamorgan the " pawning " of his " kingdoms " —as if they were his watch. Who was to act the pawnbroker's part ? And who was to advance the " large sum " on the strength of a suggestion in a private letter ? For other security there was none. Moreover, if a pawnbroker was wanted, why seek him in Ireland, when the king's recognised agent was, at this time, the queen in France ? But there is another question, which is of historical importance. Mr. Gardiner's charge against the king is that, while he was employing Ormond to arrange a peace in Ireland, he was eager to place himself in the hands of the Nuncio, " whose policy in Ireland had crossed Ormond's at every step." [1] As

[1] *History*, III. 154-155.

a matter of fact, the two men were, at this date, open foes. This, it will be seen, is a grave charge ; but is it true ?

What are the facts ? Charles had privately instructed Ormond[1] to disregard his formal dispatch of June 11 (1646) and to hurry on the Irish peace.[2] Ormond, on July 30, proclaimed the peace, which was instantly denounced by the Nuncio. But it was to Ormond that Charles looked :

> On Sept. 16 he wrote to Ormond, suggesting the seizure and fortification of a spot on the Lancashire coast as a means " of helping " him " to make use of the Irish assistance." [3]

Mr. Gardiner, indeed, can here be quoted against himself. For the situation in the summer of 1646 resembled that in the spring of 1645. At both periods the king had placed the Irish peace in Ormond's hands; and when he did so, Mr. Gardiner holds, Glamorgan was dropped.[4] Still less, while looking to Ormond, would Charles endeavour to obtain the peace through the Nuncio, Ormond's foe, whose object was not mere tolera-

---

[1] *Ibid.* p. 154.

[2] Mr. Gardiner's statements are contradictory, but only by a slip :

III. 151.	III. 153.
" On June 11 he had been forced to direct (*sic*) Ormond to abandon all further negotiations with the rebels."	" On June 24 Ormonde received the letter of June 11, in which Charles forbade (*sic*) him to abstain from further negotiation."

The first passage is the right one.

[3] *History*, III. 144.

[4] *E. H. R.*, II. 700 ; *History*, II. 176.

tion, but the subjugation of the three kingdoms to the faith of Rome.[1]   This would be even more incredible than the king's employment, the previous year, of Glamorgan as a secret rival to Ormond was pronounced to be by Mr. Gardiner himself.[2]   So much for the charge of intriguing behind Ormond's back.

But what of the statement that Charles wished to join Glamorgan and the Nuncio?[3]   If he thought of fleeing, it was to France.[4]   Yet this is

[1] " The Nuncio was of opinion that under the conduct of so zealous a Catholic as the Earl, a way would be opened for exterminating the Protestant religion from Ireland and the conversion of the king, if he should come thither ; or at least for transporting a strong and faithful army out of Ireland into England ; by the junction of which with the English Catholics, his Majesty might be restored, and the Catholic religion triumph over the Protestants in England and Scotland, who were extremely divided among themselves " (*Inquiry*, p. 253, from Nuncio's Memoirs, fo. 1,376, where the Latin runs : "ad hæresim tota Ibernia eliminandam " . . . " fides catholica in Angliâ quoque et Scotia de hæreticis inter se discordibus triumpharet "). It would be to nourish these hopes that the Newcastle letter was concocted (if, as I suggest, it was forged). It was meant to illustrate, for Glamorgan's purpose, what the memoirs term " the confidence in his Lordship testified by his Majesty in his letters to him " (*Ibid.*).

[2] " Ormond is to drive as good a bargain as he can. . . . Is it to be supposed that he [Charles] was at the same time privately authorising Glamorgan to purchase a peace at any price ? " (*E. H. R.*, II. 700). " That he [Glamorgan] had any secret instructions to abandon the Acts of Appeal and Præmunire is an idea which may be rejected as incredible " (*History*, II. 174).

[3] The Pope, it is said, shed tears on receiving a copy of this letter, from which it would seem that, if I am right, Glamorgan succeeded in hoaxing, not only the Nuncio, but the Pope.

[4] " On the 8th (July) he wrote to Ashburnham that he

not the evidence on which I take my stand. At this period we read (of the king's objects) :

It was Charles' firm conviction that he was dividing his enemies by his policy.[1]

Now if there was one step by which he would instantly, infallibly, compel those enemies to unite, it would be by throwing himself into the arms of the Nuncio and Glamorgan. The Scots, the army, the English Presbyterians would present an unbroken front. And they would be joined even by others—

at a time when all English parties were resolutely opposed to every idea which had found favour at Kilkenny.[2]

Nay, in Ireland itself, not only the Presbyterians, but Ormond and his Council, were unshakeably hostile to the Nuncio and all his schemes. Charles at the worst was no fool : he was perfectly aware that such a step would destroy his last chance of recovering, as he hoped, his kingdoms. It would be the act of a madman.

And it would, moreover, have been useless. How could Charles, even if he sacrificed all his

believed himself to be lost unless he could escape to France before August " (*History*, III. 132). Glamorgan and the Nuncio drew up (according to the latter's memoirs) a reply to the alleged letter of 20 July, urging Charles to come, as it suggested, to Ireland.

[1] *History*, III. 140.

[2] *Ibid*. p. 162. At the moment of returning this proof for press I find that Charles, in his letters to the queen (19 Aug., 31 Aug., 7 Sept. 1646) assures her that even Ormond's peace (which the Nuncio rejected) would " infallibly " hamper his negotiations in England (Add. MS. 28,857).

other supporters, hope to gain the Nuncio and his followers, when he had made it, Mr. Gardiner admits, a point of honour and of conscience never to grant those two concessions on which the Nuncio had inexorably insisted throughout as the minimum price of his support.[1] His stubborn insistence on these concessions culminated in the rejection of the treaty between Ormond and the Supreme Council (12 Aug. 1646), because it did not contain them, and in his arrest of the Council's leaders.[2] As for Glamorgan, he had " surrendered himself body and soul to the Nuncio, swearing by all the saints that he would obey every one of his commands and would never do anything contrary to his honour and good pleasure."[3] Charles, on the other hand, had firmly declared (31 July 1645) that he would " rather chuse to suffer all extremity than ever to " make these concessions,[4] and had privately assured the queen (March 1646) that he could never hope " to enjoy God's blessing " if he did.[5] Mr. Gardiner observes that " it was hopeless to expect him to change his mind,"[6] and that though " there is always something arbitrary in the selection of a limit to concession, that limit had now been reached by Charles."[7] How then could he hope for the Nuncio's help ?

Has Mr. Gardiner even asked himself how the king could " pawn " his kingdoms ? Or whether he would do so in this manner ? Or whether he

[1] See *History*, III. 39, 40.   [2] *Ibid*. pp. 156, 159.
[3] *Ibid*. p. 52.   [4] *E.H.R.*, II. 703.   [5] *Ibid*. p. 708.
[6] *History*, II. 174.   [7] *Ibid*. III. 34.

F F

wished to take a step which meant his instant
ruin?   Apparently not.   He finds a letter in
' Dircks ' (which is merely taken from Birch's
Inquiry, where it is retranslated from a Latin translation found in the Nuncio's Memoirs), and accepting its evidence without question as that of
an original authority, he charges the king with a
stupid treachery at obvious variance with all the
facts as given even in his own History.

When shall we learn, in England, how to use
our evidence?   If one document is as good as another, if their critical treatment is deemed needless,
vain is the writer's talent, and vain the student's
toil.

X

The Abeyance of the Barony of Mowbray

SEVERAL points of great interest to the student of Peerage law were raised in the Mowbray and Segrave case decided in 1877. But on the present occasion I do not propose to call attention to more than one—the alleged determination, 'in some way or other,' in favour of the Howard co-heir, of the abeyance into which the baronies of Mowbray and Segrave had fallen in the 15th century.

Anne, the child-heiress of the Mowbrays, dukes of Norfolk, was an infant of three years old at her father's death (1476) and affianced to a son of Edward IV. (one of " the princes in the Tower "), who was thereupon created earl of Nottingham, and subsequently duke of Norfolk. She died in tender years, leaving the succession to the baronies and vast estates of her house open to the heirs of her relatives, Isabel and Margaret, wives respectively of James Lord Berkeley and Sir Robert Howard. Now these ladies were the daughters of the first duke of Norfolk, son of John Lord Mowbray, by his marriage with the daughter and heir of John Lord Segrave, whose wife Margaret, countess of Norfolk, was the heiress of Thomas ' de Brotherton,' son of Edward I., and Earl Marshal. Thus the death of the little heiress proved the means of a vast accession to the fortunes of the house of Berkeley, while it virtually founded those of the house of Howard. The Mowbray baronies were divided between them, Lord Berkeley being created earl of Nottingham and Lord Howard duke of Norfolk the same day (June 28, 1483). It is a singular circumstance that the seniority of the heiresses seems to be undetermined, ' Burke ' declaring Lady Howard to be the elder, while the *Complete Peerage* of G. E. C. assigns that position to Lady Berkeley, as, apparently, did Dugdale. But in any case the Berkeleys had an equal share in the representation of this illustrious line, which makes it the more strange that the Howards should have been tacitly allowed to monopolize it as they virtually have done. In 1777 this representation, with all that it involved, passed away from the Howards to their heirs-general, the Lords Stourton and Petre ; and in 1882 the share of the Berkeleys similarly passed to their heir-general, Mrs. Milman, since recognised as Baroness Berkeley. Thus, in 1877, there were three co-heirs to the house of Mowbray, namely the *de jure* earl of Berkeley (whose right to that title has been confirmed by a subsequent decision, but who never assumed it), who inherited one moiety, and the Lords Stourton and Petre, who shared the other. The Committee for Privileges decided, however, that the abeyance of the Mowbray and Segrave baronies had been determined in favour of the Howards " previously to the reign of Queen Elizabeth," and believed that it was done by Richard III.

The first point in this decision that invites close attention is its bearing on the doctrine of abeyance. The best authorities have agreed in placing the earliest undoubted case of the determination of an abeyance by the Crown so late as 1660, the previous cases being all more or less doubtful. The Mowbray decision, however, carried back the practice *per saltum* to the days of Richard III. ! But far more extraordinary, and indeed revolutionary, was the view taken of the evidence in proof of the abeyance being determined in favour of the Howard co-heir. In the Windsor case (1660) the determination was effected by formal patent,[1] but in that of Ferrers of Chartley (1677) merely by the issue of the writ, which has since been the usual practice. But in the Mowbray case there is no evidence how or even when the abeyance was determined.

Down to the time of Lord Stourton's claim the position of the question was this. The barony of *Segrave* (though the Berkeleys had constantly included it among their titles) was believed to be still in abeyance. Mr. Fleming, Lord Stourton's own counsel, had himself admitted in the Scales case (p. 26) that the barony of Segrave is in abeyance "between Lords Stourton and Petre . . .

---

[1] See p. 361 above.

and the heir of the late earl of Berkeley." So universal was this belief that a modern barony of Segrave was created in favour of the Fitz-hardinge Berkeleys (1831). As to *Mowbray* there were doubts. Mr. Courthope, in his *Historic Peerage* (1857), referring to the Mowbray summons of 1640, held that " it may reasonably be doubted whether this writ of summons did not create a new barony instead of affecting the abeyance of the ancient dignity " (p. 340).[1] But, in any case, no other evidence than this writ, for the determination of the abeyance, was supposed to exist. In Lord Stourton's original petition it was accordingly claimed " that the Barony of Mowbray continued in abeyance . . . until the year 1640, when King Charles the First was pleased to determine the abeyance by summoning Henry Frederick Howard . . . as Lord Mowbray." This allegation, of course, ignored the difficulty that the party to whom the writ was issued was not a co-heir to the dignity at the time.

The claim, however, was subsequently altered in consequence of the discovery of Letters-missive from Richard III., including the baronies of Mowbray and Segrave in the duke's style. In

---

[1] It should be noted that, by a strange error, Courthope gave the date of this summons as " 13 April 1639 " (*sic*), and was followed in this by the *Complete Peerage* (VI. 54 ; but compare VIII. 480). This error, which is constantly repeated, probably arose from the summons being dated 21 March ' 1639 ' (*i.e.* 1640), the Parliament meeting on 13 April 1640.

THE BARONY OF MOWBRAY

Lord Stourton's "additional case" it was confidently urged by his counsel that these Letters proved (but did not constitute) the determination of the abeyance.[1]

These Letters, on which Mr. Fleming insisted so strenuously throughout, were, with singular eagerness, accepted as proof by the Committee. I append the relevant extracts from their judgment :

LORD CHANCELLOR.

"As to the abeyance of the Segrave barony, it appears to me that the Letters-missive of the 2nd of Richard III., signed by the King, would of itself be sufficient evidence that in some way or other the abeyance had been terminated by the sovereign."

LORD O'HAGAN.

"As to the abeyance, I should say that the Letters-missive of King Richard III. are of themselves, without any question being raised as to the admissibility of the garter-plates in evidence, quite sufficient to prove the determination of the abeyance of the baronies. The King recognises the determination of the abeyance ; . . . and however it may have been accomplished . . . I think the evidence with regard to the determination of the abeyance of the baronies is perfectly sufficient."

LORD BLACKBURN.

"If it [the determination] is done by a document, under the hand of a sovereign, by his sign manual, that is quite sufficient. Now here is evidence that the abeyance was so terminated. . . . I think myself, if it were necessary, it [the Letters-missive] should be construed as operating as an original grant under his

---

[1] See Additional Case, No. 27 (p. 9), and the note thereupon : "It is confidently submitted on the part of the Petitioner that the abeyance . . . was determined in favour of John Lord Howard Duke of Norfolk shortly after her [Anne's] death, and before the 24th of September, 1484 [the date of the Letters missive]."

hand to determine the abeyance; for I am not aware that the King could do more. . . . I think the Letters-missive of king Richard III. are quite conclusive upon the matter."

LORD CHANCELLOR.

"I myself do not accept that [the garter-plates] as evidence with regard to the determination of the abeyance, but I think the other evidence of the determination of the abeyance is satisfactory, namely the Letters-missive of king Richard III."

These extracts sufficiently establish the Committee's acceptance of Mr. Fleming's contention that "the abeyance of the baronies . . . was determined in favour of John Howard, the first Duke of Norfolk," [1] and that this determination, proved by the Letters-missive, "forms the sole ground" [2] for the subsequent user of the titles.

Let us first consider the consequences of the principle thus laid down. It revolutionizes the doctrine of abeyance, as hitherto understood, in the direction aimed at by Mr. Fleming in the Scales case, and thus opened the door to a new series of claims. The Leicester patent of 1784, for instance, can now be invoked as determining (or proving the determination of) the Bourchier abeyance; and other recognitions by the Crown in formal instruments, however erroneous, can now be similarly interpreted.

Incidentally, it may here be added that, according to Lord Stourton's "original case" (p. 11), the duke of Norfolk received, Feb. 24, $148\frac{3}{4}$, a general pardon "describing him by all the titles and names which could be attributed to him," but

---

[1] Special Case, p. 290.   [2] *Ibid.* p. 26.

THE BARONY OF MOWBRAY

the Pardon Roll reveals that the baronies of Mowbray and Segrave are not to be found among them.
So too with his patent of creation on June 28
preceding. This then narrows the date of the
alleged determination to February – September,
1484. And though the time and manner of such
determination, at this very early date, should have
been clearly established, we have only the Lord
Chancellor's belief that it took place "in some
way or other" on some unknown occasion.

Assuming, however, that Mr. Fleming was
right, and that, in the words of the petitioner's
case, "the abeyance . . . was determined in
favour of John Howard Duke of Norfolk previously to the 24th of September," 1484, what
evidence is there of the user of the titles by the
Howards? The petitioner was not able to ad-
duce one till 1564, when the funeral certificate of
the duchess of Norfolk styles her husband "Lorde
Mowbray Segrave and of Brews" (p. 265). And
this was dismissed, in his judgment, by Lord
Blackburn (who oddly seems to have imagined
that it was a coffin-plate inscription [1]) as "no evidence at all." With that exception the petitioner
adduced no evidence of user till the garter-plate of
1611 (p. 265). Now what is the cause of this
hiatus?

Assuming, as I have said, that the baronies of
Mowbray and Segrave were duly vested in John

[1] "The mere fact that a duke of Norfolk put upon his duchess'
coffin-plate a statement that she was the wife of the Lord Mowbray and Segrave is no evidence at all."

duke of Norfolk (d. 1485), they were obviously forfeited by the Act of Attainder in 1 Hen. VII. (p. 135). Of this there can be no question. Now the act of " restitucion " in favour of his son "Thomas late erle of Surrey " (4 Hen. VII.) expressly stipulates " that this statute of adnullacion and restitucion *extend not for the said Thomas to eny honour estate name and dignite but onely to the honour estate name and dignite of Erle of Surrey* " (p. 140).[1] This would obviously exclude the baronies of Mowbray and Segrave as well as that of Howard and the dukedom of Norfolk. Accordingly when this Thomas Howard was created Earl Marshal (2 Hen. VIII.) and duke of Norfolk (5 Hen. VIII.) he was only styled earl of Surrey and had no baronies assigned him. Now the subsequent attainders and restorations of the house could do no more than place its heads eventually in the shoes of this Thomas.

It has indeed been argued that the above provision applied only to Thomas himself, not to his heirs, and that the baronies, therefore, remained, as it were, in a state of suspended animation during his life. But this argument would, obviously, apply to the dukedom of Norfolk also, and is inconsistent with the new creation, in 1514, of that dignity, in favour of Thomas and his heirs male. Moreover, on carefully reading the act, it will be seen that its object was to deprive the earl not only of the Honours, but also of the *lands* derived from or

---

[1] Naturally enough, these words are not those italicized in the Minutes of evidence.

through his father,[1] whose great share of the Mowbray inheritance was to remain vested in the Crown, while that of the Berkeleys was assured to them by a special act which followed. Now it is clear, from the case of the lands, that the provision partially excluding Thomas excluded his heirs also.

If, then, the abeyance was indeed determined under Richard III., the baronies were forfeited by attainder and have remained so ever since.

The actual resolution, however, adopted by the Committee did not pledge them (in spite of their *rationes decidendi*) to a determination in or before Sept. 1484. Although it was avowedly on this that their decision was based, they illogically resolved—*ob majorem cautelam* we may presume—that the abeyance was determined " previously to the reign of Queen Elizabeth."

Now, either the abeyance was determined previously to Sept. 1484, or it was not. If it was not, then the earliest proof of that determination accepted by the Committee is the Act of

---

[1] " And that it be enacted by the said auctorite that this Statute of Adnullation and Restitution extend not for the said Thomas to any Honour Estate Name and Dignite but onely to the Honour Estate Name and Dignite of Erle of Surrey nor to any Manors Lordshippes Landes Tenements and other Enheritaments wherto the Kyngs Highnes was at any tyme entitled by reason of either of the said Atteyndres, other then the said late Erle had in the right of his wife, . . . or such Manors Lordshippes Londes Tenementes and other Inheritaments which if the said Act of Atteyndre had not be, shuld herafter discend, remayne or reverte to the said Thomas and his Heires by any other Auncestre than by the said John late Duke of Norfolk " (*Rot. Parl.*, VI. 410–411).

1604, which implied, according to the construction placed upon it by the petitioner, that the baronies must have been vested in Duke Thomas at his attainder (1572) ; that is to say, the abeyance was determined previous to 1572. But what is the proof that it was determined " previously to *the reign of Queen Elizabeth* " (*i.e.* to 1558) ? Absolutely none was given ! [1]

Adopting, then, this hypothesis, it is clearly far more difficult to assume the determination of an abeyance at this comparatively late epoch than it would be under Richard III., a period relatively obscure. Moreover, in this case there is no such evidence as was afforded even by the Letters-missive of 1484. We are therefore, admittedly, dependent on a retrospective induction from the Act of 1604. And to this I propose now to address myself.

The words relied on by the claimant were :

> To the Honour, State, and Dignitie of Erle of Surrey and to *such dignitie of baronies only* which the said late Duke of Norfolk forfeited and lost by the said attainder.

The word ' only ' has been understood as excluding any claim to the duke's *territorial* ' baronies.' But, in any case, these guarded words could not do more than restore to the earl such baronies

---

[1] This extraordinary expression may have originated in the petitioner's claim (Additional Case, p. 27) that the baronies " were vested in the reign of Elizabeth in Thomas . . . Duke of Norfolk," a loose expression which is by no means equivalent to " at the accession of Elizabeth."

as he could prove to have been vested in the late duke. They were not, and did not profess to be, a determination of abeyance, nor did they even name a single barony. It was urged by counsel that the only baronies they could refer to were those he claimed, which must, therefore, have been vested in the duke. But I reply, firstly, that they do not name any baronies as vested in the duke ; secondly, that even if they had, the recognition of a wrongful assumption could not operate as a creation or even a determination of abeyance.

It is the very essence of my case that the committee accepted as valid, and indeed decisive, evidence the recognition in formal documents (as in the Letters-missive) by the Crown, of minor dignities as vested in an earl or duke, although it can be demonstrated, and ought to have been shown by the Attorney General, for the Crown, that such evidence is not valid, and that the facts of the case can be perfectly explained on the hypothesis of error.

The assumption of dignities was an ancient practice. In the early days of the Tudors, Lady Hungerford, who held three baronies, took the styles of six, two of them not genuine and one in abeyance. Her contemporary, Thomas earl of Derby, took upon himself, as for instance in a warrant sealed with his seal and bearing date 8 Nov. 8 Hen. VIII. (1516), the style of Viscount Kynton, Lord Stanley and Strange, lord of Knokyn and Mohun, Bassett, Burnell and Lacy, lord of Man and the isles.[1] Yet Stanley and Strange were the only baronies actually vested in him, while his viscountcy was a fancy title taken from a 'member' of the Stranges' lordship of Ness, Shropshire. The earls of Northumberland assumed the baronies of Fitz Payne and Bryan, to neither of which had they any right. In the 16th century the Radcliffes, earls of Sussex, successively assumed the baronies of Egremont and Burnel, though (Multon of) Egremont was in abeyance and Burnel also. So too, though the barony of Latimer fell into abeyance in 1557, two of its four co-heirs, the earls of Danby and Northumberland, coolly assumed it *temp*. Charles I. (as was pointed out in the Fitzwalter case), and even had it assigned to them on their garter-plates at Windsor.[2] Lastly the barony of Badlesmere, also in abeyance, was similarly assumed by the earls of Oxford, together with a 'fancy' viscountcy of Bulbeck. And this brings us to the very reign when the similar wrongful assumption of Mowbray was recognised (I hold) in error by the Crown.

For that the Crown did so err I now proceed to show. An armorial decision of the Court of Chivalry in 1410 induced the then Lord Grey de

---

[1] Inq. p.m. of 15 Sept. 1523 in *Chancery Inquisitions*, vol. 40, No. 25 (15 Henry VIII.).

[2] It was aptly observed by Lord Redesdale (who seems to have known his business better than the Law Lords) : "You show that there were co-heirs of the barony of Mowbray ; you show that an individual assumed the title ; . . . but there is no proof of the abeyance being determined" (Proceedings, pp. 14–15).

Ruthyn to assume the baronies of Hastings and 'Weysford' [Wexford], and both these titles were duly assigned by the Crown to his heir when he was created earl of Kent, 1465 (and in 1484, 1486). Yet 'Weysford' was a fancy title and Hastings one to which the Longueville decision (1640) proved the family had no right. So retentive were the Greys of their 'plumes,' that, as G.E.C. reminds us, they "clung tenaciously to the barony of Grey de Ruthyn " even after their heir-general had proved his right to it and taken his seat. With the same tenacity the Manners family clung to the barony of Roos after it had been decided, against them, that the right to that dignity had passed to the heirs general of the earl of Rutland who died in 1587. The first duke was actually divorced by Act of Parliament as Lord Roos (1670), and the style was still used by the family at least as late as 1770 without any right thereto.[1] More striking, however, are the assumptions of the Devereux family and their heirs. Walter Devereux, earl of Essex (d. 1576), assumed among his styles the earldom of 'Ewe,' the viscountcy of Bourchier, and the barony of Lovayne : the first was a Norman countship extinct since 1539, the second also an extinct dignity, and the third a fancy title. Now my point is that these

---

[1] See *Complete Peerage*, VI. 405, 465–70. The present duke maintains indeed that "their claim to it was admitted by the Sovereign and Parliament up to the close of the last century " (*Ibid*. VIII. 500) ; but he has accepted a modern barony of " Roos of Belvoir " (1896) in its place.

titles, wrongfully assumed though they were, were
recognised *nominatim*, in the Devereux Act of
Restoration (1604), as having been " lawfully and
rightly " held by the earls of Essex ! This, as will
be seen, is evidence far stronger than that of the
Howard Restoration Act, in the very same year
(1604), which vaguely speaks of " such dignitie of
Baronies " as the Howards may have lost by the
attainder of 1572. And yet this latter Act was
actually treated as a sheet-anchor in 1877, and accepted as conclusive proof that the baronies of
Mowbray and Segrave, which were not even mentioned by name, must have been lawfully vested in
the duke who was attainted in 1572 !

The Committee and the House indeed went so
far as to resolve " that by Act of Parliament the
said Baronies were restored to Thomas earl of
Arundel . . . in the year 1604 "; but if we
turn to the Act of 1627 passed in favour of
his son, we find it speaking of " the baronies of
Fitzalan, Clun and Oswaldestre, and Maltravers,"
and annexing these " titles, names, and dignities "
with all their " places, pre-eminences, arms, ensigns, and dignities " to the earldom and castle of
Arundel.[1] Now, in spite of this Act of Parliament, no one now pretends that Fitzalan, Clun and
Oswaldestre had any existence as peerage dignities,
or were anything but ' plumes ' assumed by the
family for its own adornment. Of what possible
value, therefore, can the far vaguer language of the
1604 Act be deemed as evidence, when all that

[1] Tierney's *Arundel*, I. 132–3.

could be urged was that its mention of baronies must allude to more than that of Howard, and must consequently comprise those of Mowbray and Segrave?

To any one conversant with the practice in such matters the worthlessness of such evidence needs no demonstration.

We have now seen that, if the claim based on the Letters-missive of Richard III. be abandoned, the case stands thus: The abeyance must have been determined after the restoration of 1489 and before the attainder of 1572, but nothing is known as to how, or even when, it was done, while the only ground for supposing that it was ever done at all is an Act of Parliament at a later period, which does not state that the abeyance was determined, and does not even name the baronies in question.

So little was the supposed determination suspected at the time, that the Lords Berkeley styled themselves Lords Mowbray and Segrave constantly from 1488 to 1698, a fact which counsel, of course, kept carefully out of sight. For Mr. Fleming's argument was that all such assumptions were valid; and yet, if this one was so, there was at once an end of his case.

The view that I shall myself advance removes every difficulty. The Mowbray summons of 1640 is, I hold, exactly parallel with the Strange and Clifford summonses of 1628. All these were issued in error. It can be shown that great nobles were in the habit of annexing minor titles in the most casual manner ; and that the Crown, in this matter, so far took them at their own valuation as to allow them, in most formal documents, these ornamental appendices. Of this there are most curious examples, although they are little known. These minor titles were sometimes retained, wrongfully, by heirs-male, sometimes those of baronies in abeyance, sometimes mere inventions. Let us take the first. The strange doctrine that an earldom (in tail male) 'attracts' a barony (in fee) was advanced in the cases of Roos (1616)—now De Ros—and Fitzwalter (1668), but was disposed of by the judges in the latter. And yet the arguments in the Howard of Walden case (1691–2), now made more accessible by the publication of a House of Lords MS.,[1] are important as showing that, even at this late date, it was urged on behalf of the earl of Suffolk (heir-male) by his counsel, Mr. (afterwards chief baron) Ward and Mr. Wallop that the barony was vested in him, not in the heirs-general (in spite of the 1668 decision *ut supra*). For this they relied *inter alia* on the Strange and Clifford cases (1628), in which, as we now hold, the titles were recognised in error. Failing this, they urged that the barony was wholly at the King's disposal, without preference, to the heirs-general over the heirs-male. For this view their precedent was the case of the earldom of Oxford (1626), " in which case it was decided that the baronies were at the

---

[1] 13th Report on Historical MSS., App. V. pp. 479–489.

King's disposal."[1]   The precedents put in on behalf of the earl of Suffolk, and certified by Windsor Herald, confirm further my statements as to
the assumption of dignities.   Of these, the two
most important for my purpose are :

(1) Derby.   In this case, on the death of Ferdinand, earl of Derby (1594), the baronies
vested in him are held to have fallen into
abeyance between his three daughters.

" The Baronies, notwithstanding, were used and enjoyed by
William, Earl of Derby, brother and heir-male to the said Ferdinand, and being chosen Knight of the Garter (at his installation,
according to custom), the said William's titles and stile were proclaimed in the presence of Queen Elizabeth in 1601, which were
William Stanley, Earl of Derby, Lord Stanley, Strange of Knock-
ing and of the Isle of Man, and were also engraven upon his
plate under his arms at the back of his stall, and continue still
[1692] to be used by the present Earl of Derby, without the least
dispute, which we do esteem a good precedent " (p. 486).

(2) Oxford.   In this case the judges had reported (1626) that the three baronies in
dispute " descended to the general heirs of
John, the 14th Earl of Oxford," in 1526.

" The Baronies, notwithstanding, accompanied the Earldom,
and Aubrey de Vere, the present Earl of Oxford, when installed
Knight of the Garter, with the title of Earl of Oxford, were (*sic*)

---

[1] The judges had reported that " they, in strictness of law reverted to, and were in the disposition of, king Henry the Eighth."
But the House resolved " that the baronies of Bolbecke, Sandford,
and Badlesmere are in his Majesty's disposition " (Lords' Journals,
III. 537), 22 March 1625–6, and certified the King (5 April)
that " they are wholly in your Majesty's hand, to dispose at your
own pleasure " (p. 552), according to the judges.

also proclaimed his baronies of Bolebec, Sandford, and Badles-mere, in the presence of the King, and are also engraven upon his plate at the back of his stall at Windsor, which we do esteem also a precedent " (p. 487).

These cases have a grave bearing on the admissibility of garter-plates in evidence. Considerable stress was laid on their testimony in the Mowbray case itself ; and if that of the Letters-missive must now be abandoned, a garter-plate will not be found an efficient substitute.

One of the arguments for the doctrine of ' attraction ' was that, otherwise, ancient earldoms " should lose the plumes of their honour." This happily expresses the spirit of those great nobles who decked themselves with such plumes, too often ' borrowed plumes,' either by inventing baronies which had no existence, or by retaining those which should have passed to heirs-general. Sometimes they did both. Thus in the case of the earldom of Oxford (1626) the judges held that the baronies of " Bulbeck, Sandford, and Badles-mere " had passed away to heirs-general a century before, but that five earls, in succession, had since " assumed these titles nominally in all their leases and conveyances, and the eldest son [is] called still by the name of Lord Bulbeck." But modern research has further shown that " Bulbeck and Sandford " had never even existed as peerage baronies while Badlesmere was in abeyance, an abeyance determined by the earls themselves in their own favour, as was that of Mowbray (I hold) by the Howards. So, too, the Howards, in 1627, foisted upon the Crown "the titles and dignities of the baronies of Fitz-alan, Clun and Oswaldestre, and Maltravers," which they employed, though it is admitted that Maltravers alone was a genuine peerage barony. The Crown was actually induced not only to recognise them all (to the eternal confusion of peerage students), but to wrench them from their natural descent and entail them, together with the earldom and castle of Arundel, on the Howards by a special Act of Parliament. The same Act recognised by its preamble the pretension that Arundel was an earldom by tenure, though our better knowledge of history has shown the absurdity of the claim. Thus these baronies were made, by violence, to 'attend' the earldom, much as James I., in 1620, by a similar stretch of the prerogative, had annexed the barony of Offaley to the earldom of Kildare.[1]

The best known and latest instance of erroneous recognition by the Crown, is the patent of creation for the earldom of Leicester in 1784. In this instrument three baronies were recognised as vesting in the earl, to none of which he could prove a right.

From such recognitions it was but a step to summoning the son and heir of an earl in a barony

---

[1] In an article on 'The Earldom of Kildare and Barony of Offaley' (*Genealogist* [N.S.], IX. 202–5), cited in *Complete Peerage* (VI. 113–4), I have urged that this very barony of Offaley may have been another case of assumption, and that it is doubtful whether it even existed when James was called upon to decide by whom it ought to be inherited.

to which his father was supposed to be entitled. This was done, I suggested above (p. 337), in the case of George Boleyn's summons in the barony of Rochford; it was certainly done, by universal admission, in the case of the earl of Derby's son, summoned as Lord Strange in 1628, though the earls, since 1594, had not been entitled to that barony, as also in that of the earl of Cumberland's son, summoned in 1628 as Lord Clifford, though that barony had passed away from the earldom in 1605. It was again done in 1722, when a summons in the barony of Percy was issued in error. In all three cases the result of this error was, admittedly, the creation of a wholly new barony. My contention is that the Mowbray summons of 1640 was an error precisely similar. And as for the admission of the original precedence, it was similarly admitted in the case of Percy.[1]

An exact parallel to the Mowbray summons of 1640, a parallel of great importance for the alleged determination of the abeyance, is found in the Say summons of 1610. In 1399 the barony of Say fell into abeyance (according to the modern doctrine) between the descendants of three sisters, one of whom was the Lord Clinton who died in 1432. He thereupon assumed the style " Dominus de Clynton *et de Say*." His son went so far (1 Nov. 1448) as to grant to his kinsman James Fiennes (who was *not* a co-heir of the barony), "and to his heirs and assigns for ever, the name and title of

---

[1] It is a singular coincidence that Lord Strange was one or Lord Mowbray's two introducers in 1640.

Lord Say";[1] and the grantee's barony of ' Saye '
has descended to the present Lord ' Saye and Sele.'
Yet the Clintons continued to use the title, and
when Edward Lord Clinton, who had taken his
seat *as Lord Say* in 1536 and had been then
ranked, avowedly, as Lord Say,[2] was created earl of
Lincoln (4 May 1572) the heralds proclaimed his
style as " Sir Edward Fynes Conte de Lincoln,
Seigneur Clinton *et Say*." His grandson was returned as member for Grimsby, in his father's
lifetime (1601–4) as " Lord Clynton *and Saye*,[3] and
was called up to the House of Lords in 1610 as
" Thomas Clynton *de Say*," precisely as Henry
Frederick Howard was called up in 1640 in the
barony of Mowbray.

Again, what of the writs of summons addressed
to Lord Darcy as " Conyers de Darcie et Meynill " (1678–1680) ? Did they determine the
abeyance of Meynill, of which barony he was a
co-heir ? Or were they simply issued in error, as
were those to his relative, as " Johanni Darcy et
Meinill," from 1605 to 1629 ? And what of
' Baroness Dudley ' (1757–1762), ' Baroness Le
Despencer ' (1781–1788), and ' Baroness Cromwell ' (1687–1709), who was actually summoned
as such, in error, to two coronations ?

As might be expected, the decision of the Committee, in 1877, has opened the door to further

[1] Dugdale's *Baronage*.
[2] Dugdale's *Baronage* (from H. 13, fo. 387a, compare p. 332
above).
[3] 14th Report Hist. MSS., App. VIII. p. 279.

claims based on user and its recognition. We now, for instance, read that

the Barony of Braose was continually and uninterruptedly assumed and claimed by the Mowbray family and by their successors the Howards, both of which families styled themselves or were styled Lords Braose [1] in Charters, Letters Patent, and Funeral Certificates, and on their monuments and Garter plates. This persistent and perpetual usage of the title must inevitably cause one to think they had good reason to believe that the abeyances had been determined in their favour. Comparing the evidence available for the purposes of establishing this fact with that similarly available in relation to the Barony of Segrave in 1877, it is not an unlikely supposition that sufficient evidence could be produced to justify the Committee for Privileges in accepting the determination in favour of the Howards as an established fact. [2]

Precisely so ! If a Committee for Privileges has not yet mastered the elementary fact that titles in England, as in Scotland and Ireland, have undoubtedly been assumed, used, and even recognised in error, it is capable of accepting the wildest claims and of plunging Peerage history into utter and hopeless confusion.

To recapitulate, I claim to have shown:

(1) That the words of the Resolution, 'previously to the reign of Queen Elizabeth' (*i.e.* to 1558), are merely a careless blunder; and that what was meant was 'previously to' the death of Thomas duke of Norfolk (*i.e.* to 1572), who lived in the reign of Elizabeth.

---

[1] Unluckily for this argument the Berkeley co-heirs of the Mowbrays similarly assumed this title with those of Mowbray and Segrave (*Complete Peerage*, I. 333–4).

[2] *The House of Stourton*, II. 994.

(2) That the Letters-missive of Richard III. were vouched by the Petitioner as the proof of the determination of the abeyance (before their date), although such evidence never had been, and never ought to be accepted as the proof of such determination.

(3) That if the abeyance was then determined, the baronies of Mowbray and Segrave are now under attainder.

(4) That the determination of the abeyance previous to Sept. 1484 must therefore be abandoned as a *ratio decidendi*, and the Resolution be construed as asserting a determination between 1489 and 1572.

(5) That of such determination there is no proof, Petitioner having vouched the Letters-missive as the 'sole ground' for the user of the titles, and the Committee having deemed them essential to his case.

The moral, surely, is obvious enough. If peerage claims are to be thus decided on *ex parte* evidence, the most fatal flaws in the Petitioner's case may, as on this occasion, pass undetected.

XI

The Succession to the Crown

On the lamented death of the duke of Clarence in 1892 it was universally assumed, and was the subject of general comment, that only the life of the duke of York stood between the duchess of Fife and the ultimate succession to the Crown. But it seems to be at least open to question whether this was legally the case, and indeed whether the event of such a contingency occurring is at present clearly provided for.

It is no doubt generally believed that in the event of the succession opening to two or more sisters, the Crown, in England, would always pass to the eldest sister as of right. But it is not a question of general belief; it is a question of an Act of Parliament. Although the fact is often forgotten, the crown of these realms is held by the present royal family under the Act of Succession and under that Act alone. The descent of the crown, therefore, is determined by the wording of that Act, and the interpretation of that wording is a matter, not of supposition, but of law. I here append the actual wording of the clause limiting the succession in 12 and 13 William III. cap. 2, and by its side I print the parallel clause from the previous Act of Succession, 1 William and Mary, sess. 2, cap. 2.

1 *Will. and Mary, sess. 2, cap. 2.*	12 *and* 13 *William III., cap. 2.*
The said lords spirituall and temporall and commons assembled at Westminster doe resolve that William and Mary Prince and Princesse of Orange be and be declared King and Queene of England France and the dominions thereunto belonging to hold the crowne and royall dignity of the said kingdomes and dominions to them the said prince and princesse dureing their lives and the life of the survivour of them. And that the sole and full exercise of the regall power be onely in and executed by the said Prince of Orange in the names of the said prince and princesse dureing their joynt lives and after their deceases the said crown and royall dignitie of the said kingdoms and dominions to be to the heires of the body of the said princesse and for default of such issue to the Princess Anne of Denmarke and the heires of her body and for default of such issue to the heires of the body of the said Prince of Orange.[1]	for default of issue of the said Princess Ann and of his Majesty respectively the crown and regall government of the said kingdoms of England France and Ireland and of the dominions thereunto belonging with the royall state and dignity of the said realms and all honours stiles titles regalities prerogatives powers jurisdictions and authorities to the same belonging and appertaining shall be remain and continue *to the said most excellent Princess Sophia and the heirs of her body being Protestants.*[2]

The whole question turns on the words " the heirs of her body." Is there any precedent for construing these words as a limitation to the eldest

[1] *Statutes Revised*, II. 11.   [2] *Ibid.* pp. 94–5.

alone of two or more daughters ?   The authors of
the *History of English Law*[1] observe, in their
chapter on " The Law of Descent," that

The manner in which our law deals with an inheritance
which falls to . . . daughters may give us some valuable
hints as to the history of primogeniture.   If we look merely at
the daughters and isolate them from the rest of the world, their
claims are equal, and the law will show no preference for the first-
born.   This principle was well maintained, even though some of
the things comprised in the inheritance were not such as could be
easily divided, or were likely to become of less value in the process
of division.   For example, if there was but one house, the eldest
daughter had no right to insist that this should fall to her share,
even though she was willing to bring its value into account.   No,
unless the parceners could agree upon some other plan, the house
itself was physically divided (II. 273).

When we turn to peerage dignities, themselves
also (we shall see below) deemed real estate, we
find that, in the case of baronies, the impartible
nature of such dignities leads, not to their inheritance by the eldest co-heiress alone, but to their
disappearance by falling into " abeyance."   The
latest writer on the doctrine of abeyance is Mr. L.
O. Pike, who traces its growth and insists on the
late date of its acceptance.[2]   He cites the well-
known conclusion of the judges on the earl of
Oxford's baronies (1626) that they " descended
upon the said daughters as his sisters and heirs ;
but, those dignities being entire and not dividable,
they became uncapable of the same, otherwise

[1] Prof. Sir F. Pollock and Prof. Maitland.
[2] *Constitutional History of the House of Lords*, pp. 131–139.
Mr. Pike agrees, as a lawyer, with my criticism of the alleged
determination of the Mowbray abeyance.

than by gift from the Crown." The Lords themselves treated this opinion as extinguishing the
right to the baronies in question; for they reported
to the king that " they are wholly in your Majesty's
hands to dispose at your own pleasure." Mr.
Pike holds that " the earliest case in which anything like the doctrine of abeyance was recognised
was, it is almost certain, that of Lord Windsor in
the reign of Charles II." This case (1660), he
admits, did imply that the king's " power in relation to the barony does not extend beyond the
co-heirs and their representatives." Apart from
the fact that the writer, we have seen, was not
acquainted with the earlier action taken in respect
of this barony by king Charles I.,[1] he appears to
have also overlooked the most interesting patent
creating the barony of Lucas of Crudwell (7 May
1663).[2] There was a special proviso in this
patent

that if at any time or times . . . there shall be more
persons than one who shall be co-heirs of her body by the said
Earl, *so that the King or his heirs might declare which of them should
have the dignity*, or otherwise the dignity should be suspended or
extinguished, then, nevertheless, the dignity should not be
suspended or extinguished, but should go and be held and enjoyed
from time to time by such of the said co-heirs as by course of
descent and the common law of the realm should be inheritable
in other entire and indivisible inheritancy, as namely—an office of
honour and public trust, or a castle for the necessary defence of
the realm, and the like, in case such inheritance had been given
and limited to the said Countess and the heirs of her body by
the said Earl begotten.

---

[1] See p. 360 above.
[2] This barony is now vested in Lord Cowper.

PEERAGE STUDIES

The object of this clumsy and quite exceptional proviso, under which the barony has been inherited more than once by an eldest daughter and co-heir, was to prevent the dignity ever falling into abeyance, as abeyance was then understood. This patent was overlooked, I have said, by Mr. Pike ; for the words I have italicized should, clearly, be compared with those in the Windsor docquet : " that it belongeth to his Majesty to declare which of the said co-heirs shall enjoy the dignity of their ancestors." The allusion to " a castle for the necessary defence of the realm " is of special interest, because it seems to refer to Bracton's doctrine, ages before, that among the very few indivisible things were a castle and a *caput baroniæ*, for the reason that, if they were divisible, " earldoms and baronies would be brought to naught, and the realm itself is constituted of earldoms and baronies." [1] As for the assertion, which appears to be made, that an " office of honour and public trust " would pass by " the common law of the realm " to one of two or more co-heirs, it is directly contradicted by the case of the office of Great Chamberlain. For this most dignified " office of honour," which was an inheritance in fee, was decided by the House of Lords, in 1781, to vest *jointly* in the two sisters of the last duke of Ancaster (d. 1779) with the awkward result that there has since been no one person entitled, as of right, to that office. [2]

[1] *History of English Law*, II. 273.
[2] *Complete Peerage*, I. 207.

Having now shown that, in the case of a barony, the words " heirs of her body " were well understood to mean that two or more daughters would inherit equal rights to the barony, and that therefore a special proviso was needed to avert its becoming " suspended or extinguished," I advance to the case of an earldom. So far back as 1627 the earldom of Arundel (with appendant baronies) was entailed by Act of Parliament on " Thomas Earl of Arundel and Surrey and the heirs male of his body ; and for default of such issue, to the heirs of his body." [1] But this remainder has never come, and is never likely to come, into play. The question, however, has been raised in very recent years by the limitation of the earldom of Cromartie, in its strange patent of creation (1861), to the grantee's second surviving son, with a special remainder over to " the heirs of his body." On the death of Lord Cromartie (24 Nov. 1893), without male issue, the " heirs of his body " were represented by his two daughters and co-heiresses, and what was to become of the earldom no man could say. It was well recognised that, under the limitation, the two co-heiresses had in law an equal right to inherit the dignity, and, had it been a barony, the Crown need only have ' called it out of abeyance ' in favour of one or the other. But there was no precedent for extending to an earldom the modern doctrine of abeyance. Consequently,

---

[1] See Tierney's *History of Arundel*, p. 133 ; also pp. 137–8, on the impossibility of understanding such remainder, which Lord Redesdale (in the Lords' Reports) deemed due to inadvertence.

Burke's Peerage contained, in 1894 and 1895, the following account of the dignity, treating it as in suspension :

The limitation of this earldom being to the heirs male of the late Earl, and on failure of such to his heirs, with other remainders over, a question naturally arises as to whether or not this dignity is now in abeyance between his two daus. and co-heirs.

In 1895 the Gordian knot was cut by the Crown *mero motu suo* taking direct action.

The Queen has been pleased by Letters Patent . . . bearing date the 25th day of February 1895 to declare that Sibell Lilian Mackenzie, commonly called Lady Sibell Lilian Mackenzie, the elder of the two daughters of Francis, late Earl of Cromartie . . . is and shall be Countess of Cromartie, etc., etc. . . . And to give, grant, and confirm the said Earldom of Cromartie, etc., etc. . . . to the said Sibell Lilian Mackenzie ; to have and to hold the said Earldom, Viscountcy, and Baronies, together with all the rights, privileges, pre-eminences, immunities, and advantages, and the place and precedence due and belonging thereto, to her, and to the heirs of her body . . . in as full and ample a manner as the said Francis Earl of Cromartie or his mother, Anne Duchess of Sutherland deceased . . . held and enjoyed the same.[1]

It is by no means clear how we should describe this action of the Crown. The form employed is not the same as that which is used when a barony is called out of abeyance in favour of one of its coheiresses,[2] for in this case the strong words " to give, grant, and confirm " are introduced. In the *Complete Peerage*, indeed, the letters patent are boldly described as " terminating the abeyance of her father's peerage in her favour " ;[3] but it is not

[1] *London Gazette*, 5 March 1895.
[2] See pp. 363, 364 above. [3] Vol. VIII. 359.

too much to say that, down to 1895, the doctrine of abeyance had not been applied to the case of an earldom, and still less had such abeyance been determined by the action of the Crown. I am probably not alone in thinking that the Crown, on this occasion, may have acted *ultra vires* and have exceeded its powers in deciding *proprio motu* a legal question of inheritance. For so recently as 7 Feb. in the present year Mr. Justice Barnes, in delivering a considered judgment on the Cowley case, observed that—

The dignities of the Peerage having been originally annexed to lands were considered as tenements or incorporeal hereditaments wherein a person might have a real estate ; and although dignities are now becoming little more than personal honours and rights, yet they are still classed under the head of real property (Cruise, c. 4, 1, 1 ; C. Litt. 163).[1]

The Crown, it may be urged, is the fountain of honour ; but when dignities have once been created, they can only descend according to law, under the limitation in the patent.[2]

[1] *The Times*, 8 Feb. 1900, p. 14. The above is simply a repetition of the opening words of chapter iv. of 'Cruise on Dignities' (1823).

[2] Although the above assertion in the text would be now accepted on all sides, it is but right to mention that the early Stuart kings appear to have endeavoured, upon this point, to stretch the prerogative. It is possible that this attempt, which seems to have escaped notice, may be due to their familiarity with the Scottish system of resignation and regrant. In the Windsor case, for instance (p. 360 above), Charles I. endeavoured (1646) to bestow the old barony of Windsor, then in abeyance between two co-heirs, on one of them in tail *male*, though he seems to have thought that this declaration might be " ineffectual in

The Crown, it must be remembered, has not the power to alter the limitation even of dignities created by itself. Of this we were reminded less than three years ago, when, according to the newspapers, Lord Burton (cr. 1886) was granted an alteration in his patent enabling his daughter to succeed to the barony, but when, as a matter of fact, a fresh barony, with a special remainder to his daughter, had to be created (29 Nov. 1897) for the purpose. Indeed, it has now been laid down that, even in creating dignities, the Crown must 'play the game.' Lord Chancellor Cairns, in his judgment on the Buckhurst case, enunciated this doctrine in the words :

It is the well-established constitutional law of the country that Peerages partake of the qualities of real estate, inasmuch as they must be descendible in a course known to the law . . . it had been clearly laid down by the Committee for Privileges . . . that the Crown could not give to a grant of a peerage a quality of descent unknown to the law.[1]

Law." The same thing, however, had been done, in 1641, in the Conyers case, when the Conyers barony, with its old precedence, was bestowed on one of two co-heirs in tail *male*. The precedent had been set by James I. so early as 1604, when the old barony of Abergavenny was diverted from its legal descent in favour of the heir-male (it has since descended in tail male, though it is not known why). The Roos (1616), Offaley (1620) and Arundel (1627) cases all illustrate the efforts made at this period to divert the descent of dignities in fee in favour of heirs-male, though in the Dacre case (1604) they signally failed. It is a curious circumstance that the same tendency has resulted in the three most famous ducal castles in England, Alnwick, Arundel, and Belvoir, passing away from the heirs of their feudal lords to the families of Smithson, Howard, and Manners, who are not their present representatives. [1] *Times*, 19 July 1876.

THE SUCCESSION TO THE CROWN

In the same case the Attorney-General had admitted on behalf of the Crown that—

Although her Majesty was the fountain of honour and could ennoble those whom she chose, yet all grants of dignities must be made in accordance with the rules of Parliament and in the customary manner.[1]

It was resolved by the Committee that the challenged proviso was invalid, that is to say, that the Crown had exceeded its powers by inserting it in the patent of creation.[2]

This decision is considered to apply, of necessity, to the Cromartie patent also, which had been granted three years earlier (1861), for both patents contained, in the words of G. E. C., the same "extraordinary proviso, whereby the attempt is made to subject a peerage dignity to a shifting remainder (so that, on certain contingencies happening, it would pass from one person to another)." While on the subject of the action of the Crown in determining the descent of peerage dignities, I may glance at its autocratic treatment of the historic barony of Berkeley. On the death, in 1882, of Thomas *de jure* earl of Berkeley, the right to the

[1] *Times*, 19 July 1876.
[2] The resolution ran : "That the said barony to which the said Reginald Windsor so succeeded did not under or by virtue of the declaration and proviso in the Letters Patent cease or determine on the succession of the said Reginald Windsor to the earldom of De La Warr." Lord De La Warr had petitioned for a declaration "that the shifting clause . . . was not valid and effectual to pass the said title dignity and honour," and "that the said shifting clause in the said Letters was and is wholly inoperative" (House of Lords' Journals). This was in effect the conclusion at which the Committee arrived.

467

earldom passed to his heir male, but the ancient barony of Berkeley, which, for more than two centuries (1679–1882) had been merged in that earldom, passed, it was generally supposed, to his niece Mrs. Milman, as his heir-general. The title, however, was not assumed by her ;[1] but when she consulted me (as an amateur), I expressed a decided view in favour of her right to the dignity. In the *Complete Peerage*, also, at the request of the editor, I expressed an equally strong opinion to that effect (1885), which is there printed *verbatim* (I. 338). In that work the difficult history of this historic barony was very fully discussed, and Mrs. Milman pronounced to be " *de jure* (apparently) Baroness de Berkeley," although she had " taken no steps towards establishing her right to the Peerage." Here again the Crown intervened directly, and, in 1893, decided for itself the question of right.

The Queen has been pleased, by Letters Patent under the Great Seal . . . to declare that the ancient Barony of Berkeley now belongs to and is vested in Louisa Mary Milman . . . as the heir general of Sir James de Berkeley, Knt., in whose favour the said Barony was created in the year 1421 ; and that she and the heirs general of the said Sir James de Berkeley lawfully begotten and to be begotten for ever, shall be named and called Barons and Baronesses, and shall have and enjoy the said ancient Barony of Berkeley, together with all and singular the rights, privileges, pre-eminences, immunities, and advantages, and the place and precedence, due and belonging thereto.[2]

---

[1] *Burke's Peerage* for 1893 pointed out that this was the case even then. [2] *London Gazette*, 13 June 1893.

THE SUCCESSION TO THE CROWN

It is somewhat difficult to say what the Crown here did, or what was the actual effect of these letters patent. The question was one of right, not of favour; of inheritance, not of grace. Either Mrs. Milman had inherited this peerage dignity, or she had not. The Crown, apparently, declared that she had; but if she had, it was needless, and even prejudicial to her right, for the Crown to intervene as if its grace was required.

It must be remembered that this was a case of a barony on the origin and descent of which there had long been much controversy; and yet the Crown here decides, and sets on record its decision, that the peerage was created "in the year 1421."[1] The result of issuing letters patent in the above form has been, it appears to me, to prejudice, or at least to cast a doubt on the precedence of this barony. It is now ranked, in *Burke's Peerage*, tenth among the baronies, as a creation of 1421, being placed between Camoys ('1383') and Berners ('1455'). But it is well established that the barony enjoyed a special and very high precedence down to the time of its merger in the earldom in 1679. In a dissertation on "Precedency due to certain Baronies of ancient creation,"[2] it is pointed out by 'G. E. C.' that the Berkeleys sitting under the writ of 1421 "were allowed the precedency of the old barony." And, under Berkeley, he discusses at great length the precedency of these barons (I. 322–324, 334), pointing out that they

[1] Compare my remarks above (p. 363) on the date of the Windsor and Braye baronies. [2] *Complete Peerage*, I. 21.

were ranked immediately after the Lords De La
Warr, and that in 1661 an even higher precedency
was claimed. He also quotes in full the opinion
that I had given him on the arguments. As the
Lords Berkeley sat above the Lords Morley
(1299?) and Fitzwalter (1295?), it is obvious that
the right placing of the barony will be a matter
of great difficulty and that a protest (" salvo jure ")
will probably be required should its holder be
ranked at any state ceremonial.[1]

I have been led, in the last few paragraphs, to
discuss the decision of the right to dignities, without a reference to the House of Lords, by the
Crown itself. The Cromartie case appears to
involve the introduction of a principle unknown to
peerage lawyers, namely the application to an earldom of the doctrine of abeyance. Incidentally, I
may observe, it must greatly strengthen the claim
(if that claim should be advanced) of the present
Baroness Berkeley to be countess of Ormonde in
her own right under the creation of 1529, she
being sole heir of the body of Thomas (Boleyn),
earl of Wiltshire and Ormonde. In 1882 I
upheld this claim in a paper on " the Earldoms of
Ormond in Ireland," [2] and my views were adopted
in the *Complete Peerage*.[3]

But it is now time to insist upon my point,

[1] Compare my remarks on the precedence of the barony of
Windsor (p. 366 above).

[2] Foster's *Collectanea Genealogica*, I. 84–93.

[3] Vol. I. p. 340 ; vol. VI. pp. 139, 144.

namely that the Cromartie case proves that a limitation to heirs of the body cannot be construed, in the case of an earldom, to limit the dignity to the eldest of two or more daughters, to the exclusion of the others.[1] What ground is there for asserting that such limitation should or can be differently construed in the Act of Succession now in force ? And what tribunal has power to decide that such construction, novel as it would be, ought to be placed upon them ?

To these questions, for my part, I can see no answer, save that there is a general impression that the crown would so descend. To say that Parliament could not have meant to leave the succession doubtful, in the contingency to which I refer,—as in that case the crown would belong to no one,— would not only be a crude reply, but is disposed of by the fact that the earldom of Cromartie found itself, for the time, in like case.[2] It is quite possible that those who drew, and those who passed, the Act of Succession may have been under the above impression ; but on what grounds does it rest ? From the Conquest downwards there is no precedent till we reach the reign of Henry

[1] So well understood was this principle, that the 1702 patent for the dukedom of Marlborough avoided the phrase "heirs of the body," and contained a most elaborate limitation providing for the case of the succession opening to two or more daughters. It was specially provided that, in such case, the eldest should succeed to the exclusion of the others.

[2] It is suggested in the *Complete Peerage* that this limitation in the Cromartie patent may have been thoughtlessly introduced owing to the name happening to be Scottish (II. 429).

VII.   That sovereign, indeed, married the elder
daughter of Edward IV. ; but it would have gone
ill with any man who suggested that it was in her
right that Henry wore the crown.   Not only did
he reign in his own right, established by an Act of
Parliament, but so " especially desirous " was he
(observes Dr. Franck Bright) " of not in any sense
reigning in right of his wife " that he even postponed her coronation as queen-consort.   As for the
daughters of Henry VIII., Mary succeeded, not as
the elder,[1] but in virtue of a special entail under
that Act of Succession, which the judges declared,
when her brother was dying, they could only dis-
obey at the cost of high treason.[2]   Elizabeth, in
turn, succeeded her in virtue of that same entail.[3]

The only precedent, it seems to me, that it
would be possible to cite is the succession of
James I., in 1603, as the heir of the elder sister of
Henry VIII., to the exclusion of the heirs of the
younger sister (of whom the senior representative
is now the Baroness Kinloss).   But he did so in
direct defiance of the will of Henry VIII., which
entailed the crown on the heirs of his younger
sister ; and this will rested on the above Act
of Succession, which made its provisions binding.
Indeed, Professor Freeman went so far as to write
(biassed, no doubt, by his fierce prejudice against
hereditary monarchy) :

---

[1] Indeed, it is questioned whether her legitimacy had ever been
legally restored to her.   [2] 35 Hen. VIII. cap. 1 (1544).
[3] The will of Henry VIII. did not alter the entail, as regarded
them, created by the Act of Succession.

THE SUCCESSION TO THE CROWN

It should always be remembered that the Stewarts, reigning in defiance of the lawful settlement of Henry the Eighth's will, were simply usurpers, except so far as popular acquiescence in their succession might be held to be equivalent to a popular election.[1]

Without going so far as this, I would urge at least that no one could invoke the succession of James I., in defiance of the Act of Succession then in force, as a precedent for the interpretation of the present Act of Succession. Indeed, if it were a precedent for anything, it would obviously be for the succession of his own heirs to-day in defiance of the Act of Succession now in force!

We come, therefore, to the case of the daughters of James II. Here again there was no question of hereditary right at all. Neither daughter could so succeed in the lifetime of her brother and his heirs ; and, apart even from this fact, William and Mary were made, respectively, king and queen by Act of Parliament alone.[2] And by the same Act the succession of Anne was postponed till after the death of William. Thus it came to pass that the present Act of Succession (1701) dates from the reign of a king [3] who was actually seated on the throne to the exclusion not only of James II., but of the future queen Anne, whose 'hereditary right,' of

---

[1] *History of the Norman Conquest*, IV. (1871), 513. It is a singular illustration of the biassed views to which his prejudice could lead him that, in his hatred of hereditary right, he could uphold, as the champion of popular election, the will of Henry VIII.

[2] See p. 459 above.

[3] Queen Mary was then dead.

course, came before his own. The latter queen succeeded only, as Mary I. and Elizabeth had, we have seen, succeeded, under the special entail created by an Act of Parliament.[1] And it is under that same Act that the crown is now held.

In view of this recapitulation of facts, which, certain though they are, are, perhaps, little realized, it becomes difficult to understand how there has come to prevail the general belief that the crown would always of necessity descend to the eldest of two or more daughters when the succession opened to them. That such a belief is of old standing is seen even under Henry VIII., though at that time there was absolutely no precedent to justify that belief. In any case, however, what we have to deal with is not the existence of a general impression, but the interpretation, in a statute, of the words " heirs of her body " in a sense entirely different from that in which (it will not be denied) they are invariably construed.

We saw, at the outset of this paper, that the case I have discussed is one that came, in recent years, within the range of possibilities. Should it ever actually arise, it is not easy to see how the question raised could be constitutionally solved if it had not been previously settled by a special Act of Parliament. For if the crown were held by a doubtful title, no valid Act could be passed, and yet, without such Act, the doubt could hardly be removed. The general assumption as to the

---

[1] 12 and 13 Will. III. cap. 2.

THE SUCCESSION TO THE CROWN

descent, in such a contingency, of the crown has, I
hope it has been now shown, no foundation in fact
or in law, and appears to have its origin in a misapprehension on the part of Parliament in the past
and of the nation at large.

FINIS

Index

477

INDEX

'Attraction' of barony by earldom, doctrine of, 450–53.

Aubigny family (of Arundel), origin of, 125.

Audley, Hugh de, 207.

Augmentation, alleged grant of honourable, 132, 138, 139, 140, 144.

——, the Howard, 39–41.

Aust (Glouc.), 193.

Austria, Leopold duke of, 233.

——, arms of, 238.

Austruy, family of, 158–9, 164.

Authorities, strange treatment of, 428–9, 434.

Baalun. *See* Ballon.

Baderon (of Monmouth), 122, 191.

——, William son of, 120, 121, 122, 123, 185.

Badlesmere, barony of, 446, 451, 452.

Baelun. *See* Ballon.

Bailleul, Renaud de, 130, 131.

Bain, Mr. Joseph, 133, 134, 143.

Baker's *Northamptonshire*, 289, 291, 292, 293, 294, 295, 297, 299, 303, 322, 325.

Baladone. *See* Ballon.

Baldran, Hubert, 130.

Baldwin (de Clare, of Exeter), Richard son of, 213–4.

——, William son of, 212.

Ballon (Maine), 190, 191–2.

——, family of, in Dorset, Hants, and Somerset, 209–10.

——, Hamelin de, 189, 190, 192, 196, 198–200, 203, 204, 205, 210.

——, ——, his sons William and Mathew, 205.

——, ——, Emmeline daughter of, 202, 205.

——, ——, his grandson William, 198–9, 200.

Ballon (Hamelin de), descendants of, 199–200, 202–209.

——, Winebaud (Wynebald) de, 189, 190, 193, 194, 195, 196, 197, 198, 209.

——, ——, his sons Roger and Milo, 195.

——, ——, his son Roger, 197.

Balom. *See* Ballon.

Balun. *See* Ballon.

Bampton (Oxon.), 175, 177, 178.

—— (Devon), Honour of, 60.

Banquo, alleged ancestor of the Stewarts, 116, 118, 132, 137, 139, 142, 143.

Barkly, Sir Henry, 194.

Barnstaple priory, 215.

Barones magni of Henry I., 196.

Baronetcies, degradation of, 32.

Baronia used for one knight's fee, 203.

Barron, Mr. Oswald, 329.

Bastards not distinguished as illegitimate, 125–6.

Battle Abbey Roll, the so-called, 61.

Beauchamp (of Bedford), Hugh de, 304.

Beauchamp of Bedford, arms of, 328–9.

Bedford, earls and dukes of. *See* Russell.

Belhaven, barony of, 13.

Bellême, Robert de, 192.

Belmethorpe (Rutland), 303.

Belvoir castle, descent of, 73, 466.

Berkeley family, origin of, 72.

Berkeley, barony of, 467–470.

——, Sir James de (1421), 468.

——, ——, lord Berkeley, 435–6.

——, (Mrs. Milman) baroness, 436, 468–9.

——, baroness, 470.

——, earldom of, 436, 468.

——, lords, style themselves lords Mowbray and Segrave, 449.

INDEX

Berkeley, lords, style themselves lords Braose, 456.

——, Sir Maurice, created lord Berkeley, 356–8.

——, Thomas lord, 'sheepmaster,' 281.

Bernegger, Monsieur, of Strasburg, 242, 243.

Berners, barony of, 338, 340.

——, John lord, 332.

Bertie family, fabulous history of, 46.

Bertrand, alleged arms of, 274–5.

Betham, Sir William, 20, 68.

Blackstone on the heralds and their records, 315.

'Blanks' signed by king, 408–9, 415.

Blood, ennobling the, 5–7, 100.

Bolam (Northumberland), barony of, 190.

Boleyn, George. See Rochford.

——, Sir Thomas, 340, 356.

——, Thomas. See Ormonde.

Bolingbroke. See St. John.

Bone, an ancestral, 55–7.

Boughton Alulf (Kent), church of, 153.

——, manor of, 157–8, 162.

Bouillon, Godfrey de, 152.

Boulogne, comté of, seized by Philip Augustus, 178.

——, Eustace ("aux grenons") count of, VII.–VIII., 147–52, 153–5, 160.

——, ——, 'Goda' (of England) wife of, 147–151, 156.

——, ——, Ida (de Bouillon) second wife of, 151–4.

——, Eustace (the younger) count of, 153, 154, 163, 172.

——, ——, Mary (of Scotland) wife of, 163, 172.

——, ——, Matilda daughter of. See next entry.

Boulogne, Matilda (wife of Stephen) countess of, 159, 166, 172, 174.

——, Stephen count (*jure uxoris*) of. See Stephen.

——, Pharamus of, 160.

——, William of, 160.

——, William (son of Stephen) count of, VIII. 159, 160, 172, 174, 176.

——, ——, marries heiress of Warennes, 168–70, 172.

——, ——, his gigantic estates, 167–71.

——, ——, his death, 171.

——, ——, count of Mortain, 166, 167, 171, 174.

——, Eustace (son of Stephen) count of, 168, 172.

——, Mary (wife of count Mathew) countess of, 171, 172, 176.

——, Mathew (*jure uxoris*) count of, 162, 172, 179.

——, ——, tries to invade England, 173–4.

——, ——, obtains fresh lands there, 175.

——, ——, mortally wounded, 176.

——, Ida (his daughter) countess of, 175, 176, 178, 179.

——, ——, Reginald de Dammartin husband of, 176–80.

——, ——, Maud (his daughter), 176.

——, ——, Henry ('the warrior of Lorraine') husband of, 176.

——, the Honour of, 155 *et seq.*, 163 *et seq.*

——, ——, return of its fees, 164, 165.

——, origin of its Swan, 152.

——, its money standard found in England, 158.

Boulonnais, religious houses with

479

INDEX

Charles VI. (of France), pretended grant by, 133-4, 137, 139, 142.

Châtellerault, dukedom of, 12.

Chepstow castle, 186, 212.

Chester, the relief of, 423-4.

Cheverel (Wilts), Great, 192, 199, 204, 206.

Chichester, Adam Moleyns, bishop of, 266.

Churches, introduction of sham genealogy into, 84-7.

Chutes of the Vyne, the, 25.

Clare, family of de, 212-4.

——, Baldwin Fitz Gilbert de, 75.

——, Richard (son of Gilbert) de, 211, 214.

——, Walter (son of Richard) de, 212, 214.

——, Gilbert (son of Richard) de, 214.

Clavering, arms of, 327-9.

Clerfait, William de, 48.

Clifford (1628), barony of, 100, 449, 450, 454.

Cliffords, the founder of the, 215.

Clinton, Lord, assumes the title of Lord Say, 454.

——, ——, assigns it to James Fiennes, 454.

Clun, church of St. George of, 125.

—— and Oswaldestre, alleged barony of, 448, 453.

Coat-armour, how degraded, 316. See also Arms.

Cobden, disastrous result of his policy, 284.

Cobham, George lord, 346.

Coggeshall (Essex), 162, 168.

Co-heiresses. See Daughters.

College of Arms. See Heralds' College.

Colville, Maud de, 218, 227.

Commons, House of, long association of Russells with, 278.

Complete Peerage, The, 3, 8, 13, 15, 16, 20, 22, 25, 27-31, 33, 38, 43, 59, 70, 82-3, 90, 92, 93, 98, 100, 101-8, 110, 210, 240, 339, 340, 365, 436, 438, 447, 456, 462, 464, 467, 468, 469, 470, 471.

Conyers, barony of, 466.

——, Christopher lord, 345.

Cooke, Clarencieux King of Arms, 293, 315.

Cormeilles, Abbey of, 184, 185.

Coulthart imposture, the, 84.

Counts. See Earls.

Countship of the Empire assumed, 247-9.

——, lord Arundel's, 249.

Coucy, Enguerrand de, earl of Bedford, 233.

Courci, John de, lord of Ulster, 104, 106-7.

——, ——, his alleged descendants and his fictitious *geste, ibid.*

Courcy. See Kingsale.

Cowley (Oxon.), 158.

—— case, the, 465.

Cramond, Mr. William, 83, 87.

Crest, alleged grant of a, 141, 142.

Crests assumed, 240.

Cromartie, earldom of, 463-5, 467, 470, 471.

Cromwell, ' baroness,' 99, 455.

——, Gregory lord, 354-5.

——, Oliver, his mother's descent, 133.

——, ——, his grandfather's window, 138.

——, ——, his statue, 294.

——, Thomas (earl of Essex) lord, 333, 345, 346, 354-5.

Crown, restrictions on its powers in peerage dignities, 466-7.

INDEX

INDEX

Dover castle, reserved by Henry II., 170.

Drogo, count of the French Vexin, 148, 150.

Droitwich, St. Nicholas' church at, 175.

Dudley, 'baroness,' 99, 455.

——, duchess, 384.

——, Suttons lords, 338.

Duff family. *See* Fife.

Dugdale, Sir William, 50, 51, 67, 76–7, 128, 130, 189, 190, 195, 210, 216–7, 221–2, 228, 239, 240, 246, 261, 277, 313, 322, 332–3, 338–340, 341, 345, 360, 364, 392, 382–3, 384, 436.

Duncombes, origin of the, 29.

Dunham (Notts), 175, 177, 178, 179.

Dunkerton (Somerset), 210.

Dyrham. *See* Derham.

Dyved, 213–4.

Earl Marshal, dignity of, 109.

Earldom, alleged creation " before 1014 " of an, 90.

Earldoms, question as to abeyance of, 463–5.

Earls, taking their styles from towns, 150.

Eaton (Wilts), 201–4.

Edward the Confessor, 147–151, 182.

Egremont, barony of (Multon of), 446.

——, earls of, 44.

Elizabeth, succession of queen, 472, 474.

Ellis, Sir Henry, 151.

——, Mr. A. S., 120, 148, 195.

Ely Cathedral, Steward monuments in, 136, 137, 139.

Ely, the dean of, 135, 136.

Empson, Richard, 284.

Esmond family, alleged founder of, 68.

Essex, Devereux earls of, assume titles, 447.

——, ——, restored, 448.

Eton, 160.

Eu, William of, 187.

Eudo 'Dapifer,' devolution of his estates, 163, 167.

——, Adam brother of, 166.

Eure, barony of, 354.

Eustace, count. *See* Boulogne.

Eustache le Moine, 153.

Evidence. *See* Authorities; Deeds; Forgery; Garter-plates; Funeral certificates; Letters-missive; Records.

Evreux, St. Taurin of, 215.

Ewe (Eu), earldom of, assumed, 447.

Ewias, Harold of, 156, 165.

Exeter, Osbern bishop of, 205.

Eye, the Honour of, 167–8, 169, 171, 175, 176.

Eyton, Rev. R.W., 63, 116, 124, 125, 126, 128, 130, 131, 141, 149, 196.

Fane (or Vane) family, origin and pedigree of, 309–10.

Farnborough (Warwickshire), 325.

Faversham (Kent), 166.

Feilding, arms of, 238, 243, 247.

——, crests of, 240.

——, antiquity of family of, 247.

——, name of, its alleged derivation from Rheinfelden, 228–229, 232, 234, 236.

Feildings claim to be Hapsburgs, 14–15, 216 *et seq.*

Ferrers, family of, 32.

Ferrers of Chartley, barony of, 31–32, 437.

Ffrench, absurdity of the form, 16.

Fiennes family, origin of, 161.

INDEX

Fife, duke of, his fictitious pedigree abandoned, 82–4.

Fitzalan, alleged barony of, 448, 453.

Fitz Alan family, origin of, 115, 129.

Fitz Alan, Jordan, VII. 126.

——, ——, his descendants, VII. 126–128.

——, Walter (steward of Scotland), 115, 116, 128, 129, 132.

——, William, 125.

Fitz Count, Brian (of Wallingford), 189, 211, 212.

——, Reginald (son of Roger earl of Hereford), 201–3, 205–6.

——, ——, his son William, 198–9, 200, 205.

——, ——, his other children, 202, 205.

Fitz Flaald, Alan, 115, 116, 117, 123, 124, 125, 126, 127–129, 131.

Fitz Geralds, fabulous origin of, 69.

Fitz Osbern. See Hereford.

Fitz Payne, barony of, 446.

Fitz Rou (Rolf), Turstin, 188–9, 190, 192, 193, 194, 195, 196, 197, 210.

Fitz-Walter, barony of, 31.

Fitz-William, family, origin of, 46–50.

Flodden augmentation, the, 39, 321. See also Howard.

Fobbing (Essex), 162.

Forged pedigrees, 308–9. See also Heralds.

Forgery of documents, 141, 241, 244–5, 246. See also Worcester, Edward marquis of.

Fortescue, alleged origin of name, 61.

Foster, Mr. Joseph, 3, 14, 83, 87–8, 97.

Fox-Davies, Mr., 20, 40, 42, 53, 145, 247–8, 312, 314.

Freeby (Leic.), 305.

Freeman, Professor, 1, 2, 4–7, 20, 29, 46–7, 50–51, 52, 55, 61, 72, 73–75, 111, 114, 147–152, 154, 181–3, 187, 190, 191, 203, 213, 472.

French, origin of name, 16.

Froude, Mr., 330.

Froxmere, arms of, 253, 254, 269.

Funeral certificates as evidence, 441, 456.

Furness Abbey founded by Stephen, 168.

Gage, Sir Henry, 394.

Gairdner, Mr. James, 332, 333, 338, 352.

Gardiner, Mr. S. R., 368, 370, 371, 372–383, 385–399, 401–405, 407–415, 417–420, 422, 424, 426–434.

Garioch, alleged barony of, 11.

Garter-King-of-Arms. See Anstis; Dugdale; Heard; Segar; Wriothesley.

Garter-plates as evidence, 439–441, 446, 451–2, 456.

Genealogist, The, 4, 125, 133, 135, 136, 160, 165, 368, 453.

Genealogy, the new, 4, 112, 323–4.

——, the old, 134, 324.

——, official, 88.

——, the eccentric, 118–9.

——, monastic, 189, 198.

——, the romance of, 70.

Glamorgan, earldom of, informally bestowed on Edward (Somerset) Lord Herbert, 367–8, 374, 380, 390, 397–8.

——, Lord. See Worcester, Edward marquis of.

Glass window, the Steward, 133, 136, 138–9, 220.

484

INDEX

Glass window, the Feilding, 219, 240.

Godfrey, alleged arms of, 253, 269.

Godstow, gift of Eaton to, 201–2, 205.

Gorges, Alianore, 271–3.

——, arms of, 272–3.

Gotha, Almanac de, 78, 83.

Gotherington in Bishop's Cleeve (Glouc.), 193.

Gournai, Hawise de, 197.

Gower, peninsula of, Norman occupation of, 215.

Graunt, Walter, 287, 326.

——, William, 287.   [324.

Graziers, fortunes made by, 284–5.

Great Governing Families cited, 278.

Greenstreet, Mr. James, 274.

Grey de Powis, Edward lord, 346.

Grey de Ruthyn, barony of, 447.

Grimston family, alleged founder of, 62.

Guihenoc (or Wihenoc) of Monmouth, 121, 123, 185.

Gwent, 186, 187, 189.

——, Upper, 189, 192, 211, 212.

——, Nether, 192, 212.

Hallam cited, 342.

Hamiltons, origin of the, 89.

Hampshire, Ballon family in, 209.

Hapsburg, arms of, 238, 243.

—— descent and dignities, claim of Feildings to, 14–15, 216 *et seq.*

Hapsburgs, alleged Alsatian origin of, 244.

Harold. *See* Hereford.

Harrowden. *See* Vaux.

Hastings family, alleged origin of its name, 63.

Hastings, barony of, 447.

——, ——, its precedence, 108–9.

——, George (earl of Huntingdon), lord, 333, 338.

Hat, Lord Kingsale and his, 104–5.

Havet, M. Julien, 245.

Haye family, origin of, 125.

Heard, Sir Isaac, Garter King of Arms, 300, 302, 308.

'Heirs of the body,' interpretation of, 459, 463, 471, 474–5.

Heirs male, dignities by writ diverted in favour of, 360–361, 453, 465–6.

——, limitation to, its meaning, 371–2.

——, retain baronies in fee, 450–453.

Henry I., 213.

—— bestows Crown lands on Stephen, 168.

Henry II., grants by, 160, 163.

—— propitiates Stephen and his son William, 168, 169.

—— subsequently forces William to surrender his castles and crown lands, 170.

—— seizes the Honour of Boulogne and *comté* of Mortain on William's death, 171–2.

——, his compromise with count Mathew, 173, 174.

Henry VII., king in his own right, 472.

Henry VIII., his will disposes of the crown, 472, 473.

——, his creation of peers, 330 *et seq.*

Heraldry, 39–42, 45, 49, 50, 79, 136, 138–146, 207, 216, 238–9, 240, 243, 248, 251–3, 258, 269, 270, 272–5, 289–293, 306–7, 312–3, 316–321, 326–9.

Heralds, the, squabble over fees, 315–6.

Heralds, Elizabethan, 23, 43, 46, 50, 76, 137, 143, 301.
See also Cooke; Lee; Thynne.

485

INDEX

INDEX

INDEX

Llandovery, 215.

Llangennith priory founded, 215.

Lords, House of, unjustly charged, 5.

——, ——, 'scene' in, 279.

——, ——, abolished by Cromwell, 294.

——, ——, changes in, under Henry VIII., 330 et seq.

——, ——, in 1523, 331.

——, ——, in 1529, 331, 333–7, 341, 352.

——, ——, its decisions in peerage cases criticised, 334, 456–7.

——, ——, in 1534, 337–341.

——, ——, in 1515, 340.

——, ——, in 1536, 344–6, 366.

——, ——, use of proxies in, 344.

——, ——, in 1539, 346–7.

——, ——, precedence in, 353, 363, 366.

Lorraine, Godfrey duke of, 42. See also Boulogne.

Lou, Robert le, 298, 299, 302, 306.

Loughborough, 305.

Lovaine, origin of title, 42.

Lovayne, alleged barony of, 447.

Lovel and Holland, baronies of, 27.

Loxton (Somerset), 154.

Lucas of Crudwell, patent creating barony of, 461.

Luci, Richard de, 173, 174.

Lumley, John lord, 334.

Lydney (Glouc.), 185.

Lyon Office, its "proved and registered" pedigree of Marjoribanks, 87–8.

Lyre, La Vieille, abbey of, 184.

Lyttons of Knebworth (formerly Wiggett), the, 25–7.

Macduff, viscountcy. See Fife.

Mackay, sheriff, 117.

Madan, Mr. F., 370.

Maidstone, viscountcy of, 28.

Malet, Robert, his fief bestowed on Stephen, 167, 171.

Maltravers, barony of, 448, 453.

——, Henry Fitz-Alan lord, 335, 337.

Manners family, the, 447.

Mantes, 'Walter,' count of, 148–150.

Mar, earldom of, 90–95.

——, character and effect of Restitution Act, 90, 92–3.

Marcle (Herefordshire), Much, 204, 206–9.

——, 'Honour' of, 200.

Marjoribanks pedigree, the contested, 87–8.

Markham (Notts), West, VII.

Marlborough, Alvred de, 156.

——, heirs of first duke of, 38.

——, patent creating dukedom of, 471.

Marmoutier, abbey of, its charters, 122–3, 126.

Martley. See Marcle.

—— (Worcestershire), 296, 299, 302, 306.

Mary I., succession of, 472, 474.

Mary II., queen by statute, 459, 473.

Mascherel, Walter, 167.

Massy of Dunham Massy, the founder of, 64.

Meinill, title of, assigned to the Darcys in writs, 455.

Melcombe Regis. See Weymouth.

Merc (i.e. Marck), family of, 156–7, 164.

Merleberg. See Marlborough.

Meschamp. See Muschamp.

Meynill. See Meinill.

Moels, Nicholas de, 198.

Monbegon, Roger de, VII.

Monmouth (with Troy), 185, 187.

INDEX

Monmouth, the Breton lords of, 120, 121.

Montacute, barony of, 336.

Montacute priory, 196, 197.

Montague, Henry Pole lord, 336, 337.

Montdoubleau, Payn de, 192.

Montfort, Simon de, descent falsely claimed from, 85.

Montgomery, Arnulf de, 214.

Montmorency, de, name and arms wrongly taken, 20.

Monumental effigies altered, shifted, and forged, 83–7.

Monuments, heraldic evidence of, 137–8, 252–3.

Moray earldom, descent of the, 94.

Mordaunt, John Mordaunt created lord, 336, 337, 349, 353.

——, barony of, 351, 366.

More, Sir Thomas, cited, 286.

Morley, earldom of, 23.

Morres becomes De Montmorency, 20.

Mortain, *comté* of, held by Stephen, 167.

——, held by his son William, 169, 171.

——, promised to his son-in-law Mathew, 175.

Mortelay. *See* Marcle.

Mortimer, Isolde daughter of Edmund de, 207, 208.

Morville, arms of, 273.

Mountjoy, Charles Blount lord, 345.

Mowbray, barony of, 435 *et seq.*, 460.

——, its precedence, 108–9.

——, Henry Frederick Howard summoned (1640) as lord, 337.

Mowbray, Segrave, and Stourton, lord, 37, 40, 41, 52, 54, 56, 58, 61.

——, Alfred lord, 437–9.

Mowbrays, Anne heiress of, 435, 439.

——, Isabel, co-heiress of, 435.

——, Margaret, co-heiress of, 435.

——, their royal descent, 435–6.

—— style themselves lords Braose, 456.

——, their inheritance divided, 436, 443.

Musard, Robert, 306.

Muschamp, alleged arms of, 253.

Names of supposed ancestors revived, 21–2, 216, 247, 261, 308.

Napton, Agnes de, 218, 220, 227.

Nelson, right heir of, 38.

Neufmarché (Newmarch), Henry de, 194, 195, 196, 209.

——, James de, 196, 198.

——, William de, 210.

——, Sibyl, daughter of Bernard de, 212.

Newmarch. *See* Neufmarché.

——, Isabel, 255.

Nichols' *Leicestershire*, 217, 229, 304.

Nicolas, Sir Harris, 3, 9.

Nobility. *See* Blood; Peerage Dignities.

Norfolk, dukes of, 38, 40, 109–110.

——, dukedom of, its precedence, 109.
See also Howard.

Norfolk, Margaret countess of, 436.

Northcote pedigree, the, 71.

Northumberland, earls of, assume titles, 446.

——, origin of Percy dukedom of, 45.

Norton, Cold (Oxon.), 179.

——, ——, Augustinian house at, 177.

—— (Suffolk), 178.

489

INDEX

Norwich held by William count of Boulogne, 169, 170.
Nuncio. *See* Rinuccini.
Nutfield (Surrey), 153, 161.

Oeys (*i.e.* Oye), Eustace de, 157.
Offaley, barony of, 95, 453, 466.
Ogle, barony of, 338.
Oman, Mr., 204.
Ongar, the Honour of, 171, 174.
Ormonde, earldom (1529) of, 470.
——, Thomas, earl of, 340.
——, James first duke of, his relations with Charles I. and Lord Glamorgan (1644–7), 392, 396, 398–9, 401–7, 412–17, 419–20, 422–4, 426–7, 429–33.
Ostrewic. *See* Austruy.
Oxford (De Vere), earldom of, 450, 451–2.
Oxford, Walter, archdeacon of, 202.

Painter-stainers, 58, 60, 145.
Pancevolt, Bernard, 196.
Parish Register, discovery of a peer in, 70.
——, falsified, 86.
Parliament. *See* Lords; Commons.
Parr barony, creation of, 355.
Patent, creation by, 354–5, 358–9.
Patents of creation, invalid proviso in, 467.
——, value of recitals in, 62, 221, 240, 440, 453.
Paulett, Sir William, created lord St. John, 361.
Pauncefote, family of, 24.
Paynel family, origin of, 125.
Paynel (of Somerset), William, 206.
Pedigree-makers, pranks of, 265.
Pedigrees, attempts to tinker, 252.
——, how concocted, 227 *et seq.*

Peerage cases :—
Braye, 354, 359, 361, 362, 365.
Buckhurst, 466–7.
Clifton, 6.
Fitzwalter, 446, 450.
Hastings, 9, 11, 109.
Herries, 96.
Howard de Walden, 450.
Lindores, 100.
Mar, 90–3.
Moray, 94.
Mowbray and Segrave, VIII. 10, 110, 365, 435 *et seq.*
Oxford (earldom of), 450, 451–452, 460.
Sandys, 358.
Scales, 437, 440.
Sutherland, 94.
Vaux, 354, 357, 358, 363, 364–5.
Wentworth, 361.
Wharton, 354.
Peerage cases, evidence produced in, 361–5.
Peerage dignities deemed real estate, 460, 465–6.
——, their descent diverted, 93–5.
——, purchase of, 28, 33.
——, wrongful assumption of, 99–101, 445–8, 449, 450–456.
——, erroneous recognition by Crown of, VIII. 100, 447–8, 449–456.
——, Crown cannot alter limitation of, 466.
Peerage, vulgarization of the, 33–36.
Pembroke, Gilbert (de Clare) earl of, 212.
Pepys pedigree, the, 311.
Percy, modern barony (1722) of, 38, 100, 454.
——, arms of, 41–2.
——, origin of family of, 43–4.
——, formerly Smithson, 44.

490

INDEX

INDEX

Scandals, sundry, 28–9.

Scohies, William de, 188.

Scotland, assumption of peerage dignities in, 12, 14, 92, 95–99.

Scottish genealogy, 83, 87–90.

Scotts, male heirship of the, 89.

Seal, alleged early armorial, 49.

——, evidence of an armorial, 273–4.

——, forgery of the great, VIII. 379, 422.

Seals, strange adventures of, 231.

Segar, Garter King of Arms, 259, 293, 297, 302, 308, 315.

Segrave, barony of, 436–8, 439, 448, 449, 456, 457. *See also* Mowbray.

Serjeanties of the count of Boulogne in England, 158.

Seymour arms, 40.

Sharrington (Norfolk), 127.

Sheep, complaints of their ravages, 281–284, 286–7.

Sheldon MSS., the, 241.

Shifting clause. *See* Patent.

Shipway pedigree case, the, 85–6, 245, 276.

Shirley's *Noble and Gentle Men*, 216, 278, 296.

Shopland (Essex), 158, 159.

Signet, the, 415–7.

Smith. *See* Carrington.

Smith-Carington, fabulous origin of, 64.

Snitterfield (Warwickshire), 286, 326.

Snow, Isaac, 285.

Society, "good suburban," 316.

——, plutocratic development of, 33–6.

Somerset, Ballon family in, 209–210.

—— (or Somerset and Beaufort), dukedom of, Charles I.'s alleged creation of, 367 *et seq.*

Somerset family, origin of, 371.

Sophia, the electress, 459.

Spencer (of Cannon Hall), arms of, 317.

——, Henry (of Badby), 294, 325, 326.

——, ——, his alleged arms, 291, 306, 328.

——, Sir John (purchaser of Althorpe), 284–292, 306, 322, 324.

——, ——, his enclosed pastures, 282, 288–9.

——, ——, his brother Thomas, 286, 289.

——, ——, his father William, 286, 289.

——, ——, a grazier, 284, 287, 288.

——, ——, resides at Hodnell, 287–8, 292.

——, ——, his grant of arms, 289–291.

——, ——, his monument, 291.

——, —— (grandfather of first lord), 281, 283, 290, 292–4.

——, ——, monument of, 292.

——, John (of Hodnell), 286, 323, 324.

——, Richard, 323.

——, Robert first lord, 279–80, 285, 327.

——, Thomas (of Hodnell), 286, 287, 326.

——, —— (of Everdon), 290.

Spencers, alleged origin of, 279, 292–300, 306.

——, true origin of, 285–8, 322.

——, great sheepmasters, 279–284.

——, originally ' graziers,' 285.

——, arms granted to, 289–291, 307, 317.

——, monuments of, 293.

——, modesty of modern, 322.

——, origin of their name, 323.

INDEX

494

INDEX

Ulster office, fabulous pedigrees recorded in, 21, 69.
—— King of Arms. *See* Betham; Burke.
Uses, statute of, 352–3.

Vaillant, M. V.-J., 163.
Valentia, viscountcy of, 13.
Vanbrugh, Sir John, Clarencieux, 316.
Vane. *See* Fane.
Vaux, barony of, 30.
—— (of Harrowden), Thomas lord, 336, 337, 357, 365, 366.
——, Sir Nicholas, created lord Vaux, 356–8, 364–5.
Vavasour family, origin of, 62.
Victoria History of the Counties of England, the, 323–4.
Vignier, Jérôme, a forger, 245.
Vincent, Augustine, 241, 302, 308.
——, John, 218, 240, 241, 244.
Visitations. *See* Heralds.

Wake. *See* Hereward.
—— family, origin of, 73–5.
Wales, South, invaded by earl William Fitz Osbern, 182, 186–7.
——, the Clares in, 211–4.
——, invaded from Devon, 215.
Walesby (Notts), VII.
Warenne fief, devolution of the, 172.
Warennes, heirship of the De, 49.
Warsop (Notts), VII.
Warwick, Henry (de Beaumont) earl of, 215.
——, earls of, 22, 27.
Warwickshire, sheep farming in, 280–284.
Welsh land system, 186, 188.
Wendover, 160.

Wentworth, Martha Johnson claims barony of, 361.
——, Thomas Wentworth created lord, 336, 348, 351, 353.
——, barony of, 351, 362, 363, 366.
Westerham (Kent), church of, 153.
Weston, Segar's (spurious) pedigree of, 259, 308.
Wettingen, abbey of, 225, 227.
Wexford, alleged barony of, 447.
Weymouth, gild of St. George at, 266.
——, Russells at, 267–8.
Weysford. *See* Wexford.
Wharton, barony of, 354.
Whitsand, family of, 159, 164.
Wicken (Northants), 289.
Wiffen, Mr., 251, 257, 260, 261, 263–6, 268, 271–8.
Wihenoc. *See* Guihenoc.
William the Conqueror, 46–7, 50, 55–9, 61–3, 73, 154, 181.
William Rufus, 190, 192.
William III., king by statute, 459, 473.
Willington family, the, 221–2.
Willoughby of Parham, barony of, 100.
Wimbish, Mr., his claim to be Lord Tailbois, 350, 359.
Winchester, earls of. *See* Despencer.
Windsor (of Stanwell), Andrew first lord, 336, 337, 348, 353, 364.
——, barony of, 350, 359–361, 365–6, 437, 461, 462, 465, 469, 470.
Winterbourne-Wast (Dorset), 153, 162.
Winton, Scottish earldom of, 11.
Wolseley of Wolseley, fabulous origin of, 64–5.
Wolston priory, 128.

495

INDEX

Wolves in England, 65.

Woodward's *Heraldry*, 328.

Wool. *See* Sheep.

Worcester, Henry first marquis of, 373–5, 389, 391, 397.

——, Edward, second marquis of, informally created earl of Glamorgan, 367–8, 374, 390.

——, receives the garter (?), 369 *et seq.*

——, suspected of forging documents, 369, 379, 382, 384, 395, 399, 401–2, 405, 410–412, 427.

——, his bombast, 380, 424–5.

——, his shipwreck, 381, 407.

——, attempts to bribe Clarendon, 384.

——, his alleged 'commission patent,' 385–6, 389–392, 395.

——, his alleged power to mint, 386, 398.

——, is to raise troops and money abroad (1645), 387–8, 393–394, 397.

——, styles himself 'Plantagenet,' 390.

——, his 'instructions' for Ireland, 391, 394, 397, 412–3, 421.

——, his 'judgement' distrusted by Charles, 392, 413.

——, his Irish treaty, 396 *et seq.*

——, his alleged appointment to be Lord Lieutenant of Ireland, 398–9, 427.

Worcester, his 'special warrant for Ireland,' 399, 400, 401, 404, 405, 410, 421, 422.

——, was intended to act as go-between, 402, 420.

——, an ardent Catholic, 403, 418.

——, his character, 418–9, 423–7.

——, his military achievements, 425.

——, becomes slave of Nuncio, 433.

Wormleighton (Warwickshire), 279, 281, 284, 286, 288, 289, 325.

Worsley family, alleged founder of the, 62.

Wrestlingworth (Beds), 178.

Wriothesley barony, creation of, 355.

Wriothesley, Garter, 140, 141, 142.

Writ of summons, effect of, 5–6, 100.

——, earliest valid, 9–11, 365–6.

——, creation by, 354–5, 357–9, 361, 363.

—— to son in his father's barony, 335, 337, 454–5.

Wrottesley pedigree, the, 71.

Wyke Regis (Dorset), church of, 266.

Wyse, family of, 254.

——, arms of, 253.

Yeomen, wealth of English, 324.

Ypres, William of, 166.

LIBRARY OF DAVIDSON COLLEGE

Books on regular loan may be checked out for **two weeks**. Books must be presented at the Circulation Desk in order to be renewed.

A fine is charged after date due.

Special books are subject to
the library staff.